TEACHERS, UNIONS, AND COLLECTIVE BARGAINING IN PUBLIC EDUCATION

Anthony M. Cresswell

State University of New York, Albany

and

Michael J. Murphy

University of Utah

with

Charles T. Kerchner

Claremont Graduate School

McCutchan Publishing Corporation
2526 Grove Street
Berkeley, California 94704

ISBN 0-8211-0229-X
Library of Congress Catalog Card Number 79-91436
© 1980 by McCutchan Publishing Corporation. All rights reserved
Printed in the United States of America

Cover illustration and design by Catherine Conner, Griffin Graphics
Typesetting by TypArt in AlphaSette Times Roman

Preface

Collective bargaining has come to touch the lives of most workers and clients in public education. As a consequence, many more people now study it or have a need to know about it. Strangely, however, few comprehensive treatments of this subject have been published in the last ten years. And so those who wish to begin their inquiry into the subject must rely on dated texts written when collective bargaining in education was in its infancy, or they must wade through a variety of scattered sources. Practitioners who want to update their knowledge have a similar dilemma, as does anyone interested in a specific aspect of unionization or collective bargaining. As teachers and researchers of collective bargaining, we also have struggled with this gap in the literature. We hope that this text, which is an attempt to update the literature and provide a comprehensive, single source for all who need it, will serve immediate needs and remain useful in much the same way that earlier texts have.

The organization of the chapters reflects the idea of bargaining as an open system. This perspective, presented in Chapter 1, is intended to bring a broad unity to the many, often disparate concepts in the field. Chapter 2 describes the current state of bargaining

in education as a point of departure. As an open system, the processes
of collective bargaining and labor-management relations take place
within a context or an environment. These are discussed in Chapters
3 through 5. The process and substance are treated in Chapters 6
through 8. Chapters 9 through 11 deal with the outcomes of bargaining and lead to Chapter 12, which concludes with reflections on
unifying themes and issues. The book represents a whole, a comprehensive attempt to treat the most important aspects of the
entire collective bargaining system.

Each of the chapters in the book can, however, stand by itself
and, thus, may be useful to those who wish to study certain aspects
of the collective bargaining system in a more specialized way.
Chapter 4 on the growth of teachers' unions, for example, treats
aspects of interest to students of collective bargaining, union history,
and the history of American teachers' associations. For those
studying the interaction between the law and collective bargaining,
Chapter 5 (on the legal context) and Chapter 8 (on the contract)
should be helpful. The politics of education is covered in Chapter
6 (on governance), while Chapter 2 ("The State of Collective Bargaining") represents one of the most complete reports of demographic
data on collective bargaining available.

The integrated yet independent structure of this work should
serve several audiences. It should be a useful book for courses in
labor-management relations in education. For the beginning student,
we have tried to balance two complementary objectives: the development of useful theoretical frameworks for understanding the field
and the presentation of basic information about the subject. This
balance is reflected in each of the chapters as well as in the overall
design. We believe attention to both theory and practical content
is necessary to a working understanding of the field. And, because
it deals with the main issues in a systematic form, the book should
interest practitioners seeking to explore collective bargaining in
something other than the traditional "war stories" or polemical
style, and we hope it will contribute new insights or ways of thinking for even the experienced practitioner. And, of course, because
collective bargaining in education represents such a major share
of activity in the public sector, we think that this book will interest
students in that general sector as well.

Collective bargaining in education often seems to be cut off from the mainstream of study, both in the public sector and in general. This is unfortunate since at least half of the bargaining activity in the public sector involves schools. A source such as this should help workers in the Federal Mediation and Conciliation Service who are increasingly becoming involved in school impasse resolution, practicing lawyers, and members of arbitration panels of the American Arbitration Association. Many neutrals and other parties are asked to participate in school bargaining with little understanding of public education. This book should help them.

This isolation of collective bargaining in education from that in the private and public sectors is equally unfortunate because it deprives bargainers in education of rich sources of theory, data, and experience that have been developing over the years. Those who would focus only on collective bargaining in education necessarily suffer a loss of peripheral vision that robs them of a richness of understanding that would otherwise be available to them. We have tried to incorporate useful ideas from the private sector and other areas of the public sector and hope that this contributes, in some small way, to the development of meaningful dialogue among bargainers.

Our attempt to be integrative and comprehensive has required some difficult but necessary choices. First, it was necessary to focus almost exclusively on public elementary and secondary education. The bulk of union activity in private schools is in those affiliated with the Roman Catholic Church. Their legal and organizational structure is markedly different from that of public schools, and little is known about the style and process of bargaining in those schools. This subject deserves a separate text of its own. Higher education was excluded for different but related reasons. Public schools (elementary and secondary) and institutions of higher education are each organizationally, financially, and politically complex, and they are notably dissimilar in bargaining context and practice. To treat higher education in detail here was not practical, in our opinion. Instead of dealing specifically with these other sectors, we have tried to develop general concepts that will, we hope, help the student who wishes to explore the other areas.

The dependence we all have on others is reflected in the amount of help we had with this work. Charles T. Kerchner of the Claremont Graduate School has made two significant contributions. For one thing, because of his work on the impact of collective bargaining in education, we invited him to contribute the chapter that now appears as Chapter 10 ("Unions and Their Impact on School Governance and Politics"). Besides this, he has reviewed other sections and improved them significantly through his comments and ideas.

One of the joys of this effort has been the vivid realization of a genuine sense of collegiality and cooperation among our co-workers. They include students and faculty members at Northwestern University and the University of Utah, who have generously read drafts and unselfishly shared their criticisms and feelings. In particular, we mention Frederick Buchanan, Roald Campbell, Gregory Castle, William Hazard, Gene Jacobsen, and William Myer, who have carefully read and commented on various parts of the manuscript.

Preparation of the manuscript also required the indispensable efforts of our secretaries and typists. In particular, we acknowledge the help of Joyce Gorrell, Priscilla Nichols, France Rimli, and Debra Sibert, who cheerfully typed repeated drafts, usually under pressure of deadlines and while other duties waited.

Our greatest debt is, however, to our families who have patiently understood and urged us to work, in spite of modified vacation plans, missed ball games, and other intrusions on normal home and social existence. We hope, now that this book is done, that we can repay them for their patience and support.

Michael J. Murphy
Salt Lake City, Utah

Anthony M. Cresswell
Evanston, Illinois

July 1979

Contents

12

1

The Study of Collective Bargaining in Education: Introduction

VIEWS OF COLLECTIVE BARGAINING

Schooling is, above all, an activity of people. It involves students, teachers, administrators, psychologists, secretaries, custodians, and others. The way these people expend their time and energy is of primary importance. Aside from students, most of the people who participate in the day-to-day activities of schooling are employees. They work in a system that is dependent on people, rather than on machines. For this reason, the expenditure of time and energy by school employees is vital to any consideration of educational policy and practice. It is equally vital in relations between employees and management. This connection is the central idea on which to build an understanding of collective bargaining and labor-management relations in the schools.

We use "labor-management relations" as the generic term[1] referring to any and all types of activities through which employees and employers arrange and regulate conditions of, and compensation for, work. Some system of labor-management relations always exists where there are employees; it may not always include bilateral negotiation of terms and conditions. Where such negotiation does exist, collective bargaining is most often the central decision-making mechanism and climate-setting aspect of labor-management relations.

The term "collective bargaining," as we use it here, refers to the negotiation and administration of a written agreement between the school district as employer and an organization representing employees. This includes, of course, actual table bargaining and related actions of participants that may occur away from the bargaining table. We prefer the term "collective bargaining" to terms such as "professional negotiations," "collective negotiations," or other expressions that have been used in discussions of educational bargaining.

Bargaining as an Open System

One of our aims in writing about collective bargaining in education is to provide ways to view and understand the process of bilateral decision making that has engulfed public education in the last two decades. To view and understand means to have a perspective or frame of reference and a basis for explanation. We have conceived of collective bargaining in school districts, heuristically, as an open sociopolitical system. That means we believe the process can be usefully described in terms of a set of interacting components that exchange information and material with an environment. The components of bargaining and labor-management relations interact in the bargaining process. Information and material that originate in the environment are considered inputs that become part of the process, while information and material that originate in the process and become part of the environment are thought of as outputs. The nature of the process and its relationship with schooling are thought of as partly determined by the characteristics of the components interacting in the process itself and partly by the characteristics of the inputs from the environment. In short, labor-management relations and collective bargaining in education take place in dynamic relationship with an environment (or context as we shall sometimes call it). Understanding depends on acceptance of this proposition as a fundamental part of the design.

Inputs are composed primarily of resources, expectations, rules, and traditions. Schools, as valued social institutions, have many such inputs, and, because collective bargaining is often an important element in school affairs, it affects many of the inputs. That is why the first section of this book is devoted to a detailed examination of the environment or context in which collective bargaining takes place and how that environment contributes inputs to the bargaining process.

The second section deals with the bargaining process itself, the content of that process, and the way in which impasses occur and are treated. We hope this treatment makes clear the fact that the dynamics are conditioned largely by the nature of the influences or inputs from the environment. But it should also be clear that the internal structure and patterns of the process are important determinants of the activities and their outputs.

The immediate outputs of collective bargaining are the clauses of the negotiated contract and the changes that result from the give-and-take between the parties. Because the bargaining system is open to its environment, we expect the impact of these outputs to be detectable in terms of environmental changes, which are considered the outcomes of the process. The third section of this book focuses on outcomes. Figure 1-1 depicts our open-systems view.

Because of this systems view, we must consider not only collective bargaining (that is, the negotiation and administration of an agreement) but also teachers' unions, without which there would be no bargaining. We must also deal with the economics of education and resource allocation, for it is obvious that teachers' unions seek to affect the distribution of economic resources through collective bargaining. School governance must be included because collective bargaining seems, at times, to be at odds with conventional notions that schools are governed by boards of education acting in behalf of state legislatures and the local community. There must also be a consideration of law, for, in the American tradition of labor relations, legislatures and courts influence the behavior of parties to a bargain—both the extent to which they must bargain and the degree to which agreements can be enforced. And finally, of course, conflict and conflict resolution receive attention. Many have noted that collective bargaining is nothing more than the institutionalization of conflict, a mechanism for expressing and managing the conflict that has always existed between employers and employees.[2]

As useful as it is, this notion of bargaining as an open sociopolitical

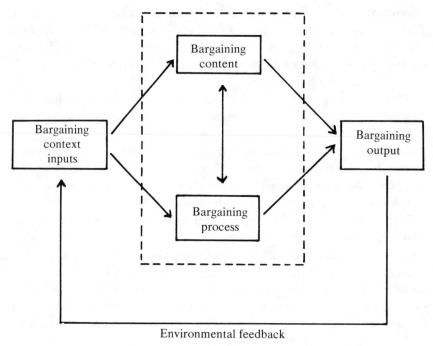

Figure 1-1
Bargaining system in education

system is not a complete frame of reference. We come to this work with a number of other assumptions about collective bargaining in education. These shape our perspective and appear as themes or parts of discussions in a number of places to follow. It is useful by way of introduction to discuss briefly each of these assumptions as a way of indicating how they may have affected the conclusions or ideas expressed in other parts of the work.

Theory and Collective Bargaining

There is no theory of collective bargaining, per se.[3] Theories from a number of disciplines and perspectives deal with parts of the process. None is dominant or generally accepted as definitive. We have, therefore, deliberately been selective. Ideas from economics, political science, sociology, psychology, and elsewhere enter into the treatment of various topics. These ideas have been used for their explanatory or descriptive value as judged appropriate.

We have attempted no synthesis of theory; nor have we attempted to produce a single conceptual scheme to cover all of the subject. That seems premature since our main focus on a single institution does not provide a broad enough base to generate theory or synthesis of theory. What we have done, instead, is use the best available theory to build a functional understanding of collective bargaining.

The "Orthodox" View

The orthodox model of labor relations is essentially two hierarchies with episodic contacts between the hierarchies at the top (Figure 1-2) in order to set the conditions of the relationship and more frequent contacts between lower-level participants in order to enforce the contract. These contacts take place largely through consultation and the processing of grievances. The barrier between labor and management is clear. The assertion in American labor continues to be that "employees work and managers manage." Or, in the case of schools, that school boards make policy, superintendents administer policy, and teachers teach. Labor relations

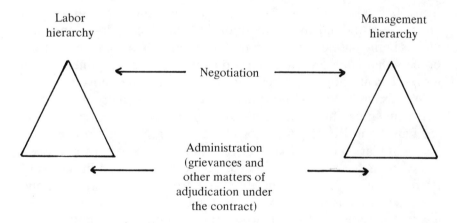

Figure 1-2
Orthodox model of labor relations

are thus viewed as an important, but quite limited, aspect of governance, and, what is even more important, agreements between the two sides are thought to be relatively inflexible and subject to change only through formal contract renegotiation.

In contrast to this orthodox approach, we suggest that collective bargaining is much more complex, that it occurs often and in many places, and that it involves many different people and issues. Because the decision process is continuous, relationships between employees and employers are subject to continuous modification or elaboration. Teachers' union officials interact on a daily basis with school management over issues that affect or *may* affect employment. In these meetings the differences resolved and the agreements struck affect working conditions and climate. The "contract" is ever being extended or modified.

Public and Private Sectors

Another departure from the orthodox view involves differences between bargaining in the public and private sectors. Almost all bargaining in elementary and secondary education is in the public schools, and a substantial body of thought holds that bargaining in the public sector is fundamentally different from that in private firms. This position is based on the arguments that public employers are not constrained by competition in a product market and that unions in the public sector can mobilize force to distort the political process that controls bargaining so as to produce bargained settlements that are not in the best interests of the community.[4]

We disagree. We acknowledge that there are many differences between bargaining in the public and private sectors, some of which are important. But the basic logic and dynamics of the process are quite similar. There is, moreover, more variation within each sector than between them. Legal and economic conditions vary from organization to organization and from state to state. Public schools in Illinois and Utah, for example, have little in the way of legal structures in the environment to constrain public-sector bargaining. But in New York and California there is extensive statutory control of school bargaining. By contrast, a firm that contracts to collect garbage for a school district in any state is a private employer and is constrained by private-sector labor laws. Many industries, including airlines and public utilities, are privately owned, but at the same time they are closely regulated by the state or federal government. We do not, therefore, find that the public-private distinction significantly advances understanding of how the bargaining process works.

BARGAINING AND THE PUBLIC INTEREST

Much of the uncertainty and debate concerning bargaining in the public sector, and its relationship with the private one, revolves around the question of what is in the public interest. In the private sector, bargaining is seen as a private activity that should be balanced and reasonably peaceful. Leaving the process largely to the parties themselves is usually seen as being in the public interest. But there is far less consensus about how to conduct public bargaining. Part of the confusion comes from different understandings of how that bargaining can serve the public interest.

Nature of the Public Interest

The term "public interest" seems to have two general meanings. The first refers to a highly abstract, general good.[5] It is built on the idea that there are practices, circumstances, or events that are generally so beneficial that their value transcends the private interests or desires of a few individuals or groups. Our constitutional rights, for example, fall into that category, as do security from foreign attack and peaceful labor-management relations.

If discussion remains at a sufficiently high level of abstraction, there is often wide consensus as to what is in the general or public interest. There is, however, no single list of circumstances or events on which all will agree. A just social order, for example, is seen as central to the public interest. But there is no common agreement on how justice should be defined or instituted in society.[6] In short, we seem to accept the fact that some *public* interests transcend private ones, and we accept certain abstractions as being elements of, or contributing to, the public interest. But consensus breaks down on more specific or instrumental means to ensure or promote that public interest. The more specific the terms, the more likely that definitions of the public interest will compete.

This competition is evident when we examine education and collective bargaining. In considering what is good for public education we must give attention to the rights and interests of *all* parties: clients and their representatives (students, parents, community), employees, and managers. All parties share a common desire for the educational systems to work well, but each can have a different view of what this means and a different idea of how goods and power should be distributed. Clients have their own, perhaps varied, desires for the system to serve their needs. Managers and school boards have a legitimate concern for protecting their legal responsibility for governance and efficient operation. Employees also have interest in the distribution of resources and power, especially concerning compensation and work rules. Each, therefore, has a competing view of what is good for education, and differences arise mainly when the *private* interests of these parties mix with their concern for the general good. This struggle between private and public interests is the basis for conflicts in collective bargaining.

As a people, we tend to reject extremes in resolving such conflicts between public and private interests. Governments are created to protect their citizens from the unbridled pursuit of private gain. But governments or other social structures that interfere too much with private affairs are seen as oppressive. In most areas of public affairs, some balance of freedom and control is desired, and collective bargaining in the public sector and the public school is one of those areas.

The need for balance is especially evident in a pluralistic society such as ours, which is characterized by unequal distribution of goods, abilities, and power, as well as wide variation in political and social ideology. One's idea of the public interest is conditioned in part by one's place in the distribution of goods and abilities and in part by one's idea of how important the public interest is when compared to private interests. A poor man who is politically conservative will favor different policies than a middle-class liberal, and those policies would likely be quite different from policies advocated by a rich man who is politically conservative. These matters are central to the way one views labor-management relations, in education or any other sphere of activity. *There will always be competing definitions of what is in the public interest*, for they grow out of the inevitable differences among individuals and groups as to resources, abilities, or ideology.

We accept, therefore, the fact that there is an inherent tension between the public and private interests involved in collective bargaining. School boards and employees' unions can act in good faith in the pursuit of their own version of the public interest and yet remain in conflict. Similarly, there are differences within groups; not all teachers in the union, or all parents, or all board members want the same thing. Conflicts both within and among the parties are, therefore, an integral part of labor-management relations.

Defining the Public Interest

As complex as the concept of the public interest is in practice and detail, there are only two basic points of view on how it is to be defined. The first is that *substantive criteria* (one or more) define the public interest. In this view, fairness, efficiency, or any other basic criterion of the good society can guide decisions on public affairs. If we believe, for example, that efficiency in the production of goods and services is the most important aspect of the public interest, a negotiated wage agreement or proposed policy could then be evaluated, assuming measurements exist, in terms of how well the agreement or policy promotes efficiency. Less efficient wage structures or laws would be judged to be not in the public interest based on the substance of the agreement and its effects. The judgment is independent of the means by which the wage was determined.

The second way of viewing the public interest is *procedural*. This approach admits that there are many possible substantive definitions of the public interest. None is necessarily superior to the others, and no combination or ordering is necessarily stable or preferable as a basis for defining what is good for the whole society. The public interest is defined rather in the preferences revealed through a fair public decision-making procedure. The judgment on whether the revealed preferences are truly in the public interest rests not on the substance of the decision but on the fairness with which it was made. Thus, what a representative government decides by fair and democratic means can be considered the procedural definition of the public interest.

This latter view seems the most appropriate one for a society with pluralistic norms such as ours, with a federal system of government limited by many checks and balances. In practice, of course, no government is perfectly representative; nor are all decisions made by fair and democratic means. But even an imperfect expression of the public interest worked out through pluralistic, political means is, in our view, preferable to any existing basis for a substantive definition of the public good.

This is not to say that substantive criteria have no place in the definition of the public interest. Efficiency, morality, and beauty are proper concerns, and there are many others. All of these concerns may have some place in determining the desirability of some policy or situation for some person or group. And the participants in a public decision-making process will surely act to achieve the results they desire. There is, however, no reason to expect that everyone will always agree on desirability; nor is there any basis for making one concern, such as efficiency, paramount. When agreement on substantive criteria is possible, then they should be used. When there is no agreement, some procedure is needed, and much of the working of our political system can be described as such a procedure. In Charles Lindblom's terms, mutual partisan adjustment takes place until a consensus sufficient for action is achieved.[7] Collective bargaining can be thought of as a special form of mutual partisan adjustment applied to specific conflicts in labor-management relations.

Bargaining and Procedural Justice

We believe that collective bargaining, though it is imperfect, is the best available means for resolving a wide range of conflicting interests between labor and management. Bargaining can be a fair procedure for distributing stakes—goods and power—in areas of dispute where there is no substantive basis for deciding who gets what. In many areas of wage policy and working conditions, there are, we feel, no generally acceptable objective criteria of fairness or efficiency. If there were a way of knowing, separate from the wage-setting process itself, what is a fair wage, bargaining would be unnecessary, but this does not seem to be the case. The dollar value of a teacher's services cannot be calculated from some measurement of the outcomes of teaching. Since there is no substantive definition of the public interest in terms of some particular wage settlement or policy, there is no way to define an objectively fair wage for any particular group of teachers.

In the absence of substantive criteria, wage policy must be set on other criteria. Of course, a district board of education may arbitrarily set a wage. A teacher could simply choose to change jobs if the wage were unsatisfactory, and, if all teachers found the wage too low, the board would have to raise it to get teachers. In cases of an individual versus a board, however, the board has a significant advantage and probably could force wages perceived as "unfair" to teachers if it chose to do so. That advantage is based on the costs to the teacher of withholding services or changing jobs compared to the cost to the school district of hiring some other teacher. Because school districts are the only public employer of teachers in an area, changing jobs usually means either changing residence or traveling a greater distance, both costly to the individual. All the school district has to do is to recruit another comparable teacher. Unless the teacher is unusually qualified or gifted, replacement costs are usually small. Given this discrepancy in costs, the individual teacher's threats to withhold services or actually leave the job are quite weak bargaining tools. Some sort of collective action is clearly in the teacher's private interest.

How are "fair" wages and working conditions established if they do not rest on substantive grounds? In the absence of such a criterion, fairness depends on the procedure by which wages and working conditions are established. A standard of procedural fairness is the appropriate one for determining wages and establishing most working conditions in school systems. In this sense we mean "pure procedural justice" as described by Rawls. That is, a distribution of shares (goods, values, and so forth) is seen as fair because the distribution mechanism is a fair one, independent of any assessment of the amounts the parties receive.[8]

How collective bargaining in schools fits in the public interest comes down, in this analysis, to an examination of the process itself. If the process itself can be fair, especially in terms of its relationship with overall governance, then it is compatible with, even necessary to, the expression of the public interest in labor matters. How, then, can the fairness of collective bargaining be judged? While no exhaustive treatment of that question is possible here, it is necessary to provide sufficient detail to make our position clear.

Since bargaining is a process based on power, fairness depends on the nature and distribution of power among relevant parties.

The meaning of power and its distribution in the bargaining relationship is, thus, central to the idea of fairness. Power, in general, is the ability to cause another person or group to act in a way they otherwise would not. Bargaining power, in our terms, is a special case of the more general concept of power in political or social systems (see Chapter 6). More specifically, bargaining power is the ability to cause a bargaining opponent to realize that conceding is more advantageous than not conceding. Adjusting power in bargaining relationships, therefore, means adjusting the ability of the parties to force concessions from one another, that is, to impose costs.

In keeping with this principle of bargaining power, one party's ability to impose costs should be kept roughly in line with that party's stakes (money, power, status, and so forth) in the bargaining if the process is to be procedurally fair. In other words, one party should not be able to make large gains over another with relatively little risk. For example, a teachers' strike may inconvenience the community. The ability to impose costs on the community provides teachers with some bargaining power. If the state requires a fixed number of teaching days, irrespective of work stoppages, teachers must ultimately work the same number of days, no matter how long a strike. The potential cost or risk to the striking teachers is fairly small. The potential gain from a salary increase is, however, great. This discrepancy, in part a consequence of state policy, gives at least the appearance that teachers have an unfair advantage.

Many features of a bargaining relationship are affected by advantages of this sort. Not all will be part of public policy or amenable to direct action. Where policy or rule structures result in such imbalances, the criterion of procedural fairness requires that the imbalances be remedied.

Our concept of fairness in the bargaining relationship, therefore, is the distribution of power in proportion to the stakes or what is at risk. The most important stakes in bargaining are money, organizational or political power, status, or potential influence in future bargains. In a fair bargaining process, one's ability to impose costs on other parties, and thus influence outcomes, should be no greater than one's stakes in the outcomes relative to those of other parties. Parties with roughly equivalent stakes, for instance, should have roughly equal power.

This is a departure from the conventional notion of a fair bargaining process as one that is balanced, presumably with respect to power. Balance implies equivalence among parties. A strictly bilateral bargaining situation, where employer and employees have roughly equal stakes, is equivalent to the one described above. Bargaining in public-sector situations is, however, better described as multilateral, which means that equal balance among several parties, each with widely varying stakes in the outcomes, is difficult to achieve. Some standard other than balance is needed for judging the distribution of power among the parties.

One alternative is to structure the bargaining relationship through public policy, which reflects government's expression of the public interest. Then the relative power would reflect not stakes, but the public perception of the best distribution, taking into account stakes and any other criteria the public desired. This approach is attractive, but it is not feasible. Preferences would presumably shift from time to time and from bargain to bargain, and the public decision-making process is incapable of making the many adjustments necessary for bargaining. Not only would it tax the public decision-making process, but such an unstable environment could also wreak havoc with the bargaining process.

Fairness in Bargaining

A more general approach, one that protects and advances the public interest through fair bargaining without attempting to control the process or burden the government, is needed. The keys to such an approach are awareness, access, and representation. We assume, first, that the parties must be aware of their stakes in the outcomes. If they are not, it is the task of the government to make the necessary information available. If parties are aware of their stakes, they will, we assume, act in their own interest given the opportunity,[9] and the opportunity is provided through access and representation. Consider members of the teachers' union, clearly relevant parties. If they have access to information about the bargaining and are properly represented by the union officers, members can act in their own interest to influence the bargaining outcomes. Bargaining should, therefore, be structured to ensure that union members are properly represented and have adequate access to the process. The same argument applies to parents of school children. They should have information about bargaining, access to the bargainers, and adequate structures of representation through which to act in their own interests. We assume, further, that their motivation to act is proportional to their stakes and that their ability to influence the outcomes is proportional to their activity and their ability to affect the representatives. In short, rather than attempting to regulate the bargaining process and the distribution of power directly, public policy should be directed toward ensuring that relevant parties have the necessary information, access, and representative mechanisms to act in their own interests. If that is assured, then the process has the best chance to be fair and produce outcomes in the public interest.

This view of the public interest suggests that the internal affairs of unions for public employees are a public concern. In the private sector this is reflected in the Landrum-Griffin amendments to the National Labor Relations Act (NLRA), which set up a bill of rights for members of the union and established certain standards and reporting rules for internal decision making and finance.[10] Landrum-Griffin provisions are a partial answer to the assurance of access and representation for union members in the private sector. But the assurance is far from complete. There are many opportunities for union abuses in the private sector. In the public sector, laws seldom go as far as the NLRA in protecting union members' rights to access and representation in union decision making. This should be a major item on the state legislative agenda. State law should include a bill of rights for members; steps for legal recourse when rights are violated; rules governing the internal government of unions, particularly the election of officers and financial records; and strong enforcement mechanisms.

By the same reasoning, access and representation for those on the client or management side of a labor-management relationship are also public concerns. School boards are supposed to represent their constituents. State laws often reflect this by providing for open meetings and public access to information about school governance. But school boards may behave in a nonrepresentative manner.[11] And collective bargaining itself is excluded from open meeting or "sunshine" laws in most states. Thus, the content of bargaining and the implications of the contract under discussion are not normally known. This could be remedied by requiring that all proposals be published when bargaining begins and that tentative agreements be available for public examination before becoming effective.

The problem of representation is more difficult. It is not a special problem of collective bargaining, but a more generic one of school (or local) governance. Unfortunately there is no simple way to make local government more responsive to, and representative of, the governed. Increased state control of financing, curricular matters, accountability, and so forth can reduce the power of local boards. Traditions of nonpartisan, low-turnout elections can further isolate the board and reduce communication with voters. There is often a strong ideological commitment to the idea of isolating boards of education from partisan concerns and "political" entanglements. These structures and traditions further complicate the problem of responsiveness and representation. Changes in structure that raise the visibility of board elections and actions will help, as will active efforts on the part of boards to obtain the views of constituents. Boards need the active support of their constituents to maintain strong positions in bargaining and ensure the balance and fairness of the process. This should be seen as an integral part of bargaining strategy and incorporated into board practices and state policy.

IMPORTANCE OF EDUCATIONAL BARGAINING

Fairness and balance in educational bargaining have importance beyond the schools. Consider the position of collective bargaining in education within the larger context of the public sector. Three facts are central: Teachers are the largest single group of unionized public employees. In terms of the proportion of workers who consider themselves professionals, bargaining in schools involves more professionalized labor-management relations than any other employment setting. And, teachers have been bargaining collectively longer than almost any other kind of public employee. These facts strongly suggest that the accumulated experience of collective bargaining in education, particularly in public schools, is an enormous knowledge base. A careful examination of that base could lead to improved understanding of unions for public employees and of labor-management relations. Much can be learned about

the nature of collective bargaining activities among professionalized employee groups. And the variety of policy settings and legal
processes found in the states and in school districts provides a rich
source of information for developing and evaluating new policies.

In short, it may indeed be very useful to consider the practice of
collective bargaining in education to be the cutting edge of labor-
management relations in the public sector. Since the public sector
is also the place where growth in collective bargaining is greatest,
the generalization may extend to the whole field. Such a point of
view suggests three areas for future work. First, there is a need to
explore the similarities and differences between bargaining in the
school and in other parts of the public sector. This will allow
scholars and policy makers to assess better how the experience and
principles developed in one area can be applied to others. Second,
serious attempts at synthesis can be encouraged to bring the knowledge and experience in other areas together with that in public
education to build a more comprehensive and useful body of knowledge about the field. The question of how different bargaining in
the public sector is from that in the private sector, especially,
needs much more serious attention. Third, collective bargaining
in public education, and in the rest of the public sector as well,
can perhaps come to be viewed more as a natural and beneficial
phenomenon overall. In that case, the process itself is more likely
to fit the description on a commemorative stamp issue: "Collective
Bargaining: A Tool for Progress in the American Tradition."

NOTES

1. This point of view grows out of John Dunlop's conception in *Industrial
Relations Systems* (New York: McGraw-Hill, 1958), and subsequent theoretical
work in Gerald A. Somers, ed., *Essays in Industrial Relations Theory* (Ames:
Iowa State University Press, 1969).

2. For example see Neil W. Chamberlain and Donald E. Cullen, *The Labor
Sector*, 2d ed. (New York: McGraw-Hill, 1971), esp. chs. 12-13; and Richard E.
Walton and Robert B. McKersie, *A Behavioral Theory of Labor Negotiations*
(New York: McGraw-Hill, 1965), esp. ch. 1.

3. The closest thing to a general theory is presented in Walton and McKersie's
Behavioral Theory. But, by their own admission, it deals with the dynamics of
process alone, rather than structure, process, and environment together. Dunlop's
Industrial Relations Systems deals with the structure and elements of the environment, but it is more descriptive than explanatory. Other attempts at basic models

are Eugene C. Hagburg and Martin J. Levine, *Labor Relations: An Integrated Perspective* (St. Paul, Minn.: West, 1978); Donald Hellriegel *et al.,* "Collective Negotiations and Teachers: A Behavioral Analysis," *Industrial and Labor Relations Review,* 23:3 (April 1970), 380-396. Socio-psychological theory is reviewed in Jeffrey Z. Rubin and Bert R. Brown, *The Social Psychology of Bargaining and Negotiation* (New York: Academic Press, 1975). Economic models are discussed by Otomar J. Bartos, *The Process and Outcome of Negotiations* (New York: Columbia University Press, 1974). Multidisciplinary approaches are found in I. William Zartman, ed., *The Negotiation Process: Theories and Applications* (Beverly Hills, Calif.: Sage, 1978). These are only examples of a large literature that still awaits a general theory or synthesis.

4. Harry H. Wellington and Ralph K. Winter, *The Unions and the Cities* (Washington, D.C.: Brookings, 1971).

5. For a detailed discussion of the concept of the public interest see Brian Berry and Douglas W. Rae, "Political Evaluation," in *Handbook of Political Science.* Volume I, *Political Science: Scope and Theory*, ed. Fred I. Greenstein and Nelson W. Polsby (Reading, Mass.: Addison-Wesley, 1975).

6. Basic alternative views of justice are reviewed in John Rawls, *A Theory of Justice* (Cambridge, Mass.: Harvard University Press, 1971). See also Arthur M. Okun, *Equality and Efficiency: The Big Trade off* (Washington, D.C.: Brookings, 1975). Problems in defining the public interest in public-sector labor relations are described in the cases reported by Richard P. Schick and Jean J. Couturier, *The Public Interest in Government Labor Relations* (Cambridge, Mass.: Ballinger, 1977).

7. Charles E. Lindblom, *The Intelligence of Democracy* (New York: Free Press, 1965); and *id., The Policy-Making Process* (Englewood Cliffs, N.J.: Prentice-Hall, 1968).

8. Rawls, *Theory of Justice*, 86-87.

9. The informed, self-interested individual is a basic component of theories of political action. See, for example, James M. Buchanan and Gordon Tullock, *The Calculus of Consent* (Ann Arbor: University of Michigan Press, 1974).

10. The development of this part of federal labor law is described in Chamberlain and Cullen, *Labor Sector*, ch. 9.

11. M. Kent Jennings, "Patterns of School Board Responsiveness," in *Understanding School Boards*, ed. Peter J. Cistone (Lexington, Mass.: Lexington Books, 1975).

2

The State of Collective Bargaining

To understand something, it is helpful to know a bit about its origins and its main features. This discussion of the history and development of collective bargaining in education provides a foundation on which to build understanding of the dynamics of the process and how it fits into the institution of public education. As an activity in the schools, collective bargaining has grown enormously and changed drastically, particularly since 1965. There is reason to believe that the rapid rate of growth and the radical nature of the changes are now leveling off, which suggests a period of greater stability that will allow refinement of the patterns and structures that have been developing.

BEGINNINGS

The earliest history of collective bargaining in the public schools in the United States is not well documented for several reasons. For one thing, it is difficult to separate the process of collective bargaining from the development of unions. Unionization or, at least, the formal organization of teachers has a long history in this country. The National Education Association (NEA) was formed in 1857; the American Federation of Teachers (AFT), in 1916. To a greater or lesser degree, these national organizations and their local counterparts have always had some interest in the wages and working conditions of teachers.[1]

Another problem for the student of bargaining history is that there is no firm agreement on what constitutes collective bargaining. Is it sufficient for the employer to recognize a union or association as a legitimate voice for the expression of teacher interest? Does it require that the parties meet formally and discuss issues of mutual concern? Does it require the execution of a formal agreement that has a binding character?

Then there is the matter of legal status. In 1935 the National Labor Relations Act set down conditions and requirements for employer-employee bargaining in the private sector. Not until 1959, however, was there any legislation in the public sector that resembled the National Labor Relations Act in scope and requirements. Legal control is constitutionally reserved to the states, and this just simply was not addressed before 1959, when Wisconsin passed the first bargaining law for the public sector.

POST-WORLD WAR II GROWTH

During the Depression of the 1930's teachers had sacrificed by taking cuts in pay. Then, during the Second World War, they again sacrificed both as consumers and in terms of relative wages. Toward the end of the war and during the immediate postwar period, the country's economy underwent tremendous expansion to meet the needs created by the war and to satisfy consumer demand following years of deprivation. But teachers did not share in the rapid wage growth experienced in the private sector. By about 1942 teachers' wages began to fall relative to the wages of other workers. Then, with the close of hostilities, a number of servicemen used the GI Bill to return to college, and many became licensed to teach in the public schools. By the late 1940's they were beginning to look for employment. These increasing pressures led to considerable activity on the part of teachers' organizations and caused considerable conflict between teachers and boards of education.

During this period, several events are worth noting. An agreement between the American Federation of Teachers Local of

Cicero, Illinois, and the Cicero Board of Education in 1944 is believed to be the first collective bargaining contract for public school teachers. This contract apparently had many of the standard features of a labor agreement, including recognition, wage rates, grievance procedures, and standards for promotion.[2] The first representation election was held in a Chicago suburb in 1946.[3] In Norwalk, Connecticut, after a strike in 1946, the teachers' association, an NEA affiliate, gained formal recognition as the official bargaining agent for teachers. In Pawtucket, Rhode Island, in the same year, AFT Local No. 930 forced the board to negotiate its proposal for salary increases.[4]

By 1947 both national teachers' organizations had begun to have second thoughts about their positions on collective bargaining. Though neither would advocate collective bargaining as such, the NEA passed a resolution in 1947 recommending that "each member seek salary adjustment in a professional way through group action."[5] By 1948 circumstances had become so bad that teachers in over thirty school districts struck their employers. It would be the 1966-67 school year before that many teachers' strikes would again occur.

Though teachers had earlier behaved militantly over wages and working conditions, it seems fair to say that the period following World War II was a turning point in the development of teacher militancy and collective bargaining as we know it today. That was when both the NEA and the AFT began a serious reexamination of their positions on teachers' welfare and the means that might be employed to improve it. The movements in the teachers' organizations are discussed more fully in Chapters 3 and 4.

The next milestone occurred in 1959, when, as has already been mentioned, the legislature in Wisconsin enacted the first comprehensive public sector bargaining law, thereby setting the stage for large-scale bargaining among teachers in Wisconsin. That law became a model for subsequent legislative activity in other states.

The rise of the United Federation of Teachers in New York City in the early 1960's gave bargaining its next impetus. That union's agressive stance on teacher welfare in New York City culminated in a bargaining election and agreement. This event seemed to loose the floodgates, and collective bargaining has grown rapidly since that time.

RAPID DEVELOPMENT: 1965-1976

Although the early period of collective bargaining in education is poorly documented, data available for the last fifteen years are considerably more complete. Two major surveys provide somewhat comparable data about the state of collective bargaining in education at two different points in time. Viewed together, these studies describe a pattern of growth and change over an eleven-year period that leads into the current state of the process and provides some indication of the direction of future development.

Both studies were surveys of a sample of public school districts. The first, conducted by Wesley Wildman, Robert Burns, and Charles Perry in 1965, covered the 1964-65 school year. Their final report also included data from follow-up study through 1968. The second major study, conducted in 1976 by Michael Murphy, gathered data about events in the 1975-76 school year. Both surveys were comprehensive in nature. They asked about a variety of collective-bargaining events in school districts, and each systematically sampled a large segment of the school population of the United States during their respective time periods.

The two surveys are important for several reasons. For one thing, they represent reasonably complete pictures of collective bargaining in those school years. In addition, they provide an empirical basis for examining collective bargaining. And, finally, because the two surveys are separated by eleven years, they serve as a useful base for determining changes taking place in the collective bargaining arena in the public school systems in the United States.

The Survey in 1965

Wildman, Burns, and Perry confined their examination of activities to school districts that had enrolled at least 1,200 students in the 1963-64 school year.[6] There were 6,023 school systems divided into seven strata for purposes of analysis. As is still the case, the distribution of school districts by enrollment size is badly skewed toward smaller districts. Over half the school districts in the sample were in the smallest stratum enrolling between 1,200 and 2,999 students in 1963-64. Only a little over 1 percent of the school districts in the United States enrolled 50,000 or more students at that time.

The survey examined three elements in the bargaining process:

teacher organization and recognition patterns, the structure and procedures for collective interaction or negotiation relationship, and instances of impasse or persistent disagreement unresolved through the normal negotiation procedure.[7]

In addition, the research team requested copies of "any and all written documents or policy statements relating to teacher organization-school management relationships at the local level."[8] The survey provided four alternative steps for organizing teachers: affiliation with the NEA at the state or national level, affiliation with the AFT, development of an independent organization not affiliated with either the NEA or the AFT, or no organization at the local level.[9]

The Survey in 1976

This study, done in cooperation with the American Association of School Administrators, used a questionnaire sent to a 10 percent stratified sample of operating school districts.[10] The fifteen-page questionnaire, which covered most aspects of union organization, bargaining practice, and experience, is probably the most comprehensive survey done to date. Unlike the earlier study, this survey covered school districts in all size strata, not just those in the larger strata. The questionnaire, like that of the earlier study, was mailed to the chief school officer in each of the districts sampled. Thus, the data gathered represents the superintendent's estimate of the state of affairs. No attempts were made to confirm these data by independent checks or against other data sources.

Teachers' Organizations

The patterns and proportions of membership in teachers' organizations and distribution among school districts remained remarkably stable from 1965 to 1976. There was, of course, a growth in the number of teachers and in the absolute membership in teachers' organizations. But the number of organizations, local and national, and their relative share of the teaching population did not vary much. The NEA and the AFT were competing for members throughout this time period, but the proportional distribution of members between the two organizations has remained about the same.

In 1965, as might have been expected, the districts reported strong NEA-affiliated representation with about 75 percent of the reporting districts having only one organization, an affiliate of

NEA. The percentage breakdown for teachers' organizations in reporting districts is shown in Table 2-1. Two observations should be made in passing. The first is that NEA-affiliated organizations had a membership monopoly in over 75 percent of the districts, and the second is that, though not shown in the table, the data in the earlier study reveal that the single-organization districts tend to be concentrated in the smaller-sized strata.[11]

Over 50 percent of the responding districts reported they accorded one organization exclusive representational rights. There are some reasons to suspect this number is too high. Exclusive representation in conventional industrial relations usage means that the employing school board has recognized a single teachers' organization to represent all the teachers in discussions concerning wages, hours, and conditions of employment. Under the agreement, the board could not meet with any other representative organization. It is likely that many districts were actually reporting exclusive representation because there was only one active teachers' organization.

Table 2-1
Number and percentage of school districts by affiliation in
a teacher organization, 1965

Organizational affiliation	Number of districts	Percentage of districts
NEA only	3,235	75.1
AFT only	17	0.4
Independent only	213	4.9
NEA and AFT	322	7.4
NEA and independent	157	3.6
AFT and independent	8	0.2
NEA, AFT, and independent	33	0.8
No active organization	323	7.5

Source: Adapted from Wesley A. Wildman and Robert K. Burns, *Collective Action by Public School Teachers,* Volume 1, *Teacher Organizations and Collective Action: A Review of History and a Survey of School District Activity, 1964-65* (Washington, D.C.: Bureau of Research, Office of Education, U.S. Department of Health, Education, and Welfare, June 1968), 59.

In some of these one-organization districts, Wildman, Burns, and Perry found that the board had specifically reserved the right to meet with any employees' organization of their choosing. Hence, though they met with representatives of only one organization, they had, in fact, reserved the right to meet with multiple organizations. In that sense, they did not have a true exclusive bargaining agreement with one organization.[12]

By 1976 nearly all districts had at least one teachers' organization. About 85 percent of the districts responding reported that they had only one active association; about 10 percent reported two active organizations. Table 2-2 contains the summary data on the number and percentage of school districts with a given number of active teachers' organizations. This table and others report data both for all districts with a thousand or more students enrolled and by each size stratum. This was done so the data would compare more readily with those of the earlier study that covered only districts with 1,200 or more students.

In 1975, NEA affiliates still held a considerable edge over AFT locals in organizational strength. In instances where there was only one local teachers' organization in a district, that organization was almost always an NEA affiliate, and it was likely to enroll in excess of 80 percent of the teachers. The NEA also holds a tremendous lead in terms of overall organization. On the average, about 64 percent of the teachers in any given district can be expected to be NEA members, whereas, only about 7 percent are

Table 2-2
Number of active local teachers' organizations by size strata, 1976

Number of local organizations	Percentage of all districts	Percentage of districts with 1,000 or more students
1	85.0	84.1
2	10.2	12.8
3	1.6	1.8
4	0.4	0.6
5 or more	0.0	0.0
None	2.9	0.7

Source: Data from "Collective Negotiations in Education," National Manpower Resources Study, 1976, unpublished.

likely to belong to the AFT. It is interesting that about 11 percent of the teachers in the United States belong to local teachers' organizations that cannot be said to be local affiliates of the NEA or the AFT. These organizations may be unaffiliated or affiliated with some other organization, or they may be jointly affiliated with the AFT and the NEA. Independent organizations tend to be found in smaller districts.

The data on the percentage of teachers organized are shown by size strata in Table 2-3. We see from the table that the AFT and the NEA have been most successful in organizing teachers in the large systems. Neither organization has been as successful in organizing the teachers in very small districts.

By and large, administrators no longer belong to teacher organizations. In the case of the primary teachers' organization, usually an NEA affiliate, respondents to the survey indicated that only in about 25 percent of the organizations were the administrators members. In over three-quarters of the districts, supervisors and administrators were barred from membership.[13]

Table 2-3

Percentage of membership in teacher organization according to enrollment of school district, 1976

| Enrollment | Teacher organization | | | |
	NEA	AFT	Other[a]	Total[b]
Less than 300	39.8	3.8	21.7	65.3
300 to 599	52.2	11.5	14.3	78.0
600 to 999	61.7	2.1	17.0	80.8
1,000 to 2,499	67.2	6.4	10.2	83.8
2,500 to 4,999	67.3	6.7	10.0	84.0
5,000 to 9,999	76.6	4.1	5.4	86.1
10,000 to 24,999	66.6	14.2	5.1	85.9
25,000 or more	66.7	13.2	2.1	82.0
All strata	63.7	6.6	11.4	81.7

[a] Nonaffiliated or jointly affiliated locals.
[b] Totals may not equal 100 percent because of rounding.
Source: Data from "Collective Negotiations in Education."

Bargaining Interactions

The most remarkable and significant area of growth from 1965 to 1975 was in the level of bargaining activity. As we have seen, at the beginning of the period teachers' organizations were well established and widely distributed in school systems, but what could be called true bargaining activity was still at a relatively low level. By the end of the period, the level of bargaining activity had more than doubled, so that most of the districts sampled were involved in some form of collective interaction. This was not a creation of a completely new pattern of behavior between boards and management and their employees. Instead, it appears to be the transformation of a form of teacher consultation with management about working conditions and compensation into bilateral negotiations. The process was a rapid one, and it now seems to be the dominant mode.

Though collective bargaining in education began earlier in some districts, it seems unlikely that a survey conducted for the 1964-65 school year caught the early period of collective bargaining activity in most school districts. Wildman, Burns, and Perry themselves observe that, in 1964-65, they could locate only nineteen "substantive, bilateral, signed agreements containing salary schedules, grievance procedures, and clauses covering a myriad of so-called working conditions and perhaps professional matters."[14] Two years later, as a result of follow-up work, the same authors report that they were able to identify four hundred such agreements. Thus, in the school year 1964-65, though there was much beginning ferment toward collective bargaining activity, there were as yet few formal bilateral agreements—the primary artifact of most serious collective bargaining activity. It may be assumed that bargaining was yet to begin in most districts surveyed.

As a result of the responses to their questionnaire, Wildman, Burns, and Perry posited the four structural types of bargaining interaction and defined them as follows:

Consultation: "Sporadic meeting between leaders of the teacher organization and the administration for the purpose of discussing matters of mutual interest, but without any active or sustained attempt by the organization to represent the teachers on questions of salaries and/or working conditions."

Testimony: "An effort by the teacher organization to present teacher views on salaries and working conditions largely through appearance of presentations (not negotiations) at regular board meetings."

Superintendent negotiations: "Meetings between the superintendent (or his representatives) and the teacher organization for the express purpose of developing mutually acceptable proposals on salaries and/or working conditions for submission to the board."

Board negotiations: "Meetings, from the onset of negotiations, between representatives of the teacher organization and the board (or committee including at least some board members) for the express purpose of developing mutually acceptable policies on salaries and/or working conditions."[15] The types are shown in Figure 2-1.

Probably because of the period in which the questionnaire was constructed, those procedures that Wildman, Burns, and Perry labeled "formal negotiation" did not necessarily result in a contract. This is particularly true in the case of superintendent negotiations,

Management participant

Style of interaction	Superintendent	Board
Informal	A Consultation	B Testimony
Formal	C Superintendent negotiations	D Board negotiations

Figure 2-1
Four collective interaction types posited by Wildman, Burns, and Perry (adapted from Wildman and Burns, *Collective Action by Public School Teachers. Volume 1, Teacher Organizations and Collective Action: A Review of History and a Survey of School District Activity, 1964-65* [Washington, D.C.: Bureau of Research, Office of Education, U.S. Department of Health, Education, and Welfare, June 1968], 49)

where it was assumed that those negotiations would result in a jointly sponsored proposal made to the board of education for their ratification and subsequent inclusion in district policy. Meet-and-confer-type arrangement would be classified under the "formal" category in this system. As we shall see from the survey done in 1976, a distinction can now be made between these types of inter-actions since, in most collective bargaining, it is assumed that a contract, and not a jointly recommended set of policies, is the ob-ject of negotiations.

Although four types of interactions were proposed, Wildman, Burns, and Perry discovered that many districts had mixed types. In some cases both informal and formal structures existed, or both the superintendent and the board were involved in the interaction (see Figure 2-2).

Several things may be noted from the figure describing the types of interaction. First, the most common interaction is formal. Over 46 percent of the districts reported some form of formal interac-tion, that is, superintendent negotiations, board negotiations, or mixed negotiations. Somewhat fewer districts reported informal interaction, and something over 16 percent reported an interaction pattern that combined informal and formal procedures. A majority of nearly 60 percent of the school districts reported that the primary interaction was with the superintendent or his staff, but in nearly 25 percent of the districts the teacher organizations interacted directly with the board of education. About 15 percent of the districts re-ported a procedure where both the board and the superintendent shared the responsibility for interaction.

Informal interactions, that is, those of a consultative or testi-monial nature, were more likely to be with the board of education than with the superintendent. On the other hand, when the inter-actions were formal, they were more likely to be managed by the superintendent. In 21 percent of the cases, however, formal negotia-tions were conducted directly with the board of education, a sur-prising situation in light of industrial practice. The prevalence of this previous arrangement in which testimony to the board was the primary mode of interaction probably explains this deviation from the common practice of managers handling the negotiations process.

Of districts surveyed in 1976, about 85 percent had some form of

PRIMARY INTERACTION RESPONSIBILITY	INTERACTION STRUCTURE			
	Informal	Mixed	Formal	
	Consultation	→ ←	Superintendent negotiations	Row total (number and percent)
Superintendent				
Number	822	127	1,384	2,333
Percent of row	35.2	5.4	59.3	
Percent of column	56.4	19.8	76.5	
Percent of total	21.0	3.2	35.4	59.7
Mixed				
Number	63	498	44	605
Percent of row	10.4	82.3	7.3	
Percent of column	4.3	77.6	2.4	
Percent of total	1.6	12.7	1.1	15.5
	Testimony	→ ←	Board negotiations	
Board				
Number	573	17	382	972
Percent of row	59.0	1.7	39.3	
Percent of column	39.3	2.6	21.1	
Percent of total	14.7	0.4	9.8	24.8
Column total (number)	1,458	642	1,810	3,910
Column total (percent)	37.3	16.4	46.3	100.0

Figure 2-2
Number of school districts by type of interaction structure
and primary responsibility, 1965
(adapted from Wildman and Burns, *Collective Action by Public Schools*,
Volume 1, 91)

collective interaction with teachers' organizations relative to wages and working conditions. The breakdown is shown in Table 2-4. Collective interactions vary from simple consultation to contract negotiations. Three kinds of interaction systems describe relationships between teachers and their employing school districts:

Consultation—meeting between leaders of the teachers' organization and the board or administration for the purpose of soliciting or discussing employee views on salaries, benefits, or working conditions. There is no explicit or implicit requirement that meeting will continue until differences have been resolved. Neither an agreement nor mutually acceptable policy is the objective of the meeting.

Informal negotiation—meeting between representatives of an acknowledged employee organization and the board or its representative to develop mutually acceptable policy or policy recommendations in matters of salary, benefits, or working conditions. Though these negotiations may differ in style and tone from contract negotiations, the main difference is that neither party expects to enter into a formal, binding agreement (that is, a contract) as a result of the negotiation. In some cases, a memorandum of understanding or some other informal document may be issued as a record of conclusions reached during informal negotiation.

Contract negotiation—meeting between representatives of a recognized employee organization and representatives of the board to engage in bilateral negotiations with the express purpose of producing a formal agreement (that is, a contract) covering salaries, benefits, and conditions of work. Meet-and-confer systems will be considered to be in this category if a contract is made or is the expected outcome.[16]

In 1976 most districts were engaged in contract negotiations. About 76 percent of all districts and about 80 percent of those

Table 2-4
Percentage of districts by presence of collective interaction, 1976

Interaction	Percentage of all districts	Percentage of districts with 1,000 or more students
Collective	84.6	88.9
No collective	15.4	11.1

Source: Data from "Collective Negotiations in Education."

districts with 1,000 or more students reported they engaged in contract negotiations. The remainder engaged either in consultation or informal negotiation. Table 2-5 shows the distribution of interaction types in the school districts.

In 1976, districts reported that, for an average of seven years, they had been engaging in their present form of collective interaction with their teachers' organizations. In that most districts reported to be engaging in contract negotiations, use of collective bargaining as we know it had become widespread by about 1968.

The vast majority of school districts acknowledge or recognize one teachers' organization to be the representative of teachers. This seems to be true in small districts as well as large districts (Table 2-6). It is probably not the case, however, that this state of affairs is the product of a competitive choice by bargaining election or some similar mechanism. Most likely, the dominance of exclusive representation arrangements results from the number of school districts that have only one active teachers' organization.

Of these districts engaging in collective interaction, about 75 percent reported that they have a contract or agreement with the teachers' organization that covers salaries, benefits, or conditions

Table 2-5

Percentage of districts by type of interaction
with teacher organization(s), 1976

Type of interaction	Percentage of all districts	Percentage of districts with 1,000 or more students
Consultation	10.9	8.2
Informal negotiation	13.3	12.0
Contract negotiation	75.8	79.8

Source: Data from "Collective Negotiations in Education."

Table 2-6

Percentage of districts by type of recognition
of teachers' representative, 1976

Type of recognition	Percentage of all districts	Percentage of districts with 1,000 or more students
Exclusive representation	91.7	91.8
Nonexclusive representation	8.3	8.2

Source: Data from "Collective Negotiations in Education."

of work. For districts with more than a thousand students, the percentage of districts with contracts is slightly higher (see Table 2-7). Contracts may last for one year, or they may cover multiple years. It would appear that most contracts have a life of one (42 percent) or two (43 percent) years; some, a life of three years (10 percent). Taken together, the information on teachers' organization and the degree of collective interaction suggest that school districts in the United States were heavily engaged in collective bargaining in 1975-76.

In the private sector, unions had to organize plant by plant and industry by industry. Unlike other sectors of the economy, however, public education had forms that could easily be translated into conventional bargaining arrangements. The organizational base was already established when the national organizations decided to endorse collective bargaining, which meant that teachers' unions were spared the expense of having to organize school by school and district by district. The fact that teachers already belonged to the NEA or the AFT allowed for the more rapid spread of bargaining and explains, in large part, why so many school districts now bargain collectively.

Another factor that has spurred bargaining has been the strong trend in the last decade for states to enact legislation that would enable or require school authorities to negotiate with their teachers. Certainly these factors, plus the tradition of discussing salaries, benefits, and conditions of work with representatives of teachers' organizations, have set the stage for the rapid spread of bargaining in public education.

Impasse

Another major area of inquiry for Wildman, Burns, and Perry was the nature and frequency of impasse. In their study, 1,688

Table 2-7
Percentage of districts with formal contract or agreement, 1976

Contract status	Percentage of all districts	Percentage of districts with 1,000 or more students
Have	75	78.6
Do not have	25	21.4

Source: Data from "Collective Negotiations in Education."

districts reporting the existence of formal negotiations also responded to a questionnaire on impasse. Of those districts, 142 or 8.4 percent reported that an impasse had occurred in their past negotiations.[17] A second questionnaire was sent to these 142 districts, and 112 responded. On those questionnaires returned, 78 of the impasses reported turned out to be, by Wildman, Burns, and Perry's definition, true impasses, that is, situations where resolution "required some action other than sustained negotiation."[18]

Analysis of the impasses disclosed by the study revealed that three impasse resolution mechanisms (see Table 2-8) were employed:

1. unilateral action by teachers including ultimate weapons such as strikes and other lesser techniques that might be advocated by the NEA or the AFT;
2. procedures involving neutral third parties, including formal procedures such as intervention by public officials outside the system, recourse to the courts, appointment of citizens' committees, and studies by a committee of educators under the auspices of the NEA; and
3. referral of the dispute to higher levels on either side on a private basis.

Table 2-8
Frequency of use of impasse resolution mechanisms, 1965

Mechanism type	Number of cases
Unilateral action	**27**
Ultimate weapons	10
Lesser techniques	17
Procedures	**37**
Formal	15
Ad hoc	22
Referral	**16**
To board	8
To consultant	8
Total	**80**

Source: From Charles R. Perry, *Collective Action by Public School Teachers.* Volume III, *Impasse Resolution in Teacher Negotiations* (Washington, D.C.: Bureau of Research, Office of Education, U.S. Department of Health, Education, and Welfare, January 1968), 12.

The patterns revealed in the table suggest that, in 1964-65, the formal procedures for coping with impasses were relatively undeveloped and unused. Of the eighty impasses turned up in the first and second questionnaires, only fifteen were dealt with by formal impasse resolution mechanisms. Surprisingly, twenty-seven of the eighty involved the use of some unilateral job action on the part of the teachers. This indicates that, in 1964-65, it was not customary to exhaust third-party procedures before resorting to job actions.

Impasses and strikes, probably the most visible aspects of collective bargaining, became much more common between 1965 and 1976. Slightly over 8 percent of the districts had experienced true impasse in 1965. Of the districts engaged in negotiation in 1975, about 35 percent experienced an impasse. The "ultimate unilateral weapon," which is taken to mean a job action, had occurred only 12.5 percent of the time in 1965. In 1975, 17 percent of districts with impasses also had job actions; thus, many more districts experienced impasse in 1975 than had experienced it in 1965, and a higher proportion of these impasses resulted in a job action.

Examination of impasse experience by size in 1975 revealed that there is a definite relationship: smaller districts have many fewer impasses than larger districts. Over 50 percent of the bargaining interactions ended in impasse in two of the three largest strata. In districts of 25,000 or more students, over two-thirds of the bargaining relationships experienced an impasse during the bargaining year. In districts of 1,000 or more students where impasses occurred, about 18 percent culminated in some sort of job action that lasted about thirteen days, required schools to be closed for two days on the average, and cost the district about $35,000 in lost revenue and additional salaries. Table 2-9 shows impasse experience for districts in each size stratum.

But, though the percentages of both impasses and job actions were higher in 1975 than they had been in 1965, two things should be remembered. First, the impasse rate was dramatically higher—an increase of over 400 percent. The impasse-to-job action ratio was also up, but considerably less high—with about 36 percent of the impasses involving job actions. Second, with the amount of bargaining activity and the impasse rate both up, the load on impasse resolution machinery has increased dramatically. In the sample of districts with 1,200 or more students in 1975, there may have been

4,200 impasses, about 2,900 of which were in districts with 1,000 or more students.

In 1965 there were relatively few established procedures for impasse resolution provided by governmental agencies, and most school districts had not developed their own. Less than 20 percent of the impasses were referred to formal resolution procedures. It appears that impasses were dealt with on an ad hoc basis at that time. In 1975 over 80 percent of the impasses were referred to third parties for assistance, nearly all of which went into mediation. About half were settled through mediation. It seems that, at the same time bargaining is becoming more formal and probably "tougher," it is being more expertly managed. Although impasses may be declared more frequently, they are also being resolved more expeditiously once declared.

Administration of Labor—Management Relations

As the relationships between employees and management change, one would expect that the structures and jobs of management would change as well. Unfortunately, the study from 1965 did not deal directly with administrative structures and personnel assignments for collective bargaining and related activities. Some patterns of administrative behavior described in discussion of bargaining interactions are, however, enlightening. From these, it is clear that, in 1965, the superintendent was a dominant figure in the handling of collective action. The superintendent was not always the bargaining representative of the board, but the basic role was established. The survey done in 1976 shows the superintendent is still the dominant figure. While the superintendent is still in a key position, however, the amount of responsibility delegated seems to have expanded since the earlier survey.

Table 2-10 shows the functional responsibilities for employment relations by size of district. In small districts, the superintendent is generally involved, but, in 23 percent of those districts, it is a board member or members. In school districts in the 300 to 1,000 student range, the superintendent is almost always directly involved, with board members playing a lesser role. Where most directly involved in negotiations, the superintendent serves as the chief negotiator only 29 percent of the time. As districts become larger, the dominance of the superintendent lessens until, in the largest stratum,

Table 2-9

Number and percentage of school districts by enrollment and impasse experience, 1976

Impasse experience	Enrollment								Row total (number and percent)
	Less than 300	300 to 599	600 to 999	1,000 to 2,499	2,500 to 4,999	5,000 to 9,999	10,000 to 24,999	25,000 or more	
Impasse									
Number	7	12	14	74	55	39	16	15	232
Percent of row	3.1	5.2	6.2	31.8	23.6	16.8	6.9	6.4	
Percent of column	23.1	15.6	16.7	37.0	40.7	51.3	43.2	68.2	
Percent of total	1.1	1.8	2.2	11.1	8.3	5.9	2.4	2.3	35.0
No impasse									
Number	24	65	72	126	80	37	21	7	432
Percent of row	5.6	15.0	16.7	29.2	18.5	8.6	4.9	1.6	
Percent of column	76.9	84.4	83.3	63.0	59.3	48.7	56.8	31.8	
Percent of total	3.6	9.8	10.8	19.0	12.0	5.6	3.2	1.1	65.0
Column total (number)	31	77	86	200	135	76	37	22	664
Column total (percent)	4.7	11.6	13.0	30.1	20.3	11.4	5.6	3.3	100.0

Source: Data from "Collective Negotiations in Education."

Table 2-10

Number and percentage of school districts by enrollment and by district employee most involved in employment relations, 1976

Employee most involved	Less than 300	300 to 599	600 to 999	1,000 to 2,499	2,500 to 4,999	5,000 to 9,999	10,000 to 24,999	25,000 or more	Row total (number and percent)
Superintendent									
Number	24	72	79	153	64	25	6	2	425
Percent of row	5.6	16.9	18.6	36.0	15.1	5.9	1.4	.5	
Percent of column	76.9	93.7	89.2	80.1	53.8	36.2	17.1	9.1	
Percent of total	3.8	11.4	12.5	24.2	10.1	4.0	.9	.3	67.2
Superintendent for business administration									
Number	0	0	0	12	19	9	6	1	47
Percent of row	0.0	0.0	0.0	25.5	40.4	19.1	12.8	2.1	
Percent of column	0.0	0.0	0.0	6.3	16.0	13.0	17.1	4.5	
Percent of total	0.0	0.0	0.0	1.9	3.0	1.4	.9	.2	7.4
Superintendent for personnel									
Number	0	0	0	5	13	14	9	7	48
Percent of row	0.0	0.0	0.0	10.4	27.1	29.2	18.8	14.6	
Percent of column	0.0	0.0	0.0	2.6	10.9	20.3	25.7	31.8	
Percent of total	0.0	0.0	0.0	.8	2.1	2.2	1.4	1.1	7.6
Director of personnel									
Number	0	0	0	0	4	10	7	0	21
Percent of row	0.0	0.0	0.0	0.0	19.0	47.6	33.3	0.0	
Percent of column	0.0	0.0	0.0	0.0	3.4	14.5	20.0	0.0	
Percent of total	0.0	0.0	0.0	0.0	.6	1.6	1.1	0.0	3.3

	1	2	3	4	5	6	7	8	Total
Director of employee relations									
Number	0	0	0	1	0	1	2	7	11
Percent of row	0.0	0.0	0.0	9.1	0.0	9.1	18.2	63.6	
Percent of column	0.0	0.0	0.0	.5	0.0	1.4	5.7	31.8	
Percent of total	0.0	0.0	0.0	.2	0.0	.2	.3	1.1	1.7
Business manager									
Number	0	0	0	6	10	1	1	0	18
Percent of row	0.0	0.0	0.0	33.3	55.6	5.6	5.6	0.0	
Percent of column	0.0	0.0	0.0	3.1	8.4	1.4	2.9	0.0	
Percent of total	0.0	0.0	0.0	.9	1.6	.2	.2	0.0	2.8
Administrative assistant									
Number	0	0	0	3	4	1	2	1	11
Percent of row	0.0	0.0	0.0	27.3	36.4	9.1	18.2	9.1	
Percent of column	0.0	0.0	0.0	1.6	3.4	1.4	5.7	4.5	
Percent of total	0.0	0.0	0.0	.5	.6	.2	.3	.2	1.7
Board member or members									
Number	7	5	10	3	2	0	0	0	27
Percent of row	27.1	18.0	36.1	11.3	7.5	0.0	0.0	0.0	
Percent of column	23.1	6.3	10.8	1.6	1.7	0.0	0.0	0.0	
Percent of total	1.1	.8	1.5	.5	.3	0.0	0.0	0.0	4.2
Contracted out completely									
Number	0	0	0	2	0	1	0	0	3
Percent of row	0.0	0.0	0.0	66.7	0.0	33.3	0.0	0.0	
Percent of column	0.0	0.0	0.0	1.0	0.0	1.4	0.0	0.0	
Percent of total	0.0	0.0	0.0	.3	0.0	.2	0.0	0.0	.5

Table 2-10 *(continued)*

Number and percentage of school districts by enrollment and by district employee most involved in employment relations, 1976

Employee most involved	Enrollment								Row total (number and percent)
	Less than 300	300 to 599	600 to 999	1,000 to 2,499	2,500 to 4,999	5,000 to 9,999	10,000 to 24,999	25,000 or more	
Other									
Number	0	0	0	6	3	7	2	4	22
Percent of row	0.0	0.0	0.0	27.2	13.6	31.8	9.1	18.2	
Percent of column	0.0	0.0	0.0	3.1	2.5	10.1	5.7	18.2	
Percent of total	0.0	0.0	0.0	.9	.5	1.1	.3	.6	3.3
Column total (number)	31	77	89	191	119	69	35	22	633
Column total (percent)	4.9	12.1	14.0	30.2	18.8	10.9	5.5	3.5	100.0

Source: Data from "Collective Negotiations in Education."

the superintendent or chief executive officer is identified as being the one most directly involved with the collective negotiations process in only 9 percent of the districts. It is more likely, in large districts, that an assistant superintendent for personnel or a director of employment relations will be the major person involved. Table 2-11 shows the involvement with the negotiator of persons in each personnel category.

The superintendent, while usually in charge of the negotiating process, is not generally the negotiator. An assistant superintendent or another central administrator is more likely to be the chief negotiator if the superintendent's office is responsible for the bargaining function. In the few districts with a director of employment relations (only about 1.7 percent) that person almost always will serve as chief negotiator. It is interesting that board members are involved in negotiations in 4.2 percent of the districts, and, in slightly over half of those districts, the board member or members also do the negotiating. The superintendent maintains general responsibility for collective bargaining, but tends to delegate functional responsibilities to various members of the staff. It is likely that the process is still considered so important that the superintendents have not yet disengaged from the bargaining process, but, rather, have simply delegated some of the duties.

The handling of the collective bargaining process in school districts does vary with district size. With larger, more functionally specialized staffs, the superintendent can delegate responsibilities. Inevitably, the responsibility for collective negotiations is one of those delegated. In districts with 5,000 or more students, the superintendent is no longer the dominant person. One might conclude from this evidence that the handling of collective bargaining varies from being a general office function in small districts to being a personnel function in larger districts, to being an employment or labor relations specialty in largest systems (see Figure 2-3).

Because most districts are small or medium in size and likely to remain so, labor relations will probably always be part of the general administrative responsibility. The generalist administrator is a strong tradition in education, and the concept of advocacy teams or specialist administrators is not widely practiced except in the largest of school districts. One usually gets to be superintendent or chief school officer by having worked through the

Table 2-11
Number and percent of school districts by negotiation role of
district employee and type of employee most involved in
employment relations, 1976

Type of employee	Negotiations Role		
	Does not negotiate	Negotiates	Row total (number and percent)
Superintendent			
Number	301	124	425
Percent of row	70.9	29.1	
Percent of column	75.7	52.7	
Percent of total	47.6	19.6	67.2
Superintendent for business administration			
Number	21	26	47
Percent of row	44.7	55.3	
Percent of column	5.3	11.1	
Percent of total	3.3	4.1	7.4
Superintendent for personnel			
Number	23	25	48
Percent of row	47.9	52.1	
Percent of column	5.8	10.6	
Percent of total	3.6	4.0	7.6
Director of personnel			
Number	13	8	21
Percent of row	61.9	38.1	
Percent of column	3.3	3.4	
Percent of total	2.1	1.3	3.3
Director of employee relations			
Number	2	9	11
Percent of row	18.2	81.8	
Percent of column	0.5	3.8	
Percent of total	0.3	1.4	1.7
Business manager			
Number	14	4	18
Percent of row	77.8	22.2	
Percent of column	3.5	1.7	
Percent of total	2.2	0.6	2.8

Table 2-11 *(continued)*

Type of employee	Negotiations Role		
	Does not negotiate	Negotiates	Row total (number and percent)
Administrative assistant			
Number	4	7	11
Percent of row	36.4	63.6	
Percent of column	1.0	3.0	
Percent of total	0.6	1.1	1.7
Board member or members			
Number	12	15	27
Percent of row	43.6	56.4	
Percent of column	2.9	6.4	
Percent of total	1.8	2.4	4.2
Contracted out completely			
Number	2	1	3
Percent of row	66.7	33.3	
Percent of column	0.5	0.4	
Percent of total	0.3	0.2	0.5
Other			
Number	6	16	22
Percent of row	28.6	71.4	
Percent of column	1.5	6.8	
Percent of total	0.9	2.6	3.5
Column total (number)	398	235	633
Column (percent)	62.9	37.1	100.0

Source: Data from "Collective Negotiations in Education."

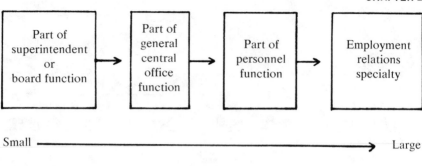

Size of district

Figure 2-3
Conduct of employment affairs

administrative chairs from building officer up through the levels. People who occupy administrative positions below the rank of superintendent are usually on their way to the superintendency. As a consequence, the chief executive officer believes, perhaps rightly, that he knows as much about any administrative function of the district as the person in the administrative hierarchy more directly responsible for that particular function. The handling of employment relations in education seems to follow in that tradition, with the chief school officer taking the major role. In fact, as has been noted, they often devote as much as 20 percent of their time to that function.

In the survey conducted in 1976, districts were asked about plans for managing employment relations in the future. The districts indicated that it is unlikely that they will change their present pattern. What this means is that most have no firm plans for hiring labor relations specialists. They do not plan to hire new labor relations consultants; nor do they plan to recruit new members to the administrative team who are labor relations specialists. Rather, they will follow two policies. First, all other things being equal, they will select a candidate for an administrative position who has had some experience or some training in labor relations over a candidate who has not. About 20 percent of the school districts will pay attention to labor relations competencies when they hire administrative personnel, and about 60 percent say that training in labor relations would give a candidate an advantage in screening considerations. Second, they plan to employ the conventional educators' technique of staff remediation: encouraging present administrators to upgrade their skills via course work and in-service development. In many instances they report either having held or intending to hold conferences and workshops on labor relations for district employees. One might conclude that labor relations, therefore, is and will remain an integral part of the administrative function and will not become a specialty area.

Table 2-12 traces the investment of time (as a percentage of total time available) for the person most directly concerned with labor relations. In larger districts, the share of time consumed tends to be higher. This has to be considered in light of the fact that, in larger districts, the person most directly responsible is more functionally specialized to accommodate a task that is growing more complex. That is why, in the smaller-sized strata, it is primarily a share of the superintendent's time that is most generally reflected in the total. In the middle strata, however, time spent is shared by an assistant superintendent for personnel or for business affairs and, in the upper-sized strata, the time spent is that of an employment relations specialist. It is likely that in larger districts the function of collective bargaining is becoming so time consuming and so complex that the superintendent has virtually been forced to abandon the labor relations area and turn it over to someone

Table 2-12

Percentage of time devoted to collective bargaining by district employee who is most involved by school district enrollment, 1976

Enrollment	Percentage of work time
Less than 300	16.90
300 to 599	9.93
600 to 999	11.85
1,000 to 2,499	17.47
2,500 to 4,999	21.07
5,000 to 9,999	25.68
10,000 to 24,999	36.87
25,000 or more	34.75
All districts	19.11

Source: Data from "Collective Negotiations in Education."

with more time to devote to it, for, in the large strata, it occupies more than one-third of one person's available time. It is unlikely that the superintendent, particularly in a large school district, could afford to spend this much time on any one activity.

Cost of Bargaining

At least two direct costs are effectively associated with the management of collective bargaining. One, time cost, has to do with the amount of administrative time available. Another has to do with the costs incurred in hiring individuals or firms to perform various functions related to labor relations. Table 2-13 shows the amount of time, as a percentage of time available both at the district level and at the building level, devoted to the maintenance of the employment relations system. It may be noted that the time cost increases until one reaches the very largest strata; then it diminishes rapidly. This is probably because school districts tend to specialize the function if they have 25,000 or more students and remove it from the general administrators' responsibility. The time commitment is still substantial, nonetheless, with an average of almost 18 percent of the total time at the district level and about 12 percent of the time available at the building level being devoted to these functions.

Table 2-13

Percentage of administrative time given to employee relations, by level or district organization and enrollment, 1976

| | Level | | |
| | District | Building | Number of districts |
Enrollment			
Less than 300	12.95	12.84	53
300 to 599	11.55	8.75	82
600 to 999	15.61	12.45	106
1,000 to 2,499	17.65	11.92	213
2,500 to 4,999	20.81	14.77	149
5,000 to 9,999	21.85	10.98	82
10,000 to 24,999	24.00	15.42	39
25,000 or more	13.90	9.25	20
All districts	17.69	12.34	744

Source: Data from "Collective Negotiations in Education."

We hasten to note that employee relations can include a number of functions that might be called personnel matters in other instances. And so, they do not necessarily represent a complete add-on as a result of collective bargaining.

The time costs and actual expenditures for the purchase of additional contract services can be summarized as a cost per pupil. Table 2-14 shows these costs for maintaining the labor relations system. In 1975 about fourteen dollars per pupil, on the average, was spent for administering employment relations. This would include, of course, both negotiating and administering the contract. The per capita costs of the system were greatest in the very small districts where negotiating and administering the contract take up much of a superintendent's time. They are relatively constant throughout most of the strata until, again, in the very largest districts there are economies of scale resulting from a specialized function. In 1976 there were about 45 million students enrolled in public, elementary, and secondary schools.[19] If it costs fourteen dollars per pupil to maintain the labor relations functions in school systems, this means that, in the United States in 1975, school systems collectively spent about $630 million on employment relations.

Trends over the Ten-Year Period

There are some problems with comparisons between the study done in 1965 and that done in 1976. Wildman, Burns, and Perry on occasion employed different definitions, reported their data

Table 2-14

Cost of employee relations per pupil by enrollment, 1976

Enrollment	Per pupil cost
Less than 300	36.94
300 to 599	11.60
600 to 999	12.02
1,000 to 2,499	13.58
2,500 to 4,999	11.93
5,000 to 9,999	11.74
10,000 to 24,999	12.23
25,000 or more	8.63
All districts	13.88

Source: Data from "Collective Negotiations in Education."

differently, and used different classification schemes. There is enough similarity between the studies, however, to derive some conclusions about collective bargaining during the last decade. In union organization patterns, for instance, it is relatively clear that few, if any, changes have occurred. Teachers are as completely organized now as they were in 1965, and the distribution of membership among national organizations has been very stable. The interaction between teachers' unions and their employers has changed rather dramatically, however. First, Wildman, Burns, and Perry found that just over half of the districts in their sample reported granting exclusive recognition rights to a single teachers' organization; by 1976, however, over 90 percent of the school districts reported engaging in this practice.

Second, it is clear that the last ten years have seen considerable formalization of the interaction processes. The percentage of districts using consultation interaction systems has declined sharply, from 37 percent in 1965 to 8 percent in 1976.[20] Altogether, about 90 percent of the districts surveyed in 1976 were engaged in informal or formal negotiations synonomous with negotiations conducted in 1965, when about 46 percent of the districts engaged in those practices.

It is clear from these comparisons that the process of formal adversarial bargaining has changed considerably in the eleven years between the two studies. The rapid development may be explained by several factors. First, there was an organizational readiness for these developments. Unlike the private sector, where unions had to create their membership base by organizing each individual work location, teachers' organizations were already in existence. In 1965, as well as in 1976, the vast majority of teachers belonged to one of the major organizations. During this period, of course, the NEA significantly altered its position on militant behavior and collective bargaining. They did this in such a fashion that their membership base was not significantly eroded.

During this period many states also adopted bargaining legislation for teachers or strengthened existing legislation. Most of these laws require school districts to negotiate with their teachers. These laws have lowered barriers to bargaining and set in motion bargaining behaviors in districts of all sizes in all parts of the country. Another organizational factor that contributed to the rapid development of bargaining was a tradition wherein teachers and school districts discussed salaries, benefits, and conditions of work. In this process of consultation and testimony, in effect long before the present era of teacher militancy, teachers' organizations had customarily been called upon by the board of education or the superintendent to present their views on salaries and other related matters. To convert this practice into formal bargaining was a much smaller step than initiating completely new relationships.

Finally, there is a strong tradition among teachers' organizations to imitate the organizational structure of larger school districts. Thus, as larger organizations have adopted formal bargaining postures, it has become "the thing to do" in smaller districts, even though the normal pressure of dissatisfaction that leads to bargaining demands might not be present. This tendency toward conformity of behavior is reinforced by national organizations, which are ever eager to train representatives from local organizations to assist state organizations and state education associations in their pursuit of bargaining competence. This supports attempts to encourage more militant postures in local organizations since the training given to local representatives almost always stresses formal adversarial technique. This training sets the stage for self-fulfilling prophecy (it is what people are trained for and what they have come to expect that a "good" teachers' organization does), even though formal bargaining might not be appropriate for a given school district or even necessary to accomplish the ends sought.

NOTES

1. Though they have evidenced a historic concern for teacher welfare, the NEA and the AFT have, until recently, differed on the importance of teacher welfare issues and on the approach to them. The NEA virtually ignored salary and working conditions during its first fifty years, preferring, instead, to concentrate on "professional" issues. Its state affiliates, however, were active, pushing minimum salaries and tenure and retirement legislation in state capitols. With the funding of the Research Division in 1922, the NEA began regular salary surveys, initiating a period when the NEA stressed information as a basis of persuasion by fact in welfare issues. This emphasis continued until after World War II, when the NEA began to take the first hesitant steps toward encouraging teachers to pursue wage interests by collective action.

The AFT, on the other hand, began with teacher welfare gains as a prime focus. For accounts of these developments, see Edgar B. Wesley, *NEA: The First Hundred*

Years: The Building of a Teaching Profession (New York: Harper and Brothers, 1957), esp. 334-341; and William Edward Eaton, *The American Federation of Teachers, 1916-1961: A History of the Movement* (Carbondale, Ill.: Southern Illinois University Press, 1975).

2. Eaton, *American Federation of Teachers,* 141-142.

3. Wesley A. Wildman and Robert K. Burns, *Collective Action By Public School Teachers.* Volume 1, *Teacher Organizations and Collective Action: A Review of History and a Survey of School District Activity, 1964-65* (Washington, D.C.: Bureau of Research, Office of Education, U.S. Department of Health, Education, and Welfare, June 1968), 34.

4. *Ibid.*, 34.

5. *Ibid.*

6. The first of the two studies was conducted at the end of the 1964-65 school year by a team of researchers working out of the University of Chicago's Industrial Relations Center. The research team consisted, at one time or another, of Wesley A. Wildman, principal investigator; Robert Burns, co-principal investigator; and Charles Perry, associate director. The study was funded by a research grant from the Office of Education and resulted in a four-volume final report published in 1968, as well as in several articles and books. These reports were written by different combinations of the three principal researchers. To avoid confusion, we refer to the generic study as Wildman, Burns, and Perry. Where a specific report is mentioned, only the researchers who wrote the report are listed.

7. Wildman and Burns, *Collective Action by Public School Teachers*, Volume 1, 46.

8. *Ibid.*

9. *Ibid.*, 47.

10. This study, "Collective Negotiations in Education," was a National Manpower Resources study, It was conducted out of the University of Utah in 1976. Michael J. Murphy served as principal investigator. Funding was provided by the Ford Foundation. Most of the data used in this book have not been previously published. Overall response to the questionnaire was about 60 percent.

11. Wildman and Burns, *Collective Action by Public Schools,* Volume 1, 59-60.

12. *Ibid.*, 48.

13. Data taken from "Collective Negotiations in Education."

14. Wildman and Burns, *Collective Action by Public School Teachers*, Volume 1, ii.

15. *Ibid.*, 50.

16. Definitions given in the questionnaire for the "Collective Negotiations in Education" study.

17. Charles R. Perry, *Collective Action by Public School Teachers.* Volume 3, *Impasse Resolution in Teacher Negotiations* (Washington, D.C.: Bureau of Research, Office of Education, Department of Health, Education, and Welfare, January 1968), 12.

18. *Ibid.*, 13.

19. U.S. Department of Health, Education, and Welfare, National Center for Education Statistics, *Digest of Educational Statistics 1977-78* (Washington, D.C.: U.S. Government Printing Office, 1978).

20. These calculations assume Wildman, Burns, and Perry's "Consultation" and "Testimony" can be equated to Murphy's "Consultation." Further, since Wildman, Burns, and Perry data include only districts of 1,200 or more students, the 1976 figure of 8 percent reflects use of consultation in districts enrolling 1,000 or more. In 1976, the consultation was used in 11 percent of all districts.

3

Development of Teachers' Unions

Recent years have been active ones in American public education. Historians will record a number of notable events, and desegregation and integration activities will undoubtedly rank high in their analysis. In 1954 the United States Supreme Court issued its momentous *Brown* v. *Board of Education* ruling on school segregation. Twenty-four years later, many large school districts still had not complied to the satisfaction of the courts. Great strides made in reformulating the way public schools are financed will also probably have lasting impact and capture the attention of historians. Then there is the conservative educational practice movement that swept the schools in the 1970's, as well as interest in reforming educational governance and involving local parents in educational decision making. But one occurrence that will most certainly capture attention and occupy many pages when the histories are written will be the rise of teachers' unions and collective bargaining.

It was in 1962 that the first major collective bargaining agreement between a teachers' union and a board of education was signed in New York City.[1] In the sixteen years that followed, over ten thousand of the nation's school districts followed suit and negotiated contracts with teachers' organizations.[2] During this same sixteen years, the combined memberships of the American Federation of Teachers and the National Education Association have grown from about 1.5 million, or about 59 percent of those teaching, to over 2.35 million, or about 91 percent of those teaching. Teachers now are one of the most highly organized work forces, not only in the United States, but in any of the Western democracies.[3]

In view of these explosive developments, the recent period may well be characterized by educational historians as the age of teacher unionization, the time when teachers' unions came of age. This chapter looks carefully at the development of teachers' unions, not just over the recent past, but over the long history of their involvement with public education in the United States.

WHAT IS A UNION?

As has been noted before, there is some semantic difficulty in talking about teachers' organizations. We have generally used the term "union" to describe those teachers' organizations that formally or informally describe themselves as "unions," as well as those that prefer to be known as "professional associations." Before proceeding, however, we should examine the nature of a union more carefully to determine whether both major teachers' organizations and their local and state affiliates can truly be considered unions.

Perhaps the most widely used and generally accepted definition of the word "union" is that supplied by Sidney and Beatrice Webb. To them, a union is "a continuous association of wage earners for the purpose of maintaining or improving the conditions of their working lives."[4] The three ingredients in the Webbs' definition are that the association be continuous, that is, not organized for some special event or time-limited purpose; that the people who associate be employees or wage earners; and that the purpose of their association be to try to influence the conditions under which they are employed.

Unions, according to the Webbs, could and would use a variety of methods to regulate conditions of employment. First, unions could formulate their own rules, specifying the terms under which employment would be accepted. These unilateral rules were and are given force by two union practices: controlling entrance into a skilled work group and restricting the availability of certain types of work to members of the association. In earlier periods, this was a function of guilds. Later, trade unions sought restrictive apprentice practices and established hiring halls. Today, professional groups seek the same measure of control through training requirements and certification procedures. The Webbs noted that craft unions reinforced solidarity by a system of "mutual assurances." Working members contributed substantial amounts ιο funds that were used to pay members who were sick or otherwise unemployed, thus assuring that they were not tempted to accept work under lesser conditions. Furthermore, craft unions employed sanctions that could be applied to members who violated the common rules laid down by the association. Much of what the Webbs called "unilateral trade union regulation" can be found operating in modern-day professional associations, such as the American Medical Association and the American Bar Association.

A second method of devising rules governing conditions of employment was collective bargaining.[5] By this, the Webbs meant a process of joint determination of work rules and agreement to abide by those rules. In short, a process of joint governance. This method would be employed, the Webbs held, in industries where unilateral regulation was not possible. In general, this joint governance or collective bargaining would be under circumstances where the union could not adequately control entry into the labor pool, where employers had the ability to choose workers, and, in general, where there was a ready supply of replacement labor that threatened a reduction in the power of the union. Finally, the Webbs argued, unions could establish rules that governed employment by persuading the legislature to enact them. This method they called "statutory regulation." Under the Webbs' definition, it is possible to include a large variety of unions, professional associations, and other groups under the definitional umbrella of "union."

Robert F. Hoxie, in his analysis of trade unionism in the United States, emphasizes the critical point that a trade union is an organization primarily devoted to the welfare of the members of that association. As such, "the economic viewpoint of unionism is primarily a group viewpoint and its program a group program. The aim of the union is primarily to benefit the group of workers concerned, rather than the workers as a whole or society as whole".[6] Elsewhere in his *Trade Unionism in the United States*, Hoxie says, the principal economic aims of the union are to prevent the lowering and, if possible, to raise the wages of all members of the group; to shorten the hours of work of the group; to increase the security and continuity of employment of the members of the group and, if possible, to secure steady and assured work for all in it; to prevent the deterioration and, if possible, to better the general conditions of employment of all members of the group—especially to better the conditions of safety and sanitation in the shop and to prevent arbitrary discipline, demotion and discharge of workers and arbitrary fining and docking of wages.[7]

Hoxie also takes note of the vast differences in power between employer and employee. He lays out a competing economic interest model wherein the worker and the employer have fundamentally opposite economic interests. The employer, Hoxie points out, is interested in minimizing the costs of labor and in maintaining competition among workers for jobs. It is in the employer's interest to exploit labor, and this is easily done where employers can bring their superior power to bear in negotiating an individual labor contract. To Hoxie, a labor union's aims were not, however, limited to those that could be classified as economic. Though he believed that economic interests would predominate, he foresaw that unions would be interested in influencing a wide variety of outcomes. This led Hoxie to coin the term "business unionism" and to argue that a union is a seller of services that will respond to the demands of client-members.[8]

Arnold Tannenbaum, in his treatment of unions, observes that "unions are organizations designed to protect and enhance the social and economic welfare of their members." Tannenbaum points out that unions are not independent organizations, but, rather, in order to accomplish their objectives, they must modify behavior in other organizations or enterprises. "First and foremost a union relates to a private or public enterprise or group of enterprises."[9] Unions are, therefore, dependent organizations. The enterprise upon which they depend "implicitly defines the membership of the union, sustains that membership, and provides the (primary economic) benefits for members which it is the purpose of the union to achieve."[10] Tannenbaum goes on to point out that customarily these benefits are not provided voluntarily by the enterprise, and, therefore, a union is at once dependent on an external organization and at the same time in conflict with it. Thus, of all organizations, a union is unique in this combined dependent-necessarily conflicting relationship.

Teachers' Organizations as Unions

The main question, again, is: Are the teachers' organizations unions? Let us examine their behavior against the major criteria of unions. First, are they a continuing association? The answer is, quite clearly, yes. Second, are they associations of employees or wage earners? Again, the answer is, most assuredly, yes. Third, do they try to influence the conditions under which their members perform their employment tasks? Again, for both organizations, the answer is yes. Do they promote unilateral regulation, collective bargaining, or statutory regulation? Again, yes. Are they organizations that are at once dependent and in conflict? Most definitely! And, finally, do these associations or organizations of teachers focus their energies primarily on the welfare of their members as opposed to the general welfare of society? Of all the major criteria, this is perhaps the most controversial—the one that has generated the greatest amount of debate and discussion in recent years.

Of the two national organizations, the National Education Association (NEA) seems more uncomfortable with this dimension of union behavior. The NEA has expended vast sums of money to create an image that reflects its concerns as being education in general and students in particular. The definition of union, however, does not require that an organization deny all interest in social or client welfare. Rather, the definition holds that a union will devote substantial energy to pursuit of members' welfare interests which may, and often do, overlap with clients' interests. An analysis of their budget priorities and activities over the last fifteen years suggests that the NEA is placing a premium on members' over clients' welfare.[11]

The American Federation of Teachers (AFT) has experienced similar tension throughout most of its history. It has championed many social and educational reforms, but it is clear, if one looks at its behavior, that the American Federation of Teachers also emphasizes members' welfare.

It represents neither a major defect in, nor a corruption of spirit for voluntary organizations to pursue the interest of members. It is unreasonable to attempt to hold the two major teachers' organizations to a situation that would favor welfare of clients over that of individual members where the two conflict. Indeed, as we shall see later, this would probably mean committing organizational suicide.

It is likely that the tremendous growth in membership is largely attributable to the fact that the members are buying services that are considered beneficial and, therefore, worth the investment.

Thus, it appears quite safe to argue that both the NEA and the AFT and their local and state affiliates are unions by most existing and accepted definitions of the term. It may also be that the term "union" is symbolically disturbing to teachers and that they will go to considerable lengths to avoid the label.

The Role of State Teachers' Associations

When one thinks about teachers' organizations in the abstract, one thinks of the NEA or the AFT. Until very recently, however, neither was really the dominant force. It was, instead, the state teachers' associations that were the primary organizations. Until the NEA implemented unified membership in the 1970's, membership in state associations was always larger. Most teachers either found it more important or more convenient to belong to their state association. As late as 1965-66, state associations enrolled about 90 percent of the teaching force, while NEA membership was only about 55 percent.[12] Eighteen state associations are older than NEA, and forty-six states have associations formed before the turn of the century (see Table 3-1). Leaders of ten state associations were instrumental in convening the meeting that led to the founding of the National Education Association in 1857.

Perhaps more significant than either size of membership or historic precedence is the strategic position of state associations. In the United States, education is a function of the several states. Fiscal and legislative influence is exercised in state capitols, and state associations are there lobbying for members' interests. These associations have been, until recently, the prime movers in obtaining such benefits as tenure, single salary schedules, increased funding, and retirement for teachers. Historically, many state associations have also informally assumed responsibility for maintaining state educational data and often drafted or. "approved" most state educational legislation.[13]

THE DEVELOPMENT OF NEA

There was no truly national organization for teachers or educators in the United States prior to 1857, but, in the summer of 1857,

Table 3-1

Dates that state associations were organized,
in chronological order

State	Year	State	Year
Alabama	1840; reorganized, 1856	Maryland	1866
New York	1845	Georgia	1867
Rhode Island	1845	Nebraska	1867
Ohio	1847	Arkansas	1869
Connecticut	1848	Colorado	1875
District of Columbia	1849	Texas	1880
South Carolina	1850	Montana	1882
Vermont	1850	Mississippi	1884
Kentucky	1851; reorganized, 1852	South Dakota	1884
Michigan	1852	Florida	1886
Pennsylvania	1852	New Mexico	1886
Illinois	1853	North Dakota	1887
New Jersey	1853	Nevada	1888
Wisconsin	1853	Oklahoma	1889
Indiana	1854	Washington	1889
Iowa	1854	Idaho	1890
New Hampshire	1854	Arizona	1891
Missouri	1856	Louisiana	1892
North Carolina	1857; reorganized, 1884	Wyoming	1892
Maine	1859; reorganized, 1902	Utah	1892-93
Minnesota	1861	Oregon	1899
California	1863	Puerto Rico	1911
Kansas	1863	Massachusetts	1911
Virginia	1863; reorganized, 1905	Delaware	1919
West Virginia	1863	Hawaii	1921
Tennessee	1865	Alaska	1922

Reprinted with permission of Macmillan Publishing Co., Inc., from *Professional Problems of Teachers,* 3d ed., by T. M. Stinnett. Copyright © 1968 by Macmillan Publishing Co., Inc.

some forty-three educators gathered in Philadelphia, at the urging of the leaders of ten state teachers' organizations, to found an organization that was to become the National Education Association.[14] The organization founded in Philadelphia was given the title National Teachers' Association. Despite the title, classroom teachers had little participation either in its founding or in its activities for the next several decades.

Given that the National Teachers' Association was a creature of state education associations, it is not surprising that there would be almost continuous tension and often friction between state organizations and the national body—tensions that would come to a head in the 1960's when the national body was finally able to assert its supremacy. By certain actions that are described later, the power of state organizations, both in determining policy for the NEA and in the ability to command the loyalty of classroom teachers, was weakened. For the first thirty years or so of its existence, however, the National Teachers' Association was little more than a debating society. About its activities, Marshall Donley says:

This propensity to talk, mainly about important sounding matters, dominated the first decades of the National Association. William T. Harris, who personally gave 145 speeches before the group, in 1891 classified the speeches delivered from 1858 through 1890. His effort revealed that the major topics had little to do with practical improvement in the teachers' lot. The favorite topic in those years was theory and psychology, followed closely by high schools and colleges, normal schools, manual training and technical schools, courses of study, kindergartens, primary grades, music education, moral and religious instruction, and philosophy of methods.[15]

During this period the National Teachers' Association changed its name to the National Education Association and merged with the National Association of School Superintendents, which then became a Department of Superintendents within the NEA. This merger was to have a profound impact on the policies and actions of the NEA for nearly a hundred years.

Reform Thrusts and Administrative Control

By the turn of the century the NEA had become an important organization firmly controlled by college presidents, such as Charles Eliot of Harvard University, Nicholas Murray Butler of Columbia University, and, later, David Starr Jordan of Stanford University. The dominance of the college presidents was supported by prominent big-city superintendents, such as Aaron Gove of Denver, William T. Harris of St. Louis, and William H. Maxwell of New York City. These men, all of whom were presidents of the NEA, and their colleagues formed what David Tyack has called an "interlocking directorate of urban elites."[16] As it was thus constituted, the NEA launched a vigorous campaign to reform the governance and administration of public education. Leaders rejected partisan political control of public education in the United States and greatly admired the structure and values that were emerging from the business sector. Their platform of reform was intended to weaken political or lay influence in educational decisions, to pursue efficiency, to replace political or lay control with elitist control, to imitate corporate business practice, and to introduce "rationality" via bureaucratic principles of organization and control.

To achieve these ends, the NEA's leaders sought allies among business and professional leaders, began a vigorous effort to professionalize the administration of education, developed and used a mythical structure that, among other things, argued that it was unprofessional for teachers to seek material gain, and attempted to gain and maintain control of the association itself. In pursuit of their goals these energetic men were remarkably successful. They not only succeeded in building their model of public education, which Tyack has called "the one best system," but they were able to build a system so pervasive that it survived long after they departed.[17]

The reform program set in motion two forces that would shape the NEA for the next fifty years. The first was the belief that the economic betterment of teaching would come through vigorous efforts to professionalize. This belief was carefully nurtured by the leaders of the NEA, and it would prevent the teachers' organization from aggressively pursuing welfare claims. On this subject, Donley says, "Some members sincerely believed that advances for teachers would follow automatically when the public realized that it should support the schools more adequately. Only a few believed that higher pay for teachers could precede a great improvement in the quality of teachers themselves."[18]

The second major thrust of the reformers was the professionalization and strengthening of school administration. The reform programs were aimed at greatly increasing the status of school administrators and enlarging their control of education. Control of NEA was important to this end, and, as a consequence, the NEA, along with the schools, was dominated by administrators until the 1960's. A classroom teacher was not elected president of the association until 1928, and it was another eleven years before the next classroom teacher would be. In fact, through 1945, only three classroom teachers had served as president. The rest were either administrators or college presidents.[19]

In the early days, of course, it would not have been expected that a classroom teacher would have been president of the National Teachers' Association or of the NEA. Officers were elected annually at a convention held in a major city each summer. All members were entitled to vote, but they had to be present to do so. In point of fact, few classroom teachers attended the conventions because travel was expensive and teachers were not affluent. Those who did attend were often men of means, that is, administrators, college presidents, and influential educational leaders. After the turn of the century it was common to "pack" the convention with teachers from the host city who were in general firmly controlled by the administrators from that city. Besides being ordered to attend the convention, teachers were told how to vote. Not until 1920 was the New England town meeting style of decision making abandoned in favor of a representative assembly.[20]

To cement their position of control, the NEA's administrator-leaders established what Wallace Sayre has called "a body of doctrine, a set of serviceable myths."[21] Within this body of doctrine there were at least four propositions that directed the organizational behavior of the NEA, retained power in the hands of the administrative corps, and prevented the NEA from adopting militant positions relative to teachers' welfare. The four propositions were: (1) that there was a unity of interest among all educators, (2) that gains for educators would follow increases in the quality of professional practice, (3) that educational institutions were organizationally equivalent to corporations in the private sector, and (4) that educational decisions should be protected from partisan interests and should be nonpolitical.

Acceptance of these myths allowed a relatively small number of individuals within the educational and business communities to exercise control over public education in the United States, and it was not until the myths began to collapse in the late 1950's that the NEA could begin to act aggressively in pursuit of the welfare of classroom teachers.

At the same time that they were advocating "professionalization" as the mechanism for increasing wages, cost-conscious administrators were manipulating the labor market to develop a cheap, compliant teaching force. One answer to their cost-consciousness lay in a feminized teaching force. Women would generally work for less, demand less say in decisions, and were less career minded.

Young, unmarried women lacked career focus, while married women were supplemental wage earners. Thus, neither group had reason to challenge administrative authority.

Another force in the gradual feminization of education was the nation's commitment to the common school and to free, compulsory education, with the cost of this education borne by a none-too-wealthy local public purse. Since everybody was to be schooled and the nation was growing rapidly, many teachers were needed. A work force that did not demand high wages was sought. The pressure led, first, to an itinerant male teaching force and then to a feminized force of supplemental wage earners or as yet unmarried women. Because of the lack of career interest, teaching was not free to develop professionally in the same way that medicine, law, and engineering were. Further, a female work force, seen as "helpless" or "inferior," would require a strong male influence in key positions to ensure that the educational system functioned well. Even without the myths, the feminization of the teaching force, and the masculinization of administration, it was quite natural that leadership responsibilities of the NEA would be handed over to administrators, even though they constituted a minority of the membership.

A small administrative force thus controlled a large teaching force. The administration drained leadership talent from the teaching work force since, as soon as members of the teaching force showed leadership capabilities, they would be quickly moved into the ranks of administration. Teachers, in turn, believed that the administrators sought their goals and served their interests. It would require a whole new viewpoint, which would develop in the late 1950's and the early 1960's, before the dominance of administrators could be effectively challenged.

Classroom teachers did not always passively accept a predominantly male administrative elite or avoid the struggle for higher pay and better working conditions. Indeed, Margaret Hailey of the Chicago Teachers' Federation championed the causes of classroom teachers and women, and staunchly advocated better pay and working conditions. In 1899 she helped organize the National Teachers' Federation, with membership open only to classroom teachers. Its immediate goal, reports Tyack, was "to put into the hands of the grade and classroom teachers a weapon keen enough to cut the NEA loose from the traditions that have bound it to the ideas and ideals of eastern university people, which the teachers describe as standing for conservatism almost amounting to stagnation."[22] Beginning in 1903, Hailey began a series of successful challenges of NEA leadership, culminating in the election of the first woman president (Superintendent Ella Flagg Young of Chicago, in 1910) and the formation of the Department of Classroom Teachers in 1913. Beginning with Young, the next four presidents of the NEA were all candidates supported by Hailey and her followers. Tyack reports that "during Young's administration and that of the next four presidents all endorsed by Hailey the NEA paid increasing attention to classroom teachers, endorsing higher salaries, equal pay for equal work, woman's suffrage, and advisory teachers councils."[23]

The old guard of the NEA was not sympathetic to Hailey and her followers. In fact, Nicholas Murray Butler is reported to have "bitterly resented Hailey and her allies."[24] Tyack reports that Butler wrote in his autobiography "of his sadness" with the victories of the Hailey forces and his feeling that the NEA had ceased being a "meeting ground of the educational aristocracy" and had fallen into the "hands of a very inferior class of teachers and school officials whose main object appeared to be personal advancement."[25]

The moment of glory for women teachers was, however, brief. The Department of Classroom Teachers was kept "weak and financially undernourished" and had scarcely more than symbolic importance in the operation of the National Education Association.[26] And the more conservative leaders of the NEA realized the need for structural reform to prevent a group like the Chicago Teachers' Federation and their allies from taking control. After a period of analysis, David Starr Jordan, president of Stanford University, proposed reform of the NEA's structure in 1919. Among other things, he called for the establishment of a representative assembly to be made up of delegates representing state and local education associations. The structural reform was adopted at the NEA convention of 1920, strategically held in Salt Lake City so that the reform might have a good chance of being passed by those attending the convention.[27] The structure adopted in 1920 was the basic one used by the NEA until the late 1960's, when it again, under pressure from militant classroom teachers, reorganized.

Organization of the NEA

The National Education Association is structured along professional organizational lines. Membership is direct, even though in recent years unified membership has been encouraged.[28] The NEA's chief executive officer is a professional administrator hired, not elected, to run the organization. As in many professional and voluntary organizations, the elected president was, until quite recently, a transient lay officer whose power was limited by the executive officer system and short tenure.

Over the years, the NEA has become a large organization. Its membership has grown substantially, as has its budget. Its journal has become the most widely read educational publication in the United States, and its research division has become a major repository of statistical data on education in the United States. It has erected impressive buildings in Washington, D.C., and, as the organization representing all professional educators, it has exercised considerable political influence on federal educational policy. In many ways the executive secretaries of the NEA have come to be recognized as spokesmen for educational interests in the United States.

The basic direction and character of the association was established by 1920 and, for the next forty years, it steadily advanced in terms of membership, wealth, and power. It continued in the direction established by its founders and leaders with little deviation from the charted course until the 1960's. The forty prosperous years provide a good idea of its functioning if one looks at the NEA's structure and some of the things that it did. First, the NEA continued trying to become *the* association for all professionals in education. It welcomed mergers with other educational groups and assigned department status to the group merged. In addition to the departments created by merger, others were created for subpopulations in the educational work force and for special functions (see Table 3-2). These departments gradually added staff and executive secretaries and functioned within the headquarters in Washington. By 1945 there were some twenty-eight departments; by 1965 there were thirty-three. The departments were designed to serve and to enroll all professionals involved with public education institutions in the United States. The departments published extensively, and each, in its own field, was quite influential. By 1975, however, all

Table 3-2

The origins of departments of the National Education Association

Department	Year	Development
Adult Education	1921	Established as Department of Immigrant Education
American Association for Health, Physical Education, and Recreation	1937	Formed by merger of American Physical Education Association (founded in 1885) and the Department of School Health and Physical Education (founded in 1894 as the Department of Child Study). Secretary to headquarters.
American Association of School Administrators	1865	Organized as National Association of School Superintendents
	1922	Established and secretary to headquarters
American Association of Teachers Colleges	1858	Organized as American Normal School Association
	1870	Became Department of Normal Schools
	1925	Merged with AATC, which had been organized in 1917
American Educational Research Association	1915	Formed as National Association of Directors of Educational Research
	1930	Became a department
American Industrial Arts Association	1942	Became a department
Art Education	1933	Became a department
Business Education	1892	Became a department
Classroom Teachers	1913	Became a department
	1940	Established headquarters at NEA
Elementary School Principals	1921	Organized as National Association of Elementary School Principals and then then became a department
	1931	Secretary to headquarters
Higher Education	1870	Organized
	1924	Discontinued
	1942	Reestablished
	1944	Secretary to headquarters
Home Economics	1930	Created as Department of Supervisors and Teachers of Home Economics
International Council for Exceptional Children	1930	Created as Department of Special Education
Kindergarten-Primary Education	1884	Grew out of meeting of Froebel Institute of North America held that year
Lip Reading	1926	Became a department

Table 3-2 *(continued)*

Department	Year	Development
Music Educators National Conference	1884	Department of Music Education was created and merged with Conference
National Association of Deans of Women	1916	Established
	1918	Became a department
	1931	Secretary to headquarters
National Association of Journalism Directors	1939	Became a department
National Association of Secondary School Principals	1917	Organized
	1927	Became a department
	1940	Established headquarters at NEA with a full-time secretary
National Association of Teachers of Speech	1914	Organized
	1939	Became a department
National Council for the Social Studies	1921	Organized
	1925	Became a department
	1940	Secretary to headquarters
National Council of Administrative Women in Education	1915	Organized
	1932	Became a department
National Science Teachers Association	1894	Organized as Department of Natural Science Instruction
Rural Education	1907	Grew out of Department of Rural and Agricultural Education
	1919	Reorganized as Department of Rural Education
	1936	Affairs administered by NEA Division of Rural Service since this year
Secondary Teachers	1886	Established as Department of Secondary Education
	1924	Lapsed
	1931	Revived
Supervision and Curriculum Development	1921	Organized as National Conference on Educational Method
	1929	Became a department
	1936	Secretary to headquarters
Visual Instruction	1923	Organized
Vocational Education	1875	Organized as Department of Industrial Education
	1919	Assumed present name

Source: Adapted from Mildred Sandison Fenner, *NEA History: The National Education Association, Its Development and Program* (Washington, D.C.: National Education Association, 1945), 153-154.

departments whose membership was not classroom teachers had divorced themselves from the NEA and had become independent organizations.

The NEA continually emphasized influencing educational practice and serving the educational community in general. It established a tradition of having study committees review some important aspect or problem of education and then issued a report intended to influence policy and practice throughout the United States. One early example was the Committee of Ten, chaired by Nicholas Murray Butler. That report, issued in 1894, had considerable influence on the development of curriculum. Shortly after the Committee of Ten, there was the Committee of Fifteen which studied the organization of school systems, teacher training, and coordination of studies in primary and grammar schools. Then the Committee of Twelve was convened in 1897 to study the problems of rural education. During the forty-years following 1920, however, the NEA moved away from the use of ad hoc or special purpose committees and began to use the departments and standing committees of the association to conduct studies and generate recommendations. The Educational Policies Commission, which was created in 1935, was to have considerable impact on educational policy and practice in the United States. It had its own professional secretary and occasionally issued major policy statements, including a set of documents on the relationship between education and American democracy. The goals established in the documents were often adopted unchanged by boards of education and school districts throughout the United States as representative of their own local goals.

Another part of the NEA that was to have considerable influence was the Research Division. This division, created in 1922, collected and reported data on nearly all aspects of education in the United States. It was generally acknowledged to have the best data available and was frequently used by the federal government. Among other things, the Research Division constantly surveyed and published the status of teachers' salaries. It also collected data and synthesized research about all aspects of educational practice in its *Research Bulletin*, which was published periodically and distributed widely. The NEA Research Division became one of the most widely quoted and authoritative sources for educational data and research information.

If one looks carefully at NEA's activities between 1920 and 1960 and compares them with activities before that period, several things emerge. It continued in the direction charted by its founders and leaders during the earlier period, but it also moved steadily from a position of being dependent upon external leaders or influential educators to one of being a large, self-sufficient organization. Work done earlier by committees and commissions was taken over by departments and divisions. The Research Division began analyzing teachers' salaries, a task formerly performed by members of the association. The Educational Policies Commission took over the task of defining the aims and purposes of education in the United States, a task formerly left to the outstanding educators of the day. And the separate departments set about in a businesslike and thoroughly bureaucratic manner to influence all aspects of education. What is striking is that, until 1920, NEA's history is laced with the presence of the great men and women of their day—influential college presidents, important superintendents, and commissioners of education. Then the bureaucracy began to transform the organization into a smooth, well-oiled, faceless machine. Its work, though influential, was not associated with prominent people; rather, it was associated with the executive secretary or with the association itself. In short, from 1920 to 1960, the NEA underwent a period of growth, organizational consolidation, and developing self-sufficiency.

There are two other things during this period that characterize the NEA's style in approaching educational problems and tasks. First, the association clearly developed a taste for consensus and consensual decision making. Second, its mode of operation was not one of open advocacy but, rather, one of attempting to persuade by education—authority derived from expertise. Given the organization of the association and its development from 1920 to 1960, it would have been difficult to have developed any other approach. Given also the diversity of membership and the breadth and scope of operations, it would have been impolitic to take an advocacy position in behalf of any one of its member groups if that position were not supported by others in its diverse constituency. Thus, the NEA could function only as a general advocate for public education. It could not afford to support the cause of teachers over the interests of administrators or school board members. In fact, the NEA exemplified the reform political structures advocated by its leaders.

A problem that always confronted the NEA was finding activities that would justify membership fees while remaining true to its concept of a unified professional association. It chose to emphasize professional matters and to avoid controversy and issues that tended to divide its diverse membership—an organizational necessity, perhaps.

The NEA's commitment to professionalism and its operating modes tended to reinforce one another. As a consequence, after the mid-1930's the association began to produce more studies and to turn out more research data, which, though it was admittedly of higher quality, tended to reinforce NEA's position as a collector and purveyor of information and also to confirm its style of operation as one that used data and facts to persuade and enforce. The biennial study of salaries is a good example. It has been noted that, until the 1960's, the NEA never expended great effort to improve teachers' salaries, although they constantly pointed out that they were substandard. Rather, they provided extensive data on the economic condition of teachers and other educational employees in the United States and supplied those to people who were in a position to make decisions: school boards, state departments, federal offices, and the like. The hope was that the data would speak for themselves and that superintendents, when they developed their budgets and presented them to school boards for approval, would utilize the data to argue for improved teacher salaries. And, more likely than not, they did.

This presented somewhat of a problem that few within NEA's ranks probably realized. As the "semiofficial" spokesman for education in the United States, it depended on the authority of the data and their reasonableness to carry the day. This was seen as a real weakness when the association was confronted by the militancy of the 1960's. It also undoubtedly caused the NEA to consider itself not so much as an interest group for education but more as an "institution." That an "institutional" style could be viewed as partisan was to come as a rude shock in the 1960's, and it was an initial disadvantage during that era of political turmoil.

THE AMERICAN FEDERATION OF TEACHERS

Early Days

The only organization that seriously competed with the NEA for the loyalty of public school teachers in this country has been the American Federation of Teachers. Founded in 1916, the AFT is now the only major teachers' organization formally affiliated with organized labor in the United States.

The AFT was not, however, the first teachers' organization to affiliate with organized labor in the United States. In 1897 the Chicago Teachers' Federation (CTF) was formed with a membership composed primarily of women teachers in elementary service. And in 1902 it voted to affiliate with the Chicago Federation of Labor.[29]

During the early years the CTF fought for higher pay, improved pension plans, and more democratic administration of the Chicago public schools. The CTF also supported a number of the social welfare causes of the day, including leading support for the successful passage of the Illinois Child Labor Law in 1903. When the union discovered that many of the large corporations in Chicago were failing to pay taxes due on their capital stock and franchises, it undertook mandamus proceedings against the People's Gas, Light, and Coke Company, the Chicago Telephone Company, and Edison Electric Light Company. As a result of successful litigation, these companies were ordered to pay nearly $600,000 in back taxes.[30] In spite of this successful attempt to recover lost revenues for the school district, the Chicago Board of Education was anything but grateful. In fact, though the district realized a considerable income bonus as a result of the suit, the board voted not to expend any of those funds to raise teachers' salaries. Despite the struggle of the CTF, pay increases were not granted until 1904.

Not only was the board not grateful, but it was quite active in opposing the CTF. In 1905 the members voted to condemn the CTF's affiliation with organized labor.[31] Despite this condemnation, the CTF continued to prosper. In 1915 the board countered with a yellow-dog contract that required teachers to agree not to join the union as a provision of their contractual status with the Chicago School District. Although the CTF contested this action in the courts in 1917, the Illinois Supreme Court held that the board did have the power to require that its teachers not belong to an organization affiliated with organized labor. The CTF reluctantly withdrew from the Chicago Federation of Labor. Later, it would have to withdraw from the fledgling AFT because it, too, was affiliated with the American Federation of Labor (AFL).

On April 15, 1916, three of the Chicago Teachers' Unions and one local from nearby Gary, Indiana, met in Chicago to form a national union. By May 9, 1916, there were eight locals affiliated: the Chicago Teachers' Federation; the Chicago Federation of Men Teachers; the Chicago Federation of Women High School Teachers; the Gary, Indiana, Teachers' Federation; the Teachers' Union of the City of New York; the Oklahoma Teachers' Federation; the Scranton, Pennsylvania, Teachers' Association; and the High School Teachers' Union of Washington, D.C. Samuel Gompers received the eight locals into the American Federation of Labor as the American Federation of Teachers in that year.[32]

Though the desire to affiliate with organized labor in the United States was never in doubt, the AFL added to the teachers' enthusiasm by announcing a position toward education that was consistent with the AFT's own platform.[33] The platform stated by the AFL not only pleased the fledgling AFT because it supported free public schools, but it also contained social planks that coincided with the beliefs of most of the leaders of local unions.

The impetus for the formation of the AFT was really threefold. First, leaders in Chicago, New York, and elsewhere recognized the necessity of a national organization of teachers and valued the support of organized labor in achieving their objectives. Second, teachers were unhappy about the conditions under which they served (low pay, poor teaching conditions, and autocratic administrative structures).

But the main impetus for the founding of the AFT lay in the perceived failure of the NEA to do something about the grievances of teachers. The leaders of the Chicago Federation of Teachers and others must have discovered quite soon that the administrators who were resisting their attempts to secure better working conditions were the same ones who were running the NEA. Margaret Hailey and the other leaders who formed the American Federation of Teachers had hoped to influence the NEA. They had been initially successful in bringing about some modifications, but by

1916 it was apparent that the NEA was not about to champion teachers' rights or teachers' causes; nor was the NEA about to become active in the area of social rights.

Although AFT leaders recognized the conservative nature of the NEA, they did not originally intend to forgo that organization entirely. For the first five years of its existence, members of teachers' union locals were actively encouraged to attend and take part in NEA's convention. It is reported, in fact, that many of the leaders of the young AFT hoped that they could ultimately be incorporated into the NEA as a department.[34]

Though the period from 1870 to 1910 in the United States was a period of unprecedented economic growth, teachers did not share in this growth. Salaries increased only slightly during this period, and the grievances of teachers, particularly those in urban areas, grew considerably. Even with obvious deprivation and the urging of AFT leadership, the NEA chose not to examine its position relative to teacher welfare; instead, it chose to condemn the AFT. Administrators and school boards, at the urging of the NEA, launched an antiunion and anti-AFT drive. They labeled belonging to an organization affiliated with organized labor as an unprofessional act; they instituted the use of yellow-dog contracts. They fired known union teachers or manipulated the organizational rewards to discourage union membership, and they actively encouraged, actually forced in some cases, membership in the NEA. During this period and through the forty years that were to follow, it often took considerable courage to be an AFT member.

During the early years of the AFT its development was actively encouraged by the AFL, which provided direct financial support for the operation of the union, both in the form of cash contributions and the employment of several AFT officers as organizers. The AFL also provided field organizers from its own staff to try to establish new locals. Leaders in local labor organizations volunteered their services to assist in drives to organize teachers. It was common, for instance, for officials from the local steel worker's union and other AFL affiliates to meet teachers and make presentations relative to the advantages of being affiliated with organized labor.

As an organizational plan, the AFT chose a conventional union model. Two primary national officers were elected, a president and a secretary-treasurer, and, as financing became available, these primary officers were employed full time in union service. There was no executive staff, as was true of the NEA, but, rather, the president and secretary-treasurer performed all executive functions within the union. To the extent that the control of a voluntary organization rests with individual officeholders, control in the AFT remained with the officers who stood for election every two years. There were no state federations active at the time, and it was to be some years before the AFT found the time or the resources to encourage the development of state federations. The relationship, therefore, was between locals and the national. Because the president and secretary-treasurer were elected working officers and there was no executive staff, the organization's leadership tended to emerge in the political rather than the bureaucratic tradition. Power was political rather than bureaucratic or corporate, and the system encouraged political factions or pseudoparties. Struggles for power were common.

By the end of the 1920's the AFT had pretty well formalized its structure and the platform that would carry it to the present day. The platform is perhaps best reflected by the eleven principles listed below:

1. The right of teachers to organize and affiliate with labor must be recognized.
2. If our children during their most impressionable years are to have the benefit of daily contact with examples of upstanding American manhood and womanhood, and not to be exposed to an atmosphere of servility in the schoolroom, teachers must be given warning and a hearing before being separated from the service.
3. The teacher must be guaranteed the opportunity to make his due influence felt in the community, working thru the school chiefly, but free to work thru all the avenues of citizenship.
4. The control of the teaching staff should be removed from the Board of Education, and placed in the hands of the professional expert, the Superintendent of Schools.
5. If our democracy is not to be crippled at its source, democratic school administration must be secured by insuring to the teacher an effective voice in that administration.
6. The schools must be removed from politics by the application of the merit principle of civil service to the employment, advancement, and dismissal of teachers, thus securing tenure during efficiency.
7. The work of the teacher, now notoriously ill-paid, determines the quality of our future citizenship, and should receive financial recognition more clearly commensurate with its importance to the community.
8. Vocational education should be encouraged, but only under a 'unit system.'

9. The people should directly control educational policies thru the popular election of boards of education.
10. A system of free textbooks is an essential of genuinely free and democratic public schools.
11. Enlightened public policy demands adequate pension provisions for public school teachers.[35]

1930-1960

The years from 1930 to 1960 were marked by considerable social, political, and economic upheaval. The period began with the worst depression the world had yet experienced, which was followed almost immediately by World War II, the largest world conflict yet seen by mankind. Then there was a postwar economic boom during which the pent-up demands from the depression and the war were vented. Finally, the country entered into a cold war period marked by extensive anti-Communist paranoia and the witch hunts of the 1950's.

During this period, two struggles characterized the AFT's existence. The first was simply a struggle for survival. Membership had grown to about 10,000 in 1920, but under pressure from school boards and school administrators, membership dropped below 3,500 by 1924, and it was not until 1934 that membership again reached 10,000. By 1946 there were over 35,000 members, and by 1952 the AFT reported 50,000 members.

Education as an institution faired badly during the Depression of the 1930's. On the National Economic League's list of paramount problems of the United States, education fell from fourteenth place in 1930 to twenty-fourth place in 1931 and thirty-second place in 1932.[36] To effect economies during these years, school boards took a number of cost-cutting steps. They increased the size of classes, thereby decreasing the number of teachers employed. They reduced teacher salaries. And they cut the length of the school day and the school year. In the state of Illinois, for example, a report issued by the Superintendent of Public Instruction showed that, in the three years between 1931 and 1934, the per capita cost of education dropped from $119 to $94; the school term was shortened by eleven days; the average teacher's salary was reduced by $385, and the number of teachers employed in the state decreased from 48,976 to 46,161.[37] To indicate the serious cost-cutting spirit that characterized public education, one needs only to look at the recommendations published by the United States Chamber of Commerce, which had previously been a staunch supporter of public education. The Chamber of Commerce, in a letter sent to all local members under the title of "Possible Fields of Economy in School Retrenchment," offered twenty suggestions for reducing local education costs, including: the transfer of supervisors to classrooms, an increase in size of classes, an increase in the number of teaching hours, and a reduction in teachers' salaries not to exceed 10 percent.[38]

Unemployment was, of course, very high during the Depression. Among professional groups, however, it was probably highest among teachers. A survey of college and university graduates done in 1932 showed that there were 21,974 unemployed graduates from fifty-four major universities and colleges in the United States. Of those, over half (12,420) were teachers.[39]

During these difficult times, it was the AFT that took to the field most actively. In Chicago the locals battled the banks and the City Council to force the city to meet payrolls. Similar rallies were held in New York and other major cities with varying success. It is likely that substantial membership gains posted during this period can be directly attributed to the vigor with which the AFT pursued teachers' interests during the Depression.

In spite of those gains, however, organizing problems and membership continued to plague the AFT. Of the locals chartered during this period, only about 56 percent survived, and the total membership was only 3.4 percent of the teaching force of the United States in 1934.[40] In 1940 George Counts stated that he thought the AFT should enroll 10 percent of the teaching force. It was his belief that there were at least that many of the nation's teachers who were sufficiently liberal and concerned to join.[41] But it was to be another thirty years before membership would pass the magical 10 percent figure.

Membership growth depends on successful organizing, and organizing for the AFT during this period was complicated by several problems. First, there was a perennial shortage of money and staff. Only through the largesse of the AFL had the AFT had been able to keep organizers in the field at all. During the Depression era, partly because of its own financial difficulties and partly because of the actions of the AFT itself, the AFL began to lose interest in the AFT and gradually withdrew their subsidies and support. One reason for this was that the AFT as a national organization was becoming increasingly liberal in its statements regarding social policy. Many AFT leaders were social reconstructionists or members of a socialist party, and some were avowed communists. The AFL, on the other hand, was growing increasingly conservative and had begun, by the late 1930's, a period of aggressive purging of Communists within the AFL and of expelling Communist-dominated unions.

A second problem that strained the relationship between the AFT and the AFL was the development of the Congress of Industrial Organizations (CIO). The CIO began as the Committee for Industrial Organization—a branch of the trade- or craft-oriented AFL. But it soon broke away from the parent organization and began operating as a rival federation, organizing nationals and internationals on an industrial-union rather than a craft-union base. Inevitably, the CIO began to challenge the organizing domains of the older AFL, and there were many jurisdictional disputes. Of the two, the CIO was considerably more the liberal, and, as a consequence, it attracted the AFT. Though the official efforts of the AFT were toward conciliating the differences between the AFL and the CIO, it was no secret that there was a large faction in the AFT who would have preferred affiliation with the CIO as opposed to the more conservative AFL. In Seattle and New York, for example, sympathy with the CIO caused the City Labor Federation, an AFL unit, to expel the AFT local from membership.[42]

The power within the AFT during this period lay with the AFT locals, which tended to have their own characteristic ethnic and geographic orientation. The New York local, for instance, was heavily Jewish in membership. The Chicago and Boston locals were predominantly Catholic. In all cases, their outlook was urban. This, coupled with their religious and ethnic identities, presented both internal cohesion and external image problems for the AFT. And the linking of these urban ethnic combinations to organized labor represented a lethal combination when the AFT began serious organizing attempts in nonurban areas or in strongly white Anglo-Saxon, Protestant, middle-class regions of the United States.[43]

The influence of the AFT was largely affected by the fact that in almost all cases its locals represented only a minority—often a

small minority—of the teachers in the school system. Only in At-
lanta and Chicago did the AFT locals at any time have a majority of
the teachers as members. Though the AFT had a national platform and goals, the minority status of its locals made it difficult,
if not impossible, for the national platform to be implemented.
The AFT simply lacked the power at the local level to force the
governance concessions required to implement its programs. The
minority status of the AFT, up until 1960, virtually dictated that
it should assume the role of critic, perennially in search of that
issue or event that would transform it into majority status and
power.

As has been indicated, the period between 1930 and 1960, in
addition to being a period of struggle for survival, might also be
characterized as a period during which the AFT was searching
for identity. Part of that search was motivated by the divergent
character of its large urban locals and part by its perennial minority status. But the major tension in the search was the one that
has always characterized unions, and it is the difficult choice between emphasizing social and economic reform as opposed to the
welfare of its members. During the 1940's, this struggle took place
between the so-called "bread-and-butter unionists," who were pushing for aggressive involvement in securing higher wages and better
working conditions for members, and the social reconstructionists.

Unlike the NEA, which devoted most of its attention to educational matters, the AFT spent a great deal of time discussing social
and philosophical concerns. The AFT was in the forefront of the
struggle for civil rights, taking early and strong stands on racial
discrimination and on the role and rights of women in education
and in society.

But the major social and philosophical thrust of the AFT during
the middle years was that of social reconstructionism. The social
reconstructionists, whose base was Teachers College, Columbia
University, viewed the school as a major force in the democratiz-
ing of American society. Their goal was to "bring into being a social
order which will secure for the common man a much larger measure
of well-being and a greater share in determining the economic,
social and political institutions and practices which condition his
well-being."[44] The school was an instrument for this social reconstruction and not an end in itself. The social reconstructionists—

John Dewey, George Counts, John Childs, Bruce Raup, Goodwin Watson, Jessie Newland, and others—were members of the AFT. They pushed their platform in the AFT as well as in the Progressive Education Association, which they also helped to found.

In the late 1930's and throughout the 1940's, the issue of Communism plagued the AFT, as it did the labor movement in the United States in general. And it was to be a problem for the AFT that would eventually take its toll in membership. Since the AFT had always been socially and politically liberal, it was only natural that some of its members would become interested in Communism during the 1930's, when it was a fashionable interest of intellectuals and liberals throughout the country. After extensive debate over Communist influence, the charters of three locals (Local No. 5 in New York City, Local No. 192 in Philadelphia, and Local No. 537 representing college teachers in New York) were revoked. By that action the total national membership of the AFT was reduced by nearly one-third.

In addition to moving decisively against Communism in its locals, the AFT had really made two statements. First, it had sided decisively with the AFL, which was putting extensive pressure on the AFT concerning Communists in locals, and, second, it had moved more decisively toward the classical American view of bread-and butter-unionism, leading the AFT to reexamine two standbys of the labor arsenal, collective bargaining and strikes.

Throughout the history of the AFT, the organization had had a special concern for teachers' salaries, which had always been poor. Teachers' salaries remained inadequate during the Depression, but, by 1947 and 1948, it was apparent that the relative reimbursement of teachers for their services was growing worse. The average salary paid a teacher in 1933-34 in the United States was $1,227. In 1947-48 the average teacher was earning $2,639. Though this meant that the salary of the average teacher had more than doubled during this fourteen-year period, the cost of living had tripled. The United States Bureau of Education issued a report stating, among other things, that, owing "to the greatly increasing cost of living, the 1947-48 average salary had less purchasing power than the lower average salary in 1929-30."[45]

The post-World War II era in the United States represented one of the greatest periods of economic growth in our history.

Business was booming, wages were increasing at a dramatic pace, and the pent-up frustrations of the Depression and the subsequent wartime crisis were being relieved—relieved, that is, in all except the public sector. Teachers were becoming increasingly desperate, and it was during this postwar era that the first signs of teacher militancy, which was to blossom in full in the 1960's, became apparent.

Organized labor in the United States won the right to free collective bargaining with the Wagner Act of 1935, which required employers to meet with duly authorized employees' organizations and to "bargain in good faith" over wages, hours, and conditions of employment. Though collective bargaining was not new in 1935, it was at that time that it received legal sanction and legal protection and enabled organized labor in the private sector to secure sizable wage and benefit gains after World War II. Teachers' unions began to look at this mechanism to determine whether it was a suitable means to their ends.

In 1944 the AFT local in Cicero, Illinois, signed the first collective bargaining contract with a board of education. The terms were quite liberal and established, among other things, a single salary schedule, a sabbatical leave program, pay for extra classes, and a grievance procedure. Still more important was the fact that it followed a relatively standard collective bargaining contract format, established the local as the exclusive bargaining agent, and provided for revision and renewal of the contract.[46] Two years later, at its convention, the AFT adopted a resolution calling for the study of collective bargaining and requiring the national office to establish a file of contracts, wage agreements, and other pertinent collective bargaining materials.

The AFT had had a long-standing, no-strike policy. The journal of the AFT (*American Teacher*) frequently printed the AFT's no-strike position:

The use of the strike is rejected as an instrument of policy of the American Federation of Teachers. The executive council and its national officers will not call a strike either nationally or in any local area of jurisdiction nor in any way advise a local to strike. The funds and facilities of the national organization will not be used to support a strike.[47]

Though it was not clear in the postwar period just what teachers' rights were relative to collective bargaining, it was clear that teachers, as public employees, had no legal right to strike.

During the troubled period following World War II, the sense of dissatisfaction among teachers grew at such a rate that, in 1946, in Norwalk, Connecticut, a teachers' local affiliated with the National Education Association, after trying to persuade the Norwalk Board of Education to hear their demands, finally called a strike. Though this was not the first strike ever engaged in by teachers in the United States, it was the beginning of a three-year period of considerable strike activity in which there would be nearly a hundred teacher strikes in the United States.

The AFT's no-strike policy had remained intact since the early years of the organization, but, by 1946, it was seriously being questioned. It is likely that the no-strike policy of the AFT had originally been drafted, not so much out of conviction that the strike had no appropriate place in education, but, rather, because public attitudes required it. Public sentiment definitely ran against strikes by public employees and exhibited concern over teachers being identified with organized labor. At its convention in 1946, the executive council of the AFT was "instructed to reexamine the no strike policy of the American Federation of Teachers and to arrange for full discussion in the *American Teacher* of the possibilities of a strike technique as a means of arousing the American public to an appreciation of the desperate needs of its children."[48] After considerable public debate on the issue, AFT delegates voted in 1947 to retain the no-strike pledge—a policy that would remain in effect until the early 1960's. During the rash of strikes by teachers in the late 1940's and early 1950's, it is clear that although the AFT did not support the local strikes, neither did they go out of their way to condemn them. The problem was compounded by the fact that data published in the monthly labor review showed that "strike action in 29% of the teacher stoppages [that] accounted for four-fifths of the days idle was taken by unions affiliated with the AFL."[49] Despite the no-strike pledge, the locals of the AFT were emerging as the most active in the strike arena. Two activities, collective bargaining and strikes, were to set the tone for the activity in the two decades that followed.

1960 and Beyond

The AFT entered the 1960's a stronger organization than it had been at any time in its previous history. Its president, Carl J. Megel, had been in office since 1954, and, under his tenure, the AFT had worked hard to build a smoothly functioning, well-financed central headquarters. There were somewhat more than 56,000 dues-paying members, and the AFT had established ten state federations, all of which had full-time executive secretaries and were active in organizing new locals. The union was operating in the black, had some investments in securities and a cash reserve of $30,000.[50] In short, things looked extremely good for the AFT in 1960. It was solvent, it was growing, and it had the benefits of continuity in leadership and little of the internal dissension that had characterized it during the 1940's. The AFT did not have long to enjoy its newfound security, however, for, in New York City, Local No. 2 was embarking on a series of events that would not only shake the AFT but would also dramatically affect the course of events in education in the years to follow.

In 1960 the Teachers' Guild of New York City, AFT's Local No. 2, merged with several small splinter groups and reorganized under the name of the United Federation of Teachers (UFT). Charles Cogen, president of the newly formed UFT, then sent word to Carl Megel, president of the AFT, that he, Cogen, believed that the city's teachers could be unionized if the AFT would help. The primary leaders of the UFT in New York City consisted of Charles Cogen, who had been president of the Teachers' Guild since 1951; David Selden, who was a social studies teacher in a junior high school in New York City until 1941, when he became an organizer for the New York local and was later taken into the national AFT office as organizer and assistant to the president; and Albert Shanker, a high school teacher in New York City who had become active in union affairs and was hired by the national office as an organizer in 1959 and was assigned primarily to the New York City area. With these three men heading the union effort in New York City, it is not surprising that the AFT was willing to act when Cogen requested aid. In October 1960 the AFT loaned the UFT $20,000 from its $22,000 reserve fund. Additional funds were raised for organizational purposes among the AFT's general membership.[51]

Not only did support come from AFT's national headquarters,

but from the AFL-CIO as well. At Megel's urging, George Meany, president of the AFL-CIO, sent personal representatives and other assistants to New York City. Walter and Victor Reuther, with their top lieutenant, Brenden Sexton, came. As a result of their appraisal, there was a heavy infusion of funds into the New York local, as well as a promise of all-out help. The AFT was taken into the rich AFL-CIO Industrial Union Department and put in the care of the department's executive director, Nicholas Zonarich, who was considered by many to be one of the country's best union organizers.

There were many reasons why the AFT's national office and the AFL-CIO chose New York at this point in time for their organizational drive. For one thing, there was no countervailing organizational force. Though there were other teachers' organizations in New York City, most were small and badly splintered. The NEA, though it had a small affiliate in New York City, had never been a major force and was unlikely to be able to develop quickly enough to interfere with the ambitions of the AFT. As the largest city in the land and the largest school district in the country, New York City and its teachers represented a very attractive plum. If the AFT were successful there, they would gain valuable publicity and momentum in their drive to organize in other cities.

Although the AFL-CIO was not, at the time, particularly interested in the AFT and had, in fact, found it to be something of a problem at times, organized labor in the United States was beginning to suffer its own membership problems. Largely because of automation, there had been a steady decline in the number of industrial jobs in the United States. Membership in the AFL-CIO was beginning to decline although the work force in the United States was increasing. It was becoming clear to the leadership of the AFL-CIO that, if this trend were to be reversed, the AFL-CIO would have to begin organizing professional and white-collar workers.[52] It was thought that, if the AFL-CIO could succeed in drawing teachers into its ranks in large numbers, the resistance of other white-collar groups to affiliation with organized labor would be greatly diminished.

A further incentive to organizing New York City lay in the fact that the political structure was conducive to such an organizing drive. Robert Wagner was then mayor, and his prolabor reputation was well known. The AFL-CIO could bring considerable pressure on the mayor to encourage the organizing drive.

To add to the situation, the UFT had barely been formed when it began to make noises about striking in New York's public schools. The first strike was called by the UFT on November 7, 1960, to reinforce demands for collective bargaining rights as well as certain working conditions. It is not altogether clear how effective this one-day strike was in actually disrupting public education in New York City. The UFT claimed that some 7,500 pickets had been out, and that 15,000 of the 39,000 teachers in the district had failed to report. The board of education's estimates were considerably lower, namely, that some 4,600 teachers stayed home that day.[53] But in any case, the strike accomplished two purposes. First, it put the board of education and political leaders of the city on notice that the union had sufficient strength to be able to disrupt the normal operation of the school system and thus embarrass the leaders of the schools within the city government. Second, it brought active political intervention from the AFL-CIO. Almost immediately, President Meany appointed Vice-Presidents David Dubinsky and Jacob Potofsky, along with Harry Van Arsdale, to a panel charged with mediating the strike. Though organized labor had not been in favor of a teachers' strike, they nonetheless were successful in their interventions with the city political leaders, and Superintendent Theobold quickly agreed to the demands of the teachers' union for a collective bargaining election and the dropping of all charges against striking teachers.

In June 1961 an election was held to determine whether the city's teachers were in favor of collective bargaining. The vote was 27,367 in favor, to 9,003 against collective bargaining. In December 1961, a second election was held to determine which organization would represent the district's 40,000 teachers at the bargaining table: the AFT local (the UFT), the hurriedly assembled and NEA-supported Teachers' Bargaining Organization, or the Teachers' Union (a remnant of old AFT Local No. 5, which had been expelled years earlier for alleged Communist leanings). The results of the election were UFT, 20,045 votes; Teachers' Bargaining Organization, 9,700 votes; and Teachers' Union, 2,575 votes.

Having won exclusive representation rights for the city's 40,000 teachers, the UFT immediately began contract negotiations with the district. Superintendent Theobold said that a total of $33.8 million was available for pay raises. The amount included money set aside for raises for supervisors as well as for teachers. This amount was not acceptable to the UFT, which at first asked for $68 million in raises but later scaled demands down to a total of $53 million. On March 22, 1962, negotiations were broken off. The following day UFT's Executive Board and Delegate Assembly voted to strike on April 10 unless the dispute was resolved. The dispute was not resolved and, after a twenty-four-hour, last-minute postponement, 20,588 of New York's public school teachers struck, closing most of the system's schools. Although the strike lasted for only one day (April 11) and the bargaining impasse lasted only about a month, by the time it was settled the mayor and city government of New York, the governor and the legislature, and the superintendent and school board were all embroiled in the controversy. To affect a settlement, the state legislature and the city appropriated an additional $82 million to the school system, and each of the city's teachers received an average pay increase of $700. Within the three years following the bargaining election in 1961, the UFT, through collective bargaining, secured salary increases amounting to about $1,500 per teacher plus "many other concessions which bite into Board of Education policymaking perogatives, reductions in instructional load, increases in specialized services and guarantees against over-large classes."[54] During the 1960's and 1970's, New York's UFT continued to prosper and grow under the successive presidencies of Cogen, Selden, and Shanker. By the early 1970's, the UFT's membership had reached 60,000, making it the largest union local in the AFL-CIO. Because of its size, wealth, and accumulated power, the UFT soon became a dominant force in the AFT and propelled its three presidents, again successively, into the presidency of the AFT.

After the significant victory in New York City, AFT locals were more aggressive in demanding bargaining elections in other major cities of the nation, and they quickly acquired majority bargaining status in most urban centers in the northeast (Boston, Philadelphia, Washington, D.C., Cleveland, Detroit, and Chicago, to name but a few). In many cases, support was forthcoming in large amounts from the AFL-CIO and the Industrial Union Department.

But in spite of its successes in acquiring bargaining representation rights in large urban areas in the 1960's, the AFT has been noticeably unsuccessful in penetrating beyond the urban industrial centers. It has had little appeal for teachers in suburban and rural school districts, which make up the bulk of school districts in the United States; nor has it been particularly successful in the South or West.

One cannot leave discussion of the AFT during this period without mentioning mergers that have taken place, often at the urging of the AFT. During the late 1960's and early 1970's there were several successful mergers of AFT locals and local affiliates of the NEA into a single local organization, notably in Los Angeles, California, and Pontiac, Michigan. Probably the most spectacular merger, engineered in large part by Albert Shanker of the UFT and the AFT, was that of the state organizations in New York. In 1972 the NEA-affiliated New York State Teachers' Association and the New York State Federation of Teachers merged to form the New York State United Teachers. Its president was a former officer of the NEA affiliate, and its vice-president was Albert Shanker, a former president of both the UFT and the AFT. This merger brought 200,000 members into the ranks of the AFT, almost doubling its membership. In 1976, much to the chagrin of the NEA, the New York State United Teachers voted to drop affiliation with the NEA, thereby becoming the state affiliate of the AFT and eliminating more than 200,000 teachers from the membership rolls of the NEA.

During the 1960's and 1970's the energies of the AFT were primarily devoted to organizing and providing limited logistical support for locals that were engaged in strikes against school districts. As the 1960's wore on, these strikes became increasingly frequent and greatly taxed the resources of the limited staff of the national AFT.[55] In addition to organizing new locals and recruiting new members, much of AFT's energy during this period was devoted to maintaining existing bargaining representation rights and winning bargaining elections in additional sites from the local affiliate of the NEA. The rivalry between the AFT and the NEA became particularly bitter, and much space in the *American Teacher* is devoted to castigating the practices and ideologies of the NEA.

In Summary

What are the major points, issues, or events that highlight the organizational history of the AFT? The first is the fact that it came about as a result of a "desire to advance the cause of the classroom teacher."[56] It grew as the result of frustrations encountered when a group of teachers and administrators, primarily from Chicago, tried unsuccessfully to influence the NEA. When this group affiliated with organized labor, they were immediately cut off by the NEA, and, as a consequence, the ties of the AFT to organized labor were strengthened. It adopted the organizational pattern of America's labor unions, and it gradually subscribed to the methods and ideologies of that movement.

Second, one thing that has affected the AFT's history is the fact that most teachers have a middle-class, antilabor bias, which means that the AFT has been denied membership and organizational opportunities because of its labor ties. It has only flourished where strongly organized trade unions have lent organizational support, and it has had little organizational success beyond metropolitan areas.

Third, the platform of the American Federation of Teachers was initially and is still a curious mixture of issues related to teachers' welfare and issues related to social reform. Interestingly, the educational goals of the American Federation of Teachers are quite compatible with those espoused by the NEA. It is not in goals or ideals that the AFT differs, but, rather, in methods.

Fourth, the AFT is identified with a crisis orientation. It has become a reactive, almost scrambling type of organization. Through most of its existence it has been perennially short of money, has had to depend upon grants and loans from the AFL, and has had an extremely small staff. Its appeal has been primarily to teachers who face a crisis and who could use organized labor's support. This has produced an opportunistic, ad hoc style of organization that is constantly looking for organizational opportunities and probing grievances among teachers. With this kind of orientation, much energy has gone into simply maintaining the organization or keeping it afloat. This historical crisis complex and crisis organization set the stage for the confrontations in the 1960's, and they have been instrumental in shaping the character and the image of the AFT.

Fifth, tension between professional social goals and teachers' material welfare goals permeates the long history of the AFT. The tension is reflected in the polarization between the Chicago-led faction (basically bread-and-butter unionists) and the New York-led faction that was more oriented toward social reform. Not until the 1960's was the AFT able to develop the welfare orientation for which it is known today.

Sixth, the AFT, during much of its history, simply lacked a national organization. It did not have, nor did it encourage until very recently, the development of the extensive network of state affiliates that have been the backbone of the NEA. It has not historically had a strong central staff and a working national office. Necessarily, therefore, the AFT has been more decentralized, with power being held primarily by the large locals. Thus, the UFT and the Chicago Teachers Union have been able to control the AFT throughout its history.

And, finally, although the AFT took up many social and educational issues of the day and although the AFT's positions on these issues have become accepted, there is little evidence to suggest that the AFT was instrumental in influencing these outcomes. Its usual minority status left the AFT incapable of carrying the day in most instances or, therefore, of implementing its program.

THE NEA CHANGES COURSE

The NEA had faced challenges from the AFT before. Its response had been to denounce labor methods and affiliations as unprofessional and to launch a membership drive with employers' support. Teachers were urged, often with some threat of job prejudice, to join the NEA and to eschew affiliation with the AFT. This approach had worked well in the 1920's. NEA's membership had grown substantially, and AFT's membership had declined significantly.

But the quick and visible successes of the AFT in New York City were clearly a threat. Although the NEA initiated its denunciation and stepped up its urging of administrators to encourage local membership, it became clear almost immediately that this would not be enough. In her study of NEA's response to AFT's challenges, Lorraine McDonnell evaluates the critical importance of the AFT victory in New York: "Not only was the NEA unprepared for such events but the actions of the AFT had an effect on the expectations of the NEA's own membership. By its success the AFT had demonstrated that with the use of militant tactics, teachers could obtain more benefits from government than they had previously received."[57]

The surprise to the NEA was not the failure of its hastily assembled Teachers' Bargaining Organization (TBO) to win the bargaining election but, rather, the fact that there was a bargaining election at all and the swiftness with which events moved. Most NEA leaders knew from the outset that they were in a less than enviable position. Even among big-city school districts, New York's is unique. Its administrative staff is very much an inbred bureaucracy.[58] Its administrative officers, by and large, were not active in national organizations of administrators; they did not regularly serve on boards and commissions of the NEA. Hence, the NEA could not expect favorable treatment from the administrative contingent.

Furthermore, the NEA was organizationally weak in New York City. At the time the UFT succeeded in getting the New York Board of Education to agree to a bargaining election, there were some twenty teachers' organizations active there. There was no strong local affiliate of NEA. The TBO was hurriedly assembled by the NEA for the purpose of having an entry in the election. The TBO was not affiliated with the New York State Teachers' Association, the NEA state affiliate; there was simply no organizational base in New York City upon which the NEA could build. In 1960 the NEA had only seven hundred members among New York City's teachers where once they had had ten thousand members.[59] On the other hand, the UFT had superior organizational and financial resources. They were able to call upon organized labor and had the support of the powerful AFL-CIO Industrial Union Department. Altogether the UFT had about $138,000 to spend on the campaign to win the support of the city's teachers in the bargaining election. During this same time, after a late start, the NEA spent about $117,000.[60]

In this struggle the UFT had the advantage in two other significant ways. First, the NEA had been opposed to collective bargaining. Nor had it had any experience in waging collective bargaining representation election campaigns. The UFT and the parent AFT, on the other hand, had been interested in collective bargaining for some time. What is probably more important is that, although the AFT had little experience in waging bargaining election campaigns, their friends in organized labor did. Because of their lack of experience, the NEA field staff was unprepared for the rough-and-tumble campaign that took place. Donley, in pointing out the campaign difficulties of the NEA, quotes T. M. Stinnett, an official of NEA:

To be starkly frank about it, NEA's staff members came up against tactics which in their relatively cloistered world they had never encountered before. After it was all over, they discovered that copies of every bit of correspondence from the NEA office reached the UFT headquarters before being received by the addressee. Mimeographed materials from the NEA office, processed by trade union members, reached the UFT before NEA personnel saw them. Members of the NEA task force scheduled to speak at one of the city's schools often were notified by telephone that their schedules had been changed only to find when they showed up that school was out and teachers had long since departed for home, or the addresses given them were not schools but vacant lots. One UFT advocate reported that he dropped by the NEA office one day to check on some NEA research data. He went from the NEA office to the UFT office and was questioned about his loyalty. Word of his visit to the NEA office had been reported by an office worker to the union before he could reach the UFT office.[61]

Stephen Cole points out that the TBO suffered an additional handicap in its opposition to the use of the strike. The UFT was on record as favoring a strike if necessary to achieve demands. To put it bluntly, the UFT knew how to talk and behave militantly and NEA's TBO did not. Cole, in his analysis of the unionization of teachers in New York City, argues that the mind-set of teachers was such that they had, by that point in time, internalized a strike ideology. The TBO, he says, "completely misjudged the temper of the teachers."[62] A TBO leader's postelection analysis supports this claim:

The only thing that TBO could have done to win was to agree to strike. I tried to convince them to do that. I said that you do not understand the temper of the high school and junior high school people and maybe not even that of the elementary school people. My experience is that teachers want a strong measure. What they want is a strike. They could not understand that and were very much surprised when they lost the election. They thought that the elementary school teachers would vote against the UFT on the basis of its strike stand. They had completely misunderstood the temper of teachers. The TBO lost in every division.[63]

Not only had the NEA misjudged the temper of the teachers in New York City but, by all indications, the leadership was also misjudging the temper of many teachers in the United States. As has been pointed out, the NEA, throughout most of its history, had not given high priority to obtaining material gains for teachers. It had concerned itself, rather, with "professional" matters and educational issues. Its strategy and counsel to teachers had been that material rewards would surely follow improved professional status. The AFT, however, by virtue of its actions in New York City, had shown teachers across the country that they could achieve gains quickly and at little personal cost. It is no wonder that the AFT became an attractive alternative for many teachers and quickly gained exclusive bargaining rights in a number of major cities.

NEA's strategy and position relative to the material welfare of teachers is understandable for several reasons. First, many leaders at the NEA aspired to professional status similar to that enjoyed by the American Medical Association or the American Bar Association, without realizing that there were significant impediments to achieving this status. The governance system of the NEA made it easy, furthermore, for administrators to dominate policymaking decisions. In 1960 the American Association of School Administrators was by far the most powerful department of the NEA. Teachers were still in a minority on all key boards and committees. On some, classroom teachers represented as little as 17 percent of the membership.[64] When it came to dramatic increases in material benefits for teachers, administrators were quite naturally ambivalent. At that time, at least, administrators served two masters— boards of education and teachers. The administrative staff of a school system is charged by the board of education with conducting the affairs of the district in a fiscally efficient manner. Translated, this has all too often meant keeping costs down so that taxes would not have to be raised to an intolerable level. Superintendents and key administrative officers were in no position to advocate large wage increases for teachers, for they knew all too well what that would mean for the budget and the tax rate.

Administrators still controlled the key machinery of the NEA in 1960, but there was considerable evidence that classroom teachers, who made up the bulk of NEA's membership, were growing restive. Although the NEA was in no mood to make demands or to call for collective bargaining, they had, as early as 1947, adopted a policy statement urging "professional group action on salary proposals."[65] The NEA policy statement called for: election of teachers' salary committees by the membership of local education association with authority to represent and act for it; study by the committee of the local salary schedule and financial conditions; submission of a plan of action to the local association for approval; approval by the board of any understanding reached by the teachers' group with a board of education and entry in its entirety into the minutes of the board; and exerting influence to prevent unprofessional acceptance of appointed replacement of teachers involved in salary discussions.[66] Just so there would be no misunderstanding or that the NEA could be accused of moving toward collective bargaining, NEA's executive secretary, William Carr, reportedly described the policy as "democratic persuasion."[67]

The NEA followed this policy over the years, maintaining advocacy of teacher involvement in salary determination and routinely feeding salary data to affiliated state and local organizations for the use of salary committees. Throughout this period, however, the NEA was careful to avoid calling for true bilateral determination of teachers' wages and benefits and scrupulously avoided terminology such as "bargaining" or "negotiation." In 1958 the NEA hired two salary consultants and began running "salary schools" for its local and state affiliates.[68]

Although the AFT victory in New York and quick succession of bargaining election victories in other major cities would provide impetus for change in NEA's position, it is quite clear that there were stirrings within the ranks even before the UFT strikes and the election successes. At the NEA convention in Los Angeles in 1960, a resolution was presented that would have moved the NEA toward endorsement of collective bargaining. The resolution read as follows:

The National Education Association recognizes that representative negotiation by teachers with their governing boards concerning conditions of employment is compatible with the ethics and dignity of the teaching profession.

Such negotiations should be conducted by teachers associations whose primary purposes are to promote the cause of education in the United States and to elevate the character and advance the interests of the profession of teaching without special commitment to any particular segment of the community.

The procedures of negotiation should be consistent with the teachers obligation to maintain the uninterrupted operation of the public schools.[69]

In the floor debate on the proposed resolution, the word "negotiation" was replaced by the word "conference," but, even as amended, the resolution was defeated by a wide margin.[70] At the convention in 1961 another resolution was proposed on the subject of teacher-board of education relationships, and this resolution was adopted by the representative assembly. This resolution recognized the legal authority of boards of education and stated that "professional education associations should be accorded the right, through democratically selected representatives using appropriate professional channels, to participate in the determination of policies of common concern including salary and other conditions for professional services."[71] By 1962, the NEA, having witnessed the success of the UFT in New York City, realized that it must take a stronger stand. Accordingly, the resolutions committee presented a much stronger proposal and, as a result, the delegates overwhelmingly passed a resolution that, for the first time, labeled the process "negotiation."

At the same convention, though the NEA continued to avoid endorsing the strike, delegates did propose an alternative (sanctions) from the floor, and the proposal was adopted by the delegates and added to NEA's policy on employment relations. In 1963 the delegates authorized the executive committee to impose and remove sanctions at the request of state and local associations, and in 1964 the NEA imposed sanctions on the state of Utah for inadequately supporting public education. Sanctions were imposed again in 1965—on the state of Oklahoma. During this period numerous local school districts were also "sanctioned" by the NEA for various unprofessional actions.

Between 1964 and 1968, the NEA would gradually modify its policy, first by deleting the section that prohibited the use of industrial methods for resolving disputes (for example, mediation and arbitration). In 1965 the word "strike" was deleted from the article that had previously banned such activity. In 1966 a resolution from the floor called for grievance procedures, and, in 1968, after the NEA had been involved with a disastrous strike through the activities of the Florida Education Association, the convention added a resolution containing provisions for "withdrawal of services." In just eight years the NEA had moved from opposition to negotiations and strikes to advocacy of both.

It is clear, from records of this period and events that occurred at the conventions, that this turnabout in policy occurred without the wholehearted support of NEA's executive secretary or principal staff members. Although the changes were gradual, it is now clear that they were not the result of a plan created and executed at headquarters. Rather, it resulted from a shift in the power structure of the association and the emergence of an urban-dominated militant leadership within its elected bodies. Not only was there a reordering of NEA's priorities, but there were also significant changes in the governance structure, leading ultimately to a change in the executive leadership of the organization.

THE NEA AND URBAN PROBLEMS

The 1960's, in the United States, was the decade of the cities. There was public recognition of the decay of America's great cities and attempts by the government to reverse the trend. On the educational scene, the problems of urban education drew increasing attention, and the federal government passed the most massive education aid bill in history in 1965. At the beginning of this period the NEA and most of its state affiliates were not particularly involved with the problems of urban education, and the organization exhibited a strong suburban-rural orientation. Within the NEA, however, an organization of urban associations, the National Committee of Urban Education Associations, emerged, and, in the early part of the 1960's, this group began to gather power within the representative assembly. The key staff leadership of the NEA saw little need to differentiate services among urban and suburban school districts, but, in 1961, the Board of Directors' budget committee proposed a one-time appropriation of $50,000 to study the development of a program for urban school systems and associations.[72] The urban associations found this response to be inadequate and, in a well-organized floor fight, the urban associations countered with a proposal for the establishment of a separate urban services division within the NEA and for the allocation of $100,000 to fund it. This proposal was initially opposed by the executive secretary and defeated at the convention in 1961, but it attracted considerable interest and, after the NEA's defeat in New York City in 1961, it became obvious that some kind of urban services division would be required. On March 15, 1962, the NEA Urban Project was established. Though this project was created to stem the union tide in urban school districts, it was to be the fulcrum for fundamental reform of the NEA.

Though the senior staff members were not particularly sympathetic to the problems of education in the big city or the problems
of teachers' associations in those locations, the younger staff members soon saw numerous advantages in the Urban Project and the
development of a forceful urban presence in the NEA. The servicing of local associations had heretofore been left primarily to autonomous state associations that collected their own dues, maintained
their own membership rosters, and elected their own officers. It
was apparent by the 1960's, however, that most state associations
were in no mood to provide services required by the urban associations and that the urban associations would have to turn to the NEA
itself for the services they required. With the Urban Project, the
staff of the NEA for the first time legitimately bypassed the state
organizations and provided services directly to local associations.
By this means they increased the visibility of the NEA among local
associations and increased the dependence of local associations
on the national organization.

These tactics follow from the basic governance structure of the
schools. The organizational control of American public schools
virtually dictates that the negotiations will occur at the level of the
local school district. Thus, the responsibility for negotiating fell
to the often poorer-equipped and poorer-serviced local associations. In conjunction with the Urban Project, local associations
could be assisted in the collective negotiation process, and ties
between national and local associations were strengthened.

In 1970, with the support of urban leaders and an executive staff
now in favor of direct ties with local associations, the Uniserv program was launched. The goal of the program was to have one professional staff member in the field for every 1,200 teacher members.
The NEA would pay $8,500 toward the salary of such a staff mem-
ber. There was, however, one important caveat: In order to participate in the program, the local association had to be an association
with a unified dues structure. This meant that teachers could no
longer choose membership in one organization without joining all
three (local, state, and national). With this powerful incentive, the
NEA was able to capitalize on the membership of local and state
organizations and thus bring its own membership and its dues
returns up to the level enjoyed by the local and state affiliates. This
arrangement was not only beneficial in terms of membership and

income, but it gave the NEA a mechanism for directly intervening in the affairs of local associations. Though Uniserv directors (professional staff members) are selected by the local associations, they are de facto employees of the NEA. The effect of Uniserv has been to establish a large, effective network of field organizers with a strong sense of loyalty to the NEA. These field agents in many cases have exerted considerable pressure on conservative state associations and their leadership.

As a result of the rapid development of collective bargaining relationships and of the Uniserv program, the NEA has assumed a configuration much like that of a labor union. The primary articulation is between the national and the local, and the national exercises considerable influence on the activities and events of the local.

THEMES

It is time to identify and elaborate on some of the themes that have emerged in this chapter. Certainly a major one that is consistent through the long history of both national teachers' organizations is their struggle for identity. They have consistently had difficulty with professional as opposed to welfare issues. Perhaps this is borne of desire for organizational status, that is, to be the powerful, professional voice of education—the ultimate authority. Yet both organizations, and especially the NEA, were painfully aware of their vulnerability to public opinion. Charges of "self-interest" could be ruinous. These organizations are voluntary, and they must maintain the support of their members to survive. This concern surfaces in a number of ways, including the NEA's early strike avoidance posture and aversion for the practice of collective bargaining. It recurs in the AFT's difficulties with certain locals that had strong leftist or Communist orientations and were not in the mainstream of American educational thought. This identity crisis probably reflects the personal one experienced by most teachers who continually ask themselves: Whom do I serve? Myself? My students? My community? My profession?

Those who were not teachers but had an interest in the governance and control of American public education were smart enough to recognize this tension and to use it to increase control. We have reported in this chapter how administrators played upon the teachers' concern over professional status. Not only was this dimension of the identity crisis exploited in the early part of the twentieth century, but it was resurrected to fight the emergence of militancy in the early 1960's. The NEA coped with the tension between professionalism and welfare by attempting to merge the profession's and members' interests. This was so successful that it became difficult for the NEA to act militantly. The invention of a language of teacher militancy by the NEA provides insight into this problem: "collective bargaining" was designated as "professional negotiation"; a contract was termed a "professional agreement." The AFT confronted the tension somewhat differently. Though it adhered more to standard labor terms and approaches, the AFT simply avoided, where possible, most welfare issues until the 1950's, preferring to devote its efforts to pressing social issues of the day.

By raising the specter of teachers' self-interest, boards and administrators were able to hold down wage costs. Teaching was repeatedly labeled a professional calling, and teachers were lauded for their dedication. The implication was that professionals simply do not pursue self-interest (*read:* "higher wages")! The difference in the 1970's may be that teachers and their organizations had decided finally to resolve the inner conflict and ambiguity over these issues. As a result, teachers can no longer be easily exploited because of them, and teachers and their organizations have become much more difficult for administrators and boards of education to control.

Another theme that emerges from the history of teachers' unions is the unique role that the NEA has played in the governance of public education. As we look back, it seems clear that the NEA was an integral part of the control mechanism of American public education during the first half of the twentieth century. It served as an arm of the reform movement that swept government and education and provided a platform for reforms. It urged school boards and citizens to trust in their professional superintendent and his staff. In some ways the NEA functioned as a quasi-governmental unit, serving as the primary data collection and research agency for public education. Maybe it even told Congress what was good for education and told teachers what was good practice. One of the functions the NEA served was to make decentralized education in the United States "safe." There is no doubt that the organization was instrumental in promoting norms that helped give public education respectability and at the same time provided fairly explicit guidelines for the behavior of teachers and the operation of school districts. Although education in the United States is decentralized and the control rests by and large with locally elected school boards, the NEA was also responsible for establishing standards of practice that were widely adopted by the diverse boards. That is one reason why the schools, although they are decentralized, are not widely divergent.

The interaction of the two major teachers' organizations is another continuing theme. Though the interaction took different forms during different periods, the presence of the "other" organization was always a consideration. In many ways the interaction is really a system of mutual dependence. The AFT was founded in 1916 because the NEA could not accommodate the more militant teachers. More militant and liberal teachers have looked to the AFT as their organization for fifty years.

But the presence of the AFT influenced the behavior of the NEA. The AFT absorbed potentially disruptive dissidents, allowing the NEA to proceed on a conservative, "professional" course. Thus, leadership challenges, such as the one led by Margaret Hailey, were few.

The fact that a more liberal rival organization existed greatly assisted NEA's organizing efforts. Threatened by the AFT, the NEA realized some of the organization's greatest membership gains by making its administrators field organizers. The AFT has, for most of this century, been the NEA's organizational bogeyman. School boards and administrators, persuaded that the AFT posed a threat to the educational establishment, were eager to support the NEA. This support, and the continuing challenge from AFT, increased the need to control the NEA. It was partly because NEA was dominated by those who ran the schools that NEA became quasi-governmental, a sort of shadow U.S. Office of Education. And, again, it was the threat from the AFT that precipitated NEA's militant reform in the 1960's.

The AFT similarly benefited from and responded to the NEA. Because it was formed by, and continued to attract, NEA malcontents, much AFT policy and behavior can be seen as reactive to the NEA. It was a reaction in several ways. First, there was certainly no advantage to mimicking the NEA. As the often struggling minority organization, the AFT had to be different, to offer an alternative. NEA, because of its size and power, could set its position; AFT was then left to choose a contrasting stance. To the extent that these choices came down to being more or less liberal than those of the NEA, or more or less militant, or more or less teacher centered, the AFT virtually had to assume the more liberal, militant, or teacher-centered stance. Its members would have had it no other way. The consequence of such repeated choices is that members share similar views and are likely to continue to hold them in the future.

But this organizationally reactive, out-of-power position has an inherent weakness. If the majority organization eventually adopts the policy of the reactive organization, then the reactive group must become more extreme or retrench. Either way, the viability of the reactive group may be threatened. In recent years, the AFT has been forced to confront this reality. If merger activity is discounted, membership in the AFT has remained stable in the past few years, whereas that in the NEA has continued to grow.

Rivalry with the NEA has affected the AFT in other ways. It has allowed, perhaps encouraged, alliance with organized labor—something not yet possible for the larger organization. The fact that NEA has maintained a large research organization and has devoted much attention to school programs allows the AFT to concede those functions and concentrate on other matters without the self-consciousness inherent in speaking for the whole field of education.

The fact that the two groups chose to develop along different organizational structures constitutes another theme. The NEA chose the professional or voluntary organizational mode. This was really an elaboration of reform management principles being advocated for school districts in the superintendent-board relationship and for city governments in the city manager-council relationship. The NEA opted for a strong executive secretary and a governing or legislative body that met infrequently. Information and management control were concentrated in the executive secretary, who was an appointed full-time staff member. The executive secretary system in the NEA also created an executive much more like a school superintendent, which undoubtedly strengthened the bonds between administrators and the NEA. The executive secretary of the NEA was seen as being its superintendent. Partly as a consequence of this pattern, the organization was conservative in its behavior, and its officers, who were elected for short time periods of usually one year, were virtual figureheads. The salary paid the president of the NEA was, until very recently, equivalent to the amount necessary to replace foregone earnings in a teaching or administrative position. The election was for a one-year period only, hardly long enough to develop an understanding of the complex machinery of a large organization.

The AFT, however, opted for a different system wherein executive responsibility was lodged in the officers. The president, who was also the chief executive officer of the union, had to stand for election periodically. As a consequence, he served a significant political as well as an executive role in the union. The fact that the chief executive officer of the AFT was elected rather than appointed because of his skill as a manager probably meant that the AFT did not have the same administrative resources or that the AFT did not devote much attention to establishing strong state-affiliated organizations. Though it cannot be said that the executive secretary system was in itself responsible for the state network and the chain of command that developed among the local, state, and national offices of the NEA, it is likely that such a system would be more comfortable for an executive secretary-manager.

NOTES

1. There were earlier contracts between teachers' unions and school boards. The earliest was probably negotiated in Cicero, Illinois, and signed in 1944.

2. Estimate taken from "Collective Negotiations in Education," National Manpower Resource Study, 1976, unpublished. This study is the most current available, and it is also the source for data presented in Chapter 2.

3. For data on membership in public and private sector unions, see Hugh Clegg, *Trade Unionism under Collective Bargaining: A Theory Based on Comparisons of Six Countries* (Oxford, Eng.: Basil Blackwell, 1976), esp. 12.

4. Sidney and Beatrice Webb, *History of Trade Unionism* (New York: Longmans, Green, 1920), 1.

5. The Webbs are generally recognized as the first to use the term "collective bargaining." See Sidney and Beatrice Webb, *Industrial Democracy* (London: Longmans, Green, 1902), 173.

6. Robert F. Hoxie, *Trade Unionism in the United States* (New York: Appleton-Century-Crofts, 1923; 2d ed. reprinted, 1966), 279-295.

7. *Id.* "Trade Unionism in the United States," in *Trade Unions*, ed. W. E. J. McCarthy (London: Penguin Books, Ltd, 1972), 37.

8. See Hoxie, "Trade Unionism in the United States," 45-46.

9. Arnold S. Tannenbaum, "Unions," in *Handbook of Organizations*, ed. James March (Chicago: Rand McNally and Co., 1965), 710.

10. *Ibid.*

11. In 1976-77 the three biggest programs in the NEA budget were: Uniserv, Independent, United Teaching Organization and Economic and Professional Security for all Educators. These three programs together claimed 44 percent of the budget. (*NEA Handbook, 1976-77* [Washington, D.C.: National Education Association, 1977], 35.)

12. For an account of the growth of teachers' organizations at the state level, see T. M. Stinnett, *Professional Problems of Teachers*, 3d ed. (New York: Macmillan, 1968), 374-376; see also Chapter 4 in this book.

13. See Laurence Iannaccone, *Politics in Education* (New York: Center for Applied Research in Education, 1967), for a discussion of the way state associations have operated in the educational policy-making arena.

14. For a detailed account of the founding of the National Education Association, see Edgar B. Wesley, *NEA: The First Hundred Years: The Building of the Teaching Profession* (New York: Harper and Brothers, 1957), esp. ch. 3.

15. Marshall O. Donley, Jr., *Power to the Teacher: How America's Educators Became Militant* (Bloomington: Indiana University Press, 1976), 13.

16. David B. Tyack, *The One Best System: A History of American Urban Education* (Cambridge, Mass: Harvard University Press, 1974), 7.

17. Tyack has used the term "one best system" to describe the model for organizing schools largely patterned on industrial practice and management. It includes centralized decision making, standardized procedures, and large, complex structures.

18. Donley, *Power to the Teacher*, 15.

19. See Mildred Sandison Fenner, *NEA History: The National Education Association, Its Development and Program* (Washington, D.C.: National Education Association, 1945), 56-160.

20. For an excellent discussion of the meaning of this reform, see Frederick Buchanan, "Unpacking the NEA: The Role of Utah's Teachers at the 1920 Convention," *Utah Historical Quarterly* 41 (Spring 1973), 150-161.

21. Wallace S. Sayre, "Additional Observations on the Study of Administration: A Reply to 'Ferment in the Study of Organization'," *Teachers College Record*, 60 (October 1958), 73-76, esp. 74-75.

22. Tyack, *One Best System*, 264.

23. *Ibid.*, 266-267.

24. *Ibid.*, 266.

25. *Ibid.*

26. Fenner, *NEA History*, 35.

27. Buchanan, "Unpacking the NEA."

28. Until recently, teachers have been able to elect membership in the local education association, the state association, and the National Education Association on an independent basis. For example, they could choose to belong to the local NEA affiliate and the state NEA affiliate but not to the NEA itself. Many teachers did just this. The Uniserv program begun in 1970 required that local associations

had to have a "unified" dues structure to participate. That is, members paid one fee, which included dues for the local and state associations and the NEA. For a discussion of the significance of this move, see Lorraine M. McDonnell, *The Control of Political Change within an Interest Group: The Case of the National Education Association*, unpub. diss., Stanford University, 1975, 120-126.

29. William Edward Eaton, *The American Federation of Teachers, 1916-1961: A History of the Movement* (Carbondale: Southern Illinois University Press, 1975), 7. About this same time, teachers in San Antonio, Texas, also organized and, in 1902, were granted a direct charter by the AFL.

30. *Ibid.*, 8.

31. *Ibid.*, 15.

32. *Ibid.*

33. For details of the AFL platform, see *ibid.*, 15-16.

34. *Ibid.*, 18-19.

35. *Ibid.*, 27-28.

36. *Ibid.*, 38-39.

37. *Ibid.*, 45.

38. *Ibid.*, 46-47.

39. *Ibid.*, 41.

40. For local survival data, see *ibid.*, 127. For membership data for AFT, see Chapter 4 in this volume.

41. Eaton, *American Federation of Teachers*, 125.

42. *Ibid.*, 132-133.

43. *Ibid.*, 175-176.

44. *Ibid.*, 74-75.

45. *Ibid.*, 140.

46. *Ibid.*, 142.

47. Stephen Cole, *The Unionization of Teachers: A Case Study of the UFT* (New York: Praeger Publishers, 1969), 6.

48. Eaton, *American Federation of Teachers*, 145.

49. *Ibid.*, 151.

50. *Ibid.*, 161.

51. *Ibid.*, 162-163.

52. Cole, *Unionization of Teachers*, 164-165.

53. Leonard Buder, "The Teachers Revolt," *Phi Delta Kappan*, 43 (June 1962), 370-376, esp. 370.

54. Stanley Elam, "Who's Ahead and Why: The NEA-AFT Rivalry," *ibid.*, (September 1964), 12-16, esp. 12.

55. For a discussion of the effect of limited AFT field staff resources, see Robert J. Braun, *Teachers and Power: The Story of the American Federation of Teachers* (New York: Simon and Schuster, 1972).

56. Eaton, *American Federation of Teachers*, 167.

57. McDonnell, *Control of Political Change within an Interest Group*, 90.

58. For a good discussion of the bureaucracy of the New York Public Schools, see David Rogers, *110 Livingston Street: Politics and Bureaucracy in the New York City School System* (New York: Random House, 1968).

59. Donley, *Power to the Teacher*, 46.
60. McDonnell, *Control of Political Change within an Interest Group*, 95.
61. Donley, *Power to the Teacher*, 49.
62. Cole, *Unionization of Teachers*, 64.
63. *Ibid.*
64. McDonnell, *Control of Political Change within an Interest Group*, 127.
65. Donley, *Power to the Teacher*, 43.
66. Eaton, *American Federation of Teachers*, 143.
67. *Ibid.*, 165.
68. Donley, *Power to the Teacher*, 42.
69. McDonnell, *Control of Political Change within an Interest Group*, 105.
70. *Ibid.*
71. *Ibid.*, 106.
72. *Ibid.*, 117.

4

Growing Membership in
Teachers' Organizations

Teachers' unions have become large organizations by most
standards in recent years. The National Education Association
(NEA), as it approaches 2,000,000 members, is now the second
largest national union in the United States. Only the International
Brotherhood of Teamsters enrolls more members. The NEA is
nearly twice as large as any union presently affiliated with the
AFL-CIO. While the American Federation of Teachers (AFT),
with approximately 450,000 members, is far from the largest union
affiliated with the AFL-CIO, one of its locals, the United Federation of Teachers in New York City, has about 60,000 members and
is the largest union local in the AFL-CIO. Between them, the NEA
and the AFT enroll about 2,133,000 members, almost 91 percent of
the nation's 2,352,000 teachers.[1] Size and membership saturation
are often used as indicators of union power and success. By either
of these standards, teachers' unions have achieved notable success.
They are large, particularly the NEA, and they have had remarkable success in enrolling those eligible as members. Education is,
therefore, one of the most heavily organized industries in the
United States. The density of its union membership is not typical
of unions here, where membership of employees in the private

sector is presently about 25 percent; it is, rather, more typical of unions in Europe, where density is high and 85 percent to 95 percent of public workers belong to trade unions.[2]

Membership in the NEA was relatively small from 1857, when it was founded, until 1918, when it began a steady climb to its present level. Reasons for the small enrollment in the early years are presented in Chapter 3. Throughout the twentieth century, however, many teachers who did not belong to the NEA held membership in state education associations that were NEA affiliates. Until after World War II, the combined membership of state associations was easily twice as large as membership in the NEA itself. Figure 4-1 shows the growth of educational associations and unions and depicts the relative difference in membership between NEA and affiliated state associations.

The same figure also shows the relative membership in the AFT from the time it was founded (1916) to 1976. Membership, which was relatively stable during the first twenty years of existence, began to increase slowly over the next twenty-five years, until, by the 1960's and the 1970's the increases were rather substantial.

Absolute membership in organizations, while it indicates size and dues-generated wealth, does not provide complete information about gains. Growth in membership may simply represent an expanding work force and the maintenance by a union of its share of that work force. Figure 4-2 shows membership for the AFT and the NEA, and combined memberships in the NEA and the AFT as a percentage of the nonsupervisory, instructional work force. This figure provides a better indication of the organizational strength of teachers' unions, for it is, in effect, corrected for growth in the work force. Table 4-1 contains membership data for the two major teachers' organizations. Both the figure and the table clearly show that growth in the NEA from 1918 onward was real growth. In addition to benefiting from a growing work force, the NEA was expanding its share through successful organizing efforts. To a lesser extent, but more noticeably in the 1960's and the 1970's, the AFT also increased its organizational penetration.

For the NEA, the figures reveal some spectacular periods of growth in the number of members in relation to the share of the work force. The years between 1918 and 1926 certainly represent such a period. Membership climbed from about 10,000 (1.5 percent

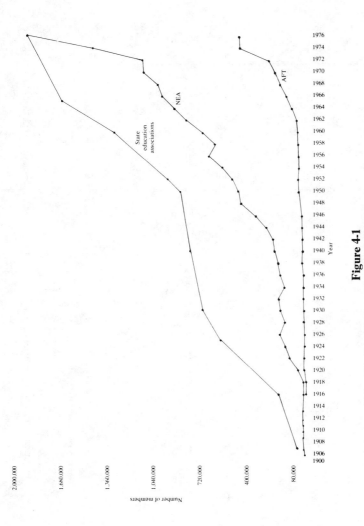

Figure 4-1

Membership NEA, AFT and state education associations

(State association data from T.M. Stinnett, *Professional Problems of Teachers*,
3d ed. [New York: Macmillan, 1968], 376)

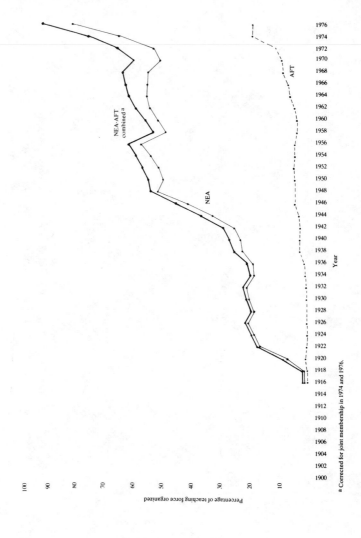

Figure 4-2

Teacher organization membership as a percent of nonsupervisory instructional work force

of the teaching work force) to 170,000 (20 percent of the teaching work force). This period probably reflects the aggressive organizing campaign carried out by school administrators in reaction to the formation and early membership drives of the AFT.

Another period of unusual growth occurred from the mid-Depression years and the beginning of the New Deal era in 1936 to the middle 1950's. This was a time of rapid economic change, from depression to post-World War II boom. Passage of the National Labor Relations Act in 1935 began a period of rapid union growth in the private sector. The parallel growth in membership of unions in the private sector and membership in the NEA during this period probably represents responses to common, underlying causes. The last period of intense growth in membership for the NEA occurred after 1970, which likely reflects the reorganization of the NEA to meet the challenge from the AFT. State association memberships were transferred to the national association to eliminate historic membership differences between the NEA and the state education associations. The growth would seem to indicate that the NEA was successful in integrating the state and local memberships and not that teachers' associations per se captured a larger share of members during this period.

William Moore and Ray Marshall, who analyzed AFT growth during the period 1916 to 1968, have identified four periods of substantial growth—1916 to 1920, 1929 to 1939, 1942 to 1947, and 1961 to 1970—and have concluded that, before 1960, membership in the AFT closely paralleled membership changes for organized labor as a whole. Inasmuch as the AFT has always had its greatest successes in areas where organized labor was strong generally and has often actively used leaders from other local unions in its organizing efforts, there might be a strong relationship between the success of organized labor generally and the success of the AFT.[3]

There can be no doubt about the fact that teachers' unions have grown substantially, particularly in the last half of the twentieth century. Growth has occurred both in actual numbers and as a percentage of the eligible work force. Nor is there any doubt that teachers and teachers' unions have changed their behavioral style and become more militant. These observations are undoubtedly related. The stance of teachers' unions on ideology and the welfare of members obviously affects individual decisions about membership.

Table 4-1

Membership of the NEA and the AFT as a percentage of the teaching force in selected years

Year	NEA membership	NEA percentage of teaching force	AFT membership	AFT percentage of teaching force	Total number of teachers organized	Total percentage of teachers organized	Total teaching force (nonsupervisory instructional)
1916	7,878	1.3	2,800	0.4	10,678	1.7	622,371
1918	10,104	1.5	2,000	0.3	12,104	1.8	650,709
1920	52,850	7.8	9,808	1.4	62,658	9.2	679,533
1922	118,032	16.3	4,500	0.6	122,532	16.9	722,976
1924	138,856	18.2	3,500	0.4	142,356	18.6	761,308
1926	170,053	20.8	3,500	0.4	173,553	21.3	814,159
1928	152,989	18.3	NA	—	—	—	831,934
1930	172,354	20.1	6,872	0.8	179,710	21.0	854,263
1932	184,394	21.1	7,356	0.8	191,735	22.0	871,607
1934	154,377	18.2	10,683	1.3	165,060	19.5	847,120
1936	165,448	19.0	16,500	1.9	181,948	20.9	870,963
1938	195,605	22.3	30,130	3.4	225,735	25.7	877,266
1940	203,429	23.2	29,907	3.4	233,336	26.6	875,477
1942	217,943	25.3	25,500	3.0	243,443	28.3	858,888
1944	271,847	32.8	29,700	3.6	301,547	36.4	827,990
1946	340,973	41.0	35,500	4.3	376,473	45.3	831,026
1948	441,127	51.2	NA	—	—	—	860,678
1950	453,797	49.6	41,415	4.5	495,212	54.1	914,000
1952	490,963	51.0	50,000	5.2	540,963	56.2	963,000
1954	561,708	53.9	45,140	4.3	606,848	58.2	1,042,000
1956	659,190	57.4	50,000	4.3	709,190	61.7	1,149,000

Year							
1958	616,707	48.6	51,000	4.0	667,707	52.6	1,267,000
1960	713,994	51.4	56,156	4.0	770,150	55.5	1,387,000
1962	812,497	54.0	70,821	4.7	883,318	58.7	1,504,000
1964	903,384	55.6	100,000	6.1	1,003,384	61.7	1,624,000
1966	986,113	55.2	125,000	7.0	1,111,113	62.2	1,786,000
1968	1,081,660	55.3	165,000	8.4	1,246,660	63.7	1,957,000
1970	1,100,155	50.3	205,328	9.3	1,305,483	59.7	2,187,000
1972	1,166,203	53.3	248,521	11.3	1,414,724	64.6	2,187,000
1974	1,467,186	64.2	444,000	19.4	1,911,186	83.6	2,287,000
1974 (corrected)	1,467,186	64.2	444,000	19.4	1,711,186 [b]	74.8	2,287,000
1976	1,886,532	75.3	446,000	17.8	2,332,532	93.2	2,502,475 [a]
1976 (corrected)	1,886,532	80.2	446,000	19.0	2,132,532 [b]	90.7	2,352,327 [c]

[a] Includes all instructional staff (certified).

[b] Corrects for approximately 200,000 in merged organizations.

[c] Accounts for 94 percent of instructional staff.

Source: Statistical Abstracts of the United States (Washington, D.C.: U.S. Department of Commerce, Bureau of the Census. annual).

Inasmuch as unions are voluntary organizations, their behavior must in some way reflect the aggregate desires of members. Otherwise, membership would decline rather than grow. Leaders or small controlling factions can distort union behavior in the short run, but, in the long run, an organization where membership is voluntary must have interests that coincide with the interests of its members. In short, given their membership accomplishments, teachers' unions must "be doing something right."

To understand this phenomenon, we must look at the situation of classroom teachers in the United States and examine the economic and political context of the organizations in which they function. Besides explaining affiliation patterns, we must account for the timing of shifts in union attitudes and behaviors. It is not enough to argue that complex economic, social, and political factors influenced the growth of teachers' unions; there must also be some attempt to explain why teachers departed from their traditional patterns of behavior in the 1960's to embark on the now familiar militant course.

A logical place to begin the search is in industrial relations literature from the private sector. Over the years considerable attention has been devoted to the formation and behavior of trade unions, and this has resulted in explanations for union growth that are widely accepted. It may be well to keep these explanations in mind as we examine the behavior of teachers' unions more closely.

EXPLANATIONS FOR UNION GROWTH AND TEACHER MILITANCY

Theories of the Labor Movement

Students of the labor movement have been attempting to explain patterns of union growth for a considerable period of time. Most theorists believe that the movement has its origin in the changes in production and pricing systems that accompanied the Industrial Revolution. As the transition was made from the guild and craft systems of the eighteenth century to the industrialized product system of the nineteenth and twentieth centuries, workers found themselves caught up in a system that deprived them of social, psychological, and economic security. The Industrial Revolution quite literally shattered the social and economic world that most people had come to know. Prior to the advent of the factory system, goods were generally produced in a small shop with a master and his journeyman. John Commons, for instance, used the shoe industry to illustrate the transition.[4] During the eighteenth and much of the nineteenth century, shoes were usually made to order. The work was done by hand in small shops servicing a relatively small geographic area, and there was little standardization of lasts.

This method of production not only characterized the shoemaking industry but also most other productive enterprises of the time. Workers shared a personal relationship with their "master," as well as a common trade. Masters were not managers but, rather, master craftsmen who, because of their status and skill, supervised the work in the shop. They also were in most cases responsible for teaching the trade to apprentices who joined a shop to learn a particular skill. Shops flourished only insofar as they did good work and there was sufficient demand in the local market to sustain them. There was little competition as we know it today. Except in the larger towns, clients could not usually choose among the products of multiple manufacturers. There were few capitalization problems, little concern for market cycles, and no need to maintain an inventory. Nor was there a stock that had to be sold.

The development of the factory system, of course, changed this way of life. Goods were no longer produced by a master craftsman and associated journeymen and apprentices. Production became centralized in factories that employed a large work force. Product markets overlapped, and factories produced goods not only for the local region but also for regions and markets many hundreds of miles away. Large investments of capital were required to build factories, buy machinery, and pay workers prior to the selling of the products.

The new system of mass production was reflected in structural changes in the marketplace. Whereas earlier the local craftsman had been both producer and retailer of the finished goods, the responsibilities of manufacturer and retailer became separate, largely because the output of large factories was simply too great to be absorbed in a local market. Custom orders were replaced by "off-the-shelf" or "ready-to-wear" merchandise. The factory owner had to be able to respond to changes in product demand by expanding or contracting according to market cycles.

Needless to say, the factory system that emerged in the nineteenth century created hardships for workers. Local producers were rapidly driven out of business, and, in order to find employment, workers had to relocate near factories. This often meant leaving small towns and moving to large cities. Social and family ties were disrupted. Perhaps as significant as the social disruption was the economic disruption brought about by the changing market structure. Producers were no longer interested in satisfying just a small, local clientele. Prices were not fixed by agreement among master craftsmen or by negotiation between client and producer as they had been in the guild system. Rather, the prices for goods became a function of the competitive marketplace, and producers became concerned not for producing a good that could be sold locally but a product that could be sold in the larger competitive market. It became important to produce goods as cheaply as possible, a competitive pressure that was rapidly transmitted downward through the work force. The incentive to keep wages low and exploit the work force became greater, and labor came to be viewed more as a cost of production than a producer of goods.

As a result of the factory system, managers as we now know them began to emerge in large numbers. To keep the factory operating efficiently, it was in the interest of the owners and the managers, who represented the owners of capital, to develop and maintain a large, cheap, compliant work force of sufficient size so that workers would have to compete with one another for available work. This kept down the wage rate and lowered the unit cost of labor in production.

Differences between owners and managers and workers also began to be exaggerated. Under the earlier craft system the master would take on journeymen only as he had trade sufficient to justify their continued employment. The factory manager or owner had much different attitudes toward labor. He could not, given the nature of the product market, take ultimate responsibility for the welfare of workers. Profit margins were sufficiently low under the competitive system that the owner or manager could not afford to maintain an idle work force. Neither could he, because of the market competition, afford a large backlog of goods. When demand slackened, there was no choice but to lay off workers until the demand for goods justified their reemployment.

It is important to note in passing that public education in the

United States has undergone structural changes that are in ways similar to the changes produced by the Industrial Revolution. During the eighteenth and nineteenth centuries, most schools were small, often with one room and one teacher. As the country grew, so did its schools. They grew from one- or two-room units to the large, complex organizations of today. During this time, individual schools were amalgamated into multischool districts, and, over time, these districts were consolidated into ever-larger districts. The growth and increasing complexity of schools and school systems have been accompanied by the development of a management system staffed by professional administrators. Thus, schools have also developed in ways that increase the tension between individuals and the organization.[5]

Selig Perlman offers one of the more important explanations of how changes in employment conditions lead to unions in his "job consciousness" theory.[6] Perlman saw three groups—intellectuals, entrepreneurs, and "manualists" or workers—as being essential to the explanation of any activity in the economic sector and as being particularly meaningful for any discussion of the rise of the labor movement in the United States. European labor movements have always had a sizable input from intellectuals. It was Perlman's conclusion after examining the American labor movement, however, that intellectuals had had little impact on the thinking of American labor. In fact, Perlman said, the United States labor movement had developed its own "home-grown philosophy." Perlman also concluded that the "mentality" or orientation of entrepreneurs and workers was quite different. Entrepreneurs, Perlman believed, are driven by a "consciousness of opportunity," that is, entrepreneurs are excited by the competitive nature of the marketplace and eager to develop and exploit economic opportunities and to acquire wealth that they can hold and pass on to their heirs. Property rights are extremely important to the entrepreneur. Workers, on the other hand, are in no position to exploit their environment; instead, they are in constant danger of being exploited. Individually they lack the resources to compete in the marketplace and, therefore, the economic market is no challenge. Beset by a "consciousness of scarcity" or "job consciousness," workers, according to Perlman, have only one chance in this free economic situation and that is to strive for ownership of jobs, that is, for collective control of hiring, firing, entry requirements, apprenticeships, and so forth. In a sense, workers, acting collectively, seek to convert jobs to property status.

Recent events seem to confirm Perlman's analysis of the motivation of labor. Civil service procedures, for example, limit the ability of managers to use competition for jobs to their advantage by expanding the concept of due process of law into the employment area. It is now generally considered unlawful for an employer in the public sector to fire an employee, that is, to deprive him of his job except by due process. Due process was intended to protect persons against being unjustly deprived of "life, liberty, or property." The extension of this protection to job rights appears to strengthen Perlman's views.[7]

Lashed by what Perlman has termed the consciousness of scarcity, workers resorted not only to collective action and collective bargaining with the employer but also turned to political action in an attempt to legislate job rights and job security. In this vein the NEA was following consistent union behavior long before the 1960's. Both NEA and its state affiliates began lobbying for tenure laws and other legislation to protect the job rights of teachers early in the twentieth century.

Among the earliest and most influential analysts of the union movement, again, were Sidney and Beatrice Webb. It is their description of the history, development, and aims of labor that probably corresponds most closely with the common view of labor practice in the United States. The Webbs recognized that the modern industrial apparatus left workers or wage earners in a powerless position relative to their employer and that the conditions of modern industry made it too easy and too tempting to exploit this powerlessness. In their opinion, the only way workers could guarantee adequate wages and reasonable conditions of employment would be to unite in trade unions and seek "the deliberate regulation of the conditions of employment in such a way as to ward off from the manual working producers the evil effects of industrial competition."[8] The Webbs believed that unions strive to adopt "common rules to govern wages, to insure a standard number of hours in the working day, and to enforce common regulations for safety and sanitation."[9] It is clear that the Webbs viewed labor unions and collective bargaining as essential to the introduction of democracy into the workplace. Democracy, to the Webbs, had two essential ingredients: an equalization of power between workers and management and a system of equitable treatment for all involved in the workplace. The Webbs did not hold to a static model of labor behavior; rather, they argued that, over time and under different social conditions, workers would adjust their behavior and utilize the most appropriate method. Through collective bargaining, wage standards would be raised, and trade unions would gradually expand the numbers of issues and problems with which they dealt.

Though the Webbs believed that workers would and should be involved in important industrial decisions that affected their welfare, they did not hold that workers should control production or technological decisions. They specifically argued, in fact, that what was produced should be a function of the marketplace, and decisions relating to technology and methods of production should be the prerogative of management. Labor, they held, had no special expertise in this area.

While the Webbs focused on the creation of work rules, Frank Tannenbaum, a labor historian, has focused on the social dislocation brought about by the factory system.[10] In exploring the impact of this system, Tannenbaum points out that industrialization and urbanization patterns broke up the social community and "left workers isolated and bewildered in a city crowded with strangers." But there was more to Tannenbaum's idea than simply the idea that industrialization caused work anomie. For, as far as Tannenbaum was concerned, there was an "organic" relationship between the worker and his job. The factory, with its wage-pricing system, both deprived the worker of his identification with the product and at the same time made him dependent upon a money-wage system in which there was little security. In short, the worker lost ties with his craft and at the same time became dependent on a large, impersonal system that cared little for his welfare. Unions, therefore, came into being both as social units and as attempts by workers to protect themselves from the uncertainties and hazards that threatened the survival both of the group and of its individual members.[11] According to Tannenbaum, the worker seeks to restore the social and economic conditions of the abandoned guild system.

In more recent years, Robert Nisbet has adopted a similar perspective when he says that the "upsurge of labor unions as well as other forms of association in the 19th Century can indeed be seen as a response to the kind of atomism that had been created by the new industrial system, with its large, impersonal factories, its rigid division between 'owners' and 'workers,' and by the sudden loss of traditional, communal context of village, parish, and extended family by so many thousands of workers.[12] Unlike Tannenbaum, who wrote earlier, Nisbet has extended his analysis into the latter half of the twentieth century and the development of unions in the public sector. With regard to the development of unions in the public sector, Nisbet says:

These public unions came into existence in circumstances analogous to those in which private unions appeared. As government agencies became larger and more impersonal, more dominated by civil service regulations and boards, with the older forms of intimacy vanishing, with the kind of personal touch that even (and especially) political bosses could offer through patronage—disappearing along with the political machine—as these conditions became more and more widespread, with elected councils, mayors, governors, and congresses seemingly powerless to do anything about them, the soil of public unionism was being prepared. It is no exaggeration, I believe, to say that the public union is the successor in many ways to the old political machine. Just as that machine offered, in its way, security to countless Americans, mostly of lower class, many of them insecure immigrants recently arrived, so does the large public union today, along with its complex of locals, offer the same kind of security.[13]

Nisbet points out that there has been a gradual decline of the power of Western governments to control events and, as a consequence, not only do state bureaucracies lack control but corporations and other associations and interest groups lack control as well. With the breakdown of the sovereignty of government, public employees have lost confidence in their employers' ability to deal with them justly and to structure an environment favorable to their existence. Lack of trust that one's employer can provide justice is a central theme in arguments for public unionism provided by the contemporary theorists, Harvey Mansfield,[14] Seymour Lipset,[15] and Alan Fox,[16] whose ideas will be discussed later in this chapter.

In 1948 John Dunlop examined the major theories of union growth and development and found that there were many similarities in the findings of each of the authors but that there were also two primary differences. Commons and the Webbs, Dunlop argued, formulated their theories primarily from the point of view of the union as a "manifestation of economic developments,"[16] whereas Perlman, Hoxie, and Tannenbaum concerned themselves more with the state of mind of workers.[17] Dunlop argues that, for any theory to be acceptable, it must take into consideration the interactions between the economic marketplace or the nature of economic institutions and the attitudes and state of mind of workers. Dunlop posits four interrelated factors that must, in his opinion, be examined if one is to understand the labor movement: technology, market structures and the character of competition, community institutions of control, and ideas and beliefs. "Technology," according to Dunlop, "includes not only changes in machinery and in methods of production but concomitant developments in the size and organization of production and distribution units."[18] As for "market structures and the character of competition," he says that the term "comprehends the growth of markets, the changes in the focus of financial control as distinguished from the size of production units, the development of buying and selling institutions in both product and factor markets, and the emergence of specialized functions and personnel within these organizations."[19]

When he talks about the wider "community institutions," Dunlop claims that the phrase "is intended to include among others the role of the press, radio, and other means of communication in society; the formal educational system for both general and vocational training; the courts, governmental administrative agencies; and political parties and organizations."[20] And, finally, "ideas and beliefs" are, in his opinion, "a short-cut for the value judgments and mores that permeate and identify a social system."[21]

Using these four characteristics, Dunlop makes some interesting observations about the nature of labor growth in the United States. First, he points out that "successful organization has required that workmen occupy a strategic position in the technological or market structures."[22] He contends that, for workers to be successful in pushing their demands and organizing a continuing association or trade union, those involved must have sufficient power to achieve at least some of their objectives. To do this, they must be in a position where they can disrupt the production process or the delivery of essential services—or they must be at a critical juncture or bottleneck in the market where they can, by their action, disrupt the larger market. Though Dunlop did not address the development of large-scale public unions as we know them today, it is clear that this strategy has been a necessary and important ingredient in their development. In their works, Harry Wellington and Ralph Winter have also pointed out the strategic importance of governmental services that are both essential and monopolistic, which means that consumers have no short-run alternatives.[23] This fact, alone, would seem to make the public sector particularly vulnerable to organization and development of strong trade unions.

In his analysis of the labor union, Dunlop argues that the nature and attitude of the work force represents another main determinant of union organization and development, and claims that a "second major condition in the emergence of organization is the view of the employees that they shall look forward to spending a substantial portion of their lifetime as workmen."[24] Again, though Dunlop was looking at unions in the private sector, this notion is particularly germane to the examination of unionism in the public sector and of teacher unions in particular. Many changes in the teaching work force over the years have affected the career-mindedness of teachers, and this situation will be examined in some detail later.

Dunlop argues that "certain types of community institutions stimulate, and others retard, the emergence in growth of labor organizations."[25] The changing attitude of the press toward unionism is an example. Certainly the legal system had an important effect on the development of trade unions as well. Passage of the Wagner Act in 1935 loosed a flurry of union activity in the United States and did more than anything up to that point to encourage union development. Then the presidential orders of John Kennedy and Richard Nixon relative to the organizing and bargaining rights of federal employees gave important impetus to unionism in the public sector. And, because public employees are generally governed by the laws of each state, one cannot discount the tremendous growth in the body of public employment law that has developed, particularly since the first collective bargaining act was passed in Wisconsin in 1959.

Underlying Cause of Public Unionism

Though Tannenbaum and other earlier theorists have dealt implicitly with the concepts of trust and equity, not until recently have these concepts emerged explicitly as means of explaining the behavior of organized labor. Expanding on Tannenbaum's notion of group protection or security derived from social arrangements, Jack Douglas has analyzed the changes in social and political orders, particularly those that have occurred in the older cities of America.[26] In comparing public unionism in Chicago and New York City, Douglas concluded that Mayor Daley's machine in Chicago was able to integrate and accommodate public unions, whereas Mayor Lindsay's organization in New York City attempted to rationalize and formalize the interaction. As a consequence, the Lindsay administration so completely destroyed the bases of trust in the old social order that the only way that order could be restored was by immense economic payoffs to the unions. What is involved in Douglas' analysis is the notion that, as governments become increasingly apolitical, specialized, and bureaucratized, it becomes more difficult for them to respond to the needs of special interests. The end result is heightened intergroup conflict and a declining confidence in the city's government. Both Douglas and Nisbet conclude that, as governments become increasingly unable to satisfy the group security needs of the population, people will turn to other associations to provide for these needs.[27] It is in this context that Douglas argues that the union provides social cohesion and responds to needs formerly met by political machines in cities.

There are several streams to these arguments of Nisbet, Mansfield, Douglas, and Lipset. One is that, as government becomes increasingly apolitical and attempts to rationalize its functions, it loses contact with clients and the ability to work with interest groups. In this context the union is viewed primarily as an interest group which will, if necessary, gradually increase or expand the interests of the members it seeks to ensure. In short, it will expand its functions from merely providing a social outlet or serving as an economic bargaining agent to providing for the social protection needs of its members. Nisbet points out that, as government loses power, associations and smaller groups inevitably gain power. The result is a growing lack of confidence in the government's ability to solve problems, and lack of confidence inevitably causes people to look elsewhere to satisfy their needs. This results in a further loss for government. In this context, government cannot function without the confidence of the governed.

In the public sector this loss of authority and confidence manifests itself in two ways. First, government loses the ability to cope with or contain increasingly powerful public unions, and, second, the members of the union, recognizing the weakening of government, lose faith in the government's ability to keep promises and to manage the work environment. As the situation deteriorates, government is seen as being unable to integrate and deal with an interest group, which means that the union interest group is driven to seek power to supply for its members the protection that government can no longer provide for its employees. This same problem is recognized by Wellington and Winter, who have argued that the public sector is unable to deal with powerful labor unions or resist their demands; hence, unions should not be permitted the right to strike.[28]

Mansfield has examined the function of social trust in public unionism from a slightly different perspective, but his conclusions are essentially the same as those of Nisbet and Douglas. Mansfield argues that the public sector has been plagued with a decline in prestige owing essentially to a loss of "public spirit" fostered by the ideas contained in classical liberalism. In the classical liberal model, as used by political scientists, it is assumed that the general interest is best served when each person vigorously pursues his own self-interest. The economic marketplace of the private sector is modeled on this assumption. Mansfield contends that the application of this classical economic liberal model to the public sector and the government is dangerous. It has the effect of eroding public confidence in municipal government as labor unions increasingly and obviously pursue their self-interest. As public confidence and, therefore, support of public servants' positions erode, public unions must exert even more aggressive behavior to preserve their self-interest. The inevitable result is a drift toward the competitive modeling of the private sector, which increases the adversarial roles in the public sector.[29]

Fox, British sociologist and student of industrial relations, has approached trust from a slightly different perspective.[30] He has observed that there are two types or models of exchange—social and economic. Social exchange normally characterizes interpersonal and most intergroup relationships. This is the system in which individuals or groups undertake certain behaviors under the expectation of some later, unspecified return or reward. Economic exchange, on the contrary, is a system wherein the terms of the exchange are explicitly stated and understood prior to the exchange. Fox notes that the two types of exchange are more functional in different environments. Most notably, economic exchange methods are utilized in the marketplace, where all are presumed to be maximizing their self-interest at the expense of others, and in situations where lack of trust in the other party precludes expectation of just or fair repayment if exchange terms are not specified. Social exchange requires that there be an element of trust between the two parties to the exchange. When that trust is absent, Fox observes, the two parties will inevitably resort to a system of economic exchange.

Labor contracts are an example of economic exchange relationships in employment relations, with the behaviors and rates of exchange between the parties specified explicitly and in detail. Thus, Fox would argue that collective bargaining, particularly the behavior that characterizes collective bargaining in the United States, where all agreements are reduced to contract form, occurs because employees no longer trust their employers. Again, the relationship is escalating and cyclical. As social interactions are reduced to economic forms of exchange, trust is further eroded, and the need for economic exchange becomes even greater. That is why more dimensions of behavior are entered into the contract and exchange expectations become more explicitly defined.

As employees' trust in their employer diminishes and attempts to define precisely exchanges between employer and employee increase, attention to and concern for equity increase as well. It has been understood for some time that peoples' judgments about fairness or equity are relative. In light of the theoretical explanations for union movements and union behavior, we would expect to encounter concern for fair treatment in three areas: social, organizational, and economic.

Stephen Cole has based his analysis of the United Federation of Teachers in New York City on the concept of relative deprivation. When discussing the situation in New York City that led to the bargaining election and subsequent strikes, Cole said:

In the case of teachers, however, relative deprivation must be viewed in the historical context. As changes outside the profession occurred, the gap between teachers and their comparative reference groups widened or narrowed; the comparative reference groups used by teachers did not change, but relative deprivation did. Just as inflation resulted in increased relative deprivation, so, too, did the introduction of the single salary schedule. Relative deprivation may result not only when comparisons are made with those who occupy a superior position, but also when those who occupy a superior position see their superiority being eroded.[31]

The growth of dissatisfaction among teachers in New York City is seen as stemming from a deterioration of relative economic returns and working conditions. Cole argues that these dissatisfactions are among the root causes of teacher militancy in New York City and of the teachers' strike there in 1962.

Relative deprivation as an explanatory system is widely used in sociology. The concept was first identified by Samuel Stouffer and later developed by Robert Merton and Paul Lazarsfeld in their massive study of the American soldier.[32] The research team was at first mystified by the discovery that a company of military police where promotion or advancement was slow exhibited higher morale than members of an air force squadron where advancement was rapid. The researchers eventually concluded that the differences lay in the fact that the members of the two groups evaluated their opportunities and successes in light of different reference groups. Members of the air force squadron, largely college educated, reflected upon the opportunities their nonmilitary colleagues enjoyed in civilian life and resented their own lack of opportunity. They saw their nonmilitary classmates getting promotions on Wall Street, establishing successful law practices, and so forth. This led them to believe they were marking time while their civilian classmates got ahead. The essential element in relative deprivation, of course, is some benchmark against which progress or achievement is measured. It may be the success of another reference group, as posited by Stouffer and Merton and Lazarsfeld, or it may be longitudinal changes in one's state. This longitudinal construct of relative deprivation, used by Gurr[33] to explain civil strife, is an essential part of Cole's analysis of the New York City situation.

Ted Gurr has identified four types of relative deprivation. The first type, illustrated in Figure 4-3, is called "aspirational deprivation," and it results when expectations rise but capabilities remain constant. Aspirational deprivation occurs when people, for some reason, progressively develop a taste for or expect greater

Key:

Relative deprivation (RD): individual perception of discrepancy between value expectations and value capabilities

Collective value position: average level or amount of goods and conditions of life that members of a collectivity have or expect to attain

Value expectations: average value positions justifiably sought by members of a collectivity

Value capabilities: average value positions members of a collectivity perceive themselves capable of attaining or maintaining

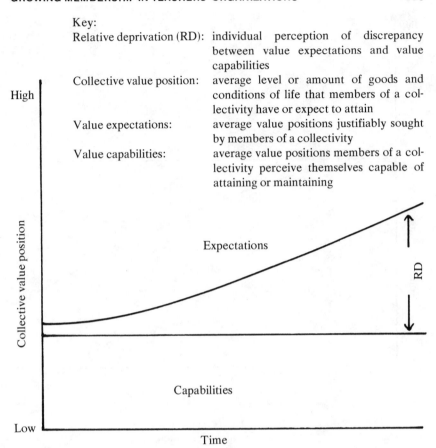

Figure 4-3
Aspirational deprivation
(from Ted Robert Gurr, "A Comparative Study of Civil Strife," in Hugh Davis Graham and Ted Robert Gurr, *Violence in America: Historical and Comparative Perspectives*. Volume II, *A Staff Report to the National Commission on the Causes and Prevention of Violence* [Washington, D.C.: U.S. Government Printing Office, 1969], 464)

achievement, but the system in which they find themselves prevents them from realizing their expectations. A second form of relative deprivation is "decremental deprivation" (see Figure 4-4), which occurs when expectations remain relatively constant over time but system capabilities decrease. This kind of deprivation could occur in situations where school systems are progressively deprived of resources or in a situation where rapid inflation erodes purchasing power. A third type of relative deprivation is labeled

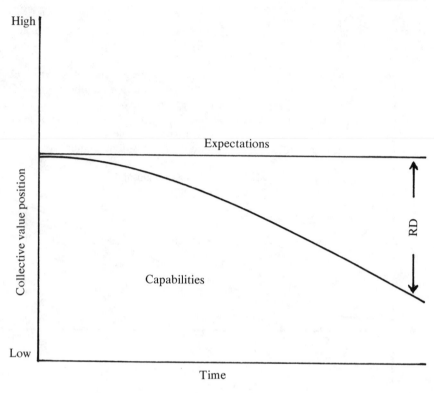

Figure 4-4
Decremental deprivation
(from Gurr, "Comparative Study of Civil Strife," 465; see Figure 4-3, above, for key)

"progressive deprivation (see Figure 4-5)." As shown in the figure, both expectations and achievement capabilities rise, but capabilities rise at a progressively slower rate. Gurr's final type allows for a state of "persisting deprivation." This is shown in Figure 4-6.

DETERMINANTS OF TEACHER UNIONISM AND MILITANCY

Though relative deprivation and Dunlop's four factors of union organization are not total explanations of the union movement, they stimulate questions about events in teacher organization and

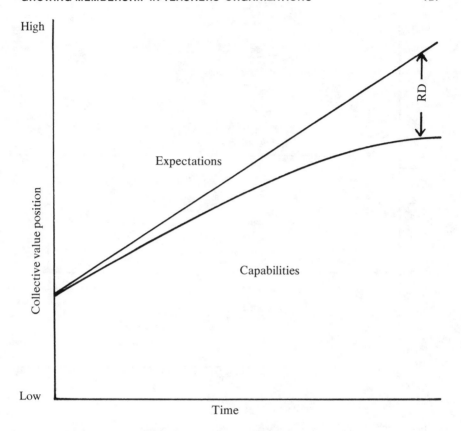

Figure 4-5
Progressive deprivation
(from Gurr, "Comparative Study of Civil Strife," 466; see Figure 4-3, above, for key)

are helpful in organizing information. The deprivational literature suggests that some form of dissatisfaction is at the root of union organization and behavioral decisions. Dissatisfaction in this case is determined by two factors: teaching conditions and what teachers expect those conditions to be. Dunlop's ideas build on this notion of relative deprivation and suggest that any explanation of union growth must also include conditions that channel or direct the response to deprivation. It seems clear from classical explanations of unionism that union organization and militant expression are but one of the choices available to workers who have identified some form of relative deprivation. Dunlop suggests that there are

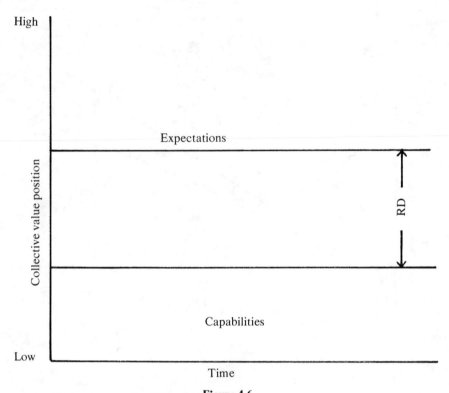

Figure 4-6
Persisting deprivation
(from Gurr, "Comparative Study of Civil Strife," 467; see Figure 4-3, above, for key)

a whole series of contextual changes and cues to help workers determine which course of action they should follow. It is quite clear, in retrospect, that contextual cues have suggested to teachers that militant organization is an appropriate response to their collective sense of deprivation. Any explanation of the teachers' union movement must, therefore, identify not only the sources of deprivation but also the contextual and internal changes that have led them to adopt the current militant posture.

Nonteaching Statuses

It is often assumed that teachers respond as teachers to problems presented by their environment. There is good evidence, however, that teachers do not necessarily respond homogeneously. This is particularly true when the problematic situation goes beyond teaching to involve status, organizational returns, or the like. In these situations, teachers respond as men or women, as young or old, as having had considerable or little organizational responsibility, as being from a middle-class or working-class background. Two things emerge clearly from research on teachers' union behavior. First, these "nonteaching statuses," as Cole calls them, seem important in determining how teachers will respond to problematic situations.[34] Second, there have been significant changes in the makeup of the teaching force relative to these statuses over the course of the last several decades.

Sex—Related Differences

Research on union membership and militant disposition has found consistant differences between men and women. Lowe found, for example, that men were more likely to join the AFT and that women were more likely to join the NEA when there were significant differences between the two organizations in terms of militancy.[35] In his study of the United Federation of Teachers in New York, Cole found that sex was a significant factor in explaining the actions of teachers relative to the strike in 1962.[36] Donald Hellriegel, Wendell French, and Richard Peterson found sex to be an important discriminate in teachers' support of strikes, and Joseph Alutto and James Belasco have found that sex and attitudinal militancy are related.[37] In a recent study, William Fox and Michael Wince also found sex to be an important determinant in occupational militancy and offered this explanation:

Several interrelated explanations of the relationship of sex and militancy may be suggested. Sex differences in militancy may reflect normative differences regarding aggression in American society, differences that may decline in the future due to the widespread resurgence of feminism. Sex differences in militancy also may be rooted in greater job dissatisfaction among male teachers, especially in regard to such salient matters as income and prestige. For more men than women, teaching is the sole or principal source of support for spouse and children. Thus, different role demands are made upon male and female teachers such that a given income is likely to seem less adequate to a male than a female teacher. Similarly, with respect to prestige, married women tend to assume the prestige conferred by the husband's occupation, thus easing the demands placed upon female teachers as opposed to males. This potential for greater male dissatisfaction with the economic and status rewards of teaching is increased by the more lucrative and prestigious alternative occupations open to men. In contrast, the alternative occupations traditionally available to female teachers are relatively few and rarely have greater prestige or income than teaching. Thus, sex differences in militancy may be rooted in feelings of relative deprivation.[38]

As has been suggested by Dunlop, the permanence or anticipation of long-term involvement in the work may be a factor in determining how one behaves relative to union organization and activity. W. W. Charters has shown that men have a higher survival rate in teaching than women, that is, men tend to teach longer and, hence, may reasonably be expected to view teaching as a more permanent career position.[39]

In a study of teacher trainee graduates from the various campuses of the City University of New York conducted between 1954 and 1955, researchers found that, five years after graduation, over three-fourths of the men but less than one-half of the women were still teaching in the public schools. And, what is perhaps equally significant, less than 40 percent of the women said they planned to continue teaching indefinitely while almost 80 percent of the men viewed teaching as a lifetime career.[40] Men not only seem to view the conditions and rewards of teaching differently, but it would appear that men must also take them more seriously since they expect to invest more of their lifetime.

Sex differences are important to an explanation of militant predispositions, but it is important to note as well that the composition of the teaching force has been shifting in recent years toward a larger percentage of males. Robert Doherty and Walter Oberer report that, prior to 1830, there were few women teachers in the common schools. At about the time of the Civil War, males were attracted to higher paying jobs in other areas and began to leave the teaching force. The proportion of women teachers increased steadily until the 1920's when a peak of about 83 percent was reached. By 1973 the percentage of women teachers had again declined to about 66 percent of the teaching force.[41] If the ratio of men to women in teaching continues to increase, this may well increase the militancy orientation of teachers as a group.

Age

Many researchers have revealed a relationship between age and militant disposition or behavior. In most cases it has been found that younger teachers tend to be more militant than older ones, even though older teachers tend to be more dissatisfied with their situation. Though the reasons for this are perhaps not as clear as those relating sex to militancy, there are several plausible explanations. One of the more obvious is the known relationship between conservatism and age. As teachers grow older, they become more conservative and, hence, less likely to support aggressive union behavior. Another explanation favored by Fox and Wince is that these differences are rooted in the generational differences of teachers. They suggest:

Beginning their careers in the late 1950s and 1960s, younger teachers had available several highly visible examples of apparently successful militancy that were not available to their older colleagues when they began their careers. The securing and enlarging of gains by blue collar workers as well as the more recent and more dramatic gains won by black militancy may well have left their marks upon younger teachers. Having perhaps the greatest impact, however, were the successes recorded by militant teachers in other communities during the 1960s.[42]

Many older teachers have vivid recollections of the Great Depression, whereas many of the younger teachers began their careers during a period of low general unemployment when there was a severe shortage of teachers. Their entry into teaching, therefore, was marked by feelings of security and a sense of freedom about expression and behavior. Students who were on the college campuses during the free speech movement, who were at the University of California at Berkeley, the University of Wisconsin, and Columbia University during the riots of the late 1960's, and who participated in the Vietnam protests of the same era have now been teaching almost ten years. No doubt these people carried with them some of the spirit they displayed on college campuses during that period.

Fox and Wince have found that teachers just entering the profession tend to be less militant. This may be their "honeymoon period" with teaching and their school board. It may also, however, be an indication that recent recruits into teaching carry with them attitudes acquired during a much more peaceful era on college campuses in the United States, as well as a generally more peaceful era in terms of civil rights activities than their predecessors experienced.

Population demographics of the 1950's and 1960's created a rapid growth in the school-age population. As schools grew, so did the size of the teaching force. The majority of the new teachers who were hired were young, and the relative age of teachers dropped during this period. In his research on teaching characteristics in New York City, Cole discovered that, between 1940 and 1960, there was a significant increase in the number of young teachers in the city's school system: "the percentage of young teachers climbed from 7 percent in 1940 to 31 percent in 1960, the year in which the UFT had its first strike."[42] Another factor that affected the age distribution of teachers was the Vietnam War, during which exemptions from military service were offered to those willing to teach in urban schools. During this same period a number of federal programs were begun to encourage the recruitment and development of teachers interested in urban problems. All of these things contributed to the decreasing average age of the teaching force, particularly in urban areas where most of the early militancy was detected.

Training

Most research on teacher unionism has also shown that there is a relationship between training and militant disposition. In early research, William Lowe discovered that teachers with master's degrees were more likely to be attracted to the AFT, whereas teachers with lesser training were more likely to join the NEA.[44] Fox and Wince also reported a correlation between training and militant disposition.[45]

It is interesting to note not only that there may be a relationship between training levels and acceptance of militant behavior but that there has also been a steady increase in the levels of training for all teachers. Doherty and Oberer report that, "as a group, teachers have more education today. All but 15% had the baccalaureate in 1965; those without the degree, mainly older women teachers in the elementary school period. By contrast, in 1920, the percentage of teachers in New York State, outside of New York City, who held college degrees was 11%."[46]

As more states adopt a five-year teaching preparation curriculum, the training of teachers will increase. And salary schedules, as they are presently designed, offer considerable inducement for teachers to acquire additional training. Should this trend toward increased training continue, one might expect teachers to grow increasingly militant as a group.

Social and Family Backgrounds

Another variable that has often shown a relationship with militancy on the part of teachers is social or class background. Teachers who come from upper-middle-class or white-collar family backgrounds tend to be less favorable toward unions and union-style behavior. The nature of this relationship, however, is far from clear. Teachers coming from blue-collar or working-class backgrounds are likely to have grown up in families in which members belonged to labor unions and supported the union movement. Though most authors have suggested that the relationship is linear, Fox and Wince report that the predisposition toward militant behavior is strongest among teachers coming from a family background where there were moderate attachments to unions. Those coming from white-collar or strongly union-oriented backgrounds tended to be less militant.[47]

Grade Level

Research findings have also shown a relationship between teaching grade levels and militancy. Teachers at the elementary level are consistently less militant than those at the junior or senior high school level. There may be many reasons for this. It is most likely, however, that these differences are rooted in the fact that there is a larger percentage of men at the secondary level and that teachers at that level tend to have higher levels of training than teachers at the elementary level. It may be that grade-level differences are entirely explainable in terms of nonteaching status differences.

Other Variables

Political affiliation, ideology, and religious background tend to affect the way teachers view teacher organizations and their predisposition to behave in a certain way. In his research, Cole concluded that Jews tend to be more militantly inclined than other religious groups, as do members of the Democratic party, though he noted that, in New York, the two statuses are closely related.[48] Fox and Wince similarly found that there were relationships between religious persuasion, ethnic background, and militant disposition.

Catholics or those who had no religious affiliation tended to be more militant than Protestants. Likewise, those with a Southern European or an Eastern European heritage were significantly more militant than those whose ancestors came from Northwestern Europe or who identified themselves simply as "American."[49] Alan Rosenthal, in his study of teachers' unions, draws similar conclusions about the effect of religion and union orientation.[50]

It is clear that there is considerable interaction among these determinant forces. Elementary schoolteachers tend to be women with less training who are more likely to have a middle-class background. Men, on the other hand, are more frequently found in the secondary schools. They often have higher levels of training and are more likely to have advanced from a working-class background. It is impossible to determine which of these variables represents a truly independent force in determining a teacher's willingness to join unions and to support their actions.

Organizational Conditions

Both Tyack and Raymond Callahan have eloquently documented the bureaucratic development of public schools in the United States.[51] They have noted how, at the beginning of the twentieth century, the efficiency movement coincided with the beginning of the development of a strong managerial presence in public education. Tyack, in particular, shows the impact of increasing size on the operation of the schools. Through the century schools have become progressively larger, and school systems have also grown, both through consolidation and demographic growth. Not too many years ago there were about a hundred thousand school districts in the United States. Today, with more pupils enrolled in schools, there are only about sixteen thousand operating school systems. The size of these systems has naturally required more formal procedures and contributed to the individual's sense of inadequacy. The increasing size of public bureaucracies has probably increased teachers' desire for organizational countermeasures, among them teachers' unions.

In a bureaucratic environment there is often a sense that one is unable to participate in the decision process. Lowe cited "the slight amount of involvement of teachers in the decision making process, particularly in curriculum matters" as the second most frequent source of teachers' dissatisfaction.[52] Belasco and Alutto, who have studied teachers' involvement in decision making in some detail, agree that those teachers who can be characterized as being in a state of decisional deprivation are also the teachers most likely to show a high predisposition toward militant behavior or have, as Belasco and Alutto have termed it, "attitudinal militancy."[53]

The many reasons for growing organizational dissatisfaction obviously include the increased bureaucratization and routinization of larger school systems. Another reason probably has to do with the increasing development of school management. Frank Kemerer and Victor Baldridge have shown, in their study of unionism in higher education, that unions tend to grow in response to managerial centralization and that they, in turn, feed or increase that centralization of power in the hands of management.[54] Teachers tend to think of themselves as professionals who are consequently entitled to be involved extensively in decisions that affect the welfare of pupils under their care. Most likely they look to prestigious professions, such as medicine and law, and envy their apparent professional autonomy. The development of a strong managerial cadre and the application of business management techniques in education probably run counter to aspirations for professional autonomy, and the attempt to curb managerial power in education may be another reason why teachers turn to unions.

One of the major analysts of teacher militancy and unionization who takes this approach is Ronald Corwin. He focuses on the tension between bureaucratic principles of organization and professional aspirations and has noted the inherent conflict between the two:

In order to increase its autonomy, however, a vocational group must challenge the parties which have been in control. And unless these authorities are willing to voluntarily relinquish their hold, the vocation will defy them by objecting, criticizing, or legal action, and more ambitious forms of militancy. Professionalization, in this sense, is a militant process and a likely source of organizational conflict.[55]

In his research, Corwin found that the more professional teachers, as measured by his battery of tests, were involved in more conflict than their less professional colleagues. Corwin believes that this "drive for status" that has characterized other emerging professions is now at work in education. Teachers are actively seeking to gain more control over their work by challenging the tradition of lay control in educational administration.

Economic Aspects

Teachers have been concerned about wage rates for a long time. The issue of higher pay for teachers has come up repeatedly in the conventions of the NEA and the AFT. Doherty and Oberer report that teachers' salaries have been low throughout much of American history:

Between 1841 and 1860 salaries for rural men teachers rose from an average of $4.15 to $6.28 a week; salaries for rural women teachers were about two-thirds of this figure. Urban men teachers earned twice as much as did their counterparts in the countryside while urban women teachers received only the same amount as rural men teachers.[56]

It has been estimated that, during the same period, the cost of maintaining a "frugal lifestyle" rose from $7.00 to $8.00 per week.[57]

William Eaton examined teachers' pay relative to other workers in 1913. He found:

The national pay average of teachers of $512.00 in 1913 was abysmally low. In that same year the United States government paid its employees an average of $1,136.00, salaried employees averaged $1,066.00, ministers averaged $899.00, wage earners averaged $594.00 and the factory workers $578.00. Even in comparison with other local government employees the $512.00 figure was only 70 percent of that of policemen and 71 percent that of firemen.[58]

In 1947-48, the average teacher's salary was $2,639. Though teachers' wages had more than doubled from the mid-Depression rate of $1,227 in 1933-34, the cost of living had tripled. Teachers in 1948, therefore, had less buying power than they had had in the Depression.[59]

It was clear that, early in the twentieth century, Margaret Hailey and the forces of the Chicago Teachers' Federation concentrated on the low salary being paid to Chicago teachers. In *The Unionization of Teachers*, Cole documents the diminished buying power of urban teachers' wages in New York City as a major factor in UFT's success.[60] In view of their aspiring professionalism, teachers' wages, many times surpassed by those of workers with considerably less education and social responsibility, have been a continuing frustration.

There is considerable evidence to indicate that teachers have been unsuccessful in raising their relative incomes. Table 4-2 shows the ratio of average teachers' salaries to per capita income in the United States since 1935. Notice that the ratio has remained very constant during most of the period except during the Depression of the 1930's, when teachers' wage rates collapsed less rapidly than did per capita income, and during the period right after World War II, when the general economy increased at a much more rapid rate than teachers' wages. Note, too, that in the most recent years the relative income of teachers has been steadily, if slightly, decreasing relative to per capita income. This would suggest that, during much of the 1970's, teachers' incomes have been losing ground relative to other incomes, and their sense of economic deprivation must, inevitably, be growing. If economic conditions are important to teachers, it seems unlikely that teachers will tolerate declining relative wages with no attempt to correct the downward trend. We might well expect to see unions grow more active and increase pressure in the immediate years to come.

Among the more comprehensive analyses of the development of teachers' unions is the one by Hellriegel, French, and Peterson; another is by Moore and Marshall. The study by Hellriegel, French, and Peterson, following the Dunlop tradition, presented a model to explain how teachers moved toward collective bargaining and collective behavior.[61] That model, reprinted here as Figure 4-7, focused on interaction between the attitudes of teachers, reinforcement from the environment, and success with various aspects of behavior. In short, teachers' behavior under collective bargaining opportunities was said to be a function of the satisfaction they achieve through various institutional functions and rewards. This satisfaction is conditioned by a series of socioeconomic factors and professional aspirations. These factors contribute to the drive for collective bargaining, which may also be enhanced or retarded by a series of external forces, including government action, competition between the AFT and the NEA, and with observation of other teachers' success in using various actions. This, coupled with the success rate of their own actions, influences aspiration levels, which in turn influence the way teachers view the situation in which they find themselves.

Table 4-2
Average annual salary of instructional staff compared to other measures of income

Year[a]	Average annual salary of instructional staff[b]	Per capita personal income[c]	Salary—per capita income ratio[d]	Average annual earnings for wage and salaried employees[e]	Salary earnings ratio[f]
1929-30	1,420	665	2.14	1,386	1.02
1931-32	1,417	465	3.04	1,198	1.18
1933-34	1,227	401	3.06	1,070	1.15
1935-36	1,283	505	2.54	1,160	1.11
1937-38	1,374	551	2.49	1,244	1.10
1939-40	1,441	815	1.85	1,576	1.12
1941-42	1,507	815	1.85	1,576	0.96
1943-44	1,728	1,150	1.50	2,030	0.85
1945-46	1,995	1,244	1.60	2,272	0.88
1947-48	2,639	1,381	1.91	2,692	0.98
1949-50	3,010	1,445	2.08	2,930	1.03
1951-52	3,450	1,697	2.03	3,322	1.04
1953-54	3,825	1,797	2.13	3,628	1.05
1955-56	4,156	1,931	2.15	3,924	1.06
1957-58	4,702	2,062	2.28	4,276	1.10
1959-60	5,174	2,193	2.36	4,632	1.12
1961-62	5,700	2,321	2.46	4,928	1.16
1963-64	6,240	2,526	2.47	5,373	1.16
1964-65	6,400	2,683	2.39	5,607	1.14
1965-66	6,935	2,880	2.41	5,838	1.19
1966-67	7,110	3,077	2.31	6,092	1.17
1967-68	7,630	3,300	2.31	6,444	1.18
1968-69	8,200	3,569	2.30	6,876	1.19
1969-70	8,840	3,825	2.31	7,334	1.21
1970-71	9,570	4,039	2.37	7,815	1.22
1971-72	10,100	4,313	2.34	8,334	1.21
1972-73	10,608	4,737	2.24	8,950	1.19
1973-74	11,185	5,204	2.15	9,647	1.16

Table 4-2 *(continued)*

Average annual salary of instructional staff compared to other measures of income

Year	Average annual salary of instructional staff	Per capita personal income	Salary—per capita income ratio	Average annual earnings for wage and salaried employees	Salary earnings ratio
1974-75	12,070	5,640	2.14	10,448	1.16
1975-76	13,104	6,124	2.14	11,219	1.16
1976-77	13,891	6,734	2.06	11,987	1.16
1977-78	14,813	7,463[g]	1.98	NA	NA

[a] School year.

[b] *Sources:* Data for 1929-30 to 1963-64, National Center for Education Statistics, *Digest of Educational Statistics, 1977-78* (Washington, D.C.: U.S. Government Printing Office, 1978); data for 1964-65 to 1974-75, *id., Projection of Education Statistics to 1984-85* (Washington, D.C.: U.S. Government Printing Office, 1975); National Education Association, *Estimates of School Statistics, 1977-78* (Washington, D.C.: NEA, 1978).

[c] Calendar year per capita personal income data have been converted to school year basis by averaging two appropriate years in each case. *Sources:* Data for 1929 to 1970, U.S. Department of Commerce, Bureau of the Census, *Historical Statistics of the United States: Colonial Times to 1970* (Washington, D.C.: U.S. Government Printing Office, 1970); data for 1971-1976, U.S. Department of Commerce, Bureau of Economic Analysis, *Survey of Current Business* (Washington, D.C.: U.S. Government Printing Office, June 1978).

[d] Derived by dividing average annual salary of instructional staff by per capita personal income.

[e] Calendar year data converted to school year by averaging two appropriate years. *Sources:* U.S. Department of Commerce, Bureau of Economic Analysis, *Survey of Current Business*; National Center for Educational Statistics, *Digest of Educational Statistics 1977-78*.

[f] Ratio derived by dividing average annual salary of instructional staff by average annual earnings.

[g] Estimated.

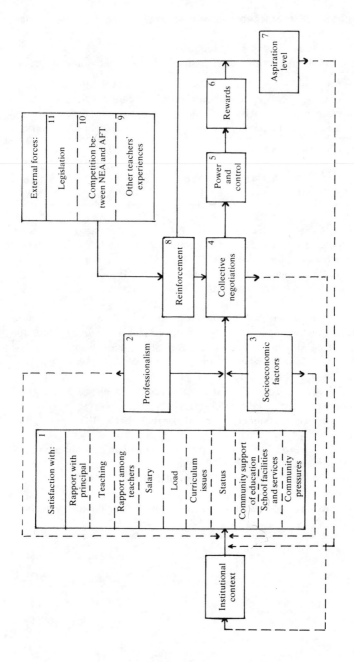

Figure 4-7

Conceptual model of factors related to teachers' attitudes toward collective negotiations

(Reprinted with permission from the *Industrial and Labor Relations Review*: Donald Hellriegel, Wendell French, and Richard B. Peterson, "Collective Negotiations and Teachers: A Behavioral Analysis," [April 1970], p. 382.

Moore and Marshall studied rates of growth of the AFT. As a result of their analysis, they concluded that four major categories of factors influence union growth: economic and work-related factors; internal, sociological factors; organizational factors; and external (social and political) factors.[62]

Conceptually, their model is quite similar to the one developed earlier and also in the tradition of Dunlop. Causal variables used by Moore and Marshall are consistent with those already identified, except for the emphasis on "external (social and political) factors," where they focus on the impact of four "community institutions": government policy, judicial system, strength of organized labor, and social movements. After analyzing changes in AFT membership over time, Moore and Marshall conclude:

A multi-causal system is necessary to account for the growth of teacher unionism. The major factors influencing secular growth are the structure of teachers' salaries; the size, composition, and location of the teaching force; and the strength and prestige of organized labor. Short-run rapid expansion in AFT membership has been the product of four factors: 1) declining economic position of the relevant teacher group; 2) favorable government policy; 3) growing support of organized labor; and 4) influential social movements.[63]

It is apparent that there is no single factor that can be endorsed as the reason teachers join and support unions. Most likely it is a series of events, aspirations, and opportunities that have combined to generate the memberships for today's militant teachers' unions.

NOTES

1. The combined membership figure of 2,133,000 is corrected for joint membership in both the NEA and the AFT held by teachers in New York State, Los Angeles, California, Pontiac, Michigan and other merged NEA-AFT units.

2. In 1973 only about 28 percent of the total public work force was unionized in the United States. This compares to 95 percent in Sweden, 93 percent in West Germany, and 85 percent in the United Kingdom. (Hugh Clegg, *Trade Unionism under Collective Bargaining: A Theory Based on Comparisons of Six Countries* [Oxford, Eng.: Basil Blackwell, 1976], 12.)

3. William J. Moore and Ray Marshall, "Growth of Teachers' Organizations: A Conceptual Framework," *Journal of Collective Negotiations in the Public Sector*, 2:3 (Summer 1973), 271-297.

4. See John R. Commons, *Labor and Administration* (New York: Macmillan Company, 1913), 210-264; also reprinted as John R. Commons, "American

Shoemakers, 1648-1895," in *Readings in Labor Economics and Labor Relations*, 3d ed., ed. Richard L. Rowan (Homewood, Ill.: Richard D. Irwin, Inc., 1976), 88-100.

5. An excellent discussion of the changes that have taken place in school organization and management systems is contained in David B. Tyack, *The One Best System: A History of American Urban Education* (Cambridge, Mass.: Harvard University Press, 1974). In his analysis, Tyack argues that the system of organization and control of schools that emerged was something more than an accident of growth. Rather, it was the result of a management ideology that developed around the beginning of the twentieth century. For a critique of this development, see Raymond E. Callahan, *Education and the Cult of Efficiency: A Study of the Social Forces that Have Shaped the Administration of the Public Schools* (Chicago: University of Chicago Press, 1962).

6. Selig Perlman, *A Theory of the Labor Movement* (Fairfield, N.J.: Augustus M. Kelley, 1928; reprinted, 1949).

7. The notion of a job as a property right is developed by William Gomberg, "The Work Rule Problem and Property Rights in the Job," in *Labor: Readings on Major Issues*, ed. Richard A. Lester (New York: Random House, 1965), 365-368. Job property rights are also developed in Arthur R. Porter, Jr., *Job Property Rights: A Study of the Job Controls of the International Typographical Union* (New York: King's Crown Press, 1954).

8. Sidney and Beatrice Webb, *Industrial Democracy* (London: Longmans, Green, and Co., 1926), 560.

9. Eugene V. Schneider, *Industrial Sociology: The Social Relations of Industry and the Community*, 2d ed. (New York: McGraw-Hill Book Company, 1969), 382.

10. Frank Tannenbaum, *A Philosophy of Labor* (New York: Alfred A. Knopf, 1951).

11. For a good summary of the views of Tannenbaum, see Neil W. Chamberlain and Donald E. Cullen, *The Labor Sector*, 2d ed. (New York: McGraw-Hill Book Company, 1971), 281-285.

12. Robert A. Nisbet, "Public Unions and the Decline of Social Trust," in *Public Employee Unions: A Study of the Crisis in Public Sector Labor Relations*, ed. A. Lawrence Chickering (San Francisco: Institute for Contemporary Studies, 1976), 28.

13. Nisbet, "Public Unions and the Decline of Social Trust," 30.

14. Harvey C. Mansfield, Jr., "The Prestige of Public Employment," in *Public Employee Unions*, ed. Chickering, 35-49.

15. Seymour Martin Lipset, "Equity and Equality in Government Wage Policy," *ibid.*, 109-130.

16. Allan Fox, *Beyond Contract: Work, Power and Trust Relations* (London: Faber and Faber, Ltd., 1974).

17. John T. Dunlop, "The Development of Labor Organization: A Theoretic Framework," in *Readings in Labor Economics and Labor Relations*, ed. Rowan, 67.

18. *Ibid.*, 68.

19. *Ibid.*

20. *Ibid.*

21. *Ibid.*

22. *Ibid.*, 70.

23. See Harry H. Wellington and Ralph K. Winter, Jr., "The Limits of Collective Bargaining in Public Employment," in *Education and Collective Bargaining: Readings in Policy and Research*, ed. Anthony M. Cresswell and Michael J. Murphy (Berkeley, Calif.: McCutchan Publishing Corporation, 1976).

24. Dunlop, Development of Labor Organization, 72.

25. *Ibid.*

26. Jack D. Douglas, "Urban Politics and Public Employee Unions," in *Public Employee Unions*, ed. Chickering, 91-107.

27. Nisbet, "Public Unions and the Decline of Social Trust," 29-31.

28. See Wellington and Winter, "Limits of Collective Bargaining in Public Employment."

29. Mansfield, "Prestige of Public Employment."

30. Fox, *Beyond Contract.*

31. Stephen Cole, *The Unionization of Teachers: A Case Study of the UFT* (New York: Praeger Publishers, 1969), 34-35.

32. Robert K. Merton and Paul F. Lazarsfeld, *Continuities in Social Research: Studies in the Scope and Method of "The American Soldier"* (Glencoe, Ill.: Free Press, 1950).

33. Ted Robert Gurr, "A Comparative Study of Civil Strife," in Hugh Davis Graham and Ted Robert Gurr, *Violence in America: Historical and Comparative Perspectives.* Volume II, *A Staff Report to the National Commission on the Causes and Prevention of Violence* (Washington, D.C.: U.S. Government Printing Office, 1969).

34. For a good discussion of the relationship between nonteaching statuses and predisposition toward militant behavior, see Cole, *Unionization of Teachers*, 76-98.

35. William T. Lowe, "Who Joins Which Teachers' Group," *Teachers College Record*, 66 (April 1965), 614-619.

36. Cole, *Unionization of Teachers*, 87-91.

37. Donald Hellriegel, Wendell French, and Richard B. Peterson, "Collective Negotiations and Teachers: A Behavioral Analysis," in *Education and Collective Bargaining*, ed. Cresswell and Murphy. 78-94; 214-239; Joseph A. Alutto and James A. Belasco, "Determinants of Attitudinal Militancy among Teachers and Nurses," *ibid.*

38. William S. Fox and Michael H. Wince, "The Structure and Determinants of Occupational Militancy among Public School Teachers," *Industrial and Labor Relations Review*, 30 (October 1976), 47-58.

39. W. W. Charters, Jr., "Some Factors Affecting Teacher Survival in School Districts," *American Educational Research Journal*, 7:1 (January 1978), 1-27.

40. Robert E. Doherty and Walter E. Oberer, *Teachers, School Boards and Collective Bargaining: A Changing of the Guard* (Ithaca: New York State School of Industrial and Labor Relations, 1967), 9.

41. According to government figures, in 1973-74 the distribution of teachers by sex in the United States was as follows:

Teaching level	Total number of teachers	Male teachers		Female teachers	
		Number	Percent	Number	Percent
All levels	2,155,448	722,868	34	1,432,580	66
Elementary	1,175,980	197,423	17	978,557	83
Secondary	979,468	525,445	54	454,023	46

These figures are from U.S. Department of Health, Education, and Welfare, *Digest of Educational Statistics, 1975* (Washington, D.C.: U.S. Government Printing Office, 1975), 50. It is notable that, although in the total teaching force women outnumber men by about 2 to 1, in secondary schools men now constitute a majority.

42. Fox and Wince, "Structure and Determinants of Occupational Militancy among Public School Teachers," 50.

43. Cole, *Unionization of Teachers*, 97.

44. Lowe, "Who Joins Which Teachers' Group."

45. Fox and Wince, "Structure and Determinants of Occupational Militancy among Public School Teachers," 55-56.

46. Doherty and Oberer, *Teachers, School Boards and Collective Bargaining*, 6.

47. Fox and Wince, "Structure and Determinants of Occupational Militancy among Public School Teachers," 55-56.

48. Cole, *Unionization of Teachers*, 79-80.

49. Fox and Wince, "Structure and Determinants of Occupational Militancy among Public School Teachers," 55-56.

50. Alan Rosenthal, *Pedagogues and Power: Teacher Groups in School Politics* (Syracuse, N.Y.: Syracuse University Press, 1969), 22-47.

51. Tyack, *One Best System*; Raymond E. Callahan, *Education and the Cult of Efficiency* (Chicago: University of Chicago Press, 1962).

52. Lowe, "Who Joins Which Teachers' Group," 615.

53. James A. Belasco and Joseph A. Alutto, "Organizational Impacts of Teacher Negotiations," *Industrial Relations*, 9:1 (October 1969), 70-74.

54. Frank R. Kemerer and J. Victor Baldridge, *Unions on Campus* (San Francisco: Jossey-Bass Publishers, 1975).

55. Ronald G. Corwin, *Staff Conflicts in the Public School* (Columbus: Ohio State University Press, 1966), 46.

56. Doherty and Oberer, *Teachers, School Boards and Collective Bargaining*, 2.

57. *Ibid.*

58. William Edward Eaton, *The American Federation of Teachers, 1916-1961: A History of the Movement* (Carbondale: Southern Illinois University Press, 1975), 48.

59. *Ibid.*, 140.

60. Cole, *Unionization of Teachers*, 22-25.

61. Hellriegel, French, and Peterson, "Collective Negotiations and Teachers."

62. Moore and Marshall, "Growth of Teachers' Organizations."

63. *Ibid.*, 293.

5

The Legal Framework of
Collective Bargaining

The statutes and legal decisions governing collective bargaining in education are subject to review and revision at any time. Labor relations in schools are, moreover, largely within the jurisdiction of state and local governments. This means that the possibilities for variety and change are limited only by the imaginations of state legislatures and the courts. Despite this, many basic issues and principles remain fairly constant, and in this chapter the issues and principles are set forth in a framework that acknowledges both the current status of the law and underlying concepts and trends.

PUBLIC POLICY TOWARD LABOR

A long history of court decisions and federal statutes documents public policy toward union activity in the private sector and highlights the actions of unions and management since at least 1806. In the public sector, in contrast, most of the judicial and legislative action related to union activity dates from the 1950's. Following Wisconsin's pioneer efforts in 1959, most state legislation on collective bargaining in schools was passed in the 1960's and the

early 1970's. Thus, the framework of laws and public policy governing labor relations in the schools emerged from principles and
precedents set earlier in the private sector. Labor laws in the two
sectors do differ, however, in one major respect: the laws for the
public sector contain more provisions for resolving impasses. The
basic structures, nonetheless, are quite similar. To show how influential the existing framework has been, it is useful to trace briefly
the development of public policy toward labor in general before
discussing how the legal framework in which schools bargain reflects ideas and issues from the private sector.

Developments in the Private Sector

Public policy toward labor in the United States originated in the
English common law. Eighteenth-century English courts held unions
to be criminal combinations, which meant that union activity, or
even membership, was punishable as a criminal offense. That
principle was first recorded in American law in the *Philadelphia
Cordwainers* case in 1806.[1] The courts later accepted the union
and its objectives as legitimate and restricted criminal prosecution
to union activities,[2] a pattern that gave way during the late 1800's
to the use of injunctions and other civil procedures against union
activities.[3]

The use of injunctions against union strikes and boycotts was
fostered by the passage of the Sherman Antitrust Act in 1890.
Although intended to prevent *employer* monopolies and restraint
of trade, the act was first tested in the United States Supreme
Court in an antistrike injunction. The landmark decision came from
the Pullman strike of 1893. The Court held, in *In re Debs*, that
an injunction against that strike was constitutional on the grounds
that the injunction was intended to prevent violence and allow the
railroads to deliver mail.[4] A later Supreme Court ruling in *Loewe*
v. *Lawlor* expanded the coverage of the Sherman Act to "any combination whatever to secure action which essentially obstructs the
free flow of commerce between the States."[5] These two decisions
provided the basis for subsequent widespread use of injunctions
against strikes and boycotts.

Congress responded to the use of injunctions against unions
by passing the Clayton Antitrust Act in 1914. It was designed to
prevent the use of antitrust laws against legitimate strikes and to

remove the federal courts from labor-management disputes. But in two decisions—*Duplex* v. *Deering*[6] and *Bedford Stone Cutters*[7]—the Supreme Court effectively neutralized the provisions of the Clayton Act and kept the door open to the injunction as a strike-breaking tool.

The framework of national policy concerning labor has been more positive since World War I. The federal government has been taking a more neutral position, encouraging peaceful bargaining, and providing mechanisms to resolve impasses. The creation of the National War Labor Board by the Wilson administration and the passage of the Railway Labor Act in 1926 reflect changing attitudes. These actions foreshadowed the four pieces of legislation that are the foundation of current national labor policy: the Norris-LaGuardia Act (1932), the Wagner Act (1935), the Taft-Hartley Act (1947), and the Landrum-Griffin Act (1959). These laws are complex and far reaching. Though a comprehensive discussion of their origins and operations can be found in the works of Archibald Cox or Charles Gregory,[8] only a brief overview of the main points is included here as a basis for discussion.

By 1932 the combined influence of the depression and growing public support of unionism led to the passage of the Norris-La-Guardia Act. It both clarified the law on strikes and union activities and provided a basis for courts to remove themselves from the center of labor disputes. The federal courts were prevented from issuing injunctions against most strikes and most other forms of union activity. The act also eliminated the concept of unions as conspiracies and outlawed "yellow dog" contracts (agreements not to join unions, which employers forced workers to sign as a condition of employment). More was left to the bargaining parties themselves, including the task of finding a working agreement. Though the Norris-LaGuardia Act has removed use of the injunction from most strikes in the private sector, the use of injunctions remains a central issue when discussing labor law in the public sector.

The New Deal brought increased interest in social legislation and support for organized labor. One major outgrowth was the National Labor Relations Act (NLRA) of 1935, also known as the Wagner Act, which created the basic framework for existing labor law in the private sector. The Wagner Act defined the rights of unions to bargain collectively and required employers to bargain in good faith. It also established a National Labor Relations Board (NLRB) to administer the provisions of the act and set up definitions and procedures to gain union recognition, to prevent unfair labor practices, and to resolve impasses.

In the first few years of operation, the NLRA seemed to favor unions. And so, in 1947, there were extensive amendments to the NLRA under the name of the Taft-Hartley Act. These amendments restricted certain union activities, such as secondary boycotts (that is, picketing other than the primary employer in a strike), union shop provisions in contracts (that is, clauses requiring employees to join the union within a certain time limit), and strikes against the federal government. The Taft-Hartley Act also stipulated a number of unfair labor practices on the part of unions (such as coercion of employees or employer, illegal strikes, and discrimination against employees), provided machinery for settling "national emergency" strikes, and created the Federal Mediation and Conciliation Service.

The legislation discussed above deals with the relationships between union and employer. In 1958 congressional hearings established the need to regulate the relationship between union and member. The hearings revealed numerous abuses, including denying members full participation in the control of the union, collusion with employers, and mismanagement of union funds. Congress responded by passing the Labor-Management Reporting and Disclosure Act of 1959, known as the Landrum-Griffin Act.[9] It provides a bill of rights for members of a union and allows members to sue the union for improper actions.

LABOR ORGANIZATION IN THE PUBLIC SECTOR

Federal Employees

The legislation discussed above applies only to the private sector; governments, at all levels, are excluded. During the 1960's there was rapid growth in the number of employees in the public sector, and in the number in unions. Between 1960 and 1970, the number of civilian employees of the government grew from less than eight million to more than twelve million. The percentage of government workers who belonged to unions grew from 13 percent to 33 percent in the same period.[10]

Until 1962 federal employees did not have the right to bargain collectively, although many were members of unions and there had been a number of illegal strikes. A labor relations framework for federal employees was established in that year by President John F. Kennedy in Executive Order 10988, which permitted employees to join unions and bargain with federal agencies over wages and conditions of employment (excluding certain agencies related to national security). Then, in 1970, President Richard M. Nixon issued Executive Order 11491, which reinforced the concepts of Kennedy's order and established a structure for the administration of labor relations at the federal level. Under these executive orders most federal employees are covered by a uniform system of regulations and administrative mechanisms. The structure set up to handle labor problems for government employees includes a Federal Labor Relations Council to administer the orders, a Federal Impasse Panel to resolve disputes and impasses, and an Office of Assistant Secretary of Labor for Management Relations to supervise union recognition and unfair labor practice processes.[11]

The situation is much more complex at the state and local levels. The responsibility for regulation of government employees at the state level lies with state legislatures. The response has been widely varied—from detailed legislation covering most aspects of labor relations to no legislation at all. Most teachers are employed by state or local governments.

State Policy toward Collective Bargaining in Education

The overall development of state and local policy toward allowing public employees to bargain collectively parallels that in the private sector. There are the same basic questions: To what extent may public employees organize and bargain collectively? Over what issues may management bargain and sign agreements? How shall strikes and impasses be handled? And the direction of change has been similar, from open hostility and legal prohibition against organized activity through gradual acceptance and support of bargaining, to the right to strike in some jurisdictions. There are, however, important differences. State policy also takes a variety of forms: statutes, case law, decision of labor boards and commissions, and administrative decisions. Each has a place in the framework of policy we discuss here.

The right of teachers to organize themselves into unions and associations is now firmly established, although this was not always so. The Chicago Board of Education prohibited teachers from joining unions in 1917 and was upheld by the Illinois Supreme Court.[12] And what amounted to "yellow dog" contracts for teachers were upheld by courts in the state of Washington in 1930.[13] But the number of public employees in unions and militancy among teachers and other workers has continued to grow, bringing greater acceptance of the legitimacy of union activity and the right to bargain in the public sector.

Negotiated teacher contracts appeared as early as 1944, but there were no major developments in the legal structure for school bargaining until the 1950's. Two notable events—the decision of the Connecticut Supreme Court in a case growing out of the Norwalk teachers' strike and the passage of the first state legislation for school bargaining in Wisconsin in 1959—illustrate alternative ways state governments have dealt with the realities of union activities among teachers and other public employees. In the Norwalk decision, the Connecticut Supreme Court held teachers' strikes to be illegal.[14] The Wisconsin statute recognized the rights of teachers to organize and bargain collectively, but declared strikes against the schools to be illegal (the basic antistrike pattern that has persisted). The statute also, however, was the first to *require* school boards (and other public employers) to recognize and bargain with employees' unions.

Recognition of formal bargaining rights for municipal employees dates back to the same period. Cincinnati began negotiating with its employees in 1951; New York's Mayor Robert Wagner issued an executive order granting limited bargaining rights to city workers in 1958. These formal steps were preceded by a history of negotiated contracts for employees of some cities, such as Philadelphia, that dates back to 1939.[15]

Following the Wisconsin statute, other states passed legislation concerning the right of public employees to bargain. By the end of 1975, forty-one states had some form of legislation requiring schools and other public employers either to bargain or to "meet and confer" with employees' unions and sign agreements. Even in those states that lack such legislation, collective bargaining has been on the agenda. In fact, in one of those states, Illinois, at least

one public employees' collective bargaining bill has been introduced every year since 1945. And, since negotiation has been
going on in states with or without enabling legislation, a large and
growing body of case law now covers labor relations in the public
sector. A brief summary of the major components of public policy
toward labor relations in schools is presented here, followed, in
the next section, by a more detailed examination of the major issues.

In an analysis of public policy toward labor relations in the public
sector undertaken in 1969, the Advisory Commission on Intergovernmental Relations (ACIR) identified four types of state policy
structures.[16] Even though details have changed, the four types still
provide a useful description:

—Avoidance of any recognition of employee organizations and silence concerning methods for resolving labor-management disputes at the local level. (In some
  states where no such legislation exists, however, local jurisdictions have established their own negotiating procedures either by ordinance, executive order,
  or on a more informal basis.)
—Strengthening the hand of city officials who may wish to seek injunctions against
  striking public employees. The statutes here deal almost exclusively with controlling strikes and ignore other facets of labor relations.
—Legislation giving certain local government occupational groups special consideration regarding organizing, presenting grievances, and negotiations. The
  groups frequently singled out include teachers, firemen, law enforcement officers,
  and utility and transit workers.
—A broad comprehensive statute setting forth policies and procedures, based on
  the meet-and-confer or collective negotiation concepts and covering all local
  employees and sometimes State personnel as well. The statutes usually offer
  the services of a State administrative agency as a third party to settle disputes.

As the states have developed and changed legislation and court
decisions, a fair amount of consensus has developed on some of the
major issues. The main areas of agreement are:
—Strikes are illegal (or closely regulated), but the automatic harsh
  penalties of the past have given way to more flexible ones to meet
  local conditions.
—Exclusive recognition of one bargaining agent for an employee
  group is the general rule.
—Supervisors are excluded from the bargaining unit.
—Nonprofessionals are excluded from the professional bargaining
  unit, but allowed in through special procedure in some cases.

—Grievance procedures, including binding arbitration, are allowed in contracts and sometimes required.
—Mediation and fact-finding may be employed for impasse resolution.
—One state labor relations agency should include all employees, although the same legislation may not apply to all.
—Representation elections should be used to determine which organization will represent the employees' group.

In spite of this broad pattern of statutory and judicial opinion, however, there are several major issues over which no clear consensus is evident:

—Management rights are defined broadly in some states, narrowly in others.
—Arbitration to settle contract disputes is still an experimental procedure, with wide variation in how or whether it is to be used.
—Union security provision, especially union and agency shop clauses, vary considerably.
—Supervisory positions are not clearly defined, so that defining membership in school bargaining units is a serious problem.

It should be stressed that disagreement is over questions for which there are no clear answers. The lack of consistency among the states is less a problem than an opportunity. By observing a variety of approaches to such difficult questions as management rights in public schools, it is more likely that sound policies will be discovered and tested.

One additional area of public policy deserves some attention. The United States Supreme Court has ruled that a school board involved with a strike may be a sufficiently impartial body to conduct hearings and dismiss striking teachers.[17] In Hortonville, Wisconsin, the school district dismissed all teachers after providing a hearing as required in state law. The dismissed teachers sued. They argued that they had been denied due process since the board, being locked in a bitter dispute with the union, could not fairly judge the question of the dismissal. The Court found that due process *could* be provided in such a case in general and that it was in this one. This established mass dismissal as a possible board response to a teachers' strike as long as the board complies with due process requirements. In times of declining enrollments and teacher surpluses, such a board tactic moves from being an empty threat to being a very real possibility. While public opinion may not approve such action, the policy structure does allow it.

THE CONTRACT AS A LEGAL DOCUMENT

At the center of the labor-management relationship is the contract. It is the center of attraction during bargaining, and it remains the central tool of personnel administration during its term. This includes the legal status of the document itself and the variations in content to be found among school districts.

The essence of a contract is that it constitutes a legally enforceable agreement between two or more parties. The parties must be legally able to enter into the agreement, and the terms must be such that they can be kept and enforced if necessary.[18] For a school board to sign and administer a labor contract, it must have the legal power to do so. Since the schools are creatures of state law, the ability of a school board to enter into such an agreement must be based in that law. This is the first and fundamental reason why there is variation among the state legal structures when dealing with labor relations in the schools. A summary of the basic characteristics of state laws is found in Table 5-1. As is shown in the table, thirty-one states have statutes *requiring* some form of contractual arrangement between school systems and employees. Of the nineteen remaining states, seventeen permit, but do not require, schools to enter into contracts with employee groups. The permission is either in the form of a court decision or an attorney general's opinion. In Texas, North Carolina, and Virginia, school boards are prohibited from entering into collectively bargained contracts with employees' groups.

Among the states that permit negotiated contracts, the most important distinction is the presence or absence of statutory structure defining the requirements and process of the bargaining relationship. In those states with some statutory arrangement, the nature of a proper, enforceable contract is, to some degree, spelled out in law. In those states without specific statutory arrangements, a contract is just what the parties, and occasionally the courts, say it is. These contracts can be little more than a salary schedule and fringe benefit package in some small school systems, but they can also be long, complex contracts of more than 100 pages in large

Table 5-1

Collective bargaining laws for state employees affecting education

State	Type of Laws			Coverage: For professional (P) personnel[d]			For classified (C) personnel[e]			For supervisors and/or administrators[g]			Union security[h]	Strike permit[i]	Blind arbitration of disputes[j]	PERBS[k]
	Local[a]	State[b]	Omnibus[c]	K-12	CC[f]	PS	K-12	CC[f]	PS	K-12	CC[f]	PS				
Alabama																
Alaska	X		X	X		X	X		X	P			X	X[m]	X[m]	
Arizona																
Arkansas																
California	X	X		X		X				P-C	P-C		X			X
Colorado		X														
Connecticut	X	X	X	X	X	X	X	X	X				X		X[r]	X
Delaware	X		X	X		X	X		X				X		X[l,m]	
Florida	X		X	X	X	X	X	X	X				X			X
Georgia																
Hawaii			X	X		X	X		X	P-C		P-C	X	X	X	X
Idaho	X			X						P						
Illinois																
Indiana	X		X	X		X	X		X	C			X		X[v]	X
Iowa	X		X	X		X	X		X						X	X
Kansas	X		X	X	X	X	X		X							X
Kentucky																
Louisiana																
Maine	X	X[m]		X		X	X	X	X	P-C	P-C	P-C	X		X[l]	X
Maryland	X			X			X			P-C			X			
Massachusetts			X	X		X	X		X				X[p]		X	X

State											
Michigan	X	X			X	X			X		X
Minnesota	X	X	X	X	X	P-C	P-C	P-C	X	X	X
Mississippi		X									
Missouri	X			X	X	X			X		
Montana	X	X	X	X	X	X			X	X^n	X
Nebraska		X	X	X	X				X	X	
Nevada	X	X		X		P-C			X		X
New Hampshire	X	X	X	X		P-C	P-C				X
New Jersey	X	X	X	X	X	P-C	P-C	P-C		X	X
New Mexico											
New York	X	X		X	X	P-C	P-C	P-C	X	X	X
North Carolina											
North Dakota	X	X			P						X
Ohio											
Oklahoma	X	X		X		P-C			X		X
Oregon	X	X	X	X	X				X	X	X
Pennsylvania	X	X	X	X	X	P-C	P-C	P-C	X^p	X^o	X
Rhode Island	X	X	X	X	X				X^p		X^p
South Carolina											
South Dakota	X	X	X	X	X	P-C	P-C	P-C			
Tennessee	X	X			P						
Texas											
Utah											
Vermont	X	X	X^q	X	X	P	P-C	P-C	X^r	X^s	X^r
Virginia											
Washington	X	X	X	X	X	P	P	P	X^t		X
West Virginia		X									

Table 5-1 (continued)

	Type of Laws			Coverage												
				For professional (P) personnel[d]			For classified (C) personnel[e]			For supervisors and/or administrators[g]					Blind arbitration of disputes[j]	
State	Local[a]	State[b]	Omnibus[c]	K-12	CC[f]	PS	K-12	CC[f]	PS	K-12	CC[f]	PS	Union security[h]	Strike permit[i]		PERBS[k]
Wisconsin	X	X		X	X	X	X	X	X	P-C	P-C	C	X		X[u]	X
Wyoming														X[u]	X[u]	X
Totals	18	7	17	31	10[f]	22	25	8[f]	25	P-18 C-13	P-6f C-5f	P-9 C-10	22	7	19	22

a Local—a law with coverage for local-level employees only.
b State—a law with coverage for state-level employees only.
c Omnibus—a law with coverage for employees at more than one governmental level.
d Professional personnel—generally, when applied to education, means teachers or personnel with similar or higher status.
e Classified personnel—generally means those below the rank of teachers; i.e., clerks, food employees, bus drivers, custodians, paraprofessionals, community colleges may be included with K-12 or with postsecondary or they may be a separate system.
f CC (Community Colleges)—this column is checked only if community colleges are mentioned specifically in law; state structures vary, and
g Supervisors and/or administrators—this column is used if state law provides coverage for any level or all levels of supervisors and administrators.
h Union security—this column is used if state law permits dues checkoff, service fees, or other forms of union security. All state laws provide for exclusive representation of organizations.
i Strike permission—this column is checked if state law provides for strike rights for education employees. All strike rights appear to be conditional.
j Binding arbitration of dispute—this column is used if state law permits the binding arbitration of contract disputes.
k PERBS (Public Employee Relations Boards)—this column is used if the state has set up a special public employee relations board or commission to administer public employee collective bargaining.
l Binding arbitration on nonfund matters only.
m Postsecondary personnel only.
n Court ruling.
o Not binding if legislative action is required.
p Mandatory.
q All state university personnel excluded.
r K-12 classified personnel only.
s Provisions unclear.
t No provision for community colleges.
u K-12 professional and classified personnel only.
v K-12 and postsecondary classified personnel only.

Source: Doris Ross, *Cuebook: State Education Collective Bargaining Laws.* Denver, Colo.: Education Commission of the States, 1978.

cities such as Cleveland, Chicago, or Los Angeles. The contract between the Chicago Teachers' Union and the Chicago Board of Education, for example, is more than 150 pages long and contains nearly 50 articles. Salary specifications alone take up over 20 pages. The absence of statutory requirements leaves individual boards and unions to work out the most agreeable contractual form.

Content

Since the content of contracts can vary so much, a comprehensive view of contract provisions (see Table 5-2) is needed. Some part (or perhaps all) of the usual provisions can then be found in the contract of any particular district. Unusual local circumstances may give rise to unique language or provisions that are not dealt with here. What this outline represents, therefore, is the basic content that can be included or negotiated; it may not, however, be included or negotiated because of state legal constraints or local decisions.

In attempting to make this outline general, we have included provisions that apply to both teachers and other employees. Any contract would be expected to have a recognition clause, but the bargaining unit named would, of course, vary according to the internal organization of representation in the school system. The Milwaukee school system, for example, recognizes unions representing over fifteen different bargaining units. Other large school systems, such as Cincinnati, may have one unit for teachers and another for all nonteaching employees. Questions related to union security are likely to be similar across bargaining units. Employee rights, in contrast, probably vary. Evaluation processes, academic freedom, and dismissal procedures have different meanings for teachers and other professional employees. For teachers, these areas are usually covered by tenure provisions in state school codes, rather than by civil service regulations that may apply to nonteaching employees. The most obvious differences among classifications of workers appear in the work rules and compensation sections. Grievance and impasse procedures are likely to be consistent, but length of contract and other terms can vary. It appears that, unless a master contract for all school employees is negotiated (and we know of none), there will be considerable differences among the various contracts under which school systems operate.

Table 5-2
Basic school system contract provisions

Section	Contents
Preamble	
Recognition	Identification of bargaining unit and membership therein
	Agreement to forgo individual negotiations
Union's rights and security	Protected organizing activity
	Dues deduction, agency shop, union shop
	Meetings, officers, general information
Employees' rights and security	Discipline
	Personnel file access
	Academic freedom
	Employee evaluation
	Seniority
	Employee termination
	Nondiscrimination
Management's rights	
Work rules and conditions	Work load
	School calendar and workday
	Work assignment and transfers
	Promotion and position notification
	Pupil discipline
	School policy and operation decision procedure
Compensation and benefits	Salary schedules
	Supplementary wage schedules
	Extra-duty, overtime provisions
	Insurance (life, medical, income)
	Leave days (sick, personal, etc.)
	Sabbatical leaves and leaves of absence
	Association leave
Grievance procedures	Detailed description of steps
Impasse procedures	Detailed description of criteria and actions
Contract terms	Length of agreement
	No strike-no lockout
	Reopen or waiver provisions

Preamble

While it is not a common feature of contracts in general, the preamble is found in several large-school contracts and deserves some attention. It seems to serve two functions. The first is rhetorical, allowing both parties to state publicly their orientation toward bargaining as evidence of their good faith and intention to reach agreement. The second possible function of a preamble is to provide the parties with some nonbinding language to start the negotiations process on a low-conflict basis. And, while the preamble does not contain operative provisions, it could provide statements of intention useful in an arbitration or judicial proceeding. If binding language is included, however, it becomes a regular, enforceable part of the contract.

Recognition and Representation

The process of establishing recognition and representation can be discussed in terms of three questions to be answered through the legal structure: What is the board's duty to bargain? How is an appropriate group of employees (the bargaining unit) to be defined? How is a representative of the bargaining unit to be chosen? Because the legal arrangements for bargaining in schools are the responsibility of state legislatures and the courts, there is considerable variation in the way these questions are answered from state to state. In spite of the variety, however, some general principles and procedures do apply.

The Duty to Bargain. The board of education's duty to bargain may come from state statute, court decision, an opinion of the attorney general, or the board's own choice. In states without collective bargaining legislation for schools, such as Illinois, Utah, and Ohio, boards are permitted to enter into collective agreements with employees, but they are not required to do so. The decision of the board to recognize a union and bargain is, therefore, less a matter of legal structure and more a question of political processes at the local level.

Where there is collective bargaining legislation covering education, a positive duty to bargain in good faith is imposed on the board. In some states, such as Pennsylvania and New York, the legislation requires all boards to enter into a negotiated agreement with teachers and other employees. The statutes specify, to one degree or another, the subjects of bargaining. In other states, such as California, the board of education is required to bargain only where an organization representing employees has been formally recognized. If no group of employees seeks or achieves formal recognition under the established process, no bargaining takes place. The legislation also establishes an administrative mechanism to establish and recognize (certify) bargaining units, to settle disputes arising out of the duty to bargain, and to adjudicate unfair labor practices.

Along with the board, the union recognized bears the duty to bargain in good faith. Both parties also have the responsibility to avoid unfair labor practices, and legal sanctions can be imposed on either party. The legal framework for bargaining in good faith and avoiding unfair labor practices is an integral part of the bargaining relationship.

The idea of bargaining in good faith is central to the duty to bargain. By refusing meaningful participation in the process, either party can frustrate the basic purpose of bargaining, which is to come to a mutual agreement. This is why the principle of bargaining in good faith has developed through the legal structure of the NLRA and laws governing public employees; it is equally important to both. The same basic standards of good faith have also been applied in both the private and public sectors. That is why it is not necessary to discuss this concept as though it were a special aspect of negotiations in the schools or in the public sector.

The parties representative of management and labor must participate actively in the negotiations and make a sincere effort to agree.[19] Good faith is a matter of *intent*, and intent is neither observed nor reported reliably. A finding of bad faith, therefore, can only be an inference based on behavior. A discussion of what constitutes good faith is thus an examination of *bargaining tactics*. Part of the question of good faith in bargaining depends on management's refusal to negotiate certain issues on the grounds that to do so erodes the rights of management. What is properly a subject of negotiations is considered scope of bargaining and is dealt with in that section.

A legal determination of good faith in bargaining occurs only when one party accuses the other of bad faith and the case comes before a labor relations agency or court. An inference of bad faith can be based on either the substance of the proposals or conduct when bargaining. Proposals that indicate bad faith may be unreasonable, so that no responsible negotiator or representative could accept them. It can also be an indication of bad faith for an employer to offer fewer benefits or to refuse to grant any concessions over and above those existing,[20] but there can be extenuating circumstances. For example, the New Jersey Public Employee Relations Commission found that a severe economic crisis could justify an employer's limiting wage proposals to existing levels.[21]

Bad faith may also be inferred from such bargaining conduct as take-it-or-leave-it proposals that indicate refusal to deviate from the beginning position through long negotiations; dilatory tactics, such as shifting positions whenever agreement seems to be reached; unnecessarily complicated proposals; pointless questioning of the opponent's proposals; or unreasonable fragmentation of bargaining sessions.[22] This is not intended to be a complete list of behaviors indicating bad faith; rather, these are examples. No single behavior of either party is sufficient to result in a finding of bad faith. Courts and labor relations boards examine the entire process of bargaining, and it is a consistent pattern of behavior that constitutes a failure to bargain in good faith.

Some tactics are not usually taken as evidence of bad faith. For instance, neither party is required to make any particular concession. Refusal to change any particular position, even though the result is a stalemate, does not mean bad faith if the position is genuinely and sincerely held.[23] Nor is other evidence of hard bargaining, such as long negotiating sessions or strong demands, sufficient to indicate bad faith. It is only the *overall pattern* indicating an absence of intent to reach agreement that constitutes failure to bargain in good faith.[24]

Unit Determination. Three sets of competing concerns are involved in the problem of unit determination: the union's interest in having the most powerful and effective bargaining unit; management's interest in having a structure of bargaining units that makes the labor relations process most advantageous for management, and government's interest in structuring the labor-management process so as to produce peaceful relations and workable agreement. Some accommodation of these competing concerns is necessary before one can define an employee group that is appropriate to the work situation and contributes to a stable and productive bargaining relationship. The key term is "appropriate"; it is the basis for legal arrangements that define bargaining units.

An inappropriate unit definition could interfere with a successful relationship in a number of ways. Some employees, for example, might be poorly represented, or the unit could be too small to be effective, or the range of employees covered could present an unmanageable set of divergent interests, or previous patterns of associations could be broken. These and other considerations affect unit determination.

The states' approach to the question of unit determination usually follows existing concepts of the NLRB, which employs a "mutuality of interest" criterion as the primary basis for deciding appropriateness of the unit. The NLRA excludes professionals from nonprofessional units unless they are admitted by mutual consent, and security personnel must be in a separate unit. Other than those exclusions,[25] appropriateness is based on similarity of skills, history of collective bargaining, desires of the employees, and extent of existing organization by unions. There is no definitive boundary in the law between supervisory and other employees. Hence, the main unit determination problem in schools is separating management from nonmanagement personnel.

These same basic principles are reflected in many of the state collective bargaining laws and decisions of labor relations boards. But there is wide variety in how they are applied, especially in relation to the question of separating management from workers in the bargaining unit. The Iowa Public Employee Relations Board has excluded supervisory personnel from teachers' bargaining units, in direct application of the statute, but it has extended the exclusion. The Iowa board held that curriculum coordinators were management personnel since "they act, in fact, as representative of the district." But department heads are not management since they exercise no independent authority and act only as representatives of their departments.[27] By contrast, the New York Public Employee Relations Board held that participation in collective bargaining with the teachers' union is the main criterion of management status. Principals are not, therefore, management, and they are entitled to representation by their own bargaining unit since they do not have a "significant role" in bargaining.[28] Typically, however, most states provide for a single unit for teachers, from which supervisory personnel, by one definition or another, are excluded, and, in most cases, if principals and other management personnel are to bargain, they must have a separate unit.[29]

The central problem when separating supervisory from other employees in bargaining is to avoid conflict of interest. Employees' organizations and employers alike require solidarity among their membership. Divided loyalties weaken the organization's ability to take tough positions in the bargaining process. And, perhaps even more important, there can be damaging leaks of information from one side to the other that are much more likely when personal and organizational boundaries are not clear. Thus, the term "confidential employee" is included in legislation and labor relations board rulings, designating workers that may not be part of a bargaining unit since they have access to critical information. The courts have even upheld a school board rule against employing a teacher who was married to a principal in the same district.[30] Since there are so many supervisory and quasi-supervisory positions in school districts, this issue comes up repeatedly in labor disputes involving school personnel.

A different, but equally troublesome problem arises in the determination of nonprofessional bargaining units. Most state bargaining laws provide that certified employees (that is, teachers and other professionals) be in different units from noncertified employees. How the nonteaching employees of the school are to be organized, however, is not immediately clear. For some, such as bus drivers or custodians, there are unions that specialize in their functions, and they could form bargaining units along functional lines. But in many school systems, especially smaller ones, a separate bargaining unit for each specialization among nonteaching employees would be ill advised. The result would be a proliferation of small bargaining units and an impossibly complex labor relations operation. Other than the very largest urban school systems, boards of education do not employ sufficient numbers of workers in the skilled trades or other job categories to justify separate bargaining units. Even in some large cities, such as Cincinnati, Ohio, most of the nonteaching employees are organized in a single bargaining unit represented by AFSCME (American Federation of State, County, and Municipal Employees). The state laws do not provide definitive answers on how nonteaching employees should be organized. The same basic criteria and procedures that apply to teachers are used for the rest of the school's work force. This appears to be functional since the basic principles for determining bargaining units in the private sector are well established, and they apply directly to most nonteaching workers in the schools and other government units.

Once the criteria for defining an appropriate bargaining unit are set, a procedure is needed to determine the composition of a specific bargaining unit each time that issue arises in a school. Existing state legislation requires several approaches. In some states (for example, Hawaii) there is a long list of categories of employees that might form separate bargaining units. In other states, such as California, the law provides only that supervisory personnel may not be in the same bargaining units as teaching or nonteaching employees. The specific determination of what is a supervisor is left to the state public employee relations board. A third approach is to permit teachers and supervisors in the same bargaining unit, if they so choose, as in Alaska, Connecticut, or Maine. And a fourth approach establishes criteria to determine the appropriateness of the unit and a process for determining the composition of the unit through the state labor relations board while the statute remains silent on the specific question of supervisors in the unit. Florida, Massachusetts, and Nebraska, for example, leave the determination of the unit to a state body.

Statutes and existing contracts provide a number of mechanisms for recognizing a representative for the bargaining unit. If there is no dispute, either by the employer or by some other group of employees, an organization may become the recognized representative by simply providing some evidence that its members are a majority of employers in that bargaining unit. That evidence can be obtained through a variety of ways. The California statute, for example, requires "current dues deduction authorizations, or other evidence such as notarized membership lists, or membership cards, or petitions designating the organization as the exclusive representative of the employees."[31] If the employer disputes this claim, or a competing organization challenges it, a representation election is held, provided the competing organization can demonstrate it represents over some minimum proportion (such as 30 percent) of the employees. Where a state labor relations agency exists, it usually conducts the election. Otherwise, the parties must determine the election procedure by mutual consent. In either case, the choice of "no representation" ususally appears on the ballot.

Once a representative organization is chosen and officially recognized or "certified" by a state agency, it is usually referred to as the *bargaining agent* for that unit. It remains the bargaining agent for those employees unless or until it is challenged and displaced by some other organization. The challenge can come from another organization proving membership over some minimum (such as 30 percent), or from an employer's claim that a question of representation exists. A challenge of this type is usually resolved by another representation election. Thus, there is always the potential threat to the bargaining agent that it will be replaced by some other organization.

Freedom of Choice in Representation

The democratic principles of majority rule and free choice expressed in the mechanism for choosing a bargaining agent mean little if the choice is not, in fact, free. That is why the legal framework of selection defines as an unfair labor practice any form of coercion of the workers in their choice of a bargaining agent. The details of rulings vary from state to state. But, by collecting principles from the NLRA and state rulings, we can compose a basic list of unfair labor practices involving employees' freedom to organize and choose representation.

It is an unfair labor practice for an employer to induce or attempt to prevent the employee from joining a labor organization or to make nonmembership in an organization a condition of employment; to interfere with the union activities of employees, use spies or information to learn about union activities, or prohibit solicitation for union membership in nonwork areas or hours; to threaten reprisals or promise benefits to workers to prevent them from engaging in union activities; to use antiunion propaganda so extreme as to seriously compromise the election conditions (although antiunion propaganda per se is not prohibited); to dominate or support a union (such actions as forming a company union, financial assistance, providing company facilities, checkoff, soliciting membership for a union, or influencing union officers are prohibited); or to discriminate in employment, promotion, tenure, or working conditions on the basis of union membership or activities.

Labor organizations and their members are also prohibited from interference with employees' rights in representation disputes. More specifically, they cannot threaten reprisals or violence against employees who do not join or support a union, physically harm or intimidate employees from reporting to work, pressure an employer to discriminate against employees on the basis of union membership, or use economic coercion, such as withholding insurance or retirement benefits.

Scope of Bargaining

Public policy controlling scope, that is, what is to be bargained, goes to the heart of the labor-management power relationship. For those issues which *must* be bargained, the law grants the union power of joint determination of school policy. For those issues which *may not* be bargained, the law grants the board the power of unilateral determination of school policy. For those issues which policy says *may* be bargained, the union's role in joint determination depends on its ability to force management to negotiate. How policy is structured, therefore, can have important consequences for both sides. Thus, questions of scope are major legal and legislative matters in bargaining policy.

There is considerable lack of agreement as to what should be included in a collectively bargained agreement. The Wisconsin labor relations statute requires board and unions to bargain "in good faith, *with respect to wages, hours, and conditions of employment* [emphasis added] . . ."[32] That is, the statute obliges employers to negotiate wages, hours, and conditions of employment. If there is to be bargaining at all, there is seldom disagreement over including wages and hours in the agreement. It is the phrase "conditions of employment" that raises fundamental issues. Management attempts to preserve a large area of discretion isolated from the pressure of negotiations. And the employees' groups attempt to influence as broad a range of "conditions of employment" as possible. It is in part a question of power: the more powerful the bargaining side, the greater control over what is bargained. But it is also a matter of law: the scope is defined by statutes, court decisions, and labor relations board rulings. It is the legal aspect of scope that is taken up here.

In terms of our outline of the content of bargaining, issues of scope are most prevalent in the sections of the contract we have called:[33]

> Union's rights and security
> Employees' rights and security
> Management's rights
> Work rules and conditions

In any of these areas the employer can refuse to negotiate on the grounds that the matter is one of "management rights," or the union can insist on negotiating. How these questions are resolved determines the scope of the agreement.

The central legal questions concerning the content of bargaining are: What *must* be bargained? What *may* be bargained? What *may not* be bargained? In terms of the NLRA, these questions refer to the *mandatory, permissive,* and *illegal* content of bargaining. The framework of policy for conducting labor-management negotiations provides a set of answers to these questions. The scope of bargaining is affected by more than just statutory arrangements for negotiation. The state school code determines in part what may or may not be bargained. The specific organizational and political context of the school district affects what the parties want to bring to the bargaining table. But the political and organizational forces affecting the scope of bargaining (see Chapter 10) must work within the legal structure.

Mandatory Subjects

The definition of what are mandatory subjects of bargaining defines, as well, management rights and prerogatives. Management is clearly interested in maintaining as broad a definition of its rights as possible and, consequently, as narrow a scope of bargaining as possible. The union's objectives are just the opposite. There is bound to be persistent and serious conflict over the scope of bargaining, regardless of the legal definition. Thus, the statutes and legal decisions define the general framework in which many specific questions of scope of bargaining are decided.

The basic principle on which scope of bargaining rests comes from the private sector. In the language of the NLRA, the required substance of bargaining includes: "rates of pay, wages, hours of employment, or other conditions of employment."[34] For a private employer to refuse to bargain with employees' representatives on these matters constitutes an unfair labor practice. An employer found guilty of an unfair practice can be subject to legal sanction imposed by the NLRB or the federal courts (for example, an injunction).

This basic definition of the required subject of bargaining — wages, hours, and other conditions of employment — is reflected in the states' bargaining laws, but with important modifications. The California statute further defines and limits the meaning of "conditions of employment":

> The scope of representation shall be limited to matters relating to wages, hours of employment, and other terms and conditions of employment. "Terms and conditions of employment" mean health and welfare benefits . . . , leave and transfer policies, safety conditions of employment, class size, procedures to be used for the evaluation of employees, organizational security . . . , and procedures for processing grievances . . . .[35]

By contrast, the Michigan statute does not go beyond the language of the NLRA and defines the mandatory subjects of bargaining to be "wages, hours, and other terms and conditions of employment."[36] But regardless of how far the statute goes in defining specific subjects that must be bargained, the definition will remain incomplete. The statute merely establishes a rough outline; the details are filled in by decisions of state labor relations agencies and courts. And in states without bargaining laws, the outline and details of the legal framework are determined by the courts and at times by opinions of the attorney general. It is useful, therefore, to examine the most pervasive and important issues on which these skirmishes are based.

Delegation of Authority

Boards of education are creatures of state law; all of their powers are delegated to them by the state. A basic principle of law is that these delegated powers must be exercised and cannot be delegated to some other agent.[37] Taken by itself, that principle indicates that nothing the board is required or empowered to do by the school code should be limited by a negotiated contract or delegated through the contract to some other agent. Under a school code alone, for example, the board would not be allowed to negotiate teacher dismissal procedures beyond those already in the law, as was ruled by the Illinois and Ohio Supreme Courts.[38] Neither could the board consent to binding arbitration of grievances since that would delegate power to the arbitrator. The same principle would apply to any other statutory power of the board.

But the principle of delegation of authority cannot stand alone. States' bargaining statutes may require employers to negotiate certain items, such as binding arbitration of grievances. This statutory requirement can supersede the school code. The Pennsylvania Supreme Court upheld a contract providing arbitration of grievances involving the dismissal of nontenured teachers. Because Pennsylvania had a bargaining law requiring arbitration of school grievances, the delegation of power was ruled legal.[39] While this seems directly contradictory to the decision of the Illinois court above, it is not. In the absence of a state bargaining law, the Illinois court decided on the basis of the school code. In the presence of a bargaining law, the Pennsylvania court placed the bargaining law above the school code on that particular subject. Courts in other states with bargaining statutes have consistently held that subjects not specifically excluded by the law are negotiable and do not generally constitute illegal delegation of authority.[40] The question of illegal delegation of authority depends on the definition of scope of bargaining that exists in a statute, whether it be the school code or the bargaining law. Where the two conflict, the courts seem inclined to hold that the bargaining statute takes precedence.

This role for the courts is consistent with their general duty to determine and interpret legislative intent. On the basic question of delegated authority, courts tend to interpret legislative intent in ways most favorable to the board's basic power to operate the schools. In the absence of an expressed power to bargain, an implied one can be seen as an extension of the authority to operate the school. This implied power to bargain does not, however, set clear boundaries for what must or may be bargained.

In spite of variations in the definitions of scope in statutory and case law, some topics—wages and salary schedules; contingent benefits, such as leave policies, health and medical insurance, retirement benefits, life insurance; and a large variety of associated fringe benefits—are consistently in the mandatory bargaining area. Working conditions that are closely related to hours and work load are usually mandatory as well, but there are important aspects of teachers' working conditions that are closely tied to the educational policy prerogatives of the board of education: class size, school calendar, length of the school day. Related to the length of the school day are questions concerning teachers' extracurricular activities, attendance at meetings, and in-service educational training programs.

The main responsibilities of the school board are to hire and fire staff, establish school taxes and budgets, and determine educational policies and programs. In the absence of any statutory requirement, the board may not delegate these basic authorities through negotiation or any other means. Where there is a statutory requirement to bargain, some of the components of the board's delegated authority may be controlled through the bargaining process or a contractual agreement to use binding arbitration. In short, there is, either in the school code or bargaining statute, a defined core of the management rights and authority of the board. These may not be properly negotiated. That core is the illegal content of bargaining. Disputes over what specific issue lies within that core are settled either by a state labor relations agency or state court.

Permissive Subjects

Between the mandatory and illegal subjects lies the wide range of subjects that may be negotiated if the two parties agree. Within the concept of bargaining in good faith, either party may refuse to discuss any of these permissive issues without legal penalty. Whether any permissive issue actually becomes the subject of bargaining depends on the bargaining power of the two parties. If the teachers' union were to insist on negotiating, say, a procedure to evaluate teachers, in many states the board could refuse. If the teachers were unable, through bargaining tactics, to change the board's position, the issue would be dropped. Or the union could file an unfair labor practice charge against the board on the grounds that they were bargaining in bad faith (again, provided there exists an administrative mechanism to do so). Then it would be up to a labor relations agency or court to rule on whether that bargaining subject was mandatory. If it were, the board would be guilty of bargaining in bad faith if it refused to deal with evaluation of teachers and would be ordered to bargain. If the subject were to be considered either permissive or illegal, the board could not be forced to discuss it, and the charge would be denied.

Where there is a well-established pattern of labor relations agency rulings and court decisions, the parties to the bargain have a basis for determining the legal boundaries of negotiations. It is, obviously, much easier to refer to an existing ruling on a subject than to undertake the long and costly process of litigation or labor review. This is one advantage of an existing statutory arrangement for determining the scope of bargaining. In the absence of such an arrangement, only the school code defines the illegal subjects of bargaining, and only a court can settle an otherwise intractable dispute. Everything else is permissive. The opportunities for litigation and prolonged conflict over scope are, therefore, much greater.

Scope and the Public Interest

The central policy issues embedded in the question of scope are, of course, *where* and *how* the boundary should be drawn. This problem lies at the center of the power relationship between the parties. Lewis Kaden's illustration points up the essence of the conflict.[41]

I have heard a teachers' union president talk of his frustration at the bargaining table in dealing with the scope of negotiations. When he suggests that the discussion turn to wages, the Board of Education responds that they do not control the purse. When he suggests that they negotiate about room assignments, study hall responsibilities, and patrol obligations, the Board responds that these are subjects within the management prerogative. When he indicates the teachers' desire to negotiate over curriculum development and experimental programming, the response is that these are matters of policy.

Management's desire to keep scope narrow and labor's pressure to broaden it are clearly understandable in terms of power. The union's greatest power is in bargaining, so union pressure to increase scope increases union power at the expense of management.

If it were simply a matter of relative private power, the private sector concept of balance would be appropriate. As elected or appointed public officials, however, boards of education are responsible for serving the public interest. Thus, they receive a grant of power—management rights—to control the schools. But where states recognize that the public interest is also served by successful labor-management negotiations, much control is exercised through joint decisions. One view suggests that scope should be narrow, leaving most control to the board so they can exercise their sovereignty in the public interest; this gives the board greater power.

The other view allows scope to be determined more within the bargaining relationship; this balances power. The variety in existing state policies reflects the difficulty of achieving this balance.

An erosion of management rights through an expansion of scope can thus be seen as damaging the public interest, primarily by diminishing the sovereignty of the local government. As Joan Weitzman puts it, "sovereignty, as it applies to labor relations, refers to the government's power to fix, through law, the terms of [its] employees' employment. This power is unique, unalterable, and unilateral."[42] To the extent that it allows decisions to be made contrary to the interests of all citizens, a broad scope of bargaining is seen as evidence of excessive union power. Public policy that tightly limits scope through law can prevent public school (and other public sector) unions from exerting undue influence on the working of local government.[43] This argument rests on the questionable assumption that the public sector of employment is fundamentally different from the private, particularly because it is monopolistic and provides essential services. Determination of the scope of bargaining cannot, therefore, be left to the dynamics of the bargaining process; it must be controlled by some higher level of government and supposedly removed from the undue influence of unions.

This clear distinction between the public and private sectors has been seriously challenged by, among others, John Burton and Charles Krider, Anthony Cresswell, and Hervey Juris and Myron Roomkin.[44] The view they express is, in essence, that the differences between the private and public sectors, while they are real, are neither consistent nor large enough to warrant a wide divergence in basic policies that would treat the sectors as being fundamentally distinct. Some public services—parks, garbage removal, transportation—are not necessarily monopolistic. Some private services—for example, private utilities and fuel delivery—are often essential. And not all public services are essential at all times; schools, for example, are closed for many weeks of vacation during the year. So the case that scope of bargaining in education should be legislated is weakened.

Instead, peace between labor and management is best ensured by policies that rely primarily on balance of power and mutual accommodation at the bargaining table. It follows, then, that scope should be left largely to local determination through bargaining rather than handed down by fiat from a higher power. If management has insufficient bargaining power to protect the public interest in bargaining, that problem should be addressed directly. Policies to increase the managerial or political strength of the school board would be such direct means. Scope of bargaining thus determined through reasonably balanced local interests may fit local needs better than a narrow, uniform scope originating at the state level.

Union Security

The central issue in terms of union security is the extent to which the employer will agree to assist the union in collecting members or revenues. The principal methods are:

Closed shop—only members of the union may be hired (at present the NLRA prohibits closed shops and no state laws permit them for schools).

Union shop—employees are required to join the union within some stated period of time after hiring (at present only Oregon and Pennsylvania permit union shop agreements for school systems).

Agency shop (or service fees)—the employer agrees to collect a fixed fee (roughly equivalent to union dues) from nonunion members or makes payment of these fees a condition of employment.

Dues checkoff—employer collects union dues by deduction directly from paychecks and pays sum to union.

No statute currently requires any of these (or any other) union security provisions in negotiations; it is a question of whether they are permitted. A summary of current state statutes is found in Table 5-3. For the states not mentioned in the table, there is no specific legal provision regarding union security, and so, in those states, these issues could be considered permissive bargaining subjects (except for those states that do not permit contracts).[45]

Grievance Procedures

Any contract may provide within it means for enforcement and interpretation of the terms and provisions. A lease, for example, might require a security deposit from a tenant, which the landlord then holds as a means of enforcing the terms of the lease. A construction contract may contain penalty clauses whereby the contractor loses revenue for late completion. Similarly, labor agreements

Table 5-3
States with legislation allowing union security provisions in contracts

State	Dues checkoff	Service fees	Union shop
California	X	X	
Connecticut	X		
Delaware	X		
Florida	X		
Hawaii	X	X	
Indiana	X		
Iowa	X		
Maryland	X		
Massachusetts	X	X	
Michigan	X	X	
Minnesota	X	X	
Montana	X	X	
Nevada	X		
New York	X		
Oregon	X	X	X
Pennsylvania	X	X	X
Rhode Island	X[a]	X[a]	
Vermont	X[b]	X[b]	
Washington	X	X	
Wisconsin	X	X	

[a] Professional personnel only.
[b] Nonprofessional personnel only.
Source: Doris Ross, *Cuebook.*

often include a grievance procedure as one means of further interpreting and enforcing the terms of the contract after it has been signed. The employer may use various disciplinary measures to assure that employees meet the terms of the contract; employees have the grievance procedure to help ensure that the terms of the contract are followed by the employer. When an employee or the organization feels that an employer is improperly administering the contract, they can file a formal, written allegation called a grievance. The grievance procedure in the contract outlines the steps required to settle the grievance.

The establishment of a grievance procedure has become commonplace in contracts owing to the complex nature of labor relations and the impossibility of creating a foolproof contract. Some means is usually necessary for the orderly resolution of contract disputes that arise either out of badly constructed elements of the contract or errors or abuses on the part of management. Including the grievance procedure in the contract shows that both sides accept the procedure as being fair and are prepared to bind themselves to the results.

The exact details of a grievance procedure will, of course, depend on the nature of the school systems and the contract involved, but certain elements are common. The first step or level in the procedure usually requires that a formal statement of the grievance be filed by the employee, or his or her representative, with the immediate supervisor. This provides an opportunity for the worker and supervisor, who is quite often the source of the grievance, to solve the problem at its source. If it cannot be resolved there, the grievance is processed in steps through the levels of the organization until it reaches the superintendent or board. The employee and the administrator at each level have the option of agreeing to a mutually satisfactory resolution, which would stop the procedure at that point. If no resolution is available at the top of the school system, the final step is often binding arbitration by a mutually selected neutral party. By submitting the grievance to arbitration, the employer and employee agree to be bound by the outcome, unless one side feels the award is illegal. If so, either side can appeal through the courts.

Thus, within the framework of the contract, the parties to the bargain establish what amounts to a system of labor-management jurisprudence. In Neil Chamberlain and Donald Cullen's terms:

The resemblance between the grievance procedure and the judicial procedure is evident. There is an effort to apply the general "law" (the agreement) to specific situations, with an eventual determination—if need be—by an impartial judge. The grievance process has therefore been called the "compliance process," or the basis for the building of an industrial jurisprudence.[46]

Through this orderly process, the employee is protected from arbitrary decisions and actions on the part of the employer, and the administration of the contract can be adjusted to the realities of the workplace.

Contractual grievance procedures apply to all employees covered by the contract, whether or not they are members of the bargaining unit. The law or the contract generally requires the union to represent the individual employee and process his or her grievances fairly. The union generally has some discretion over which grievances it chooses to process, however, and how far they are carried. This control allows the union to eliminate trivial grievances or to control the costs of grievances, but it can also bring the union into conflict with the right of individual members to prosecute their own grievances. Under federal law, members may sue to force unions to process a grievance only if the union's actions in refusing have been arbitrary, discriminatory, or in bad faith. The same standard is common in related decisions by state courts.[47]

Impasse Procedures

Resolution

In its simplest sense, "impasse" means that bargaining is no longer progressing toward agreement. The existence of an impasse is a threat to the bargaining relationship and the public interest since it implies that, rather than make any concession, the parties are ready to risk open hostility, long delays in reaching agreement, and perhaps a strike and its related costs. Somehow the stakes at the bargaining table have become so high that any retreat from a position is quite difficult. When stakes are that high, the parties are more likely to engage in extreme forms of behavior that may damage the bargaining relationship and impose serious costs on the clients of the school and the public. Peaceful resolution of impasses is, therefore, usually treated as a public policy problem.

The statutes and courts of many states have constructed procedures for dealing with impasses and moving the parties back to bargaining. That can be done through providing a mechanism for defining and recognizing impasse; providing for third-party intervention to help resolve differences and get the bargaining moving again; and creating sanctions to discourage certain forms of impasse-breaking tactics, such as strikes and lockouts, and providing inducements to come to agreement.

Impasse provisions in the legal structure of labor relations, in education or elsewhere, form a central feature of public policy. The possibility of impasse and the costs of a strike to both sides are the primary forces driving the parties to agreement, which means that any legal machinery involving impasses directly affects the power relationship between the parties. This is where the central dilemma of public policy toward labor relations, particularly in the public sector, is most obvious. Public policy has two partly conflicting objectives: to allow the parties to come to agreement through a process of free collective bargaining and to protect the public interest. The first suggests letting the parties work out the impasses the best way they can and tolerating strikes as the necessary price of fair labor relations. The second requires that some external controls be applied, recognizing that some costs of impasse exceed even the need for fair labor relations. The most familiar examples of the latter kind of controls can be found in cases where strikes constituted a national emergency under the terms of the Taft-Hartley Act, or when injunctions are imposed against strikes by public employees.

There is no clear answer to this policy dilemma. No mechanism yet proposed to resolve impasses or prevent strikes is uniformly agreeable to all parties. Imposed resolution of impasses, such as mandatory arbitration, is opposed by school boards as a violation of sovereignty. Yet many of those same boards seek injunctions to force unions back to work or to bargaining. The absence of any mechanism risks long and costly strikes. In light of this difficulty, we attempt here to describe existing impasse machinery rather than to propose solutions or ideal policies.

Procedures

There are five legally defined or regulated processes for resolving impasses: mediation, fact-finding, arbitration, strikes and lock-outs, and injunctions. Although this section defines and discusses only the legal framework within which each of these processes operates, they are more than just legal processes. They are tactical weapons in bargaining, and they affect the power relationship between the bargainers (see Chapter 9).

While there is some variation among states, the legal arrangements for controlling and resolving impasse have some similarities. In the public sector there are basically four legal interventions— mediation, fact-finding, arbitration, and injunctions—available to deal with impasses. These interventions are the mechanisms needed to resolve impasses legally. Strikes and injunctions are discussed separately at the end of this section.

Mediation is the least formal and perhaps most widely used form of intervention. A mediator is simply a neutral third party who meets separately with the two bargaining sides and tries, through persuasion and communication, to bring them back to bargaining. The mediator has no power to force the parties together or to impose an agreement. To be effective, a mediator must have the confidence of the parties to the degree that they will communicate with each other through that person. Of course, gaining trust is only in part a matter of the mediator's legal status. Mediation services are obtained most often through the Federal Mediation and Conciliation Service, which has offices in major cities, or through a state labor relations agency. A mediator must be mutually acceptable to both sides, and the cost is usually shared by the parties or by a state agency.

Mediation is an attempt to bring the parties together directly; *fact-finding* is an indirect approach. A fact finder (or team of fact finders) studies the bargaining positions of the parties and gathers information about the relative merits of the proposals. The report that evolves is then made public in the hope that full disclosure of the bargaining positions and supporting facts will bring public pressure to bear on the less reasonable party and encourage a change in position that will allow both parties to move again toward agreement. As with mediation, the choice of a fact finder depends on the mutual agreement of the parties. The person or team may be supplied by a state labor relations agency or be independently chosen by the two parties.

The distinction between fact-finding and arbitration becomes fuzzy in practice because of the variations in the way the procedures are used. In the private sector, *arbitration* means the process by which agreement is reached by parties voluntarily submitting the dispute to the neutral third party. If the parties involved agree to be bound by the arbitration decision, it is called "binding"; otherwise, it is referred to as "advisory." When the settling of a new contract is involved, the process is called "interest" arbitration, and, if the dispute is over administration of an existing contract, it is usually called "grievance" or "rights" arbitration.

As used in the public sector, however, mediation and fact-finding acquire some of the characteristics of arbitration since, under some state arrangements, arbitration lacks much of the voluntary character that it has in the private sector. States such as Oregon, Connecticut, and Minnesota require binding arbitration. In Maine and Rhode Island binding arbitration is used to resolve nonfiscal issues at impasse; fiscal questions are left to the parties to be resolved. A third approach is to require fact-finding with nonbinding recommendations, thereby turning the fact-finding process into advisory arbitration. This approach is followed in several states, including Vermont, New Hampshire, and Nebraska. Other states, such as New York, New Jersey, and Hawaii, allow binding arbitration by mutual consent of the parties. Virtually every combination of the mechanisms for resolving impasses is represented somewhere in the variety of legal provisions created by the state legislatures.

One special feature, now found in some form or other in four states, deserves some attention: "final (or last best) offer" arbitration. In this process, the parties submit only their final offers to the arbitrator, who is bound by law to choose, *without modification*, one or the other of the offers. The entire contract package may constitute the final offer, or individual parts can be handled separately. The arbitration can also be limited to fiscal issues, with the parties left to agree on nonfiscal matters on their own. It is argued that final offer arbitration should lead the parties to settle before reaching the arbitration stage, or at least make their final offers reasonable enough to appeal to the arbitrator. In conventional arbitration, it is argued, the parties believe the arbitrator will usually "split the difference," so the parties tend to enter arbitration with exaggerated demands. Experience with the final offer form of arbitration has shown that it can be effective in some circumstances, but the results are not uniform.[48]

Another legal element of arbitration is the scope of topics considered arbitrable. School districts and other civil divisions of the state are, as we have pointed out, restricted in the decisions and powers they can delegate. Where a statute specifically requires arbitration, or defines the areas where it may be voluntary, the question is more easily dealt with: whatever is negotiable is arbitrable. Where the scope of bargaining is poorly defined or where the limits of arbitration are not clearly established, however, arbitrability becomes an issue. In Illinois, for example, where the scope of bargaining is not clearly defined, the Supreme Court has ruled that a school district may not agree to arbitration where a grievance involves the statutory power of the board, such as the hiring of professional staff.[49] Delegation of such a statutory power to an arbitrator is not permitted.

The question of arbitrability is first faced, of course, by the arbitrator, who can refuse to make an award in areas judged to be not arbitrable. If an award is made, however, the employer has the option of appealing the award through the courts on the grounds that the bargaining statute or school code has been violated. As there is more bargaining and arbitration in the states, a body of case law defining the scope of arbitration will develop in much the same way case law and labor relations board decisions define the scope of bargaining.

Legal processes to deal with bargaining impasses require some triggering mechanism. To initiate processes to resolve impasses before they were needed would result in unnecessary costs and interfere with the bargaining process. Should intervention be delayed too long, however, a tense bargaining situation might result in damaging conflict before anything could be done. Most of the statutes provide for mediation or fact-finding at the request of the parties involved. But the parties do not always agree to declare an impasse or decide what sort of intervention they want. That is why state bargaining statutes often provide several mechanisms to initiate intervention. Several states include a timetable for automatic impasse steps.

Pennsylvania's statute, for example, provides a schedule tied to the budget submission date for the school district. The schedule illustrates how a sequence of impasse resolution procedures can be used to mandate a long period of intervention before all means are exhausted (see Figure 5-1). The schedule establishes a set of orderly procedures that both parties know in advance will be followed, and it mandates a minimum bargaining time before a strike is allowed. Although Pennsylvania is one of the few states that allows strikes, the same sequence of procedures is common to other bargaining statutes. Mediation and fact-finding are explicitly provided for or permitted in all the statutory states, with twenty states allowing or requiring some form of arbitration as a final step.

Where a timetable for intervention is not present, impasse may be declared by the parties, by agreement, or by one party, or by the state labor relations agency. In states with bargaining statutes, the law generally provides a method of selecting neutral third parties for mediation, fact-finding, or arbitration. In nonstatutory states, the parties are free to determine their own methods. In Illinois and

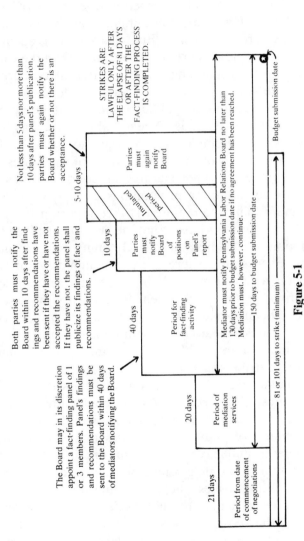

Figure 5-1

Time period intervals for the impasse procedure
(from Pennsylvania School Boards Association. *Act 195* (Harrisburg, Pa.: the Association, 1973)

Ohio, two states with much bargaining but no statute, the state education agencies assist school systems in obtaining competent neutrals for mediation and fact-finding.

Strikes and Injunctions. In the private sector, the strike has long been recognized as a central, indispensable element of collective bargaining. With a few exceptions, injunctions against strikes in the private sector are not allowed. But legal sanctions against strike activity by public employees are the rule, rather than the exception, in the legal arrangements among the fifty states. Strikes are viewed as affronts to the sovereign power of state and local governments and as serious disruptions in public services that many consider essential or for which there is no easy alternative. As a result, few states allow school employees any right to strike, with a few statutes remaining silent on the issue. Many of the states without bargaining statutes have other statutes or court opinions prohibiting strikes. Of course, these prohibitions do not prevent strikes. Most of the more than two hundred strikes reported in 1976 were in states with strike prohibitions. What the law does is place the anti-strike injunction in the arsenal of bargaining tools available to management. Even states where there is a limited right to strike have injunction mechanisms built into the law. In Pennsylvania, the statute provides that, even when the statutory impasse resolution steps have been exhausted, a strike may be prohibited when "such a strike creates a clear and present danger or threat to health, safety, or welfare of the public."[50] This makes the injunction a possibility in any strike situation.

In the event of a strike, the injunction is not, however, automatic. Management must first decide to seek court intervention. The threat of an injunction may be more potent than the act itself since the punitive nature of injunctive penalties may solidify union resistance or generate public sympathy for the union.[51] Where management seeks an injunction, judges may not always oblige. And, even in states that outlaw strikes, the courts may invoke the standard of "clear and present danger to public safety" and deny an injunction for strikes that pose no such threat.[52] Local courts may, in fact, be reluctant to intervene in some labor disputes, and, if so, they can often find technical reasons for not granting an injunction or for delaying its enforcement. In one Illinois case, the district court delayed a hearing over a weekend on a technical flaw in the management complaint. By the following Monday, the teachers had decided to return to work.

Once an injunction has been granted, union officers and members who continue strike activity can be fined and imprisoned. The contempt powers of the court may be invoked to take criminal action against strikers, or the bargaining statute may provide for fines against the union itself (New York State's Taylor Act). Criminal prosecution of union officers or members is possible under the contempt powers of the courts, but it may be counterproductive: A union leader being marched off in handcuffs often becomes a hero to union members and inspires their resolve to continue a strike. Union leaders can also evade the court by temporarily moving out of its jurisdiction. In the St. Louis teachers' strike of 1973, union leaders simply crossed the Mississippi River into Illinois and directed the strike from there.[53] Fines against the union affect the entire membership, but large fines, if they are actually levied, can result in hostility that interferes with labor relations long after a strike ends. The injunction can be a potent bargaining tool on the side of management, but it has limitations and costs for both sides.

SPECIAL PROBLEMS OF SCHOOLS AND LABOR RELATIONS

Public policy toward labor—whether teachers or other workers— has dealt with a set of common questions: What are the rights of workers to organize? How should the employer-employee relationship be structured? What are the rights and duties of the parties in bargaining? What should be bargained? How should strikes and impasses be regulated? The answers to these questions are only determined in part by the policy structure itself. Because they are also determined in part by the nature of the institution involved, it is useful to examine the special characteristics of schools in relation to these six questions.

The Teaching Function

The nature of teaching may lead to some special legal problems. The work of teaching involves close, personal contact between the professional (teacher) and the client (student). A teacher has the status of both subject expert and role model in most situations.

A teacher is expected to influence the growth and development of children, in emotional and ethical, as well as intellectual, ways. There has always been tension between teachers' rights to freedom of religion, speech, and academic expression and the protection of the students from indoctrination and propaganda. In matters related to curriculum, the right of the teachers to deal with controversial subjects is well established. And the rights of teachers in such matters as religious objection to flag salutes and political protest are well defined. In the matter of labor disputes, the line between free speech and improper conduct may, however, be different. The law is not well defined in this area, so we will only discuss the kind of question that may arise.

One important question concerns the extent to which issues in a labor dispute may be introduced into the classroom. Teachers have been disciplined for wearing buttons or referring to a current contract issue in the classroom. Teachers have used conferences with parents to argue for a union position in bargaining. Treatment of labor history could be biased, especially in history and social studies classes, by high levels of conflict in the labor relations of the school. In each of these instances teachers could use the teaching process to gain advantage in a labor relations situation.

Some of these actions, such as propagandizing students on labor issues, are clearly proscribed by the ethics of the teaching profession. Teachers' organizations neither advocate nor support such behavior, but that does not settle the matter. Unscrupulous teachers may do so, regardless of ethical standards. And innocent teachers could be wrongly accused of bias in their teaching. The lack of clear standards or precedents for judging such matters is a serious problem where schooling and bargaining coincide.

Deliberately distorting teaching is clearly unethical; wearing an armband or button referring to a labor dispute is somewhat more difficult to judge. The same is true of discussing bargaining issues with parents at conference time, or other use of the teaching role to union advantage. Freedom of speech, both symbolic and direct, is a protected right. To abridge that right justifiably requires showing some substantial danger or damage to the public good. The question then becomes a matter of determining how much damage might be caused by these particular kinds of teacher behavior. Since bargaining is largely a political process, community support is an important element in the relationship between the two parties. It is to either party's advantage to have as much parent and student support as possible. If the teachers use their actions to gain support among school clients, there may be some advantage when bargaining. How much cannot be known; nor is it clear that *only* advantage will result. Should parents and students be offended by teachers' armbands or the introduction of labor matters into other contexts, such behavior could lose support for teachers.

Two kinds of action are clearly needed. It is most important that teachers' organizations take responsibility for defining clear ethical standards for their members governing the introduction of labor-management issues into the teaching process. The organizations should then be prepared to enforce those standards when necessary. At the same time, school boards and administrators should recognize this as an area where clear, enforceable policy is required. It is in the interest of both sides to be sure that the labor-management elements of the school do not interfere with either the quality or credibility of the educational program.

Tenure and Seniority

Almost all public school teachers in the United States are covered by some form of state tenure or continuous contract law (only two states have no such law). These laws provide that, after a given probationary period (usually three years), teachers have a continuing contract and may be dismissed only for cause following some process of hearing or review. (During the probationary period teachers usually can be dismissed without specific charges or hearing procedures.) Tenure laws can come into direct conflict with the provisions of negotiated contracts and with the best interests of the educational program if the dismissal of both probationary and tenured teachers is involved.

In dismissing teachers because of programmatic or financial cutbacks, state school codes generally provide only that nontenured teachers be dismissed before tenured. Within the ranks of tenured teachers, the law usually requires no distinction according to length of service. But seniority provisions in contracts often require a board to lay off or dismiss teachers according to that standard. The problem comes in defining length of service: Is it length of service in the district? At the grade level? In the subject matter?

In a special program? All are possible definitions of seniority, but with important implications for educational programs. Suppose a school system facing the need to reduce staff had started a new primary-grade reading program in one building, with plans to expand to four other elementary buildings in stages. Suppose, further, that all primary-grade teachers were tenured, but the ones in the experimental program were lower in seniority, defined as total length of service at a particular grade level. The school district might then be forced to delay or destroy the new program by dismissing the teachers instrumental in its development. The higher the degree of specialization or program differentiation in a district, the more troublesome this sort of seniority problem is likely to become. It is even possible that poorly constructed seniority systems could deter some kinds of program development.

These special problems, taken with the more general problems and issues in the legal structure of bargaining, illustrate one point clearly. The legal structure provides the basic context of public objectives and constraints for labor relations in education, but it does not answer all the questions or solve all the problems. The legal framework guides practice in some areas, but merely follows in others. The field of labor relations is undergoing constant change, as is the social and political environment in which it exists. While it is necessary to understand and use the legal structure, it is also necessary, in the educational setting, to look beyond that structure both to the institution itself and to the changing nature of the institutional environment.

NOTES

1. *Philadelphia Cordwainer's Case*, in *Documentary History of American Industrial Society*, ed. John R. Commons *et al.*, 10 vols. (New York: Russell and Russell, 1958; originally published in 1909-1911), III, 59-248 (1806).

2. *Commonwealth* v. *Hunt*, 4 Met. (Mass.) III (1842).

3. For overall treatments of the origins and state of public policy toward labor, see Archibald Cox, *Law and the National Labor Policy*, Industrial Relations Monograph Series, No. 5 (Los Angeles: Institute of Industrial Relations, University of California, 1960); and Benjamin J. Taylor and Fred Witney, *Labor Relations Law*, 2d ed. (Englewood Cliffs, N.J.: Prentice-Hall, 1975).

4. *In re Debs*, 158 U.S. 564 (1895).

5. *Loewe* v. *Lawlor*, 208 U.S. 274 (1908).

6. *Duplex* v. *Deering*, 225 U.S. 443 (1925).

7. *Bedford Cut Stone Co.* v. *Journeymen Stone Cutters*, 274 U.S. 37 (1927).

8. Cox, *Law and National Labor Policy*; Charles O. Gregory, *Labor and the Law*, 2d ed. (New York: W. W. Norton, 1961).

9. The amendments cited above are incorporated in the National Labor Relations Act, as amended, P.L. 101, 80th Congress. This discussion does not include attention to the extension of the NLRA to the health care and hospital sector. See 29 U.S.C.A., ch. 11.

10. James W. Robinson, James T. Turner, and Roger W. Walker, *Introduction to Labor* (Englewood Cliffs, N.J.: Prentice-Hall, 1975).

11. For more details on legal aspects of labor relations in the federal government, see Taylor and Witney, *Labor Relations Law*, ch. 21.

12. *People* ex rel. *Fursman* v. *Chicago*, 278 Ill. 318 (1917).

13. *Seattle High School American Federation of Teachers* v. *Sharples*, 159 Wash. 424 (1930).

14. *Norwalk Teachers Association* v. *Board of Education*, 83 A.2d 482 (1951).

15. Advisory Commission on Intergovernmental Relations, *Labor-Management Policies for State and Local Government* (Washington, D.C.: U.S. Government Printing Office, 1969), esp. ch. 2.

16. *Ibid.*, p. 19.

17. *Hortonville Joint School District* v. *Hortonville Education Assoc.*, 96 S.Ct. 2308 (1976).

18. Contracts that are outside the power of the district to make are called *ultra vires* contracts. For a discussion of the impact of *ultra vires* contracts on school district liability, see William R. Hazard, *Education and the Law*, 2d ed. (New York: Free Press, 1978), pp. 520-523.

19. *NLRB* v. *Truitt Mfg. Co.*, 351 U.S. 154 (1956).

20. *Stevenson Brick and Block Co.*, 160 NLRB 21; and *Continental Insurance Co.* v. *NLRB*, 495 F.2d 44 (1974).

21. *State of New Jersey and Council of New Jersey State College Locals, N.J.S. F.T.* P.E.R.C. #CO-12, E.D. No. 79, August 14, 1975.

22. These points are based on material in Harry H. Wellington, *Labor and the Legal Process* (New Haven, Conn.: Yale University Press, 1968); Bernard D. Meltzer, *Labor Law*, 2d ed. (Boston: Little, Brown, 1977), and also on *Borg-Warner Controls*, 198 NLRB 726 (1972), *NLRB* v. *Truitt*, 351 U.S. 149 (1956), and *NLRB* v. *American National Insurance Co.*, 343 U.S. 395 (1952).

23. *Continental Insurance Co.* v. *NLRB*.

24. *NLRB* v. *Cummer-Graham Co.*, 279 F.2d 757.

25. William A. Rutter, *Labor Law* (Gardena, Calif.: Gilbert Law Summaries, 1973), p. 49.

26. Where an issue of inclusion in an existing unit arises, the NLRB has conducted so-called "Globe Elections" that allow employees to choose between a separate unit or merger. *Globe Machine and Stamping Co.*, 3 NLRB 294 (1937).

27. *Davenport Community Schools* v. *Davenport Education Association*, Iowa Public Employee Relations Board, No. 72, October 30, 1975.

28. *Cedar Falls Education Association* v. *Cedar Falls Community School District*, Iowa Public Employee Relations Board, No. 26, April 17, 1975.

29. *Government Employee Relations Reports*, No. 644, February 16, 1976. A comprehensive review of the status of supervisors is found in Stephen L. Hayford and Anthony V. Sinicropi, "Bargaining Rights Status of Public Sector Supervisors," *Industrial Relations*, 15:1 (February 1976), 44-61.

30. *Keckeisen* v. *Independent School District 612*, 509 F.2d 1062 (1975).

31. California Educational Employment Relations Act, Art. 5, Sec. 3544.

32. Wisconsin Stat. Ann., 111.70 (1)a.

33. It is necessary to note, in passing, the selection problem presented here. Each state has a different legal structure for school labor relations (albeit with many comparable features). Within the matter of scope, literally dozens of specific issues can arise, from questions as fundamental as class size to those as minor as whether the union has access to bulletin boards. A discussion of each issue in the context of each separate state legal structure is beyond both the available space and our objectives. Instead, we focus below on the major issues and the most general legal principles. A summary of recent legal actions is found in "Special Report: Teachers and Labor Unions," GERR, Ref. file 170, 41: 301 (Nov. 26, 1979).

34. National Labor Relations Act, Sec. 9a.

35. California Educational Employment Relations Act, Sec. 3543.2.

36. Michigan Stat. Ann., Sec. 423.215.

37. Hazard, *Education and the Law*, 364-365.

38. *Illinois Education Association Local Community High School District No. 218* v. *Board of Education of School District No. 218*, 320 N.E.2d (1974); and *Dayton Classroom Teachers Association* v. *Dayton Board of Education*, 41 Ohio St. 2d 127 (1975).

39. *Board of Education of the School District of Philadelphia* v. *Philadelphia Federation of Teachers, Local No. 3 AFT*, 346 A.2d 35 (1975). See also *Fairview School District* v. *Fairview Educ. Association*, 368 A.2d. 842 (1977).

40. For example, the New York Court of Appeals found that class and staff size were both bargainable and arbitrable. *Susquehanna Valley Central School District* v. *Susquehanna Valley Teachers Association*, New York Court of Appeals, No. 388, October 1975.

41. Lewis Kaden as quoted in Joan Weitzman, *The Scope of Bargaining in Public Employment* (New York: Praeger, 1975), 4.

42. Weitzman, *Scope of Bargaining in Public Employment*, 8.

43. For a detailed exposition of the point of view, see Harry H. Wellington and Ralph K. Winter, *The Unions and the Cities* (Washington, D.C.: Brookings Institution, 1971). See also John H. Metzler, "The Need for Limitation upon the Scope of Negotiations in Public Education," in *Education and Collective Bargaining*, ed. Anthony M. Cresswell and Michael J. Murphy (Berkeley, Calif.: McCutchan, 1976).

44. See John F. Burton and Charles Krider, "The Role and Consequences of Strikes by Public Employees," *Yale Law Journal*, 79:3 (January 1970), 418-443; and Anthony M. Cresswell, "The Public Interest in Public Sector Bargaining: Management Rights v. Management Power," in *Critical Issues in Education*, ed.

Lou Rubin (Boston: Allyn and Bacon, 1979); Hervey A. Juris and Myron Roomkin, "Education and Collective Bargaining: Sui Generis?" Paper presented at the American Educational Research Association's Annual Meeting, 1978.

45. The U.S. Supreme Court found agency shop clauses constitutional in *Abood* v. *Detroit*, 97 S. Ct. 1782 (1977).

46. Neil W. Chamberlain and Donald E. Cullen, *The Labor Sector*, 2d ed. (New York: McGraw-Hill, 1971), 259.

47. Federal law is based on *Vaca* v. *Sipes*, 386 U.S. 171 (1967). State policy is discussed in Kenneth J. Rose, "The Duty of Fair Representation in Public Sector Collective Bargaining," *Journal of Law and Education*, 5:1 (January 1976), 77-89.

48. James L. Stern *et al., Final-Offer Arbitration* (Lexington, Mass.: D. C. Heath, 1975), is a detailed study of experience with this procedure for public safety workers.

49. *Illinois Education Association* v. *Board of Education of School District 218,* 340 N.E. 2d 7 (1976); and *Board of Trustees of Junior College District 508* v. *Cook County College Teachers' Union*, 343 N.E.2d 473 (1976).

50. Pa. Act 195 (1970), Art. X, Sec. 1003.

51. David L. Colton, "Influence of an Anti-Strike Injunction," *Educational Administration Quarterly*, 13:3 (November 1977), 47-70.

52. This point is discussed at some length by Hugh D. Jascourt, *Public Sector Labor Relations* (Chicago: International Personnel Management Association, 1975), 40-43. He points out that even in states where strikes are illegal, courts have been unwilling to grant injunctions in all cases and often require evidence of good faith bargaining and exhaustion of impasse procedures.

53. Colton, "Influence of an Anti-Strike Injunction."

6

School Governance and
Collective Bargaining

In collective bargaining, power is exercised to resolve inherent conflicts of interest. Both compromise and cooperation are necessary to achieve effective operation of the schools. Much the same could be said about school governance, where power is exercised, conflicts are resolved, and cooperation is achieved toward the same ultimate end of effective operation. It is useful, however, to distinguish between bargaining and governance. Bargaining actually seems to fit into the larger process of governance. Not every issue or decision in the operation of schools is collectively bargained, and yet bargaining can affect virtually any issue or decision. To understand how collective bargaining fits into school governance, it is necessary to explore the meaning of both ideas and the boundary between them.

Both bargaining and governance are thought of as processes, that is, a series of events and interactions among a variety of participants. Both processes take place in a somewhat stable structure, that is, a set of rules and expectations that indicate how events are to occur and how the participants are to behave. Making a school budget is, for example, an important element of governance. Board members, administrators, and other individuals and groups take part in building the budget, which usually requires a timetable, rules of procedure, expectations, and assigned tasks. Similarly, negotiations take place according to a timetable and within rules and laws, with roles and specialized tasks assigned to the participants.

There are many issues and conflicts involved in the operation and control of schools. They can range from decisions of the United States Supreme Court to choices of what brand of floor wax to use. It is obvious that different processes and structures are used to make different decisions.

To describe how bargaining fits into this complex situation, we have constructed a framework for discussing the process and structure of bargaining and governance. The framework organizes the elements of governance according to the substance of the issue involved, the nature of conflict and cooperation, and the power of participants.

MODES OF GOVERNANCE

The concept of governance—that process by which decisions are made about the control of public education—is at the center of the framework. The view is fundamentally a political one whereby governance is considered the political process of making decisions about the important stakes involved in schooling. In Gerald Sroufe's words:

"Stakes" means jobs, money, prestige, influence, status, or even acceptance of ideas. People care enough about such stakes to try to actively influence their distribution. To this end they develop and husband their influence, and seek to use it wisely to affect the distribution of stakes. "Politics ain't beanbag."[1]

This is little more than the application to schools of Harold Lasswell's classic definition of politics as "who gets what, when, how."[2] Collective bargaining and labor-management relations are part of this distribution of stakes; they are affected by and in turn affect it. Almost all of the potential stakes in school governance can be directly or indirectly involved in the bargaining.

The exercise of influence or power is central to this political dynamic. Used in Edward Banfield's sense, influence is the ability to get another to act, think, or feel as one intends.[3] Influence is exerted in the governance process through essentially the same mechanisms as it is in any other social process. The basic tools are rewards and punishments, expertise and information, control through rules or formal authority, and friendship.[4] Since friendship is ubiquitous and, thus, not a special part of any particular mode of action, it does not receive much attention here. When one examines the other means of exerting influence, it becomes clear that there are important differences in how these means are used in varying aspects of school governance, and it is these differences that provide the basis for describing connections with bargaining.

Consider the contrast between an arbitrator deciding the outcome of a grievance and a curriculum director choosing a new series of science texts. Both are parts of the governance process as defined here, and important economic and political stakes can be involved. In the arbitration, however, the mechanisms of influence are defined by the contract and the rules governing the arbitration process, which make these the basis for deciding who wins and loses. Participation and flow of information are determined by the labor-management relationship. The structure of decision making is similarly defined. In the textbook decision, in contrast, the basis for decision rests on expertise or the desire to maximize the attainment of certain objectives, and the process is controlled through the regular authority structure of the school system. Any attempt to use one set of procedures, criteria, and patterns of participation for both decisions would encounter resistance. Many of the decisions that are part of school governance are as varied.

We have identified four modes of governance in school systems that can be distinguished in terms of variation in the control of the basic tools of influence. Variation is expressed in terms of different *participants* in the process, different *criteria* for allocation of values, and different *rules* or structures. Participation is the basis for applying expertise or controlling information. Decision criteria determine the allocation of rewards and punishments. The rules and structures reflect the authority relationships in the decision process.

From this point of view, modes of governance for schools (and for other sorts of organizations as well) can be clearly distinguished from one another. In this discussion they are called "public," "bureaucratic-professional," "labor relations," and "private." The *public* mode is the one most often considered the main process of governance. It is the policy-making mode, where elections, laws, government machinery, and public participation are the dominant elements. The *bureaucratic-professional* mode refers to the internal governance of the school (or related agencies). It is the bureaucratic process wherein the professional staff makes the day-to-day decisions that determine general operations. Bureaucracy and professional decision making are closely linked in school governance. The judgment of professionals about how best to conduct the school is the basis for many decisions. These decisions are not, however, made by individual professionals acting autonomously. They are made in the framework of institutional rules and control mechanisms characteristic of bureaucracies. Decisions are supposed to be rational and orderly. Since it is not accurate to refer to this aspect of governance as either strictly professional or strictly bureaucratic, we use the combined term to indicate the mixed nature of the process. It is the *labor relations* mode that is based in the bargaining and contract administration processes. It usually focuses on terms and conditions of employment, but it can overflow into more general concerns. The *private* mode involves decisions concerning private property and actions. Ownership and individual rights are the main concerns.

The Elements of Governance

We can describe the way collective bargaining fits into and interacts with the overall structure of governance in terms of these four modes and show specific differences among their main elements (see Table 6-1). The modes of governance described in the table are not unique to schools (or other educational institutions). They are common to many organizations. Any organization can have some, perhaps small, component of labor relations—whether unions are present or not. All organizations affected by law and government have a public mode. And there is some component of private and bureaucratic-professional governance in any organization as well. The modes and their components provide us with a way of describing salient differences among organizational events and how the labor relations process fits into the rest of the governance process.

Consider four hypothetical decisions commonly made in school systems, and how the relative importance of the different modes of governance would vary among them (Table 6-2).

Table 6-1

Collective bargaining and modes of governance

Mode	Element	Component of governance mode
Public	Participants	Public officials (elected and appointed) Organized interest groups Corporations and individuals Courts and quasi-judicial bodies (commissions etc.)
	Structure	Legal framework of public decision making: formal rules and procedures of legislatures, school boards, etc. Pattern of influence and organizations of formal interest groups or alliances Relative influence determined by political power
	Criteria	Compromise among plural interests and actors The "public interest" or maximizing social welfare Legal precedent or statute law
Bureaucratic-professional	Participants	Qualified professionals with recognized expertise in the field (education or some component thereof) Identified clients, to a limited degree
	Structure	Rational or formal decision procedures of identifying alternatives, weighing comparative advantage, and choosing course of action May take place in professional associations, informal work groups, or formal committees established by employer Relative influence determined by expertise and authority
	Criteria	Objective criteria of effectiveness in terms of benefit to the client Maximization of benefit to specific client group (i.e., students) Professional ethics and standards
Labor relations	Participants	Labor organizations and members (acting as members) Labor relations staff of school district or union

Table 6-1 *(continued)*
Collective bargaining and modes of governance

Mode	Element	Component of governance mode
		State labor relations board or agency (if there is one)
		Courts, on occasion, and other levels of government in some situations (i.e., legislatures in passing laws)
	Structure	Formally recognized bargaining process
		Grievance procedure
		Impasse and dispute settlement process (e.g., mediation, arbitration)
		Informal bargaining or conferring between labor and management during contract
		Relative influence determined by bargaining power
	Criteria	Mutual acceptability to the two organizational parties
		Peace and stability in the labor relations system, taken into account often by third party in dispute settlement
		Gaining comparative advantage over the opponent in a future bargain
Private	Participants	Owners or those with proprietary claim on the organization or process in question
		Courts or public officials, where questions of law and property rights are concerned
	Structure	Degree of ownership or proprietary claim as determinant of relative influence, but no formal structure necessary
		Due process of law for settlement of dispute involving property rights
	Criteria	Maximum benefit to owners in proportion to their claim of ownership
		Assurance of due process in dispute settlements and other safeguards of property rights

Table 6-2

Relative importance of governance modes in four school districts

Decision	Governance mode			
	Public	Professional	Labor relations	Private
Choose new board member	High	Low to medium	Low to medium	Low
Assign teachers to classes	Low	High	High	Low
Send band to summer camp	High	Low	Low	High
Choose new reading materials	Low	High	Low	Low

The first decision mentioned in the table, recruitment and election of new members of boards of education, is among the most public of governance processes, with a variety of possible means of public participation.[5] There may be some bureaucratic-professional participation, with the superintendent influencing the choice, or the actions of a member of the administration, particularly the superintendent, may become an issue in the election. There may also be some activity of teacher organizations, such as endorsing the election of certain board members. That is why the importance of bureaucratic-professional and labor relations modes is low to medium in those categories. Questions of private property are unimportant here.

Staff selection and assignment is generally treated in schools as an internal, administrative decision, affected or constrained by negotiated agreements in some cases.[6] This is the type of issue which may or may not be in the labor relations mode, depending on whether there is a formal agreement and on the relative power of the parties. If the teachers' union is sufficiently powerful in the bargaining process, it may be able to force staff assignment decisions, or at least part of them, more into the labor relations mode.

The summer camp decision is definitely not part of the regular administrative or political mode of governance. Such decisions usually involve the heavy participation of parent and community groups and volunteers, which places it in the private mode. It may become a political cause célèbre if a major conflict arises, but, otherwise, it would have little effect on the public mode.

Choosing new reading materials is clearly a decision in the bureaucratic-professional mode. That would probably require an objective review of the quality of the materials, as well as the participation of teachers through committees—perhaps including parent or community members. In some districts the structures for curricular decision making are determined in part through the bargaining process, but the decision itself is most likely to be treated as a rational process, with benefit to clients being the main objective.

It should be made clear that these modes are often mixed in practice. There are few decisions where participation patterns, criteria, or decision rules are restricted to one pure mode, as described above. What the modes provide is a classification technique or description of the patterns into which governance decisions tend to fall and a way of discussing relative distribution of power and sources of conflict over how decisions are made in school systems.

The Labor Relations Mode

The notion of a labor relations mode of governance draws first from John Dunlop's concept of an industrial relations system and the product of that system—a web of rules.[7] For schools that engage in bargaining, the web of rules from the labor relations mode is not the only one; there are also legal and professional rules. Because these webs partially overlap, some areas of schooling, such as discipline policies, may be covered by all three. Corporal punishment would, for example, be covered by legal and school board policy. Some discipline rules may be specified in the contract or prescribed by professional ethics (for example, not to lose control and strike a student in anger). Our analysis expands this overlapping "web of rules" concept and applies it to an institutional setting, rather than to society at large.

The administrator must deal in all modes and negotiate with each participant. Neil Chamberlain and Donald Cullen conceive management's unique role to be coordinator of bargains.[8] The administrator must balance one bargain against the other to keep the operation functioning. Bargains are often in different modes, each requiring varying skills. The public must be dealt with one way;

unions, another; students and parents, a third; and so forth. This view of administration guides our analysis. The intent here is to discuss how the administrator can coordinate bargains in the several modes in such a way as to keep a workable level of cooperation and still leave room for innovation and development.

Power and Conflict

Because we are dealing with modes of governance, power is a central concern. Participation, structures, and criteria differ for each mode, which means that there are differences in power. The ability of the union to affect outcomes is greater in the labor relations mode than in the others. In labor relations, all major events require union agreement. In public decision making, the union is one of many groups with influence, but usually no veto power. In the bureaucratic-professional mode, union members are participants, but in different roles and with different rules, and are constrained by professional norms. These differences in power and objectives are the key links among the modes of governance.

All four modes of governance must function together to some degree for a school system (or any other organization) to work at all. If differences in power and objectives led to nothing but conflict, the system would be paralyzed. Strikes or parents' protests are common examples of the consequences of intense conflict over governance. The resistance of individual parents to busing is a case of decisions made in a private mode (household or neighborhood group) coming into conflict with decisions made in a public mode (enforced by legislatures or courts). A school strike is generally the result of a school board refusing to shift funds or control from the public or bureaucratic-professional mode (school board policy) to the *labor relations mode* (the contract.) While these episodes are temporary, they emphasize the need for a minimum of cooperation among the modes of governance.

Cooperation across modes is problematic, however, since there are different structures and distribution of power among them. Administrators tend to make most of their decisions according to a bureaucratic-professional mode. Dale Mann's study of representational roles among administrators, for example, demonstrated that over 60 percent acted as trustees, that is, made decisions according to their own professional knowledge of what was best, while another

30 percent acted as delegates of the board, acting in the public or bureaucratic-professional mode.[9] In these modes political tradition and public legitimation give the administrator and the board greater power. That is why they are likely to resist shifting decisions to labor relations where their power is diminished.

There also tends to be a norm favoring rational approaches to decision making—the bureaucratic-professional mode—in school affairs, and elsewhere. How decision procedures and criteria are controlled is part of the power relationship. As Jeffrey Pfeffer notes, "In the allocation process, there are typically available a number of legitimate, objective criteria. Organizational members use power and influence to have those legitimate criteria selectively used that tend to favor their own relative positions."[10] There is likely to be a shifting of criteria and decision structures or a mixing of modes as participants seek to increase their own relative power in the decision process. There is not likely to be any long-term stable balance in this process. Rather, modes of governance, as well as relative influence, continuously shift as the circumstances and levels of conflict change.

Conflict and cooperation are, thus, the main forms of interaction between labor relations and the other elements of school governance. The forms and sources of conflict and cooperation are, therefore, central to the overall picture.

Bases of Conflict

Conflict is seen here as an interaction between organizations. The adversarial nature of bargaining in schools has been the main focus of other analyses, most notably Myron Lieberman and Michael Moskow's basic treatment of the subject,[11] and Charles Perry and Wesley Wildman's empirical work,[12] as well as Ronald Corwin's studies of militancy.[13] Four mutually incompatible actions or situations can be sources of conflict: limited resources, control of arrangements that influence the availability of or access to limited resources, role expectations, and values and ideologies.[14] Resources include not only physical goods and money but status and power as well. Status and power are not, of course, limited in the same sense that physical resources are. But status and power are meaningful only in situations where they are unevenly distributed. Their distribution in organizations is, therefore, a source of competition.

In an organizational setting there are structures and arrangements that affect access to, or power over, resources. A job, for example, is a scarce resource. An evaluation system that determines who will get a job is an organizational arrangement that strongly influences or controls the allocation of jobs. Participation in or control over the evaluation process can thus be as desirable as controlling access to the job itself.

Because organizations are the parties in labor relations, there can be conflict over differing role expectations. By way of illustration, one major source of role conflict arises for administrators directly involved in bargaining. They must maintain a cooperative, collegial relationship with the professional staff outside negotiations and an adversarial one at the bargaining table. Role conflicts can also affect teachers. Militant, strong support of a group can conflict with professional norms of autonomy and altruistic commitment to service.

Both the subject matter of education and its place in the political arena can make a value conflict inevitable. Commitment to local control of schools, for instance, is a major ideological battleground. Many see teachers' unions as usurping the traditional local control of schools, particularly where state or national teachers' organizations are active and visible. The question of whether public employees should have the right to strike is often argued on ideological grounds as well. Such ideological arguments are often combined with questions related to scarce resources or role conflict, making the resolution of conflict quite tricky.

Bases of Cooperation

While the potential for conflict in school labor relations is great, the purpose of the system is to resolve conflict and to maintain a workable agreement; this requires cooperation. The need to agree, an implicit part of the labor relations system, gives rise to the sharing of specific instrumental objectives in the labor relations system itself. For example, competition over scarce resources can be transformed into a cooperative search for new resources to meet the needs of both parties. Similarly, role conflict can sometimes be resolved by new organizational arrangements that are the result of a search by both parties to the negotiations. Both the generation of new resources and the changing of institutional arrangements in

the school are common examples of cooperative interactions between negotiations and other spheres of educational policy action.

Cooperation and conflict are obviously essential elements in the
governance process, but how they are manifested depends on the
substance at hand. The basic sources of conflict and power do not
change, but their operational expression does. And so it is necessary to examine in some detail the substantive components of
governance, especially in the labor relations mode.

COMPONENTS OF GOVERNANCE AND LABOR RELATIONS

The substance of labor relations in schools contains four main
elements: the wage-effort bargain, bargaining power and intraorganizational bargaining, union recognition, and decision participation. These are the main issues in the labor-management
relationship, and they link most directly to other modes of governance. They are also elements of the school situation that are similar
in many ways to labor relations in other settings. Some minor issues
arising in collective bargaining may not fit readily into this context,
but the basic process used in discussing this topic will apply generally to the rest of the bargaining.

The basis of the labor agreement is the *wage-effort bargain*.
The employer offers a wage in return for some level of effort.
In other words, "the contract is: work for pay."[15] But total compensation considerably exceeds the wage itself when contingent
benefits, such as health insurance, retirement plans, leaves, and
holidays, are included. The level of effort is also affected by a
number of variables that have direct cost consequences. In schools
this would be such things as class size and elements of working
conditions such as office space, clerical assistance, teachers' aides,
and other supportive staff. All of these have measurable economic
consequences and appear as costs to the employer. Because effort
is contingent on both work load and working conditions, these
factors are included in the general category of the wage-effort
bargain.

The wage-effort bargain reflects some specific action indicating
agreement between teachers and school boards. While they are
not always collectively negotiated, salary levels are usually uniform
for teachers at a given education and level of experience. The

salary schedule, which is uniform and applies to all the teachers whether or not there is a union, establishes the salary for each level. The agreement of the school board is expressed in formal adoption of the schedule; individual teachers accept an employment contract for the scheduled salary. Even in the absence of a salary schedule, there is a wage-effort bargain. But in those situations it would be between the individual teacher and the board on a case-by-case basis.

The recognition of an organization to represent teachers or other employees can be a problem in two ways. Where collective bargaining does not exist, the board of education must decide whether to recognize a bargaining unit for the teachers. In some states, school boards are required by statute to recognize and bargain with a representative of the teachers. In other states, such as Illinois, Ohio, and Utah, school boards may legally refuse to recognize or bargain with any teacher organization.[16] Where recognition itself is not an issue, the form and extent of recognition can cause controversy in a bargaining agreement. By recognizing a bargaining agent for an employee group, the board legitimizes and admits a new organizational actor to the policy-making process, sets up a new structure of relationships, and comes under an additional set of legal procedures and constraints governing the bargaining relationship.

Even where bargaining is well established, the problems related to recognition of an organization do not disappear. Teachers, along with most other employees, can change the representational organization. Whether the teachers in a particular school system are represented by an affiliate of the National Education Association (NEA), the American Federation of Teachers (AFT), or an independent union, other alternatives are always available to some degree. Every union leader knows that, if an organization represents the interests of its members badly, another group may step in, especially in the many areas where there is active competition between NEA and AFT state affiliates.

Just as union leaders know another organization can step in, they also know that other union members are waiting to take over as officers. The same reasoning applies to members of the school board and other representatives at the bargaining table, but the problem of representation in organizations is more complex.

Both sides of the bargaining dyad are in fact combinations of diverse interests. Richard Walton and Robert McKersie call the process through which the diversity internal to the organizations is reconciled "intraorganizational bargaining":

> The organizations participating in labor negotiations usually lack internal consensus about the objectives they will attempt to obtain from the negotiations, and this is especially true for the labor organizations. Different elements of the organization may have different ideas about the priorities assigned to the various objectives being pursued, or they may disagree on what should be minimally acceptable for the total contract. Disagreement can also exist around strategies and tactics . . . .[17]

The levels of disagreement within each side and the success of the representatives in reconciling these differences are tied in part to the governance and administrative structures of the schools. To the extent that they are, intraorganizational bargaining is part of the governance process.

The role of the teacher as a member of a labor organization is intimately tied to professionalism. Teachers as professionals are likely to have diverse opinions about what is best for the schools and for their job situation. But the ideology of professionalism also includes the concept of participation in the governance of the organization. Early in the teachers' unionism movement, militancy was considered antithetical to professionalism. More recently, however, militancy and professionalism have moved closer together, even though there is still variation among teachers' attitudes since militancy is in part dependent on such factors as age, experience, and family background.[18] These important differences among teachers in commitment to militant action, desire to participate in decisions, and desire for high professional status require the union to bargain intraorganizationally.

Sources of conflict and cooperation vary according to decision and action. The concepts of public, bureaucratic-professional, and negotiated decision modes allow us to examine the sources of conflict and cooperation in light of educational policy making and labor relations.

Wage-Effort Bargain and Resource Allocation

The wage-effort bargain between school boards and teacher groups is integral to the overall resource allocation function of both the school board and the administration. Teachers compete for resources with alternative uses within the school system, as well as with other public employees, for a share of the tax dollar. This competition is a central source of conflict among teachers, administrators, and school boards, as well as a source of cooperation among the antagonists. Resources flow to, and are distributed within, school systems by several means. Funds flow from federal, state, and local revenue systems. Budgets are made within schools. Staff, pupils, and physical goods are assigned. Because all of these decisions can affect the work load of employees and the funds available for wage bargaining, resource allocation decisions are a central link between labor relations and other modes of governance.

Federal Government

Because of the organization of the funding process at the federal level of government, conflict between teachers and other actors in the school system is minimized. Separate agencies within the United States Office of Education and other education-related parts of the executive branch deal with separate areas (education of the handicapped, vocational education, educational statistics, and so forth), and teachers and administrators in each separate area advocate their own special interest.[19] Teachers and clients of, say, vocational education, cooperate to influence executive agencies on behalf of their special programs. There is no single body representing teachers and administrators at the broader level of the entire profession, and controversy over broader questions is not related to the problem of the wage-effort bargain or other aspects of labor relations at the local level. The only possible exception to this would be labor conflict as a source of tension between teachers and administrative groups. If the tension were sufficiently high, it could interfere with the cooperative lobbying efforts of national organizations in Washington.[20] But the advocates themselves do not openly compete for funds at the expense of some other educational program. A united front is the general rule.[21]

Because competition for resources at the federal level is not directly related to labor relations issues at the local level, participation in the federal funding process is not organized around employer-employee groups but around the functional or programmatic divisions within education. The participation of teachers and employees is, therefore, more likely to be in a cooperative mode.

The structure of participation reflects this cooperative mode. The Committee for the Full Funding of Education, for example, is a coalition of interest groups formed to press for increased federal appropriations to education. Representatives of teacher organizations also sit with administrators on the many advisory committees that influence policy in federal executive agencies. The same is true of the many program-related interest groups that act as advocates for particular categorical programs. Access to participation may come through appointment by a teacher organization, such as the NEA, but the participation itself, where federal funding is involved, does not generally reflect the labor relations system.

The same reasoning applies to the criteria for what constitute good federal decisions. Since the interests are not clearly divided along lines related to labor relations, neither are the policy objectives. This is reflected in the national legislative objectives of both teachers' and employers' organizations. Where matters of funding are involved, there is, once again, generally a united front.

State and Local Funding

The mechanisms of state and local funding of education are so closely connected that their relationship to the wage-effort bargain cannot be usefully separated. A large proportion of the revenues of local schools comes directly from the state. The proportions vary from close to 90 percent in Hawaii to about 8 percent in New Hampshire, with the national average being around 43 percent.[22] What is more important is the fact that the mechanism of state support of education is directly tied to local financing, and the whole system is determined by the state legislature. The total amount spent on education and the allocation of those resources among alternatives within the school system are, thus, jointly determined by local school authorities and the state government.

The basic questions related to labor relations are the same for both levels: What will it cost to employ teachers? What is received in return? The two levels of government deal with the same policy problem. But the responsibility for allocating most resources is divided between local and state action. The state government determines how to generate revenues and the general purposes and functions to which resources are to be allocated. But determining wages and program expenditures remains the responsibility of the local school board. There are two major exceptions: the establishment of minimum or maximum salaries for all school systems in the state, or the provision of additional funds for the operational budget of local school systems to cover the cost of a wage agreement with the teachers' union. Usually, only large-city school systems can assemble enough political support in state legislatures to seek special funding successfully, but such direct interventions are only a small part of the finance process. Indirect links between the process of wage determination at the local level and the operation of the overall school finance system are more significant.

Participants and Objectives

Financing and the wage-effort bargain involve the same types of participation. At the local level, individual school boards and administrators bargain with individual teachers' organizations. The school boards are influenced by parent and other interest groups, as well as by local and state governments. Many studies of school finance and politics at the state level have identified the same set of major actors. At the state level they are state teachers' organizations, the school boards' association, and so forth. As the actors are closely related, so are the interests. Nothing has illustrated this more forcefully than changing relationships among the major state-level educational interest groups in places where there has been serious conflict involving collective bargaining. In those states there had been patterns of cooperation among school-related organizations in seeking increased funding. But the pressures of adversary relationships and the divergent interests growing from the labor relations process have caused some of these coalitions to disappear, and conflict has increased among associations in states where coalitions did not form.[23]

The officers and staff of state school boards and of teachers' and administrators' organizations can be key actors in the determination of state policy. They convey the interests of their constituents to the elected officials. They organize lobbying efforts by the members. They maintain active newsletters, telephone communication, and other contacts between their membership and the legislature. These are the same people who assist local school systems in the conduct of labor relations, especially where collective bargaining is difficult. These activities are designed to serve the interests of each organization's membership. Where the objectives of different memberships converge, there can be cooperation among the organizations; where they diverge, conflict is, of course, the result.

On the basic question of funding education relative to the rest of the state budget, the common interest of all school groups is clear, but it is not always reflected in the manner of seeking resources. A pattern has emerged in which the process of seeking educational funding at the state level has come to reflect the labor relations process at the local level. The central problem at both levels is the same: to convince the taxpayer or legislator that the requested resources should be assigned to schools instead of to other uses and that tax rates should be maintained or increased. The pattern in some places has been for all educational interests to unite in an effort to influence the public decision makers. This pattern is being replaced by one where employers take a tough stand on wage demands based on budget constraints. Then strikes, strike threats, or the political influence of large teachers' organizations are mobilized to force public decision makers to increase the available budget. The specific tactics may vary from state to local levels, but the basic strategy is the same.[24]

Distinguishing conflict from cooperation in this dynamic requires closer analysis. One key factor is how strongly the employer—the school board—is motivated to increase or decrease costs. When bargaining in the private sector, there is a need to keep labor (and other) costs down because the market for a firm's products is competitive, and there is a desire on the part of owners to receive as great a return on their investment as possible. If costs get too high, prices must increase. Then the firm's products cannot compete in the market, and both sales and profits suffer. That is why both managers and owners are strongly motivated to control labor costs. In cases where labor costs rise, management may even have the option of replacing some of the workers with less costly machines. Banks, for instance, have installed computer terminals that perform many of a teller's functions.[25]

In public institutions the matter is less clear. There are real limits to what taxpayers will tolerate, but that limit is not precisely known. Nor is it clear whether any particular public official wants to minimize costs. In a given situation peaceful labor relations might be more important than holding down the price of a wage settlement. Public officials may even advocate a particular program or expenditure category and favor increased salaries and the allocation of other resources for that purpose. There are certainly school board members who see themselves as champions of education and favor expanding budgets and increasing salaries to attract the best teachers. Other school board members see themselves as guardians of the public purse; they feel they were elected to keep taxes as low as possible. There are also members who are less interested in any particular expenditure level and more concerned with maintaining or increasing their base of support. Depending on the particular situation, the political orientation of some board members would lead them to take a tough stand or to make concessions in the interest of a peaceful settlement. Certainly the same can be said for legislators and other state officials.

Policy and Bargaining Structures

Many aspects of the state and local situation have significant implications for determining wage-effort bargaining in the schools. The organization of schooling into what are usually small, special-purpose governments with strong local ties is also a salient structural feature. The same is true of the number and distribution of membership in teachers' organizations at the state and regional levels. Lastly, the internal organization of budget making in the school affects the possibility that teachers can participate in fiscal decision making at the local level.

The structure of the school's finance system and the establishment of wage-effort bargaining are closely linked. The finance system is tied directly to the distribution of wealth and fiscal resources among the school districts in a state. Differences in the distribution of financial resources produce mixed motives and conflict in the process of wage bargaining. Important variables in both financing and wage determination vary substantially across a state. One of the most important is the variation in average salaries paid. Wages are highly correlated with ability to pay (local wealth) in most school systems, and so rich school systems pay more, in general, than poor ones.[26] That is why there are great regional differences in terms of competition for teachers and cost of living. Since any school finance decision at the state level has distributional consequences, the representatives of school boards and administrators are not likely to agree completely on what policy to support.

In some situations, the distributional aspects of state funding policies affect teachers' organizations also. The most obvious case is a state where NEA and AFT affiliates actively compete. AFT locals tend to be concentrated in urban areas, regions often differentially affected by the finance system. Urban-based AFT organizations would, therefore, advocate fiscal systems that favored the cities. In states where AFT membership is concentrated mostly in one or two major cities, the state organization may be largely uninterested in the overall state finance system and confine its activities to obtaining increased aid for the cities.

Interactions between bargaining and financial decision making extend to the local level as well, even though the structures are different from those at the state level. Revenues are raised and allocated locally through the tax-rate-setting and budget-making processes. One of the main resource allocations is the establishment of wage-effort bargaining; it is established in the bargaining mode. The wage-effort bargain has direct consequences for the school budget, and budget decisions can affect salaries and working conditions. It is useful, therefore, to think of the budget decisions as a combination of bureaucratic-professional, public, and negotiated decisions.

The public elements of the finance decision system extend from the state to the local level. For any particular state school finance system, the board affects the total amount of available resources by manipulating local revenue (or, to some small degree, seeking and obtaining additional state or federal grants). Often school boards must seek the approval of the electorate or some other governmental unit for the actual allocations in the budget. Those are the public elements of the finance process. The professional elements are the allocation of funds among programs and alternative uses for each classroom, school, and program area. The basic wage-effort element of the budget process is setting the amount to be offered as benefits to teachers and other employees. That figure is determined by the wage, fringe benefit, and working condition clauses in negotiated contracts, or by policies set by the board in the absence of a contract.

Individual teachers can participate in determining local resource allocations in each of the three modes. Obviously, as members of the labor organization, their input to the union position and willingness to support the organization contribute to the bargaining process. But teachers also participate as professional members of the formal and informal organization of the school. Budget preparation often includes the participation of teachers through the submission of budget requests in program areas, and participation in department- or building-level budget review processes. They can participate through local political activity, as well, either as members of the teachers' organization or some other citizens' group.

The expected objectives in these three modes of participation are somewhat divergent. A teacher, as unionist, is presumably concerned with maximizing individual benefits and achieving gains for the organization. A teacher, as professional participant in the budget preparation process, would be expected to act on behalf of the most efficient use of resources to obtain the educational objectives of the school system. A teacher, as lay citizen, could conceivably prefer lower taxes and thus lower salary costs. These differences in objectives are potential sources of role conflict for the individual teacher.

Possibilities for conflict in expectations also exist when school board members participate in the local wage-effort bargain as well. School boards can be seen in one light as advocates for more education, seeking the most resources possible for the schools from the public purse. But when those resources are going largely toward paying teachers' salaries, too eager an advocacy role can appear to be spineless capitulation to the selfish demands of the teachers' union. The board must somehow be a tough bargainer (directly or indirectly, through the person at the table) and claim that the public will tolerate no further spending. At the same time, it must seek funds from the public it paints as being so unwilling to pay. These conflicting expectations can lead to uncertainty on the part of individual board members and to disagreements among members of the same board. It is expected that there will be multiple and often conflicting objectives and tactics on the part of school boards and employers. That is, they cannot always agree on what would be a proper wage-effort bargain.

Another interaction of interest is in the competition for public resources among government employees who rely on the same tax base as the schools. This is particularly obvious in districts that are coterminous with other governments, such as cities, townships, or counties. The competition may be explicit when school budgets must go through the same channels as other services. Or the competition may be less visible if budget and tax-setting structures are separate. The consequences for the schools may be troublesome where the school budget is the only tax decision that goes to the electorate on a regular basis. It has been common in these cases for voters to express general resistance to rising taxes by defeating educational tax and bond issue referenda.

More extensive taxpayer resistance has appeared in the form of statewide referenda on tax rate ceilings or cutbacks. The first successful statewide action of this type was the California constitutional amendment passed by referendum in 1978 (the so-called Proposition 13). It limited local real estate tax rates to 1 percent of market value and caused substantial declines in local revenue in many cases. The immediate effect was the layoff of over eleven thousand employees of local governments and the idling of almost thirty thousand workers in the educational system when summer school was canceled. The longer-term effects are not yet known. Similar efforts to limit or cut back spending are underway in other states, either through constitutional amendments or legislation.[27] The overall effect is to increase the difficulty of raising revenues and to put more pressure on public officials to hold the line on wages.

Internal structures of the school may affect the wage-effort bargain as well. Some states, such as Illinois, have separate boards of education and administrative structures for elementary and secondary schools. In this situation it is common to find a wage differential in favor of secondary schoolteachers. Maintaining the differential may be an objective of the secondary teachers, and eliminating the differential may be an objective of the elementary organization.[28] Schools with a departmental organization (or similar internal division of function) often have pay differentials for teachers with administrative responsibility. Specialized teaching functions and counseling may also carry pay differentials, as may teaching positions funded largely by outside sources, such as special or vocational education. Similarly, the manner in which extracurricular and after-school programs are structured may determine the assignment of these duties and thus become a part of the wage-effort bargain. While these may be important matters in local situations, there is so much possible variation among school systems that an exhaustive treatment of all of the internal structural variations is not possible here. It is possible, however, to say that virtually any element of the internal organization of the schools can affect either the cost of teaching or the level of effort required. Whether or not each of these organizational issues does become a part of the process of negotiations is essentially a matter of how the scope of bargaining is determined—a question discussed in detail in Chapter 5.

Recognition

In one sense, the issue of union recognition and representation cannot be separated from either the wage-effort bargain or participation in making decisions. If recognition and representation did not imply a requirement that the board bargain and allow teachers expanded participation in making decisions, there would be no issue. But important consequences flow from these actions, so they become salient in their own right.

It would appear, on the surface, that recognition of a bargaining unit is a clear-cut matter; either a bargaining unit exists, or it does not. But the issues go deeper. Wage-effort bargaining and participation in decisions occur in every school, regardless of the existence of a formal bargaining process. Local teachers' associations, affiliated with the NEA, existed in thousands of school systems long before the AFT became a major force or before the NEA sanctioned bargaining and strikes. In a sense, they were and are recognized by the board of education since the associations typically meet on school property, often on schooltime. Even where bargaining does not exist, an association salary committee might informally discuss questions related to salaries and fringe benefits with the board. Committees of the associations might review curriculum questions and participate in other school-planning processes. The key differences between formal recognition and this informal activity are that no contract exists to bind the board and so the actions or decisions of the association are only advisory. The board retains full, formal authority and has the option to ignore the desires of the local association. This type of participation in making decisions is best described as being in the bureaucratic-professional mode.

Full board authority no longer exists where a board recognizes a bargaining agent for teachers and negotiates a contract. Loss or sharing of authority from the public or bureaucratic-professional mode, and the loss of power it implies, is a central issue in recognition and representation. Our interest is in how and why a school board relinquishes authority and enters into a bargaining relationship with an organization representating its professional employees.

Recognition is simply a formal board action agreeing to negotiate a contract with a representative (or representatives) of teachers (or another group of employees). It is not a commitment to agree on any particular issue or even necessarily a commitment to bargain in good faith; it is only an agreement to enter into the bargaining process. Recognition does imply that a bargaining unit exists, that is, that some organizational mechanism has been established to define membership in the unit, to choose persons who will represent the teachers' interests, and to secure the agreement of the teachers to the negotiated contract. The bargaining unit may be an affiliate of the NEA, or the AFT, or independent, or some combination of all three. The question of how representation works is the substance of intraorganizational bargaining for the teachers. Its connection with the rest of the school organization is explored here.

That connection can be described in terms of three modes of governance: public, bureaucratic-professional, and negotiated. Through the process of recognition and representation, the board of education transfers part of its authority to establish and implement school policy from the public and professional mode to the negotiated one. That is what agreeing to bargain means. That transfer implies changes in participation, structure, and objectives in the policy process. Two basic questions of participation are raised: Who is to participate in the recognition decision itself? And, through recognition and representation, who are the new participants in the policy process? The issues of structure are more numerous since moving to a formal negotiation process involves new legal and political machinery for the policy process. New objectives are introduced, from the teacher organization and from the bargaining relationship as well. These include the need to maintain the bargaining relationship and to satisfy the expectations of constituents as to how the bargaining process is to proceed.

Participation and Objectives

The fundamental question of participation concerns *who* makes the decision. There are a number of possible alternatives, given the variations in school policy making. There are also the related questions of whether this variety is to be maintained, or whether the same basic framework is to be imposed on all labor relations issues through federal legislation for all public employees. Since these two questions are rather closely related, they can be examined together.

Conflict arises over the question of who is to make representation decisions because, under different circumstances, the power could rest at different levels of government. The federal government has some power to regulate the relationships between state and local governments and their employees.[29] Although that power is limited, there has recently been pressure for federal legislation to regulate public employees' bargaining, and some bills have been introduced that teachers' organizations have actively supported. In the absence of federal legislation, however, the power to regulate state and local public employee relationships rests with the governors and legislatures of the states. Where no state provision exists, local option governs, and school boards are free to accept or reject bargaining.

As with any other governmental arrangement, these different structures confer differential advantages on the actors in the decision processes. Teachers' organizations have uniformly favored legislation at the state (and now federal) level mandating collective bargaining.[30] The more teachers are organized, the greater the organizational resources of the teachers' union. The more school districts bargain, the more teachers will organize. And, if it is possible to get all school districts in a state bargaining through one legislative act, this would mean that teachers' organizations would not have to devote resources to a district-by-district organization and recognition struggle. On the other hand, if the objectives of the school boards and administrators are to minimize the extent of bargaining and limit the interference of teachers in policy making structures, it is in their interest to oppose a state mandate. That would force teachers' unions to divert resources from bargaining to organization and recognition drives.

In states where school systems have mixed bargaining or no

bargaining, there will likely be mixed opinions. The teachers' organization that has the best chance to create new locals in unorganized districts or where nonbargaining affiliates exist would favor a state mandate for bargaining. But the effect of any new mandate on school systems that already bargain is uncertain. Those systems may be neutral or even oppose legislation since the advantages conferred by some new, externally imposed structure might change the balance of power.

Along with disputes over legal arrangements, there are ideological bases for recognition conflict. The ideological commitment to local control of schools is particularly strong among school board members and local administrators. Legislation that limits local discretion in matters of recognition and representation also diminishes local control. Not only is the decision moved to a higher level of government, but the legislation typically constrains the participation of school management in the choice of representation. The right of workers to self-determination of representation is firmly established in both federal and state statutes governing collective bargaining. There seems to be less need for support of localism among teachers' organizations than among boards and administrators.

There is also an ideological commitment among school officials to what we have called "bureaucratic-professional criteria" in making school decisions. That is, choices of educational policy and action should be based on "what's best for the kids," as determined in some objective way. This ideology is sometimes expressed as a desire to keep schools out of politics, where, presumably, partisan interests and self-interest replace the good of children as objectives. Recognition of a bargaining agent necessarily implies moving at least some educational policy matters out of the bureaucratic-professional and more into the negotiated policy sphere where objective criteria no longer control. Teachers argue that this will aid students since bargaining improves the lot of teachers and, thus, their performance. The other side argues that teachers' self-interest replaces concern for the good of their students. Since there is little evidence to support either position, the conflict is best classified as ideological.

SCHOOL POLICY AND THE BARGAINING STRUCTURE

Recognition of a bargaining agent implies both the shift of decisions into the negotiated sphere and the redefinition of some roles in the school structure. An adversarial relationship between teachers and the administration is institutionalized. To the extent that administrators accept norms of collegiality and consensus regarding teachers, the adversarial relationships produce conflicting demands. One is, presumably, open and cooperative with colleagues, sharing information and resources freely. One is, presumably, guarded and hostile with adversaries, holding information and resources closely and demanding quid pro quo in all interactions. A school or other organization cannot operate if a relationship continues to be overwhelmingly adversarial; even the bargaining process requires both adversarial and collaborative elements. As Walton and McKersie point out, "labor negotiations present few pure-conflict issues and few problems which individually allow parties direct mutual gain."[31] Administrators, board members, and teachers must, therefore, accommodate conflicting expectations for the type of relationships they must maintain.

Formal recognition also legitimizes the teacher organization as another authority structure in the school policy system. This can create or exacerbate role conflict in adversarial and collaborative relationships. In any school district there is an informal authority structure that includes members of the teaching staff. And there is likely to be a teacher organization in the more formal sense in most school systems, regardless of the status of bargaining. The informal social system of the school provides motivation, job satisfaction, and support. "Collective alliances," Sergiovanni and Carver hold, "are simply attempts to formalize informal groups and relationships . . . [which] exist to help teachers make a better adjustment to their school lives by satisfying human needs and by protecting teachers from a potentially, if not actually, hostile organization."[32] Corwin takes the idea a step further by proposing that, "as teachers as a group develop more cohesiveness they will develop autonomy with respect to both administrators and laymen outside the organization."[33]

An organization that provides autonomy and protects teachers from the organization of the school makes conflicting demands on teachers and administrators. Teachers may be asked to choose between allegiance to the union or to the school institution, as in a work stoppage. Administrators may recognize the positive contributions to teacher effectiveness and wish to encourage loyalty to the peer group, but at the risk of encouraging allegiance to alternative authority. This particular type of role conflict can appear in many aspects of school governance, especially participation in making decisions.

Participation in Making Decisions

Two characteristics of schools are central to the place of labor relations in making decisions. One is the fact that schooling is a labor-intensive process. The other is that the primary work force — those who do the main job of the enterprise — consider themselves to be, or aspire to become, professionals. Much of the organizational structure and patterns of practice in schools is consistent with the notion of the teacher as professional and provides a major basis for conflict and cooperation in the labor relations system.

The labor-intensive and professionalized nature of the schooling process is a pervasive concern in labor relations. The teacher, along with co-workers, manages the school activities of a group of children. And, although there is immense variation among teachers and school situations, some generalizations about that work are possible. First, there is seldom close supervision. The teacher's minute-to-minute decisions and choice of teaching technology are largely not, therefore, externally directed. Teachers also have wide discretion in dealing with children, as well as discretion in assigning relative emphasis among the general objectives set down at the administrative levels of the system. In addition, individual teachers or work groups (such as a department) choose among multiple technologies (different texts, materials, methods, and so forth). Teachers make these decisions based on their specialized training, experience, and concern for the good of their students, and it is these aspects of teaching that characterize it as a profession.[34]

The labor-intensive nature of teaching is simply an expression of the resources used, most of which are the activities of people, rather than machines, in contrast to, say, an airline. The large amounts of discretion exercised by teachers increase the labor-intensive nature of their work and affect the allocation and use of the principal resources of the school system—teachers' and students' time.

Any conflict that arises in terms of labor relations is not over whether teachers should make important decisions in the operation of schools; that is already a basic characteristic of the system. Instead, the issues arise over expansion of teachers' discretion into areas previously closed to them; reduction of teachers' discretion, that is, the removal of decision-making authority; or transfer of the main locus of decision from the public or bureaucratic-professional mode into the negotiated one.

The conflict involved here can be considerably more complex than conflict in the wage-effort bargain. Teachers may want to participate in decisions regarding the allocation of scarce fiscal resources, but all decisions have some fiscal consequences. Conflict in this area can arise over moving teacher evaluation policy questions from the sphere of public policy into that of negotiation, for the evaluation of teachers affects salary and promotion. But the conflict can also be over ideology or role concept. The ideology of professionalism, for example, includes a commitment to evaluation by peers rather than by supervisors or clients. Moving evaluation to the negotiations mode moves it closer to congruence with a professional ideology.

The bases for cooperation are just as complex, although cooperation, given the pattern of shared decisions just outlined, is also a component of any school operation. Part of the need for cooperation grows from the nature of the teaching process itself. Teachers' actions must be individualistic, flexible, and tailored to the diverse needs and characteristics of their pupils. School policy and rules must be more general and inflexible to meet the more universal objectives of larger communities. Articulation of the general with the specific requires the close and continuous cooperation of the teachers, among themselves and with the administrative structure of the schools. And, with respect to the educational substance of schooling, teachers, administrators, and members of the school board share the same basic concern for the achievement of the pupils. Instead of concentrating on the broad base of cooperation, we have selected areas of direct conflict that involve collective bargaining, participation in making decisions, and the operation of schools. Each area is outlined to show the interactions between collective bargaining and the overall structure of school governance.

Personnel Evaluation and Dismissal Procedures

Evaluation of staff is the means through which management defines what is desired behavior and promotes that behavior among the employees. Without the carrot of promotion and salary increase or the stick of discipline or dismissal, the process of employee evaluation would have little power. But these are not strictly management tools. Teachers are strongly interested in evaluating their own performance, and, as a profession, they are concerned with discipline and dismissal of their members. Lortie has provided pointed evidence of teachers' frustration and concern for evaluation. The teachers he interviewed said:

I feel like chucking it all—at times it all means nothing to me. I do what I feel I ought to do. No one can ever know how it affects the students, no one can know what they're thinking, or how my teaching affects them now or in the future. There are so many intangibles.

It is very difficult to evaluate a teacher . . . One teacher may be marvelous at getting across subject matter—the children may have suffered every minute they were in there but they learned something. Another teacher may not teach quite as much, but what she teaches, she teaches well and certain ideas that she gets across to them have very lasting value, though they might forget little things that she taught them. Self-evaluation is the most difficult of all.[35]

Teachers' organizations are also interested in achieving the best performance from their members, but not at the expense of what they have gained in the wage-effort bargain. Organizational objectives also include maintaining fair procedures for teachers, ensuring due process in dismissal, gaining increased peer control over teacher evaluation, and enhancing the job security of members. Maximizing management control and productivity is at least partially incompatible with achieving further teacher control and job security, and it is these incompatibilities that are the sources of conflict.

Evaluation and dismissal procedures are related to control of two scarce resources in the school system: *fiscal*, implied in the jobs themselves, and *status and power*, involving the assignment of rewards and punishment within the school system. Because both are valued items, controlling the arrangements concerning them can become competitive. When teachers participate in evaluation decisions, management's discretion is constrained (except in the unlikely event that teachers and administrators have precisely the same objectives). As evaluative procedures become part of the contract and are subject to negotiations, they are removed from the bureaucratic-professional mode of governance, and even the technical aspects of evaluative methods can be decided on bargaining-related grounds rather than objective criteria. The process of evaluation can also become directly linked with the machinery for contract administration and more closely associated with the grievance procedure. This is a negative consequence from the management perspective insofar as it constrains individual school administrators from applying evaluative processes in ways that fit the administrator's objectives. From the teachers' perspective, the argument runs that performance would be improved to the extent that teachers collaborate since teachers would then have greater understanding of, and support for, the evaluative process, which would increase their motivation.

The teacher's role in setting objectives is worth closer examination. As any workers, especially professional ones with long periods of training behind them, teachers have substantial investments in their own knowledge, teaching techniques, and prepared materials. While this investment cannot be precisely valued, the difficulties encountered in attempting innovations that threaten these investments are adequate testimony to their importance.[36] There are, of course, educational objectives implicit in teaching skills and behaviors, as well as arrangements. If these are the same as the objectives of an evaluative procedure, conflict is less likely. But, again, an exact matching of objectives is quite unlikely. That is why teachers are motivated to participate in and affect the evaluative process. They want to bring it more into line with their own objectives and professional investments. This is not meant to imply that teachers refuse to change or make new investments—only that these changes are costly and likely to be resisted at least to some degree by many teachers. Conflict of this sort is inherent in the nature of the teaching staff as the major human capital resource of the school system.

Curriculum

Participation in curriculum decisions is also related to teachers' status as the major component of the work force. The curriculum plan of the school system largely determines what teachers are to do. Thus, it is a central factor in the working environment of teachers and a fit subject for bargaining. At the same time, however, the curriculum is the expression of the objectives and policies of the school board and school clientele and is, therefore, their prerogative.

Teachers are typically involved to some degree in curriculum planning and development (but not necessarily as part of collective bargaining process), but the major objectives and subject choices are made by school boards and often by state or federal legislation.[37] And so it is obvious that sharing of decisions and control is already built in to some degree. The issues in bargaining revolve around the degree to which sharing is part of the negotiations mode or reserved to the bureaucratic-professional and public mode of school governance.

If it were possible to distinguish clearly between "policy" and "implementation" in curriculum matters, the issue of who should control which decisions would be less important. Objective and value-based decisions on curriculum questions could be made in the public mode by the board and other governments. The bureaucratic-professional mode would then provide optimal means to achieve the stated ends and advance the preferred values. Where the means touched on the wage-effort bargain in important ways, instrumental questions could be reviewed in the bargaining process. But the teacher is the main instrument in any curriculum, and the values and objectives cannot be separated from the means. There is, moreover, a question of professional status. The training of teachers includes attention to what should be taught as well as to how it is taught. So teachers have their own ideas of what the curriculum should be and what objectives should be pursued. These ideas may conflict with the school clientele, even if collective bargaining is not involved.

In light of the ambiguity about where curriculum decisions belong and how means can be separated from ends, it is useful to describe a continuum of curriculum decisions ranging from those that are clearly policy to those that are clearly instrumental, with several demarcations along the way. Choices at the policy end are abstract, value laden, and can be implemented in a variety of alternative ways. Choices at the instrumental end are highly specific, concrete, based on objective criteria, and operational. The choice to offer a course of instruction in astronomy, for example, would clearly be a policy decision. What kind of telescope to purchase for a course would clearly be a bureaucratic-professional decision. If teaching astronomy meant that teachers had to return to work in the evenings (when the stars are visible), compensation for that would clearly be related to working conditions and a fit topic for negotiation.

When the choices are as clear as these, little conflict is likely. The problems arise when the choices are more ambiguous: At what grade level should the astronomy course be offered? Should a new teacher be hired or a present staff member be directed to prepare to teach the new course? Should an astronomy unit be inserted in the present courses for all teachers? In matters like these, arguments over ideology and available resources can arise.

Role conflict and competition for resources are closely related in this area. One set of role expectations for teachers includes a commitment to improvement of instruction as a part of altruistic service to the children. Curricular innovations that promise improved instruction but imply great costs to individual teachers create an uncomfortable situation. Resisting new programs on the grounds of high personal cost violates the norm of selflessness. But the professional norms of self-determination and autonomous expertise offer an alternative. Teachers can aim at channeling curriculum decisions through processes that afford effective control of costs at the same time they seek improved instructional methods; collective bargaining is such a process.

This does not mean that teachers commonly seek to have curriculum decisions included in the bargaining process. That would be a direct frontal assault on the policy-making role of the board and would be likely to spark intense conflict, both on ideological and strictly legal grounds. The relevant negotiations issue is the structure of curriculum decision making, particularly the role of teachers in those processes. Fundamentally, this is an ideological conflict over lay as opposed to professional control. It can be translated into a deliberation over decision-making structures and the relative advantages conferred on each party by any particular feature of the structure. Structures that allow teachers veto power over curricular changes would, for example, be clearly to the advantage of the union. In contrast, a structure that made teachers a small minority in a curriculum council composed also of parents and administrators may place the board in a stronger position to control outcomes.

Another key element in the structure of curricular decisions involves incentives for teachers to review and revise the curriculum.

Many incentives and procedures could fall into the working conditions category: Are teachers required to attend curriculum-planning meetings after school? Do teachers receive extra pay (or release time) for curriculum development work? How will assignments to curriculum work be controlled (that is, within or outside of the contract)? These are basic questions related to resource allocation and competition that would generate conflict whether or not they were part of the bargaining process. Then there is the additional problem of disagreement among the parties as to whether these are proper matters for bargaining.

Discipline

As with curriculum, questions related to student disciplinary policy have the potential to spark conflict. Handling discipline problems is part of the day-to-day job of teaching, so disciplinary policy and procedure are integral to working conditions, but disciplinary policy decisions are expressly reserved to the school board in most state school codes. Because disciplinary policies reflect community values and objectives, they are in the public decision mode, but the bureaucratic-professional mode is also directly involved since disciplinary procedures should be designed as part of the overall instructional program and work to achieve specific instructional objectives, as well as maintaining control. The matter of control is also related to a teacher's personal security on the job and the presence of violence in schools. Finally, disciplinary procedures involve relationships between teachers and administrators in the areas of evaluation of teaching and authority.

The way disciplinary policy and bargaining interact depends on the nature of the problem. One type of discipline, "instructional discipline," is part of the teaching function and is administered directly by teachers while working with students. It relates to maintaining a classroom atmosphere conducive to good instruction and obedience to teachers' instructions and assignments.[38] The other major type, "institutional discipline," involves order and personal security in the overall school operation. It consists of rules against such acts as running in halls, smoking, leaving the building during the day, carrying knives, and so forth. In both areas teachers and administrators employ punishment procedures to control or promote certain student behaviors. To be credible and effective, disciplinary actions must be supported by the school authority structure, but the two types involve different aspects of the teacher-school governance relationship.

Instructional discipline varies from teacher to teacher, class to class, subject to subject, even child to child. So what is "proper" instructional discipline is left to the discretion of the individual teacher and thus must vary greatly throughout a school system. Any disciplinary policy that attempted to enforce precisely uniform rules and behaviors across all teaching situations would be unrealistic. Yet teachers must be confident that their judgment will be supported by the punishment apparatus of the school system, which is controlled essentially by administrators. The administrator, by contrast, must limit discipline variation out of concern for maintaining consistent standards of fairness to children and adherence to overall school policies. Teachers do vary in terms of fairness, ability to control pupils, and adherence to general policy principles. That is why administrators cannot uniformly ratify teachers' disciplinary actions. Where there is disagreement on these grounds, some appeal procedure is common.

Instructional discipline is closely related to the teaching process, the relationships between teachers and administrators, and the level of effort expended by teachers in their classroom duties. It is in the interest of teachers that they participate in the making and administration of disciplinary policy. If that participation is part of the bureaucratic-professional mode of governance, the actors are individual teachers, administrators, and those specifically named in the discipline and punishment procedures of the school (such as parents, counselors, social workers, truant officers, and so forth). Resolution of specific conflicts may vary from school to school, or from time to time in the same school system. Keeping disruptive students out of class can reduce teacher effort and may increase achievement. Administrative backing increases teachers' autonomy, self-esteem, and efficacy in the eyes of the pupils (that is to say, because the teachers' threats are credible to those threatened, the threats are more effective). If the teacher is able to exclude problem pupils and shift responsibility to some other portion of the system for remediation of problems, the teacher's task is simplified.

By contrast, it is in the administrative interest to maintain some discretion in backing teachers' discipline actions, thereby reducing responsibility for resolving problems outside the classroom. Conflicts between teachers' actions and school policy must be resolved by the administrator, not the teachers. Resources must be found to provide remedial work for pupils excluded from regular instructional programs. Administrators may also wish to avoid confrontations with hostile students and parents. As the teacher's discretion in discipline matters increases, the administrator's diminishes. Resources must be shifted, indirectly, to assist the classroom teacher, and conflict resolution is shifted more to the administrative role. This means that the conflict involved between teacher and administrator is both resource and role based.

In addition, students punished are entitled to due process, and it must be provided by the school system. Disciplinary hearings and public participation in some punishment processes are required for certain severe cases (such as suspension, expulsion, and corporal punishment).[39] In this respect, the school governance structure is even further constrained. This, in turn, constricts the area of autonomy available to the teacher and provides more possibility for conflict between what the teacher feels is needed for proper discipline and what the administrative structure of the system can sanction.

When these conflicts enter the labor relations process, however, a new set of interactions is involved. The nature of bargaining and contract administration means that discipline issues handled in that context will be linked to nondiscipline matters as well. There can evolve two discipline administration channels: the formal authority structure of the school system and the grievance procedure for areas covered in the contract. Both involve teachers and administrators. But one (the grievance procedure) includes the teachers' organization as a formal actor, a strict set of procedures, and a narrow legal framework. Policies set in contracts constrain the administration from making changes within the life of the contract. Discipline questions can be resolved in bargaining only by trade-offs with other parts in the contract.

Conflict arising over institutional discipline is less complex. It has two main components: how the system will provide for individual teacher security from student violence and what demands are placed on the teachers for maintenance of institutional discipline. Both are basically questions involving competition for resources, although assignment of teachers as institutional disciplinarians (such as hall guards) is in part a professional role question. The presence of these actions in the negotiations mode interacts with others only insofar as the contract constrains decisions or reallocates resources away from other areas involved in institutional discipline.

Administrative backing of teachers' actions is a common source of conflict in schools.[40] Wherever a policy action affects teachers' autonomy, classroom practice, effort, or professional status, it has potential as an issue for participation in making decisions and, thus, for the bargaining process. But it is clear that the placement of any of these issues in the negotiations mode introduces the additional criteria and participants of the bargaining process into what are otherwise bureaucratic-professional decision areas. A narrower, more complex decision process (bargaining and grievance procedures) replaces bureaucratic-professional or public mechanisms. How well that mechanism works depends in part on the nature of the issues themselves. That we have discussed above. But success in bargaining depends in part on the internal conflict resolution of the parties themselves. That brings us to intraorganizational bargaining.

Representation and Intraorganizational Bargaining

Collective bargaining is, among other things, a representative process. The bargainers act on behalf of many interests—their own and others. And so understanding the total process depends in part on analysis of representation.

When used in the context of bargaining, the term can have multiple meanings. In its most basic sense, representation is a process by which one person (or group) acts in ways intended to serve the objectives of some other person or group as well as one's own. Parents can represent children, wives can represent husbands, and this happens in a variety of other situations beyond the formal representative processes of government. Representation is *political*, to use Easton's definition of the political process, when some person or persons from a group are seen as acting on behalf of that group in the authoritative allocation of values.[41] It can be a legal selection process, such as the election of a senator or a delegate to a political convention, or extralegal, such as might occur in a church or voluntary association. Within labor relations, representation can take on a much narrower meaning, referring to the process through which a labor organization is chosen to act on behalf of the workers in a particular industry or in relation to a particular employer. In this sense, the "representation election" is the voting process where workers choose an agent to represent them in bargaining and contract disputes.

Our main interest here is in political representation, of which the narrower form of union representation is just one example. The main elements of the political representation process are groups: the groups that select representatives and the assembly of representatives that makes decisions and conducts the business of labor relations. Teachers are one group; they select a bargaining agent. The voters of a school district are another; they select a school board. The board represents the voters; the bargaining agent represents the teachers. We can also distinguish groups within groups, such as militant versus nonmilitant teachers, conservative versus liberal board members, and so forth. For the labor relations process to work, a minimum level of consensus must be reached among these groups. Board and teachers must agree among themselves on objectives and tactics. The bargaining group must agree on the conduct of bargaining and eventually ratify a contract. How consensus is reached within teacher and board groups is the substance of representation and intraorganizational bargaining.

The manner in which these groups are represented in the bargaining and labor relations of the schools parallels the general governance processes in the system. Although the specific substance and structure may differ, the same basic political representation exists for the bargaining process and the rest of the school policy system.

Management

Conflict on the management side of bargaining arises from the same basic sources as conflicts between the parties: different objectives and expectations among the actors. The administration of the school is far from monolithic. While the school board is part of the governance structure, it is composed of part-time laypeople who are responsible for policy in the school system but devote only a portion of their time to those tasks. The administrative group is composed of the superintendent and central office administrators who work with the board on higher levels of policy administration, and the operational or building-level administrators who work with teachers and other workers in direct supervision of the instructional program. All of these administrative actors are affected in one way or another by the activities of factions and interest groups in the community served by the school. These interests may differ from each other as well as from the positions and policies of the school board and give rise to conflicts among the actors because of differences in role expectations or ideologies or competition for a position of advantage in the distribution of resources.

The relationships between board and administrative staff are the main sources of role and control conflict. There is, first of all, little consensus over what role the superintendent and board should play in the bargaining process. The conflict from the superintendent's perspective involves the different sources of authority in his role. Bidwell identifies three sources of authority in school administrative structure: public trust, bureaucratic role, and collegiality (among the instructional staff of the school).[42] A superintendent who takes a clear position on the management side as spokesperson for the school board in bargaining invokes authority through bureaucratic role and public trust, but diminishes collegiality by becoming an adversary of the teachers. By taking a neutral role, the superintendent may increase collegial authority but diminishes public trust and, by being cut off from the board, may also affect his or her bureaucratic role authority. In order for the management side of bargaining to achieve solidarity on the substantive issues of bargaining, these questions of role must be settled. To the extent that there is conflict over these basic role identifications between superintendents and school board, there will be interference with consensus on the substantive bargaining issues.

Conflict can also arise from division of authority within the administrative structure. There can be differences of opinion about how principals and other operational administrators are to fit in the management team. An important source of principals' authority is the collegial relationships with the teaching staff. Clear identification on the management side as an adversary of teachers can, therefore, have serious consequences for principals and other building-level administrators. Again, solidarity on the management side depends on a clear definition of these role expectations as well, so that conflict on that dimension can be resolved. The principals and supervisors are key middle managers in both overall and contract administration. Their role must be clear in order to be properly represented in the bargaining process.

The participation of board members in the bargaining process is another source of disagreement. Board members may differ in their interests in or ability to participate in the bargaining process. If some board members participate and others do not, cleavages can develop within the board itself that result from different knowledge and perception of the conduct of bargaining. As Schelling points out, a main component of bargaining power is the ability to bind oneself to a course of action.[43] A single board member as a bargainer cannot bind the rest during bargaining. A divided board does not present a firm stand to the opposition. It can also be more difficult for the negotiation team to control the flow of information to the board and public during negotiations if members of the board are negotiators.[44] Direct participation by board members in negotiations also can threaten the role of the superintendent as chief executive officer. Keeping both the board and the superintendent out of the bargaining process has the advantage of giving the bargaining team some tactical flexibility. It is easier, for example, for the chief negotiator to characterize the position of the board and superintendent if neither is present.

Representation also involves relationships across the bargaining table. There are two problems of conflict resolution: within the organizations and between them. For external bargaining to proceed compromises and concessions must be made between management and labor. That can only come through compromise and concession within each side's organization, through some representational process. But, if the representational process does not fit with the bargaining process, the necessary resolution of conflict is prevented or, at best, inhibited.

The representation process can mismatch the requirements of bargaining a number of ways. Aside from role conflicts, the management side can be divided ideologically, as, for example, on the closely related question of how board members are to represent the public interest. Harmon Zeigler and Kent Jennings studied school board members' feelings on their representational roles.[45] Most felt they were trustees, chosen to do what is best for the schools as they see it, rather than to follow the instructions or expressed desires of a constituency. But there were also many board members who viewed themselves as delegates, expected to act on the instructions and desires of their supporters. Disagreements as to representational role can divide the board and cause conflict with administrators and the school clientele.

The bargaining relationship has certain basic requirements that are more consistent with the role of trustee than that of delegate. Bargaining takes place in closed session, usually with clear ground rules restricting external communications during the process. To maintain consensus on one side, it may often be necessary for public information on the terms of an agreement to be kept vague. Concessions must be made, and some demands traded off against those of the opponent. The interpersonal relationship among the bargainers themselves may be fragile and sensitive to the actions of "outsiders." All of these factors suggest restricted participation in the bargaining and restricted flow of information from the process.

This is not consistent with a delegate orientation in the board or similar expectations from the clients of the school. A delegate cannot receive instructions on issues of which constituents are ignorant. Constituents with a special objective will be unlikely to compromise when their objective is traded off for some concession in which they have little interest. A board member chosen to represent, say, a Spanish-speaking faction would be unlikely to agree to trade an expanded bilingual program for a clause concerning new teacher aides. Moreover, a clientele composed of active interest groups that sees the members of the board as delegates will be more likely to press for so-called "sunshine laws" requiring public bargaining and multilateral participation in bargaining, with even parents' unions at the table.

In contrast, the role of trustee for board members fits with the basic requirements of bargaining in the usual sense. This suggests that structuring a successful bargaining system requires attention to the expectations of the constituent groups for representational roles. It may even mean adaptation of the traditional mode of bargaining to fit the requirements of a local situation. While there has been some experience with "sunshine laws" and some attention to multilateral bargaining, too little is yet known to suggest what effects they have on the processes or outcomes of bargaining.

Two other ideological divisions in the school clientele relate directly to bargaining. An orientation toward community development and decentralization of government (and schools) is at least partly incompatible with social (and racial) integration.[46] This issue is usually tied to a desire for more direct lay control (as opposed to professional control) of school policy. Decentralization is usually seen as a means of enhancing lay control and diminishing the power of professional bureaucracies. Of course, both decentralization and increased lay control have been vigorously opposed by teachers, particularly in the bargaining process. As representative of the clients, the board must balance its objectives on these issues with the necessity to reach agreement with teachers. In some urban areas, such as New York and Detroit, this issue has complicated bargaining and led to bitter confrontations.

Distributional Issues

Disagreements on decentralization and lay control of schools are not strictly ideological in origin. They have important implications for the board in bargaining over allocation of resources in the schools, particularly in relation to control over hiring and assignment policies. What is involved are advantages in the policy-making process that can be used to influence the distribution of resources in favor of one party or another. Variables that appear to have some importance in allocating resources are size of the bargaining unit, tax effort or burden, residential distribution of minority groups, and criteria for membership in the bargaining unit.

Other things being equal, there appear to be important links between size of the bargaining unit and bargaining advantage. Teachers' unions oppose decentralization, which places personnel policies in the hands of many small units within large cities. Assuming a relatively homogeneous membership, the advantages to the teachers of a centralized organization are clear: a broader base of dues-paying members to support bargaining activities, greater impact of a strike or slow-down, and more diversity and internal dissension on the management side.

The effects of size on the board side of bargaining are less clear. Some factions with strong support in subsections of the district may favor decentralized personnel administration and bargaining. This would be particularly true in large districts. But other factions would favor centralized administration, especially organizations with established lines of communication and influence with a central board of education.[47]

The distribution of tax burden in a school system may be another source of conflict. Not all residents of a school district have the same preferences or ability to pay for public schooling. Some simply have less income. Some (large property owners) are more vulnerable to school taxes. Then there are families with many young children that benefit more from school services, and so forth. Different levels of spending obviously have varying impacts, so the board must form a working consensus with the economic as well as the ideological factions of the district. Because bargaining is the central resource allocation process of the school system, the same economic factions that have a general interest in school financing would also have a particular interest in a salary settlement.

The political faction which has the most direct and personal interest in the outcome of bargaining is, of course, the teachers' organization. Its most direct influence in those outcomes is through normal bargaining mechanisms. Teachers, like any group of citizens, may, however, act as an organization to influence the decisions of public officials. At the local level, teachers' organizations may influence the outcome of bargaining indirectly by political actions directed toward the school board or other elements of local government. Supporting or opposing candidates for the school board is one direct means. While this has not been a common action of teachers, it has been a tactic in some areas where the stakes were large, such as in the election of community school board members in New York City.[48] Teachers may also attempt to influence other governments that affect the bargaining or budget processes for the schools, such as the mayor of a city school system.[49] In addition, teachers may try to influence local bargaining through the state legislature by lobbying for specific bargaining legislation or for changes in financing so that more funds are available for bargaining at the local level. In fact, the record of teachers' organizations in legislative activities at the state level has been rather good.[50] And, of course, any other channel of influence normally available in the political process is available to teachers' organizations seeking to affect board policies outside bargaining.

There is some question as to the desirability and the effectiveness of this manner of political activity by teachers and other government

employees. One side of the argument, represented most compre-
hensively by Wellington and Winter, holds that, by virtue of their
special position in the bargaining, especially by use of the strike as
a weapon, public employees' unions distort the political process and
force contracts that are not good public policy. Because of their
strength, these unions dominate what should be, as the argument
goes, a pluralistic political process, with all interests given a fair
chance to influence the outcomes. In the opinion of Wellington and
Winter, the strike is the key:

The private sector strike is designed to exert economic pressure on the employer
by depriving him of revenues. The public employee strike is fundamentally different; its sole purpose is to exert political pressure on municipal officials. They
are deprived, not of revenues but of the political support of those which are in-
convenienced by a disruption of municipal services. But precisely because the
private strike is an economic weapon, it is disciplined by the market and the benefit/
unemployment trade-off that imposes. And because the public employee strike
is a political weapon, it is subject only to the restraints imposed by the political
process and they are on the whole less limiting and less disciplinary than those of
the market.[51]

They feel that this may have such a distorting effect on the political
system that public employees' strikes will become "an institutionalized means of obtaining and maintaining a subsidy for union members."[52] The strike is not, of course, the only means of exerting
political influence. But the strike is seen as the central source of
union power from which the other means of political intervention
flow.

That unions of public employees participate in the political
process is not challenged. That they are as effective as Wellington
and Winter argue is less clear. The results of the distortion claimed
should include much higher salaries in governments with unions
(or which allow strikes) than in those without. What evidence there
is on this question is far from conclusive, but it usually shows that
union activity has little effect.[53] The lack of market constraints
is not true for all types of public activity, and governmental services
are not uniformly essential. For example, Burton and Krider contend that government functions can be separated according to how
essential they are, with prohibition of strikes for some, such as
police and fire services, but with others, such as teachers, parks,
and so forth being allowed to operate much as they might if they

were in the private sector.[54] In fact, some services, such as refuse collection, could be placed in the private sector through contracting, relieving the municipal government of direct responsibility for labor relations in that area. Education seems to fall somewhere between the strictly essential service, and the one that can be easily contracted out. So there may be some rationale for some constraints on strikes by teachers, but strict prohibition of strikes is more difficult to justify. And legal prohibitions, besides being ineffective in eliminating strikes, may also have little deterrent effect.

That leaves open the question of how much power teachers' organizations (or other groups of public employees) should have, which is best left to the political arena. This discussion simply recognizes the importance of employees' groups as a political force in affecting the bargaining relationship. Because they are connected with local, state, and national labor organizations, employees' unions have the mechanisms at hand to affect management by directly pressing demands on the policy-making process. Management, too, has the means to resist and have impact on its own, as do other participants in the political arena. We see no single best answer to the question of balancing power among them, but this is not a labor-management issue per se. As we have tried to show, the public and bureaucratic-professional modes are linked to bargaining in many ways. And the power that either side can exert in bargaining depends on the larger political structure. So the overall balance question is one for that structure as well. In other words, one should not attempt to achieve an overall balance of power among the many actors in school governance by manipulating the labor relations mode alone. That mode is best left to function as freely as possible, with imbalances in political power adjusted through the larger political process.

NOTES

1. Gerald E. Sroufe, "Evaluation and Politics," in *The Politics of Education*, Seventy-sixth Yearbook of the National Society for the Study of Education, Part I, ed. Jay D. Scribner (Chicago: University of Chicago Press, 1977), 290.

2. Harold D. Lasswell, *Politics: Who Gets What, When, How* (New York: McGraw-Hill, 1936).

3. Edward C. Banfield, *Political Influence* (New York: Free Press, 1961).

4. These follow from J. R. P. French, Jr., and B. H. Raven, "The Bases of Social Power," in *Studies in Social Power*, ed. D. Cartwright (Ann Arbor: University of Michigan Press, 1959).

5. See Frank W. Lutz and Laurence Iannaccone, *Public Participation in Local School Districts* (Lexington, Mass.: D. C. Heath, 1978), esp. chs. 1 to 6.

6. William B. Castetter, *The Personnel Function in Educational Administration* (New York: Macmillan, 1976).

7. John T. Dunlop, *Industrial Relations Systems* (New York: Henry Holt, 1958), p. 13.

8. Neil W. Chamberlain and Donald E. Cullen, *The Labor Sector*, 2d ed. (New York: McGraw-Hill, 1971), 223-225.

9. Dale Mann, *The Politics of Administrative Representation* (Lexington, Mass.: D. C. Heath, 1976). The same results are reflected in L. Harmon Zeigler and M. Kent Jennings, with Wayne Peak, *Governing American Schools: Political Interaction in Local School Districts* (North Scituate, Mass.: Duxbury, 1974).

10. Jeffrey Pfeffer, "Power and Resource Allocation in Organizations," in *New Directions in Organizational Behavior*, ed. Barry M. Staw and Gerald R. Salancik (Chicago: St. Clair Press, 1977).

11. Myron Lieberman and Michael Moskow, *Collective Negotiations for Teachers* (Chicago: Rand McNally, 1966).

12. Charles R. Perry and Wesley A. Wildman, *The Impact of Negotiations in Public Education* (Worthington, Ohio: Jones Publishing Co., 1970).

13. Ronald G. Corwin, *Militant Professionalism* (New York: Appleton-Century-Crofts, 1970).

14. This follows from the fundamental sources of conflict discussed in Kenneth E. Boulding, *Conflict and Defense: A General Theory* (New York: Harper and Row, 1962).

15. Edwin F. Beal, Edward D. Wickersham, and Philip Kienast, *The Practice of Collective Bargaining* (Homewood, Ill.: Richard D. Irwin, Inc., 1972), 325.

16. The legal structure of school bargaining is covered in detail in Chapter 4. For an overview of state bargaining laws, see Doris Ross, *Cuebook: State Education Collective Bargaining Laws* (Denver, Colo.: Education Commission of the States, 1978).

17. Richard E. Walton and Robert B. McKersie, *A Behavioral Theory of Labor Negotiations* (New York: McGraw-Hill, 1965), 281.

18. Corwin, *Militant Professionalism*, 173-197. See also Joseph A. Alutto and James A. Belasco, "Determinants of Attitudinal Militancy among Teachers and Nurses," *Industrial and Labor Relations Review*, 27:2 (January 1974), 216-227; and Stephen Cole, "Unionization of Teachers: Determinants of Rank and File Support," *Sociology of Education*, 41:1 (Winter 1968), 66-87.

19. These groups are described in detail by Stephen K. Bailey in *Education Interest Groups in the Nation's Capital* (Washington, D.C.: American Council on Education, 1975).

20. The overall process of federal policy making for education is discussed at length by Norman C. Thomas, *Education in National Politics* (New York: McKay, 1975).

21. While educational interest groups may be competitive on other grounds, they share a common interest in federal funding. See *ibid.*, 135-145.

22. *Digest of Educational Statistics, 1979* (Washington, D.C.: U.S. Government Printing Office for the National Center for Education Statistics, U.S. Department of Health, Education, and Welfare, 1979), 70.

23. This process has received considerable attention in the literature. In particular, see Frederick M. Wirt and Michael W. Kirst, *Political and Social Foundations of Education* (Berkeley, Calif.: McCutchan, 1975), esp. ch. 7; Michael Usdan, "The Role and Future of State Educational Coalitions," *Educational Administration Quarterly*, 5 (1969), 25-42; and Michael A. Cohen, Betsy Levin, and Richard Beaver, *The Political Limits to School Finance Reform* (Washington, D.C.: Urban Institute, 1973).

24. The overall process of state decision making for education is treated by Roald F. Campbell and Tim Mazzoni, *State Policy Making for the Public Schools* (Berkeley, Calif.: McCutchan, 1976). For case studies of individual states, see Richard Lehne, *The Quest for Justice* (New York: Longman, 1978); and Edward R. Hines, *State Policy Making for Public Schools of New York* (Columbus: Educational Governance Project, Ohio State University, 1974).

25. A more complete discussion of the relationship between wages and costs in the private sector can be found in Albert Rees, *The Economics of Work and Pay* (New York: Harper and Row, 1973).

26. The studies of school finance demonstrating this relationship are voluminous. The literature is reviewed in Walter I. Garms *et al.*, *School Finance* (Englewood Cliffs, N.J.: Prentice-Hall, 1978); and Joel Berke, *Answers to Inequity* (Berkeley, Calif.: McCutchan, 1973).

27. *School District Expenditure and Tax Controls* (Denver, Colo.: Education Finance Center, Education Commission of the States, 1978).

28. There is some evidence that the onset of collective bargaining in schools with pay differentials between elementary and secondary teachers works to reduce the size of the differential. See Gary A. Moore, "The Effect of Collective Bargaining on Internal Salary Structures in the Public Schools," *Industrial and Labor Relations Review*, 29:2 (April 1976), 352-362.

29. The power of Congress to regulate some aspects of state and local governments' labor relations was upheld in *Maryland* v. *Wirtz*, 392 U.S. 183 (1968). But an attempt to extend wage regulations to those same governments was ruled unconstitutional in *National League of Cities* v. *Usery*, 426 U.S. 833 (1976). In light of these two decisions, the extent of federal power in this sphere is unclear.

30. For an expression of the teacher associations' point of view on federal collective bargaining legislation, see Terry Herndon, "The Case for Collective Bargaining Statutes," *Phi Delta Kappan*, 60:9 (May 1979), 651-652.

31. Walton and McKersie, *Behavioral Theory of Labor Negotiations*, p. 161.

32. Thomas J. Sergiovanni and Fred D. Carver, *The New School Executive: A Theory of Administration* (New York: Dodd, Mead, 1973), 99.

33. Ronald G. Corwin, "Models of Education Organizations," in *Review of*

Research in Education, Volume II, ed. Fred N. Kerlinger and John B. Carroll (Itasca, Ill.: F. E. Peacock, 1974).

34. These generalizations about the administrative context of teaching come from Dan C. Lortie's discussion of teachers' autonomy in "The Balance of Control and Autonomy in Elementary School Teaching," in *The Semi-Professions and Their Organization,* ed. Amitai Etzioni (New York: Free Press, 1969); Charles E. Bidwell, "The School as a Formal Organization," in *The Handbook of Organizations,* ed. James G. March (Chicago: Rand McNally, 1965); and Corwin, "Models of Educational Organizations."

35. Dan C. Lortie, *School Teacher* (Chicago: University of Chicago Press, 1975), 143-146.

36. A comprehensive review of this literature is found in Gerald Zaltman, David H. Florio, and Linda A. Sikorski, *Dynamic Educational Change* (New York: Free Press, 1977). A detailed and behavioral view of the problems of changing teachers' curricular behavior can be found in Seymour Sarason, *The Culture of the School and the Problem of Change* (Boston: Allyn and Bacon, 1971).

37. The political aspects of curricular decision making are analyzed in Wirt and Kirst, *Political and Social Foundations of Education,* esp. ch. 10. A more general review of that literature is found in Paul E. Peterson, "The Politics of American Education," in *Review of Research in Education,* Volume II, ed. Kerlinger and Carroll.

38. This definition corresponds to what Dunkin and Biddle refer to as "classroom management and control." They review the literature on that subject in Michael J. Dunkin and Bruce J. Biddle, *The Study of Teaching* (New York: Holt, Rinehart and Winston, 1974), ch. 6.

39. The United States Supreme Court has ruled that students are entitled to due process in many school discipline actions. The major decisions on this issue are *Goss* v. *Lopez,* 419 U.S. 565 (1975) and *Wood* v. *Strickland,* 420 U.S. 308 (1975). For a discussion of these cases, see Ronald J. Anson *et al.,* "*Goss* v. *Lopez* and *Wood* v. *Strickland,* Implications for Educators: Proceedings of the National Institute of Education Conference," *Journal of Law and Education,* 4:4 (October 1975), 565-616.

40. This point is described by Corwin, *Militant Professionalism,* 122-125.

41. David Easton, *A Systems Analysis of Political Life* (New York:Wiley, 1965).

42. Bidwell, "The School as a Formal Organization."

43. Thomas C. Schelling, *The Strategy of Conflict* (Cambridge, Mass.: Harvard University Press, 1960).

44. Walton and McKersie, *Behavioral Theory of Labor Negotiations,* 313-335, treats this as a problem of intraorganizational bargaining tactics.

45. Zeigler and Jennings, *Governing American Schools* 121-123.

46. This point is made by Wirt and Kirst, *Political and Social Foundations of Education,* 90.

47. An example of this in Chicago is described in Paul E. Peterson, *School Politics* (Chicago: University of Chicago Press, 1976), 242-243.

48. See George LaNoue and Bruce L. Smith, *The Politics of School Decentralization* (Lexington, Mass.: Lexington Books, 1973).

49. This process is discussed by Diane Ravitch, *The Great School Wars* (New York: Basic Books, 1974). See also Marilyn Gittell, *Participants and Participation* (New York: Praeger, 1967).

50. This subject has received some attention in recent political studies; for example, see Mike M. Milstein and Robert E. Jennings, *Educational Policymaking in the State Legislature* (New York: Praeger, 1973); and Campbell and Mazzoni, *State Policy Making for the Public Schools.*

51. Harry H. Wellington and Ralph K. Winter, *The Unions and the Cities*, (Washington, D.C.: Brookings, 1971), 26.

52. *Ibid.*

53. This particular topic has received considerable attention in the literature on labor relations. For a detailed discussion, see Chapter 11.

54. John F. Burton and Charles Krider, "The Role and Consequences of Strikes by Public Employees," *Yale Law Journal*, 79:3 (January 1970), 418-443.

7

The Process of
Collective Bargaining

Attempting to be systematic and analytical about bargaining is a little like attempting the same approach with marriage. Both subjects are ubiquitous in that almost everyone has some understanding of and has had some experience with each. But understanding and experience vary enormously according to a person's background, point of view, objectives, and station in life. Both subjects have great emotional and political impact and can rouse sharp, often violent social conflict. When the adjective "collective" is added to "bargaining," the possibilities for differences in opinion expand, and the problems of analysis multiply. Since our objective is a systematic, basic review of the collective bargaining process, possibilities for confusion, difference of opinion, and emotion must be considered. This requires both a basic and a comprehensive approach to what is a difficult and multifaceted subject. The approach is outlined briefly to aid in the discussion of the collective bargaining process that follows.

FRAMES OF REFERENCE

The bargaining process is discussed, first, in terms of three layers or levels that are represented schematically in Figure 7-1. At

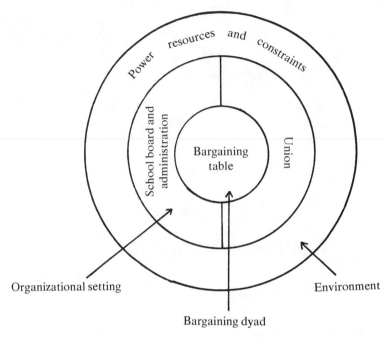

Figure 7-1
Bargaining frames of reference

the center of the circles shown in the figure is the bargaining table, indicating that the behavior of the immediate parties to the bargain — the negotiators themselves — is the primary consideration. That is where we find the essence of two-party bargaining, with its fundamental characteristics and dynamics. This area is surrounded by the organizational setting for the bargaining where the union as an organization is on one side and the school system is on the other. Our attention there centers on the relationships between the bargainers and their constituencies and on the way organizations affect the bargaining and vice versa. Moving beyond, to the largest area shown, we find the political and economic context of collective bargaining, including attention to the way bargaining may be affected by the legal and political forces in the society, especially sources of power and constraints in the environment. This approach borrows heavily from John Dunlop's conception of industrial relations, especially where the relationships between the bargaining power of the parties and their environment are involved.[1] Our goal here is somewhat different from Dunlop's. We are not interested in a construction that deals with the whole of the labor-management relationship. For us, such a construction is just a device to order the presentation of ideas while we examine the bargaining process.

The examination begins at the bargaining table, proceeds to the organizational context, and ends with the environment, thereby following one of our fundamental premises: that bargaining is a political process that takes place in an organizational and economic environment. The interaction of the parties at the table is the center of attention, and it is only when the basic dynamics of that process are understood that one can discuss bargaining in its organizational setting. And the organizational setting, in turn, largely determines how the bargaining relationship interacts with the environment, which is the final consideration.

The three levels of analysis are examined in terms of conflict, power, and strategy—central elements of any discussion of bargaining, regardless of the level of analysis. Exploring the meaning of these general concepts will serve as a useful introduction to the process of bargaining.

Conflict

Labor-management relations constitutes one of many areas in life characterized by basic and unavoidable conflict. The sources of that conflict have already been discussed in some detail, and, at this point, we are interested in what conflict means in terms of labor-management relations and the general mechanisms by which it is resolved.

We view collective bargaining as a means of resolving conflict, that is, its purpose is to find compromises whereby parties in conflict over labor-management issues can work constructively with each other. The sources of conflict are not removed, the compromises are not necessarily permanent solutions, and the cessation of open conflict is usually temporary. But bargaining does generally produce an agreement that allows an operation to proceed in a productive manner.

The general notion of conflict that underlies this discussion is taken largely from Kenneth Boulding's analysis, although other work is related.[2] Conflict is a situation wherein two or more parties seek ends that are incompatible, and the parties are aware of their own wishes and those of the other party or parties. Teachers, for example, may demand that an average class have only twenty-two students or that a raise in salary be 8 percent. The school board, in turn, might expect that the average class have twenty-five students and that salary raises be limited to 4 percent. Awareness of these incompatible objectives leads to behavior that contributes to either conflict or its resoltuion. If the workers have little power, management may simply dictate the outcome. If power is better balanced between the two parties, however, negotiation may be required in order to reach a compromise.

In some situations the parties' aims are completely opposed, as in total warfare. Such situations, which are rare, leave no room for negotiations. Labor-management conflict is better described as part conflict and part mutual dependence: the union needs the employer to provide jobs; the employer needs the union to represent the workers and stabilize the relationship. In terms of schools, some get along very well without a union of teachers or other employees, but, throughout this discussion, it has been assumed that unions exist in a school system because there is sufficient desire on the part of workers to form and support one. Even if a particular union were to disappear, the demand and motivation that remained would generate conflict between workers and managers. If a union and a bargaining relationship were not present to resolve the conflict, both employer and employees would suffer.

This mutual dependence aspect of a bargaining relationship can be expressed in economic terms as well. In a perfectly competitive market there would be no incentive to negotiate; prices, including wages, would be set by the market. Similar jobs would have equal pay, and equivalent workers could expect equal wages.[3] But schools, as well as most other forms of employment, do not operate in a perfectly competitive market. The board of education has the option of offering higher wages for services, in return for a peaceful labor-management relationship. Even though higher wages increase the price of schooling, the board has this option because there are no local competitors offering the same product at a lower price. Teachers and other workers have an incentive to negotiate with their present employer, rather than incurring the cost of finding another employer offering higher wages. This is especially important in the current labor market where there is an oversupply of teachers.

Both parties, therefore, have incentives to engage in and incur the costs of bargaining in the hope of resolving conflict to their own benefit.

There can also be situations where the negotiated resolution of a conflict results in *both* parties gaining relative to their expectations, which makes it useful to distinguish between *distributive* or constant-sum bargaining and *integrative* or nonconstant-sum bargaining.[4] In distributive bargaining the conflict is such that one party can only gain at the expense of the other. The sum of benefits on both sides is a constant, as in negotiations over wages, and each dollar gained by the union is given up by the board. In integrative bargaining, a process closer to problem solving than the distribution of shares, both parties can gain simultaneously. A negotiated mechanism for teacher participation in curriculum decisions may, for example, result in both greater satisfaction for teachers and a better curriculum development process for the board.

It should be recognized that not all labor-management conflict is resolved by collective bargaining between union and board. Conflict may arise in areas not covered by a contract or in areas where the contract gives the power to resolve issues to management. Choice of curricular materials or transfer of staff are two such areas. Other matters may be settled by informal, individual negotiations between teachers and administrators; differences of opinion over subjects to be taught or methods to be employed can be handled in this manner. The basic dynamics of negotiations and the existence of conflict in these cases may resemble those in collective bargaining. Other than to recognize this individual aspect of bargaining in the schools, however, we do not devote further attention to it. We concentrate, instead, on the collective aspects of labor-management bargaining and now shift our attention to the place of power and strategy in that process.

Power

There are two basic ways to approach power in the bargaining relationship. Power can first be thought of, in terms of social influence, as the ability of one party to move another party through a range of outcomes.[5] This range of outcomes encompasses a variety of values, both positive and negative, for the parties. By this definition, party A has more power than party B if A can cause

B to move B's bargaining position farther than B can force A to move A's position. It is assumed, of course, that one party would only force another to move to a bargaining position more favorable to the party promoting the move. In a school bargaining situation, teachers would be said to have more power if they could force the board to concede 5 percent on a salary package if the teachers were only willing to concede 3 percent. The conclusion that the teachers had more power would be true in this case only if each percentage of concession had the same value for both parties. Where money is involved, this is probably a tenable assumption.

This definition provides a basis for inferring the relative power of bargaining parties from their actions. But it does not allow much insight into how one party is able to force the other through a range of outcomes. From another point of view, the definition represents an outcome more than a description of power.

A definition emerging from the study of the economics of labor relations defines bargaining power through a consideration of relative costs. By this definition, party A's bargaining power is A's cost of disagreeing to B's terms relative to A's cost of agreeing to B's terms,[6] or:

$$P_a = \frac{\text{cost of accepting B's terms}}{\text{cost of rejecting B's terms}}$$

where P_a is the bargaining power of party A. This definition makes clear that bargaining power is a strictly relative concept that is directly dependent on the parties' subjective calculation of their own costs.

Consider the bargaining situation for the school board and teachers' union referred to above. Suppose that the parties are meeting to discuss their current bargaining positions (or "terms" in the sense of the definition): the teachers are asking a 12 percent raise; the board is offering a 4 percent raise. No agreement has been reached since, for both sides, the cost of accepting the other's terms is greater than the cost of rejecting them. Suppose, further, that the teachers' union simultaneously reduces its demand to 9 percent and convincingly threatens a strike if the board refuses to agree to those terms. Those actions would have the effect of decreasing the board's cost of agreement (from conceding 8 percent to conceding 5 percent) and increasing the costs of disagreeing (incurring a strike). The result could be a sufficient reduction in the board's bargaining power to force acceptance of the teachers' terms.

Bargaining power in this sense becomes a matter of perceiving the costs of one's own and another party's actions. These costs are always subjective, depending on each party's view of the consequences of action. For example, consider the threat of a strike. If the board believes that the teachers will follow through on their threat, the threat is credible, and the board must assess the possible costs of a strike. These might include loss of state aid, public dissatisfaction and loss of political support, disruption of the school program and of learning, or residual hostility among staff and administration. The teachers could suffer similar losses, as well as loss of pay and diminished prestige in the eyes of many in the school community. Each side has some rough idea of the cost factors for the other, but neither can know exactly how important each factor is to the other side. Even without this precise knowledge, one side may attempt to manipulate the other's perception in an effort to gain bargaining power. Some school boards have been known to publish and distribute detailed booklets describing what parents should do in case of strikes. This effort to minimize disruption would demonstrate the board's resolve to accept a strike. Such a tactic would reduce the cost of a strike to the board and thereby increase its bargaining power.

Strategy

The behaviors just described can be thought of as elements in a strategy employed by the board to achieve its objectives in the bargaining process. Understanding these and other elements of strategy is essential to a grasp of bargaining interaction. But the concept of strategy itself is complex and deserves special attention.

Strategy, like power, has different shades of meaning. The early military analyst, Carl von Clausewitz, defined strategy to mean "the employment of battle as the means towards the attainment of the object of war."[7] This definition captures the essence of the idea: the organization and use of means, or tactics, toward the achievement of an end. In the military setting, this is clearly an interactive situation, where the choice of means is in part contingent on some idea of what the enemy might do.

When applied to nonmilitary conflict, the notion of strategy retains this basic form. Thomas Schelling refers to the term as it is used in the language of games of strategy as activities "in which the best course of action for each player depends on what the other players do. The term is intended to focus on the interdependence of the adversaries' decisions and on their expectations about each other's behavior."[8] This is the general meaning of strategy that we employ in this discussion of bargaining. That is, bargaining strategy, a plan or course of action intended to achieve the bargainer's objective, takes into account interdependence of action and expectations about an opponent's behavior. Knowledge of the opponent's behavior cannot, however, be complete. The best strategist can estimate accurately what an opponent will do under certain situations, but such estimates leave room for error. Because strategy is based on interdependence of actions, it must include alternative courses of action that are contingent on opponents' choices. A board initiating strategy might include an offer of, say, 3 percent on a salary package *if* the teachers were to drop their demand for smaller classes. If the demand for smaller classes were to stay on the table, however, the salary offer would then be only 1 percent. Or the union could plan to leave the bargaining table altogether if the board were to refuse to concede at least 2 percent at the next session. Each of these possible behaviors or choices can be thought of as tactics of bargaining. Strategy is the use of alternative tactics to achieve the bargainer's objectives, taking into account the actions an opponent might take. It is the actions or tactics that constitute the bargaining process.

The choice of strategy and tactics thus requires some understanding of the overall process—an understanding based on the intuitive judgments of an experienced bargainer, or on formal models of the bargaining process, or on some combination of the two. This is the principal reason why some modeling of the bargaining process, intuitive or formal, is essential to the design and execution of strategy.

THE BARGAINING DYNAMIC

Collective bargaining requires a number of sessions. In each session negotiators for each side propose and discuss terms of a contract, and they eventually agree on the specific language of that contract. As we have noted, the terms proposed by both sides are in conflict, that is, they are incompatible. The fundamental purpose of the bargaining process is to turn incompatible terms into an agreement. This can happen if one side abandons its terms and accept the other's, if both sides modify their terms (make concessions) so that the results become compatible, or if the parties discover and accept new terms, better in some way than either of the original proposals.

Abandoning one's terms to accept the opponent's is simply a unilateral concession. So bargaining can be thought of as either making concessions, causing your opponent to make concessions, or finding new, more acceptable terms. This formulation is equivalent to Richard Walton and Robert McKersie's concepts of distributive and integrative bargaining, which are used below.[9] In practice, the two forms of bargaining are not easily distinguishable. Conceptually, however, they are sufficiently different to warrant a separate discussion.

Much that transpires in an actual bargaining session is not, or at least does not appear to be, related to either making concessions, forcing others to make concessions, or finding new terms. The apparent irrelevance of much bargaining behavior and language can be attributed to the fact that collective bargaining is fundamentally a social and psychological process that is part of a continuing relationship. The parties are interested in finding an agreement *within the framework of the existing relationship*. Since it is basically a conflictual relationship, some activity is directed at simply maintaining dialogue through periods of stress, and this *is* part of the process of causing the opponent to make concessions. No one can make concessions if they break off the bargaining process. More attention is devoted to this element of bargaining in the sections on cooperation and social influence.

Bargaining and Concessions

A central question related to the tactics of bargaining is why and how much to concede. And, as it turns out, this is directly related to the question of why one bargains in the first place. These two questions are taken up together. The first inducement to bargain comes from imperfections or rigidities in the school's labor market.

Only when the parties think the bargaining transaction is better than the alternative do they have the incentive to settle.[10] Once the decision to bargain is made, the problem of a concession strategy remains.

Concessions as Exchange

In determining possible concessions, the first consideration is the nature of bargaining as exchange. The initial terms proposed are not likely to be acceptable to either side and are usually much more than either expects in the final agreement. This is a logical approach where neither party can accurately estimate how much the other is likely to concede. To get fully as much as possible, one begins beyond the conceivable range and works toward the estimated target. The opponent does the same thing. One side wishes to persuade the other side to concede as much as possible, while yielding as little as possible oneself. Each concession, therefore, is in exchange for a similar concession by the opponent, and it is through such exchanges that both sides converge on an acceptable middle ground and eventually reach an exact settlement. If the bargaining is in terms of dollars, as it is in salary negotiations, the process can be represented as in Figure 7-2.

In the figure the vertical dimension is dollars in a salary settlement. The horizontal dimension represents the process of concession over time. The initial positions of the parties are some distance apart and converge to an eventual settlement at time t_d. The size of any particular concession is represented by the vertical distance between any two connected points. The figure shows an example concession by the union, C_{u7}, as the amount given at the seventh session or exchange. If we assume the union began the exchange process, then it would be followed by a concession from the board, represented by the distance C_{b7}, followed by another concession by the union, and so forth.

Both parties know that some concessions are necessary. But their size and timing is one of the central strategic problems of the bargainer. To illustrate, consider the simplest distributive bargaining situation: parties negotiating wages in dollars. The units of the bargaining exchange are clearly known, and each dollar has exactly the same value for both parties over the entire bargaining range. This latter assumption means that the first dollar conceded at the

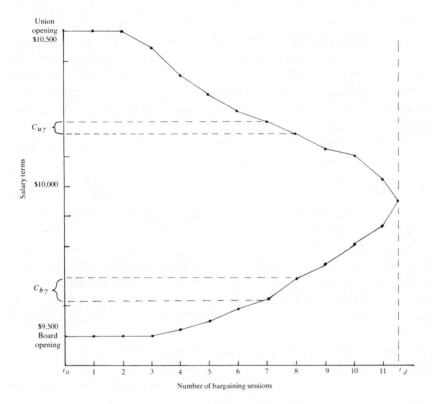

Figure 7-2

Hypothetical pattern of bargaining concessions

beginning of the bargaining period has the same value for both sides as the last, as do all dollars between. Based on these simple but unrealistic assumptions, there is no incentive for one party to concede more in each exchange than the dollar amount conceded by the opponent. In fact, the outcome of the bargaining would be determined by the opening proposals of the parties, and the settlement would be exactly halfway between where the parties began. The whole bargaining process would be reduced to the status of a guessing game wherein each side would struggle to introduce the more extreme opening proposal.

Subjective Utilities

The situation outlined above is not the way bargaining proceeds. The assumptions, instead, must be incomplete descriptions of how bargainers perceive their situation since concessions at the beginning of the process are usually much larger than the last few, hard-fought fractions of percents as bargaining approaches the deadline. And seldom are concessions matched on a strictly equal quid pro quo basis. Bargainers behave, instead, as though the dollars (or other units of bargaining) are not at all equal and, further, as though the values associated with the currency of bargaining differ between the parties. Models of distributive bargaining invoke the concept of "subjective utilities" to explain the observed dynamics of the bargaining process.

Subjective utilities are thought of as units of value as they are perceived by the bargainer (or bargaining organization). They are related to, but not the same as, the units actually exchanged (say, dollars), and the subjective utility (or value) of those dollars to the bargainer is expressed as the "utility function." An example of utility function is shown in Figures 7-3 and 7-4. We assume that the current starting annual salary for teachers is $9,500 and, for simplicity's sake, that other salaries are pegged to that figure.

Figure 7-3 shows the union with a very low utility for a decrease in salary. This is consistent with the generally accepted practice of beginning negotiations at the current level in all but the most extreme circumstances. The value of salary increases climbs slowly at first, since small increases are expected and taken for granted. Utility then rises rapidly with the size of the settlement up to a point where concern for the negative consequences of a large salary raise comes into play. A large raise could result in serious cutbacks in jobs, public resistance to tax increases, or other reactions that could diminish an employer's ability to maintain the system in a manner beneficial to the union and its members.

Figure 7-4 shows a management utility function dropping slowly with small wage increases, and more rapidly as the settlement rises. Both the financial and political costs to the board of large salary increases account for the sharp downward slope of the curve in the higher salary ranges. The figure also shows the board with

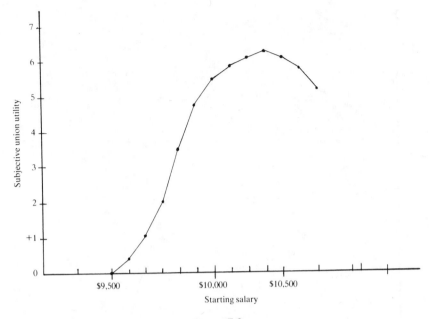

Figure 7-3
Union salary utility function

a slightly decreasing utility for a decrease in salary. This reflects a possible desire on the part of the board to maintain a work force of a given quality, or the intangible factors associated with providing a "fair" wage or pattern of leadership among a group of districts.

The notion of wage leadership and strong pattern bargaining is supported by evidence from schools in metropolitan areas, where the labor force is fairly mobile and the possibilities for wage competition are strong.[11] The notion of wage leadership or pattern setting also can be used to support the claim that a district attracts the "best" teaching staff. Since there are no productivity measures for teachers or objective indexes of quality other than education and experience levels, the board may claim that the highest-paid teachers in the region are the best for that reason alone.

The notion of the board's desire to maintain a work force of a given quality is quite complex on close examination. The wage necessary to maintain a teaching force of given quality would

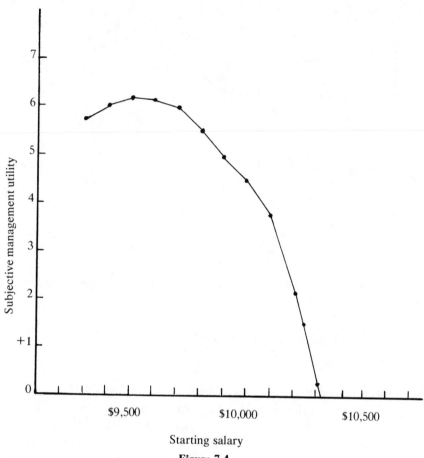

Figure 7-4
Management salary utility function

vary both with the supply of teachers in the local labor market and with the wages available in alternative employment.[12] The notion of quality in terms of a teaching staff has no standard definition, and the salary level needed to maintain a work force of a given quality may differ from that necessary to attract workers. Because the rate and nature of staff turnover affects the perception of management on this account, the assumption of a decrease in management's utility function for a salary decrease may not be reasonable under all circumstances. There have, in fact, been effective salary cuts during the term of the contract in some large cities forced by financial exigencies to shorten the school year and lay off staff in the spring. The effects of these program reductions are not fully known. Boards might prefer not to shorten the school year or effect salary reductions in similar ways since the political repercussions could be serious and the effect on the achievement of the students could be detrimental. These questions await systematic study.[13]

The utility functions in Figures 7-3 and 7-4 are drawn on separate vertical axes to reflect the concept that the utilities scales are subjective. The units on each scale are arbitrary; the union scale cannot be thought of as equal to that of management. The curves represent only the value of one concession relative to other concessions in the value scheme of the side making the concession. In addition, the shape of one side's utility function is usually not known to the other, and each side takes great pains in the course of bargaining to hide actual preferences.

Resistance Point and Settlement Range

The shape of the utility function indicates that each party has an optimum value for a salary settlement, that is, a salary with the highest utility. There is also a range of salary values near the optimum where the utility remains fairly high. Salary settlements within this range should be acceptable to the parties, even though the associated utility is less than the maximum. There are also salary settlement figures that would be unacceptable to one side or the other, and, as the utility gets below a certain point, resistance to settlement becomes high. Walton and McKersie have referred to this as the "resistance point," and so will we.[14] The union negotiator who settles below the resistance point risks being put out of office, or the membership might insist on replacing one representative organization with another. A negotiator for management who agrees to a settlement below management's utility resistance point risks being replaced as management's representative, and management may reject the entire contract. In this discussion we are assuming that management's resistance point, RP_m, is $10,000 (see Figure 7-5).

Given these resistance points and the opening proposals of the parties, we can define the "bargaining range" as the amounts between the union's opening proposal of $10,500 and management's opening proposal of $9,500. Normally neither side expects settlement

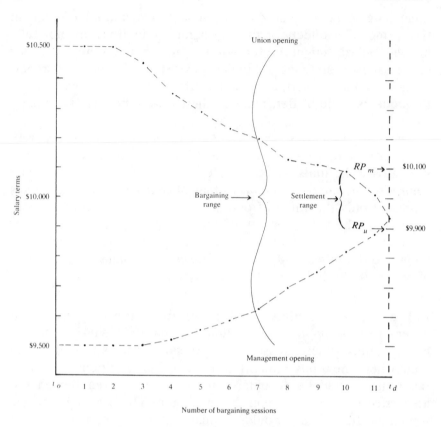

Figure 7-5
Convergence of salary bargaining to agreement

at or near those points. Once either side makes a proposal, however, it is not expected to go back. This means that offers below $9,500 and demands above $10,500 are outside the normal bargaining range. If the union's resistance point is low enough or management's resistance point is high enough on the salary scale, there can be, as there is in the example presented here, some overlap. In this case it is between $9,900 and $10,100. This is referred to as the "settlement range." Unless something happens during the bargaining to change resistance points, the final outcome would be expected to fall between these two points, which are shown in the figure. The figure illustrates the notion of bargainers proceeding through a series of concessions with a particular range of possible outcomes in mind. It does not indicate how the particular range or individual concessions are determined. Reference to the utility function for settlements does not help much in this regard. In order to deal with these aspects of the bargaining dynamic, a model requires some consideration of the costs of disagreement, or incurring a strike, and some conception of the way bargainers interpret and try to influence each other's concession and bargaining behavior.

Concession Rate

Formal models of bargaining generally account for the basic negotiations process in terms of the negotiator's joint consideration of two costs: the cost of disagreeing with the current set of proposals and the cost of agreeing to the opponent's current proposal.[15] Treating these two as separate calculations introduces some complexity into the discussion and some behavioral questions as well. Analytically the two costs are separable, but they cannot be estimated separately. At any point in the process one bargainer must either accept an opponent's proposal or continue bargaining (unless negotiations are broken off, which is a separate topic). The decision to accept a proposal "now" must be based in part on a notion of how that proposal might change later. So the choice is, to some degree, a gamble.

If bargaining is to continue, the bargainer must choose a concession for the next round of negotiations. That concession may be zero or any value up (or down) to the opponent's current proposal. Since these actions take place over time, the choice of any particular concession can be thought of as the choice of a "concession rate." Each move or offer extends the time of the bargaining and brings the line of concessions closer to the deadline. To understand how costs of agreement and costs of disagreement are related requires some understanding of concession rate.

We suggest that bargainers choose a rate of concession for their current situation that is based on an assessment of where the overall pattern of bargaining is leading relative to their own resistance point and optimum outcome. That is to say that the bargainer's choice at any particular stage of the process is based on a projection or extrapolation of the overall pattern of concessions out to the expected deadline. The choice takes into account the cost of continued bargaining and the estimated cost of the pattern of concessions implied by past behavior of the bargaining parties.

This conception is based, first of all, on the existence of a deadline to end bargaining that is mutually agreeable to both parties. The deadline itself can be the subject of negotiations, but in school systems it is likely to be related to the opening date for school and the corresponding termination date for the current contract. In schools, therefore, setting a general deadline for bargaining is not a major issue. As the opening of school approaches, or if bargaining extends into the school year, the establishment of specific deadlines for settlement may become an important issue; it can even be shifted on a day-to-day basis near the point of settlement. Either way, the existence of an explicit deadline agreeable to all parties is considered normal.

Projected Concession Rate

Projecting the current situation to the deadline can be thought of as a combination of a learning process and use of a behavioral template built from past experience. Some formal models of bargaining suggest that the bargainer learns to judge the expected behavior of an opponent by adjusting expectations according to each new concession observed. Suppose the teachers' negotiator began the bargaining with a number of fairly large concessions. The board's negotiator could then reasonably expect the amount the teachers would accept in the final settlement to be far below that in the original proposal. In other words, the overall rate of concession for the teachers would be high, and the board's negotiator would have "learned" that the teachers would make many large concessions. If the teachers then began to reduce the size of the concessions and got "tough," the board's negotiator would be forced to adjust the original projection to a somewhat lower rate of concession: another aspect of learning or adjusting behavior to new information. A perceptive negotiator should be able to develop an accurate projection of future concessions based on past actions.

But the bargainer's projections may be based on more than observations in the immediate bargaining. Previous experience with this or similar bargains may indicate that a particular overall pattern or behavioral template is valid for predicting the opponent's behavior. The same negotiator in the past may have consistently begun with large concessions and then gotten tough as the bargaining proceeded. Or another negotiator may have tended to mirror the opponent, matching large concessions to large concessions, small to small, and so forth. So the learning process that goes on during bargaining may require adjustments to an expected pattern of concessions built upon past experience as well as the extension of behaviors observed in the current bargaining.

In laboratory studies of bargaining behavior, two patterns of bargaining are generally found to be most effective in producing optimal solutions to the bargaining problem beneficial for both parties. One is the "start tough, get progressively softer" one. In this pattern, opening moves are small and competitive, with the size of concessions increasing as cooperation builds. The other pattern, which is similar, is referred to by H. Kelley as "systematic."[16] That is, the bargainers find a pattern of sequential exchange that gives each the desired information about the other and establishes a pattern of yielding that both see will lead to a satisfactory agreement.[17]

The expected patterns may shift over time as well. Charles Perry and Wesley Wildman found schools engaged in what they called "crisis bargaining" early in the history of the relationship. By that they meant a delaying of important concessions until near the deadlines, with a rush of movement to reach agreement at the eleventh hour. But they note that this pattern shifted to more gradual concessions later in the bargaining history. But these are longer-term processes not directly of interest within a particular set of negotiations.

Consider the situation shown for the pattern of bargaining from Figure 7-2, but only up to the point of the seventh bargaining session (Figure 7-6). Since we have assumed that the union began the process of concessions, it is the union negotiator's turn to choose a move for the eighth session. In this conception of the process, the union's negotiator has developed a pattern of expected behavior for management's negotiator, based on past performance. Let us suppose that the union bargainer expects management concessions to follow a smooth curve of slightly decreasing radius up to settlement at approximately $10,000, which is well within the union's settlement range and close to the optimal utility. Let us suppose that the union's negotiator believes this to be the best outcome

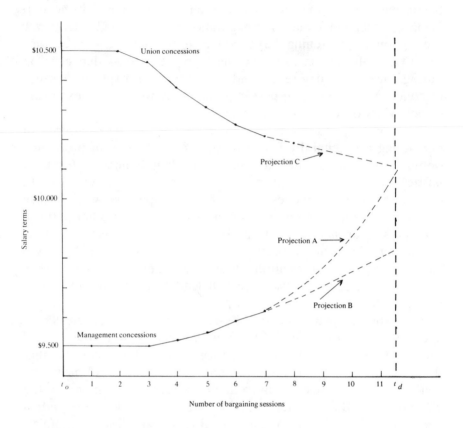

Figure 7-6
Projection of expected bargaining patterns

that can be expected under the circumstances and wishes to establish a concession pattern that will reach that point. He or she would
simply choose a concession rate that meets the deadline at $10,000
and make an offer at the eighth session that reflects that rate (a
proposal of approximately $10,180). As long as management's con-
cessions match the pattern expected by the union, the union would
continue to make concessions at that rate. If management's concessions deviate largely from the union's expectations, some adjustment would be necessary, either in the concession rate or in bargaining tactics, to return to a pattern leading to an acceptable
settlement.

Characterizing the bargaining exchange in this way focuses our attention on three critical aspects of bargaining behavior: the choice of a pattern or behavioral template for projecting the opponent's past behavior into future bargaining, how the negotiator interprets and adjusts to the opponent's actions relative to that expected pattern, and how the negotiator attempts to influence the nature of the opponent's concessions through bargaining tactics if the expected pattern or outcome is not acceptable. In the example above, the key choices are the shape of the curve of expected concessions, the decisions that the chosen curve represents the best to be expected "under the circumstances," and the decision to attempt to stabilize or change the concession pattern relative to its current state.

This approach to model bargaining does not by itself explain why bargainers would make these choices; rather, it indicates the central strategic elements in the process. The union could have interpreted management's rather large expected concession rate as a sign of weakness. That could lead to exploitation, with the union choosing an even lower concession rate to force the opponent into even greater concessions. Similarly, projecting past concessions using a straight line rather than a curve would lead the union to expect a much lower outcome or possible impasse (Projection B in Figure 7-6). This would be a signal to increase concession rates to avoid impasse, or attempt through bargaining tactics to move management's rate up, or some combination of these. These tactical choices would depend in part on the individual characteristics of the bargainers and in part on their assessment of the opponent's power and costs of impasse. Each of these merits separate attention.

Strike-Impasse Costs

The possibility of an impasse or strike is a constant threat in any bargaining situation. Until a contract is finally signed and ratified, each move in the bargaining interaction has implications for the probability of a strike, and, therefore, the possibility that each party will incur additional costs. The importance of a strike at any point in the bargaining is a combination of the subjective estimate of the probability of it occurring and the estimated costs associated with it. Thus, if one party feels a strike is remote, they will be relatively unconcerned about strike costs, even if those costs would be high.

The estimate of the probability of a strike is based on the projection of the current pattern of concessions to the deadline. Consider Figure 7-6 again. The union's assumption of Projection A (large management concessions) would suggest low probability of a strike. Assumption of Projection B would greatly increase the union's estimate of the possibility of a strike, especially since management's position at the deadline in that projection is below the union's resistance point. Faced with that situation, the union's representative would be forced to consider what course of action to take to reduce costs. Continued adherence to the present pattern would make a strike virtually inevitable, and conceding to management's pattern would mean serious loss of expected utility.

Relative strike costs at this point would be a major consideration in determining the course of action. If the union felt the costs of striking were much higher for management, perhaps because of strong community resistance to disruption of the school schedule, it could maintain a low concession rate and let the high cost of striking (for management) provide the pressure to meet the union's demands. If, however, the union felt strike costs were too high (say, because of low membership enthusiasm or loss of support for officers), it would have to take steps to reduce the concession gap. Where strike costs are so disparate, the union would probably be forced to increase its concession rate, undertake some action to generate support among the membership for a job action, or employ some other bargaining tactic in an attempt to change management's pattern. Calculations to estimate the costs of agreeing and disagreeing are based on both projected concession rates and strike costs. Power, as we have defined it, is thus related to these projections. But we have also seen how such projections require estimates of the future behavior and intentions of an opponent, as well as one's ability to influence them. These estimates and particularly influences are tied to the larger range of bargaining tactics that can be employed—tactics that can influence the outcome of bargaining and are, therefore, integral parts of the discussion of power and strategy.[18]

Threats and Promises

These two bargaining tactics are considered together because they are closely related in two basic ways. Both consist, first of all, of binding oneself to a future course of action regarding a bargaining opponent. A "threat" binds one to punish or impose costs on an opponent. A "promise" binds one to reward an opponent. Both can be considered inducements to the opponent to concede, by either raising the cost of disagreeing or reducing the cost of agreeing. A second way they are related is that both tactics are heavily dependent on the credibility of the act (how strongly the party making the threat or promise is bound, or perceived to be bound, to the future course of action). To be "bound" and to be "committed" to a course of action are usually used synonomously, and we follow the same practice.

There is, however, an important difference between threats and promises as they are used in bargaining. A promise is usually made with the expectation that it will be carried out. It is hoped that the opponent will see the mutual benefits to be gained by responding positively and act so as to collect on the promise. The union might promise, for example, to recruit volunteers from among its members for after-school programs if the board were to drop its contract demand to make the programs mandatory. A threat, in contrast, is made for the opposite reason. If the threat is successful, the threatener will *not* have to take the threatened action. A strike hurts both parties; a strike threat, if it is successful, gains the desired concession from management without requiring the union to act.

In either case, however, the success of the tactic depends on commitment or credibility. What constitutes successful commitment is central to the discussion of both threats and promises. Since commitment tactics differ somewhat, they can be treated separately.

Threats

The success of a threat depends on three elements. The first is making the threat contingent on the fact that the opponent, or threatened party, can actually make the desired response. It does the union no good, for example, to threaten a strike in order to force the board to relinquish hiring decisions to the union. Boards of education are usually bound by state law to make those decisions. The second element needed to make a threat effective is to make the threatened party believe that the threat will in fact be carried out. If management knows that the rank and file of the teachers' union will not support a strike on that issue, the threat, since it is not credible, is ineffective. And the third element required is that the threatened party must feel that the costs of conceding under threat are lower than they would be if the threat were carried out. If management feels it can tolerate a strike longer than the union can hold out and that the ultimate result will be the union's capitulation, the threat of a strike has little force.

Negotiators who use threats in an effort to achieve impossible concessions are often inexperienced. Whether a concession is possible is easily determined, and this is usually done. Understanding what is feasible for the opponent requires analysis of the organizational and environmental situation more than the use of bargaining tactics.

The third element of a threat, comparing costs of conceding with the consequences of refusing, is based on the subjective utilities of the threatener and the threatened party. If management's strike costs are low, for example, compared to the cost of the concession demanded, the decision may be to accept a strike (or whatever else may be threatened). In constructing a threat, then, the threatener must make some estimate of the opponent's utilities for the consequences of both conceding and not conceding. For instance, in deciding to threaten a strike if a salary demand is refused, the union must calculate the values management assigns both to the strike and to the salary concession. Whether choosing to use a threat or respond to one, an estimation of one's own and the opponent's subjective utilities is needed, and this is no different from estimating subjective utilities for ordinary concessions. The union must also consider its own strike costs relative to the value of the concession demanded, in case the threat is ineffective. The same line of reasoning would apply, of course, to management's choice regarding the use of some other threat.

That leaves the second element of a threat, its credibility, as the central feature that needs further discussion. The element is clearly described by Schelling:

The distinctive character of a threat is that one asserts that he will do, in a contingency, what he would manifestly prefer not to do if the contingency occurred, the contingency being governed by the second party's behavior. Like the ordinary commitment, the threat is a surrender of choice, a renunciation of alternatives, that makes one worse off than he need be in the event the tactic fails; the threat and the commitment are both motivated by the possibility that a rational second player can be constrained by his knowledge that the first player has altered his own incentive structure. Like an ordinary commitment, a threat can constrain the other player *only insofar as it carries to the other player at least some appearance of obligation*; if I threaten to blow us both to bits unless you close the window, you know that I won't unless I have somehow managed to leave myself no choice in the matter [emphasis added].[19]

The importance of this appearance of obligation or credibility in the making of threats has been painfully illustrated in the behavior of terrorists and other criminals who hold hostages, and in the responses of governments to these actions. By physically connecting themselves to explosives or providing some other evidence of their fanaticism, terrorists emphasize their absolute commitment to carrying out threats toward their hostages. If the threatened party or government believes that the terrorists are committed and that there is no other way to prevent the threatened act, the only choices are to concede or risk sacrificing the hostages. The government of Israel, the target of much terrorist activity, has announced and adhered to an equally extreme policy: *no negotiations with or concessions to terrorists*. This is equivalent to announcing that the cost of *any* concession whatsoever is greater than any action a terrorist could take. This sort of commitment, if credible, takes bargaining power away from potential terrorists.[20] The equivalent in a bargaining situation would be for one side to commit itself, publicly and in advance of the bargaining, to no concessions on a particular issue (say, binding arbitration of grievances) and make clear its willingness to take any consequences. A union, if it believes this commitment, is faced with the prospect of conceding the point or striking. And the board has also given notice than any consequence, strike or otherwise, is worth bearing rather than to yield on that issue. Again, the whole calculation hinges on the credibility of commitment to a single position.

Two basic types of commitment tactics available in a threat situation are either to convince the opponent that one's own incentive structure or utilities are so arranged that fulfilling the threat is a foregone conclusion or to appear helpless to do anything but fulfill the threat. Walton and McKersie discuss the union negotiator's tactic of raising members' expectations so that they will not allow him to act in any other way than the one threatened. They note that this type of tactic "comes as close to effecting an irrevocable commitment as any to be observed in collective bargaining because it may effectively alter the strength of the membership's aspirations." But the tactic is not without serious risks. They go on to point out that the negotiator who "can convince his opponent that he has no control over his membership or that his 'hands are tied' on a particular issue may gain some bargaining advantage at the negotiating table, but he must suffer the consequences should his opponent not accommodate his adamant position."[21] Public or board member aspirations can be raised in the same manner to achieve a similar effect on the side of management.

This tactic can be thought of as the use of information as a source of power. The negotiator is in a position to feed information to his or her constituency in such a way as to raise expectations about the outcomes of bargaining. The constituents do not have access to this information except through their negotiator. In addition, the negotiator uses real or tactically fabricated knowledge of the constituent's attitudes to convince the opponent of high expectations. In either case, the bargainer is manipulating information that he or she is in a unique position to have and to control.

Convincing the opponent of one's incentive to fulfill the threat involves some other tactical alternatives. Walton and McKersie discuss two commitment tactics of this type: emphasizing the intrinsic viability of the demands and identifying officials with the demands.[22] The appeal to the intrinsic viability of the demand can be thought of as a use of legitimate power. It appeals to the principles or values of rationality or integrity that form the basis of trust necessary for any bargaining exchange. Identifying officials with the demand involves two aspects of social power. The authority or expertise of the officials may lend strength to the demand, and such support increases the cost of reneging on the threat by adding loss of face or image to other costs.

Related to changing the incentive structures are tactics intended to convince the opponent that the utilities have *really* been changed. The most direct ways are to act in small ways as though they had by making preparations for executing the threat (as discussed above), by making or carrying out small threats, or by any other sort of verbal or nonverbal behavior that emphasizes the importance of the shifted incentives in controlling one's actions.

It should be clear from this discussion that the use of threats in the bargaining situation is complex and sensitive. In fact, the credibility of the threat is perhaps the most important element. After all, credibility is a matter of predicting the opponent's behavior. If there is no record of similar actions in the past, the prediction would be unreliable, at best, and probably not effective. Charles Perry and Wesley Wildman found, for example, that in relatively new bargaining situations threats made by teachers' unions were ineffective. Before there was an actual test of power, management acted as though teachers' threats were empty, not based on real organizational strength or commitment.[23]

Another aspect of the use of threats deserves some attention. Threats are fundamentally hostile aggressive acts, although they obviously vary widely in terms of seriousness and potential for damage. Some of the damage may be to the long-term viability of the bargaining relationship, as well as to the likelihood of final agreement. Both threats and promises have been shown to increase the probability of early concessions by opponents. But threats increase hostility in the relationship and decrease prospects for a mutually acceptable outcome.[24] Promises, on the other hand, tend to increase both liking in the relationship and prospects for agreeable outcomes. Thus, the choice of alternative threat strategies itself includes some costs and benefits that should be part of the decision-making process.

Promises

The ability of one party to reward the other, that is, to use control over future benefits as a source of power, is the basis for the efficacy of promises as bargaining tactics. As with threats, a promise is a commitment to the opponent. But it differs from a threat. As Schelling points out, "the promise is required whenever the final action of one or of each is outside the other's control. It is required whenever an agreement leaves any incentive to cheat."[25] The example discussed above illustrates the basic characteristics of a promise used in the bargaining process. Suppose that one aim of management is to require teachers to supervise certain extracurricular activities, rather than to ask them to volunteer to do so for small fees (the current practice). Management's demand is based on the assertion that too few teachers volunteer. The union obviously could make several tactical responses to this demand. It could counterpropose increasing the wages paid for these activities, but this could interfere with other economic objectives. The union could concede some other point in return for management's dropping that demand: a trade-off based on some estimate of relative utilities. The union could threaten to take some serious action, such as breaking off bargaining, if the proposal were not dropped. Or the union could offer some future benefit to management in return for a concession on that proposal. One such promise would be to take the responsibility for organizing and recruiting volunteers for these activities, thus relieving management of the responsibility.

In order to accept that trade-off, management must believe that the union will follow through on its promise. Credibility is as essential here as it is in a threat situation, and so the tactical use of promises must include some sort of commitment. One is a pledge of reputation, which stakes a possible loss of public image along with possible damage to the bargaining relationship as the basis of commitment. Making the promise public increases these same stakes, as does including such a pledge in the contract, where legal action may be taken to enforce compliance. Making actual preparations for carrying out the promise increases the likelihood of the promise being fulfilled and, thereby, its value as a reward. Schelling points out that the ability to make such commitments is essential to entering into contracts or other promissory relationships. Someone who cannot be sued, such as a minor child, cannot be bound to a promise and thus cannot legally or functionally enter into a commercial contract. A union or management that cannot keep a promise is in the same position.

Promises and Threats as Information

Beyond being used as tactics, promises and threats can be an important source of information in the bargaining process. Both underscore a demand or bargaining position. Tying a demand to a particular action (threats to impose a future cost or promises to confer a future benefit) indicates the value of that demand to the party. Unions do not threaten to call a strike, nor management negotiators threaten a lockout (management's equivalent of a strike) lightly. The value of the action threatened or promised puts a sort of price tag on the demand.

Some research indicates that the use of threats and promises results from an inability to employ other tactics successfully. These devices are more likely to be used in situations where the bargainer finds other sources of influence ineffective.[26] As for the size of threats and promises, this indicates a party's attitudes toward an opponent. The size of a threat or promise usually depends on some judgment of what will motivate the opponent: too small a threat is ignored, too large a threat is not credible; too small a promise is insulting; too large a promise can be seen as a bribe. The party on which such tactics are practiced can, in turn, develop some idea of how an opponent sees one's own utilities and attitudes.

Problems of Commitment

Clearly the effectiveness of threats and promises depends on credibility and on strength of commitment. But irrevocable commitment is incompatible with the give-and-take necessary for bargaining. Commitment tactics must be used judiciously if strategy is to be successful. Both parties, when bargaining, must be able to revise or even abandon previous commitments if they are to reach agreement. So "leaving a back door open" or "not getting painted into a corner" are familiar expressions when determining bargaining strategies. In terms of bargaining power, this means not letting the cost of changing one's mind or backing down preclude the option to do so.

Consider a board threat to break off bargaining until the union makes a particular concession, say, dropping a demand for a section on evaluation of teachers in the contract. A threat made in absolute terms and backed up by public statements and posturing (the board negotiator might tell the local paper that discussion of anything having to do with evaluation will be allowed "over my dead body") leaves little room for maneuvering. The same negotiator might, in contrast, privately have told the other team that management "did not expect to include any discussion of evaluation on the agenda and insistence on doing so could lead to a halt in negotiations." The basic threat is the same, but such phrases as "did not expect" and "could lead" leave some room for maneuvering.

If a commitment is seen by either party as undesirable, one or the other can attempt to reinterpret the original position. There may even be some incentive for one party to assist the other in revising a previous commitment. Again, Schelling's treatment of the subject is enlightening:

when the opponent has resolved to make a moderate concession one may help him by proving that he *can* make a moderate concession consistent with his former position, and that if he does there are no grounds for believing it reflects on his original principles. One must seek, in other words, a rationalization by which to deny oneself too great a reward from the opponent's concession, otherwise, the concession will not be made.[27]

This could involve some creative reconstruction of past behavior, or simply a new agreement revising the previous commitment. Whatever specific technique is used, it involves a cooperative effort where it is to both parties' advantage to allow revision.

Communication with constituencies or the public beyond the bargaining area makes revising commitments particularly difficult. If the commitments were only between the bargainers in the first place, they could be handled as the bargainers saw fit. When commitments are to or concerning others and they are made public, revision may be much more costly in terms of reputation or the security of the bargainer's position. The bargainer loses power to control this aspect of bargaining through sharing information about commitments with constituents or other publics. If bargainers are able to regulate the flow of information from the table, there is less difficulty. If bargaining is public or open to observers who can report independently to constituents, however, the management of information is more difficult. In such cases, more care must be taken to ensure that room to maneuver is built into the positions taken and the commitments made in the bargaining exchange.

The external framework of school operations also provides mechanisms that complicate the commitment process. Most state school codes include timetables for the construction and approval of school budgets and for informing teachers of dismissals. School codes typically provide a minimum time (say, sixty days) before the closing of school for notifying nontenured teachers who will not be employed the following year. Tentative school budgets must be published, and statutes require public display or hearings. Thus, the school board is required to make certain external commitments that are difficult to modify, and they must often be made far in advance of the usual time that contracts are settled. Since the contractual settlement often has a major effect on the budget and the number of teachers to be employed, the board must regulate external commitments to leave some negotiating leeway. This can be done by building contingency funds into the budget or otherwise "hiding" funds to mask the amount available.[28] Some school districts have also taken to dismissing all nontenured teachers formally at the end of each school year and hiring back only those needed after the contract and budget are determined.

Besides forcing premature commitment, bargaining circumstances can include elements (tactical maneuvers or simply factors in the environment) that block the ability of either party to make firm commitments. The financial arrangement for schools often places the budget maker in a situation of uncertainty about revenues, particularly from state and federal sources. This can block the board from making firm commitments on economic items. Boards, as well as teachers' or other employees' organizations, may also be badly divided internally and unable to take firm positions. Bargaining during the summer often removes the teachers' organization from close communication with the rank and file, thus limiting communication and the building of a credible base for commitment. Tactics that block or complicate commitment include severing communications, limiting time to develop commitments, or simply ignoring or ridiculing the opponent's behavior.[29] Union leaders have been known to leave the school district, or even the state, to avoid communication or the execution of a threat, thus preventing the board from carrying through on a commitment. David Colton reports, for example, how officers of the St. Louis Teachers' Union crossed the Mississippi River into Illinois to avoid injunctions and subpoenas resulting from a strike in 1976.[30] Regardless of the method, blocking an opponent's commitment has the same basic effect: the less an opponent has invested in the position, the easier it will be to change or abandon that position and make a concession. Thus, the tactics are tied to bargaining power.

SOCIAL STRUCTURE OF BARGAINING

To this point we have concentrated on tactics and strategies designed to have a direct effect on utilities and concession behavior. But the range of actions available to bargainers is much broader. Bargaining power, and thus effectiveness, can be affected by the social and physical structure of the process. An examination of the social structure moves us from the bargaining dyad to the organizational frame of reference (see Figure 7-1).

At its core, bargaining takes place between two individuals, typically the chief negotiators for the two sides. But understanding the process requires looking beyond the protagonists and noticing, in particular, how the nature of the social setting and social interactions affect the process. Central to this understanding is a clear picture of the structure and components of the bargaining relationship. That relationship is reflected in the conduct of bargaining itself and in the day-to-day workings of the educational program; it is examined, here, in terms of its central problems and its social components and how these relate to the conduct of bargaining and the larger process of labor-management relations.

A successful bargaining relationship can be thought of as: maintaining a working balance between excessive competition and excessive cooperation; influencing the opposing bargainer and organization to change or hold various positions; and maintaining an atmosphere of trust, both within the bargaining process and with the side the bargainer represents. From our point of view, these goals can never be completely or finally achieved. There are constantly changing elements in the bargaining situation, the organizational setting, and the environment that preclude stability, and so the task of the bargainers (and other participants) is to keep adjusting behavior and other controllable factors to maintain a functioning relationship.

The elements of the bargaining relationship that have some impact on cooperation-competition, trust, and influence can be grouped for discussion around three factors: the characteristics of the people involved, the roles that make up the social structure of the relationship, and those elements of the situation that are related to the interactions between parties. Roles, that is, collections of behaviors that make up the bargaining process (and related behaviors in the administration of the agreement and so forth), are the key concepts. Bargaining behaviors can be thought of as conditioned by the attitudes and predispositions the bargainer brings to the process; the expectations the bargainer perceives significant others hold for his or her behavior; personal skill and knowledge about bargaining; and purposeful plans and strategies for achieving bargaining objectives including related tactics. These elements can be thought of as interacting with the nature of the situation in which the bargaining takes place to produce the process itself, and they stem from the personal characteristics of participants and the nature of the bargaining situation.

Many aspects of the bargaining situation can conceivably affect the process. Here, for convenience, they are arranged into seven groups: bargaining power (described earlier), prevailing norms and ideology in the organization and the environment, organizational structure and demands, the presence of third parties and audiences, the nature of communication channels, physical setting of the interactions, and time limits and deadlines. These elements can interact with each other as well as with the role of the participants in a complex and dynamic process. A diagram of the main interactions is found in Figure 7-7.

The solid arrows represent main flows of effects, such that the bargaining relationship is a product of the roles of the participants. These roles are in turn determined by two sets of factors: personality characteristics and the nature of the situation. The situation, in turn, is a result of the organizational setting in which bargaining takes place and the nature of the environment, with the environment affecting the situation directly as well as through the

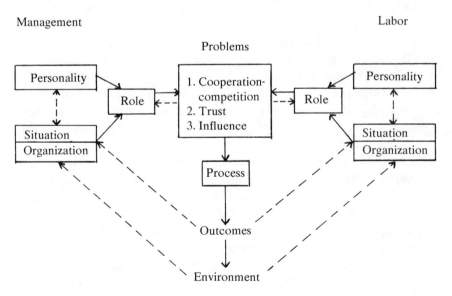

Figure 7-7
Components of the bargaining relationship

organization (as in, say, a newspaper article reporting "secret" bargaining information that could affect both the climate of the bargaining relationship and the status of the bargainers in their own organization).

The broken lines represent secondary and feedback effects. They show that bargaining interactions can change the role of participants. Significant success of cooperative initiatives could, for example, result in one bargainer changing to a more cooperative predisposition for future exchanges. Similarly, outcomes of bargaining can be reflected in later situational or organizational climates. A bargainer forced to concede all but a small salary increase for younger teachers, for example, would likely encounter diminishing support from that faction within the union. Also, norms and expectations for bargaining behavior will influence the personal characteristics of those chosen for bargaining roles, thus the broken arrows between situation and personality.

There is a complex interaction among cooperation-competition, trust, and influence. Cooperation in this sense requires both mutual agreement on concessions that constitute the distributive part of the bargaining and integrative approaches necessary to solve labor-management problems in the course of reaching overall agreement. Without cooperation, agreement and an operational relationship would be, of course, impossible. Yet the extremes of cooperation — one side capitulating or both sides colluding—eventually destroy the relationship by undermining the legitimacy of the participants in the eyes of their constituents, a legitimacy upon which they ultimately depend for support. The fundamental competitive nature of the relationship must be maintained.

Trust is an essential element in this balance. Without some trust and support between the sides, cooperation would be impossible. It is necessary to examine more closely why trust is central to the relationship. When used in this way, trust has two related but distinguishable meanings. With respect to bargaining, it means the strength of one's belief that an opponent in a competitive situation will, in the interest of maintaining the bargaining relationship, restrain himself or herself from exploiting any concession or risk taken. With respect to the representative nature of collective bargaining, trust means the strength of belief of those represented that participants will behave so as to optimize the outcomes in terms of their constituents' objectives. Without some trust relative to one's bargaining opponent, there is no incentive to take risks or make any but the smallest concessions; there is, especially, little incentive for integrative initiatives. One builds trust in the bargaining dyad by exchanging concessions, allowing gain and avoiding extreme exploitation. But this behavior can be viewed by the constituents as a violation of their trust in the bargainer to represent their interests. Being too trusting in bargaining interferes with good representation, and being too good a representative interferes with building trust in bargaining.

This interaction relates, further, to the problem of influencing bargaining positions or commitments. Trust is necessary to most influence strategies; each party must believe that the other party has authority to enforce concessions made and agreements reached—that is, each side must believe that the bargainers can hold their constituency to a negotiated position. A bargainer for management would not ordinarily take a tentative agreement to the school board for approval without some confidence in the union negotiator's ability to obtain ratification from the union, or vice versa. The ability to make and deliver on commitments is thus a consequence of interaction between bargainers and between bargainers and their constituencies.

Balancing cooperation, trust, and influence can thus be seen as weighing the value of the bargaining relationship against representing a constituency's interest. There is clearly no single solution or firm answer. The relationship and the bargaining that results are affected by the changing situation and behaviors of the participants. In terms of the model in Figure 7-7, the role of the participants changes and adjusts continuously according to the influences of the people in the role and the situation in which they find themselves. These are treated as the main components of the bargaining relationship.

The basic view of the social structure of a bargaining system (see Figure 7-7) is similar to a number of conceptions of what determines bargaining behavior. The three main components of system—person, role, situation—are used by Daniel Druckman to organize a large body of empirical and theoretical literature about negotiations.[31] The dual influence of institutional (situational) factors and individual characteristics on behavior is based on Jacob Getzels and Egon Guba's model of social behavior.[32] Walton and McKersie's model of the forces affecting the bargaining relationship includes four antecedents or determinants: contextual factors, personality, social beliefs, and instrumental thinking and planning.[33]

The model presented here groups instrumental thinking and planning with personality as individual behavior. Social beliefs are divided into attitudes and predispositions, which are considered individual characteristics, and expectations and norms for bargaining behavior, which are received from the situation. Jeffrey Rubin and Bert Brown describe bargaining in terms of four sets of variables: structural context (part of the situation), behavioral predispositions of the bargainers, interdependence of bargainers (cooperation-competition, trust, and commitment), and social influence strategies (purposive actions of the bargainers).[34] In short, these views of the structure of the bargaining relationship share common components. The model used here groups and arranges them in a simplified way to show the connection between bargaining process, structures, and the organizational setting.

The Bargainer's Role

Having described the overall social setting of bargaining, we now turn to the way in which the setting interacts with bargaining actions and outcomes. Earlier in the chapter we discussed the basic elements of bargaining behavior—concessions, threats, and promises in terms of economic concepts of costs and utilities. But these actions take place in, and are influenced by, the social structure of the bargaining relationship. In addition, these basic actions take place in a flux of many complex verbal and nonverbal actions in the bargaining setting and in the relations between the bargainers and their constituents. The entire complex of actions are what we refer to as the bargainer's role.

In the economic description of bargaining, the basic motive is clear: maximize the benefits in terms of the bargaining objectives. From the point of view of the overall social setting, however, motives are far less clear. The boundary-spanning nature of the bargaining role described above means that individual participants in the process experience role conflict, that is, incompatible expectations for how they should behave. Also, a wider range of social influence tactics are available to them to augment the basic tactics of concessions, threats, and promises. In the simple models of bargaining, moreover, the actions are viewed as conscious, rational choices among known alternatives. Bargaining as social behavior is thought of as a combination of those actions with unconscious or intuitive actions resulting from attitudes, predispositions, and personal and situational limitations inherent in the bargaining situation. That is, the pressures of time, fatigue, limited information, emotions, and inadequate skill or experience combine to make actual bargaining behavior often seem irrational or even silly. The actions of participants in the bargaining relationship are similarly influenced by many factors in ways that are not fully understood. So no analysis will produce a complete or definite explanation for behavior. Instead, we concentrate on the main items and the extent of existing knowledge.

Personality, Cooperation, and Trust

Cooperativeness and competitiveness are viewed as different ends of a continuum. The continuum represents the degree to which one seeks to maximize joint outcomes with an opponent rather than to defeat or surpass the opponent. A highly cooperative bargainer would seek an agreement best for both sides; a highly competitive one, an agreement in which he or she got the most. In a somewhat different basic personality orientation toward bargaining, the individualistic one, the bargainer attempts to maximize his or her own gain regardless of the other's gain or loss. This type is suitable for certain kinds of laboratory bargaining and game situations. In collective bargaining, however, power, gain, and loss are relative. An individualistically oriented person may participate in bargaining, but his or her gain could only come at the other's expense. That person would shun integrative bargaining opportunities, which would certainly be viewed as competitive behavior by the opponent. One cannot really go one's own way in a collective bargaining situation.

The degree of cooperativeness in a bargaining process can be a consequence of the predispositions the bargainers bring with them, or something happening in the situation. Bargainers who are predisposed to be cooperative do, as would be expected, behave more cooperatively in a bargaining situation.[35] Since cooperation is necessary to reach an agreement, cooperatively disposed bargainers would be expected to reach faster, lower-conflict agreements, other things being equal.

There is also an interaction between the cooperative-competitive nature and the interpersonal orientation of the bargainers. Interpersonal style reflects a bargainer's reaction or sensitivity to the actions of others in a relationship. A person with a high interpersonal orientation would be quite responsive to the degree of cooperativeness or competitiveness exhibited by the opponent. Cooperative bargainers tend to be more responsive or sensitive than competitive ones, which means that they tend toward behavioral assimilation.[36] That is, they tend to act toward their opponent as their opponent acts toward them. They view the world as being composed of other competitors. Two cooperative people paired as bargainers are more likely to fall into a cooperative pattern and reach agreement quickly. If one is cooperative and one competitive, it is likely that the cooperative one will switch to a competitive style in response to the opponent, leading to more conflict and slower agreement.

A number of other attitudinal aspects of personality have been studied in relation to cooperativeness in bargaining interactions. Low cooperation and high competitiveness are associated with high authoritarianism. The same is true of people who tend to be dogmatic, Machiavellian (manipulative and exploitative of others), and low in self-esteem. Cooperativeness is associated with higher levels of self-esteem and need for affiliation (friendship). Those with a high need for achievement tend to be more competitive.[37]

Cognitive style or decision style is also related to cooperativeness. Some elements of this style are associated as well with a sensitive interpersonal orientation. These include high tolerance of ambiguity, a tendency to attribute control of events to external (rather than internal) causes, high levels of cognitive complexity (or abstract thinking), and low risk preference. These traits can be interpreted as sensitivity to the cues or information in the bargaining environment.[38] People in whom these sensitivities are well developed are more able to recognize and respond to opportunities for cooperative exchange in a situation.

Aside from personality and cognitive style, some other personal characteristics have also been found to affect cooperativeness in bargaining relationships. In general, males tend to be lower in interpersonal sensitivity than females; men tend to maximize their own objectives to a greater degree. When bargaining with people of the same race, blacks tend to be more cooperative than whites. And same-race pairs tend to be more cooperative than mixed-race pairs. Also, large differences in social status between bargainers produce more competitive and exploitive behavior on the part of the higher-status person, resulting in less cooperation overall. Interestingly, intelligence, as measured by tests, does not seem to be related to bargaining behavior in any consistent way.[39]

Taking these relationships together, it is possible to describe, in rough terms, the personal characteristics that will produce the most cooperative or competitive bargaining. The cooperative bargainer will be one who is personally secure, has a low need for personal power or achievement, is high in self-esteem, and values friendship. He or she will have a flexible and complex cognitive style and be low in authoritarianism and dogmatism and high in abstraction. He or she will be basically trusting and cooperative and highly sensitive to behaviors and cues from the bargaining opponent. In contrast, the most competitive bargainer will also have high sensitivity to the opponent, but that will be accompanied by a high need for achievement and power, a tendency toward Machiavellian manipulation, and a general lack of trust. Persons low in interpersonal sensitivity, aside from these other traits, would not be effective bargainers since ability to perceive and correctly respond to others' behavior seems to be an essential part of the bargaining role.

Along with the cooperative-competitive nature, a predisposition to trust varies with individuals. The greater the predisposition, however, the more cooperative one is likely to be in a bargaining relationship. Trust and cooperativeness seem to be closely related.[40]

Skill, Knowledge, and Cooperation

The amount of cooperation actually observed in the bargainer's behavior is also in part a matter of conscious choice. This conscious choice is a consequence of the bargainer's decisions on strategy and tactics, for strategy and tactics are based on what the bargainer believes the constituency wants as well as on personal judgment. Judgment, in turn, is based on skill in assessing a situation and knowledge of an opponent and the bargaining process. In other words, a bargainer may be highly disposed to be cooperative, but choose to be highly competitive (or vice versa) for strategic gain or to meet the expectations of a constituency. Effective bargaining may require a number of shifts in style over the course of bargaining, depending on the tactical positions of the parties. And from one contract to the next, the external economic or political environment may cause a change in expectations. Some minimum level of cooperation and trust is necessary to maintain the bargaining relationship. But above that minimum, the bargainer who can control the level and type of cooperation to fit the circumstances is likely to be more effective than one who, for personal reasons or because of organizational constraints, is bound into one style or another.

There is some reason to believe that skill and knowledge, especially when these result from bargaining experience, can lead to changes in structure. New bargaining relationships are often characterized by rigid expectations on the part of constituencies and reduced maneuvering room for bargainers. Better-established bargaining relationships often evolve into a situation where there is less communication with constituencies and their expectations are less rigid. This allows bargainers more opportunity to cooperate and make concessions.[41] It seems that bargaining experience leads both sides to create a structure that allows more cooperative exchange by reducing the rigidity of expectations and the amount of communication with constituencies. This is a key example of interactions among the situation, the social structure of the situation, and the bargaining process.

There is little evidence, however, of any clear or uniform progression from less to more cooperative structures. The choice of a cooperative or competitive pattern is a product of too many factors other than experience of the bargainers. Management may see a chance to gain back past losses. The union may change leaders or feel threatened by a rival organization. A number of other conditions may shift the basic pattern.[42] Experience and bargaining sophistication will facilitate cooperative bargaining, of course, but only if that is the desired pattern.

Influence, Commitment, and Personality

How a bargainer uses or reacts to influence and commitment strategies is tied to personality. Developing bargaining strategy and tactics depends on some choice among methods of influence. The choice is based on an assessment of how the other side will react.

Influence can be exerted through rewards or punishments (in bargaining terms, concessions, threats, and promises), friendship, expertise, or control of information. Each of these means can be expected to interact in some way with the personality dynamics of the persons involved. Patterns of concessions, which constitute the level of cooperation or competition, have been discussed. The focus in this section is on the other influence techniques.

The way threats and promises interact with personality relates to the concept of "face," that is, perception of one's capability, strength, prestige, or reputation in the eyes of significant others.[43] Saving or restoring face is a major component of bargaining, even though it may seem to be unrelated to the tangible issues on the table. Intangible matters can become bargaining issues and shape the course of the process.[44] Carl Stevens' notion of the paradoxical position of face in bargaining illustrates: to get agreement one must yield (show weakness), but strategy requires strength.[45] Maintaining an image of strength, even though yielding, is important. Maintaining face simply for strategic purposes is not necessarily related to personality, but face is also related to self-esteem. Social disapproval can result from appearing weak, acquiescent, or vulnerable to illegitimate force. As a result, bargainers often go to great lengths and incur heavy costs to avoid losing face or to restore face once lost.[46] Persons low in self-esteem or with a high need for power or prestige would be expected to place great importance on the appearance of strength. This can be exploited by the opponent, especially if one bargainer can be influenced to concede on important tangible issues in return for saving or restoring face. This also suggests that the bargainer cannot reliably estimate the importance of any issue in terms of its tangible value alone; an accurate assessment must include intangible considerations as well.

Threats and promises link directly to maintaining or restoring face since any threat or promise makes face an issue to some degree. In making a threat the bargainer risks loss of face by failing to carry through if the threat does not work. When faced with a threat, the opponent risks loss of face by showing weakness. Similarly, making a promise risks loss of face if the promise is rejected or if one is fooled by a false promise. The choice of a threat or promise strategy requires a careful assessment of the value of face, along with the tangible issues at stake.

The need for friendship or affiliation can also be a personality trait connected to influence tactics. Friendship among opponents in bargaining is a common and often significant element in the overall relationship. Because bargaining is a marginal or boundary role in the organization (see below), participants in bargaining may often have more in common with each other than with other individuals in the organizations they represent. A person with a high need for friendship, as opposed to a need for power, will be more vulnerable to tactics involving withdrawal of friendship by the opponent. This would be particularly true, of course, in long-standing relationships, but could be a factor at any time.

The need or desire of one bargainer to be liked, or friendly with, the opponent can be the basis for a number of tactics.[47] One side will dissociate itself with positions the other does not like, using "it's nothing personal," or "I'm only following orders" as disclaimers. One can also imply that maintenance of the relationship is contingent on some particular concession or action by the other. Or friendship can be the basis for continuing discussions when an apparent impasse is reached. In any case, the value of the relationship to the parties becomes an element in the overall exchange process.

BARGAINING AND THE ORGANIZATIONAL STRUCTURE

Linking the bargaining relationship to the larger social setting includes recognizing that the role of participants in the process spans organizational boundaries. In general, the functions of acquiring resources from the environment or returning outputs requires some specialized unit.[48] There are a number of special activities in organizations, including bargaining, that require roles "whose activities place them at organizational boundaries for the purpose of affecting exchanges with the environment."[49] Bargaining structures are best thought of as spanning boundaries between the school system and its labor organization. We should, therefore, consider the influence this has on the behavior of the occupants of these roles and the consequences for the conduct of the bargaining relationship.

The most important element of the boundary-spanning role is that it has two sources of salient messages about expectations and behavior: the constituent organization and the opponent. These messages revolve around the levels of cooperation and competition desired by the two sides, as well as the levels of trust and commitment. Because fundamental conflict is inherent in the structure, the role demands some balancing. In describing the expectations and organizational demands arising from the position of the bargainer, it should be kept in mind that the situation referred to includes both the organization that the bargainer represents and the link to the opposition.

There are complex interactions in the way constituency expectations for cooperation-competition in the bargaining relationship affect the process. A bargainer's choice of competitive or cooperative actions depends, it appears, on pressures from his or her own constituency and on the perception of pressures from the opposing bargainer. The key to the interaction seems to be whether the bargainers have some room to exercise their own judgment. When the constituent groups on both sides agree on how their bargainer should behave, those expectations can have a strong effect on the bargainer's actions. Thus, a bargainer told to be cooperative will usually act accordingly, even in the face of a competitive opponent, and vice versa. When the expectations are not clear, however, the situation becomes more complex. Where there is little or inconsistent pressure to be cooperative, bargainers tend toward more competitive behavior when facing a competitive opponent. That is, the bargainer appears to exercise individual reactions to the opponent in the absence of strong organizational messages about what style of bargaining is expected. A bargainer who knows that the opponent's behavior is freely chosen can respond in kind.[50]

In other words, bargainers seems to "excuse" a competitive opponent if the opponent appears to be forced into competitive behavior by constituency pressure or accountability. But if the opponent freely chooses to be competitive, that choice is met by intensified competition in return. This is a specific example of findings that, in general, demonstrate that the degree to which the bargainer's personality affects the process varies with the constraints; fewer constraints lead to more personality influence.

The way in which organizational expectations affect bargaining is tied, as well, to the communications process among bargainers and those represented and the presence of alternative communication paths. The first is a matter of the specific mechanism of accountability between the organization and the bargainer, the power of the bargaining unit in the organization, and the general influence of third parties on cooperation and concessions in bargaining. The basic premise is that, the more open the communication, the more constituency expectations will affect bargaining and the less power the bargainer or the bargaining sub-unit has in the organization. Then there is a special case of disinterested third parties being involved in the bargaining as either observers or mediators; communication with them is treated separately.

Organizations—school board and teachers' or employees' union— come to bargaining with many expectations; not all can be met if an agreement is to be reached. The bargaining role requires controlling commitment of the organization to expectations before bargaining in a way that leaves some room to compromise and building commitment to the package of compromises that makes up the agreement. At the same time bargainers must avoid becoming committed to public positions from which they cannot retreat without great loss of face or credibility. All of these role imperatives require some control of constituency and of communications concerning bargaining so that participants in the bargaining process have increased power with respect to outcomes. In short, this is a reciprocal relationship. To influence the outcomes of bargaining, the bargaining sub-unit must be able to influence the organization and bind it to the agreement made at the table.[51]

Accomplishing this role task requires a communication pattern that keeps the members of the constituency well enough informed to ensure consensus and permit them to adjust their expectations to outcomes. It does not mean a communication pattern that provides the constituency with a detailed knowledge of the bargaining or of positions taken privately at the table. This balance, in turn, requires organizational commitment to the bargaining process and clear role expectations for the bargaining unit that enable it to make decisions and maneuver at the table. Studies of municipal governments and school districts show that the power of the bargaining structure is affected by organizational factors, especially commitment to the process, and that relationships evolve to place more control in the bargaining structure.[52]

The alternative to a bargaining structure with some control of information and built-in flexibility is one with strong constituent advocacy and accountability for the bargainers. This alternative, which builds considerable pressures on the bargainers to maintain the organization's position, results in less flexibility and less likelihood of agreement. This is particularly true if the constituency is part of the bargaining audience. It seems that, as Rubin and Brown note, "excessive commitment and advocacy may be in neither the bargainer's nor his constituency's best interest."[53]

The problem of communication and advocacy is compounded by the public nature of most educational systems. The school board is a public body and part of a federal system of government. The full power to govern school affairs and resources is spread across three levels of government, with multiple points of access and influence. Consequently, the union has the opportunity to attempt influence through alternative elements of the organization that are not formally part of the bargaining process. These include the school board itself (unless the board is fully engaged in the bargaining process), municipal or county government in some states, state legislature or departments of education, and the federal government. Particularly in large-city systems, all levels of governments may be involved in a labor dispute simultaneously. This provides opportunities for what Thomas Kochan calls multilateral bargaining, where more than a pair of participants or organizations are involved.[54] For school systems the other party could be the city government, the state board of education, or the legislature. In such a situation the control of the bargaining structure is clearly threatened, and communications and expectations are more difficult to manage. The role of the bargainer is expanded to include political interactions with the other participants, especially for the management side. In fact, it is not uncommon for multilateral strategies by teachers' organizations to result in a teachers' advocate on a school board or other governmental body influencing the bargaining process. In these cases control of information and maintenance of maneuvering room become even more critical tasks for the bargaining structure.

There is also some evidence that the governance structure of the school and of the bargaining are linked to conflict levels.[55] Certain structures may be more vulnerable to conflict or less conducive to resolution. These include management of communication, structures to control or resolve conflict may require ways to limit dissent, penalize or control extreme positions, or enforce majority rules. If existing conflicts in or out of the bargaining are controlled or resolved, cooperation is more likely.

The result is quite different for third parties who are seen as impartial or who have some authority or expertise. Their presence in the bargaining structure seems to build pressure for agreement. Two interrelated mechanisms seem to contribute to this effect. The third party may facilitate the process by improving communication between parties, finding new alternatives, or reducing hostility. What is more important, the third party offers a possible release from accountability. A bargainer can more easily accept an offer from a mediator without loss of face than he or she can from the opponent.[56]

The other major pressure for agreement that is part of the bargaining structure comes from time limits, or deadlines, and these are an integral part of any collective bargaining arrangement. The image of mounting tension as the strike deadline approaches is classic in collective bargaining tradition. But it has become a tradition because the time limit is a fundamental element in the relationship. The logic is simple: the basic reason for incurring the cost of a concession is to reach agreement; and, if agreement is not reached, the cost of the consequences will exceed the cost of the concession. The deadline enforces the costs of not agreeing. If failure to reach agreement is "free," there is no incentive to concede. All that is left is integrative bargaining, which can never settle all issues.

But the need for time limits does not explain the so-called eleventh-hour effect, wherein many concessions are delayed until the last minute. An outstanding example of this is found in the Camp David negotiations between Israel and Egypt. Accounts report that most of the major concessions were made in the last few hours of the summit meeting, even though the participants had been bargaining for many days without major success.[57] Clearly the parties wanted to reach agreement. But a concession made early in the bargaining is viewed differently from one made at the end, even when they are otherwise identical. An early concession implies more are coming. A late concession implies that some yielding was necessary to obtain the agreement, but no more are to be expected. A flurry of late concessions signals to constituents that the bargainer did the best he or she could, holding on to the last. Early concessions lead one to suspect that the representative could have done better. In short, time remaining until a deadline modifies expectations. The more time, the greater the expectation that there will be further concessions; the less time, the stronger the conviction that the best deal has been made.

BARGAINING AND THE PHYSICAL SETTING

The location of the bargaining is the principal component of the physical structure. A neutral site, where neither party is the host or guest, has a different effect on the relationship than a site controlled by one party or the other. Bargainers on their own home ground tend to behave more assertively than their opponents,[58] and the guest may tend to assume a subordinate status. The observation that, if negotiations take place on one's home ground, this can be an advantage is generally held to be true judging by the preference for a neutral site in situations where the site depends on mutual consent of the parties.

The social roles of "guest" and "host" may be so strongly established for most people that bargaining behavior is affected, in spite of the adversarial nature of the relationship. Or the host's control of the physical environment may enhance his or her perceived power in the eyes of the guest. It may also be that territorial instincts or socialization patterns raise the anxiety levels of those on an opponent's territory and interfere with assertiveness and cognitive processing. Agreeing to meet on another's ground may be seen as a concession and consequent sign of weakness even before the bargaining on issues begins. This area of bargaining behavior has not been extensively studied. These alternative explanations of the importance of the bargaining site remain speculative.

This chapter represents an attempt to present a comprehensive overview of the bargaining process in relatively condensed form. The emphasis has been on the cost of concessions strategies, the determinants of cooperation and competition, and the mechanisms of social influence. The view of bargaining is one of complicated interactions, uncertain influences, and unknown results, which, we believe, provides an accurate reflection of the state of theory and understanding of the process. One can account, in very general terms, for why bargainers behave as they do, why concessions are made, and how agreements are reached, and a successful working understanding of bargaining for the practitioner or student of bargaining should be built on concepts such as these. There has been no attempt to "explain" the bargaining process in a determinate way; that remains for the future.

NOTES

1. John T. Dunlop, *Industrial Relations Systems* (New York: Holt, Rinehart and Winston, 1958).

2. Kenneth Boulding, *Conflict and Defense: A General Theory* (New York: Harper, 1962).

3. For a detailed discussion of this point, see Albert Rees, *The Economics of Work and Pay* (New York: Harper, 1973), esp. chs. 4, 5.

4. These terms follow the definitions developed in Richard E. Walton and Robert B. McKersie, *A Behavioral Theory of Labor Negotiations* (New York: McGraw-Hill, 1965).

5. This is the definition developed in J. W. Thibaut and H. H. Kelley, *The Social Psychology of Groups* (New York: Wiley, 1959). It is also discussed in Jeffrey Z. Rubin and Bert R. Brown, *The Social Psychology of Bargaining and Negotiation* (New York: Academic Press, 1975).

6. This view of power is presented in Neil W. Chamberlain and Donald E. Cullen, *The Labor Sector*, 2d ed. (New York: McGraw-Hill, 1971). This view is also basic to economic models of bargaining behavior. See J. Pen, "A General Theory of Bargaining," *American Economic Review*, 42:1 (March 1952), 24-42; and Otomar J. Bartos, *Process and Outcomes of Negotiations* (New York: Columbia University Press, 1974).

7. Carl von Clausewitz, *On War*, Volume I, tr. J. J. Graham (London: Routledge, 1966; originally published, 1908), 165.

8. Thomas C. Schelling, *The Strategy of Conflict* (Cambridge, Mass.: Harvard University Press, 1966), 3. Schelling goes on to note that this is not the military use of the term, but we interpret this to mean only that warfare is not the referent.

9. Walton and McKersie, *Behavioral Theory of Labor Negotiations*, 4-5.

10. See Myron Joseph, "Approaches to Collective Bargaining in Industrial Relations Theory," in *Essays in Industrial Relations Theory*, ed. Gerald A. Somers (Ames: Iowa State University Press, 1969).

11. In general, studies show that bargaining has little effect on salaries, but there is some evidence that there are regional effects. See Jay Chambers, "The Impact of Collective Bargaining for Teachers on Resource Allocation in Public School Districts," *Journal of Urban Economics*, 4:3 (July 1977), 324-339; and Donald Gerwin, "An Information Processing Model of Salary Determination in a Contour of Suburban School Districts," *American Educational Research Journal*, 10:1

(Winter 1973), 5-20 (reprinted in *The Employment of Teachers: Some Analytical Views*, ed. Donald Gerwin [Berkeley, Calif.: McCutchan, 1974], 152-184).

12. The evidence that teachers' salaries are strongly affected by salaries in comparable employment is plentiful. See Anthony M. Cresswell, Hervey A. Juris, Leslie Nathanson, and Kathryn Tooredman, "Impact of State Labor Relations and Finance Policies on Educational Resource Allocation," paper presented at the annual meeting of the American Educational Research Association, 1978; Alan L. Gustman and M. O. Clement, "Teachers' Salary Differentials and Equality of Educational Opportunity," *Industrial and Labor Relations Review*, 31 (October 1977), 61-70; John D. Owen, "Toward a Public Employment Wage Theory: Some Evidence on Teacher Quality," *ibid.*, 25 (January 1972), 213-222.

13. The shortened school year in Chicago in 1977 did not appear to affect achievement (Bureau of City Wide Testing, Department of Research and Evaluation, Chicago Board of Education, 1977), but there is some evidence of long-term impacts on student attitudes. See Robert Hashway, "Long Range Effects of Teachers' Strikes on Student Attitudes," *Educational Research Quarterly* 2:1 (Spring 1977), 12-21.

14. Walton and McKersie, *Behavioral Theory of Labor Negotiations*, 41-44.

15. The discussion of concessions here follows from Anthony M. Cresswell, "A Sequential Model of Collective Bargaining in Education," in *Education and Collective Bargaining: Readings in Policy and Research*, ed. *id.* and Michael J. Murphy (Berkeley, Calif.: McCutchan, 1977). It is similar to that in Gary Yukl, "The Effects of the Opponent's Initial Offer, Concession Magnitude, and Concession Frequency in Bargaining Behavior," *Journal of Personality and Social Psychology*, 30:3 (September 1974), 323-335. Other learning models of bargaining are described in Bartos, *Process and Outcomes of Negotiations*, ch. 4.

16. See H. Kelley, "A Classroom Study of the Dilemmas in Interpersonal Negotiations," in *Strategic Interaction and Conflict: Original Papers and Discussion*, ed. K. Archibald (Berkeley, Calif.: Institute of International Studies, 1966).

17. This general process is discussed by Rubin and Brown, *Social Psychology of Bargaining and Negotiation*, 69-278.

18. For discussion of the political and economic consequences of a long teacher strike, see Richard P. Schick and Jean Couturier, *The Public Interest in Government Labor Relations* (Cambridge, Mass.: Ballinger, 1977), esp. chs. 2, 3.

19. Schelling, *Strategy of Conflict*, 123.

20. Israel departed from its no-negotiation policy in one case long enough to mount a military action in which the terrorists were killed and most hostages were rescued. While effective once, it is unlikely that this strategy would succeed again.

21. Walton and McKersie, *Behavioral Theory of Labor Negotiations*, 104.

22. *Ibid.*, 105.

23. Charles R. Perry and Wesley A. Wildman, *Impact of Negotiations in Public Education* (Worthington, Ohio: Jones Publishing Company, 1970), 72.

24. Rubin and Brown, *Social Psychology of Bargaining and Negotiation*, 283-286.

25. Schelling, *Strategy of Conflict*, 35.

26. Rubin and Brown, *Social Psychology of Bargaining and Negotiation*, 280.

27. Schelling, *Strategy of Conflict*, 35.

28. John F. Hulpke and Donald A. Watne. "Budgeting Behavior: If, When, and How Selected School Districts Hide Money," *Public Administration Review*, 36:6 (November/December 1976), 667-674.

29. Walton and McKersie, *Behavioral Theory of Labor Negotiations*, 114, 116.

30. David L. Colton, "The Influence of an Anti-Strike Injunction," *Education Administration Quarterly*, 13:1 (Winter 1977), 47-70.

31. Daniel Druckman, "Social Psychological Approaches to the Study of Negotiations," in *Negotiations: Social Psychological Perspectives*, ed. *id.* (Beverly Hills, Calif.: Sage Publications, 1977).

32. Jacob W. Getzels, "Administration as a Social Process," in *Administrative Theory and Education*, ed. Andrew W. Halpin (New York: Macmillan, 1958).

33. Walton and McKersie, *Behavioral Theory of Labor Negotiations*, 208.

34. Rubin and Brown, *Social Psychology of Bargaining and Negotiation*, 35-39.

35. See Margaret G. Herman and Nathan Kogan, "Effects of Negotiators' Personalities on Negotiating Behavior," in *Negotiations*, ed. Druckman; see also Rubin and Brown, *Social Psychology of Bargaining and Negotiation*.

36. Rubin and Brown, *Social Psychology of Bargaining and Negotiation*, 185.

37. Laboratory studies showing the results are reviewed, *ibid.*, ch. 7. Similar results for actual bargaining situations are reported by L. Tracy, "The Influence of Non-Economic Factors on Negotiators," *Industrial and Labor Relations Review*, 27:2 (January 1974), 204-215.

38. See Herman and Kogan, "Effects of Negotiators' Personalities on Negotiating Behavior."

39. These observations are discussed in detail by Rubin and Brown, *Social Psychology of Bargaining and Negotiation*; see also James T. Tedeschi, ed., *The Social Influence Process* (Chicago: Aldine-Atherton, 1972); and K. W. Terhune, "The Effects of Personality in Cooperation and Conflict," in *The Structure of Conflict*, ed. P. Swingle (New York: Academic Press, 1970).

40. See B. R. Schelinker, B. Helm, and J. T. Tedeschi, "The Effects of Personality on Behavioral Trust," *Journal of Personality and Social Psychology*, 25:3 (March 1973), 419-427; Rubin and Brown, *Social Psychology of Bargaining and Negotiation*, 183.

41. Perry and Wildman, *Impact of Negotiations in Public Education*, 133-136.

42. Walton and McKersie, *Behavioral Theory of Labor Negotiations*, 201-208, have a detailed treatment of this issue.

43. Bert R. Brown, "Face-Saving and Face-Restoration in Negotiation," in *Negotiations*, ed. Druckman, 276-277.

44. Rubin and Brown, *Social Psychology of Bargaining and Negotiation*, 131-133.

45. See Carl M. Stevens, *Strategy and Collective Bargaining Negotiations* (New York: McGraw-Hill, 1963).

46. Anthony M. Cresswell and Daniel Simpson, "Collective Bargaining and Conflict: Impacts on School Governance," *Educational Administration Quarterly* 13:3 (Fall 1977), 49-69.

47. Walton and McKersie, *Behavioral Theory of Labor Negotiations*, chs. 6, 7, discuss attitudinal change tactics in detail.

48. Daniel Katz and Robert L. Kahn, *The Social Psychology of Organizations* (New York: Wiley, 1966).

49. Stacey J. Adams, "The Structure of Dynamics of Behavior in Organizational Boundary Roles," in *Handbook of Industrial and Organizational Psychology*, ed. Marvin D. Dunnette (Chicago: Rand McNally, 1976).

50. *Ibid.*

51. The mechanisms of control and influence in school settings are discussed in Perry and Wildman, *Impact of Negotiations in Public Education*, and, in general, in Walton and McKersie, *Behavioral Theory of Labor Negotiations*.

52. Thomas A. Kochan, "Determinants of the Power of Boundary Units and Interorganizational Bargaining Relations," *Administrative Science Quarterly*, 20:3 (September 1975), 434-452. See also Perry and Wildman, *Impact of Negotiations in Public Education.*

53. Rubin and Brown, *Social Psychology of Bargaining and Negotiation*, 54.

54. A model of multilateral bargaining appears in Thomas A. Kochan, "City Government Bargaining: A Path Analysis," *Industrial Relations*, 14:1 (February 1975), 90-101.

55. Cresswell and Simpson, "Collective Bargaining and Conflict," The relationship between conflicts and structure is covered in Joseph A. Sarthory, "Structural Characteristics and the Outcome of Collective Negotiations," *Educational Administration Quarterly*, 7:3 (1971), 78-79 (reprinted in *The Employment of Teachers*, ed. Gerwin, 376-386).

56. Richard E. Walton, *Interpersonal Peacemaking: Confrontations and Third-Party Consultation* (Reading, Mass.: Addison-Wesley, 1969); see also D. F. Johnson and W. L. Tullar, "Style of Third-Party Intervention, Face Saving and Bargaining Behavior," *Journal of Experimental and Social Psychology*, 8:4 (July 1972), 319-330.

57. For a general chronology of the events, see *Time* (October 2, 1978).

58. D. A. Martindale, "Territorial Dominance Behavior in Dyadic Verbal Interactions," *Proceedings of the Seventy-ninth Annual Conference of the American Psychological Association*, 6 (1971), 305-306.

8

The Contract

Central to labor-management relations is the contract, an explicit framework of agreements and procedures with a specified life span. It becomes the touchstone or main reference point in the relationship between school workers and administrators. While it by no means provides a complete picture of the labor relations system in schools, the contract in force reflects the current situation and indicates something about the history of the relationship through the pattern of rules and compromises that have evolved. To understand the meaning of the contract and its place in the labor relations system, it is useful to examine the contract as a document (what it contains, and how it is typically organized), in terms of language (the words and how they are interpreted in the work situation), and as an artifact (physical evidence of the history and development of the labor relations system in the school district).

In spite of the way one views the contract, one major issue constantly crops up and goes beyond the contract to become a part of bargaining and to affect the power of the parties: what and how much should be negotiated. This is known as the "scope" of the contract, and cherished values and ideological positions are part of this consideration. It is useful to attempt to separate such questions from other, more straightforward ones of a factual nature. In this discussion of the content of a contract, we do not advocate what we believe should be included in contracts. The discussion, instead, is a comprehensive one that allows mention of most of the matters that might be negotiated.

THE CONTRACT AS A DOCUMENT

Agreements in force in school districts range from one- or two-page contracts that deal only with salary and benefits to longer, more complex ones of over a hundred pages that cover most aspects of school operations. The more complex ones, often found in large cities, reveal a long history of bargaining and cover a great variety of special programs and work situations.

The written agreement that results from collective bargaining has some of the characteristics of an ordinary commercial contract and an individual employment contract, but it is fundamentally different from both. Like the commercial contract, it is an agreement, enforceable in the courts, describing some mutually beneficial exchange, such as a lease, where the use of an apartment is exchanged for a monthly rental fee. The commercial contract is motivated by each party's self-interest, and the transaction is usually temporary. The labor contract, which also has a fixed term, differs, however, in that it is part of a permanent relationship and is written with an eye to future bargains and work conditions. Workers are hired individually under a written or implied employment contract, but their work is largely governed by the labor contract. Robert Gorman notes:

By articulating and absorbing a host of rules and regulations for carrying on the day-to-day continuing activities of those employees, the labor contract functions more like a statute or a code of regulations than it does a bilateral agreement. Moreover, the union, although a legal entity with the power to contract, does not speak for a single monolithic constituency but rather for an amalgam . . . whose ambitions, needs and interests frequently come into conflict.[1]

The document itself is not a *definition* of the labor relationship; rather, it is a *product* of it. Nor is the contract ever complete since practices, informal agreements, and compromises in the workplace, as well as grievances, continually modify the written terms. As with a statute, the real impact is determined more by implementation and interpretation than by the letter of the law. With these observations in mind, we can examine the document.

In some important respects the development of labor contracts in schools differs from that in other organizations in the public and private sectors. In the absence of teachers' unions, boards of education generally apportioned salaries according to a published, uniform schedule, where wages for teachers are determined by years of experience and level of education.[2] Most states require a written employment contract for individual teachers. Boards of education typically have written policies governing terms and conditions of employment. There is often a local teachers' organization, usually an affiliate of the National Education Association or a state association. This organization, formed for primarily professional and social purposes, has provided a basis for union-like activity. That is why collective bargaining for teachers and other employees does not usually require the development of written policies or uniform salary arrangements; by and large, these exist. What teachers would like is to change the mode in which these policies are made from the bureaucratic-professional or public one to the labor relations one. The contract records which decisions and policies have been moved into the labor relations mode.

Preamble

Before describing the details of rules and working conditions, contracts often contain a section wherein the parties express some general principles or feelings about the bargaining relationship. This section, usually called a preamble, is not usually enforced since it seldom contains specific terms. The language rarely is meant to gain benefits for either the employer or the employee. But it can still have potential advantages for both sides.

By broadening the language of the preamble, the board risks extending the scope of the agreement by implication. Statements of intent and descriptions of the opponent can also be taken into account when considering contract matters. If there is to be a preamble, therefore, careful crafting of language is necessary. Benefits may accrue to both sides if a cooperative spirit can be conveyed in the preamble. The language may appear pretentious, but, at the beginning of a contract developed out of conflict, it signals the parties' willingness to make a public statement of mutual support.

The following passages from an agreement in Chicago illustrate the point:

It is recognized that teaching requires specialized qualifications as well as educational requirements and that the success of the educational program depends on the maximum utilization of the abilities of teachers who are reasonably well satisfied with the conditions under which they work, who are assured of fair reward and security in their profession, and who are cooperatively working for the achievement of an effective program of education.

It is the intent of both parties that all discussions and conferences growing out of this agreement be held in an atmosphere of good faith, confidence, and mutual respect.[3]

Beyond the rhetoric, clear statements of intent to act in good faith may be useful in any litigation growing out of the administration of the agreement.

Negotiating the language of the preamble at the beginning of negotiations may be beneficial since a precedent for agreeing to neutral language may help get things started. If the language is negotiated at the end of difficult bargaining, its conciliatory tone may calm and heal.

Structure of the Union-Management Relationship

In terms of the three modes of decision making in schools— bureaucratic-professional, political, and labor relations—described in Chapter 5, the section of the contract of interest here outlines formal arrangements for the labor relations mode. Where state law regulates the bargaining process in public schools, some specifications for labor relations structures usually appear in the law itself. Our concern is with how that structure develops as a result of the bargaining process. The law provides boundaries and constraints; the contract fills in the details.

The Parties to the Bargain

Recognition that an organization represents the workers in the negotiating process is, of course, the first step in structuring the relationship. The contract generally specifies the name of the organization, recognizes its status as exclusive representative of the workers covered, provides some description of the criteria for membership in the bargaining unit, that is, workers covered by the specific contract. In some states recognition of an exclusive representative is a mere formality since the law requires that only exclusive recognition be awarded. In states without formal legal frameworks, it is possible for the employer to recognize more than one organization as representing the employees. In these cases some sort of proportional representation or confederation of employees' organizations is necessary. In Tucson, Arizona, for example, a negotiating council made up of representatives of the competing employees' organizations actually represents the workers at the bargaining table. In Illinois, another state without a collective bargaining law for public employees, there are districts where several organizations have formed confederations to represent all of the teachers in bargaining. In any case, the organization named in the contract as the recognized bargaining agent represents all of the workers covered by the contract, whether they are members of the organization or not. And that organization is responsible for fairly representing those employees.

The definition of an appropriate bargaining unit is a critical component of the structure of the labor relations system, particularly in schools. There are two central issues: whether professionals should be in the same unit as nonprofessionals, and where to draw the dividing line between managerial and nonmanagerial workers. Underlying both issues are the policy objectives of creating a bargaining unit with common interests and of promoting the stability and effectiveness of the bargaining relationship.

Teachers have a clear community of interest with other professional education workers, such as counselors, psychologists, and others. They have roughly the same status, salary, and level of responsibility in the operation of the educational program. This is less true for teachers' aides and other so-called paraprofessionals. In some large cities, such as Chicago, these workers are in the same unit as the teachers. Elsewhere, as in Detroit, they form a separate unit. A case can be made for both arrangements. The teachers work side by side with aides and share the same working conditions and problems. Because there are fewer aides than teachers, however, aides might have trouble competing in the bargaining process.

The same facts can lead to opposite conclusions. There is an inherent competition for resources between teachers and aides. The relative number of each represents a series of trade-offs in the allocation of instructional resources—more aides can mean fewer teachers, or vice versa. Aides and kindred workers, because they are a numerical minority in the instructional staff, may not be well represented within a bargaining unit, especially when teachers have higher status in the system, enjoy the advantages of tenure, and supervise the work of aides.

It is generally in management's interest to keep the aides in the same unit as the teachers, for this means one less contract to negotiate. The trade-offs between aides and teachers can be handled within the bargaining unit, and the management team can avoid union efforts to pit one side against the other. It also seems to be in the teachers' interest to have aides and other paraprofessionals in the same unit in that it is easier to control competition for the instructional dollars and limit the number of aides to that needed by teachers. Other things being equal, however, nonprofessional instructional staff might be better off in its own unit. How this question is ultimately settled is a matter of negotiations in most instances, and the recognition and unit determination sections of the contract spell out the results.

In judging the appropriateness of the bargaining unit, as it is determined through local negotiation, state labor relations agencies and the courts have employed a set of criteria resembling those discussed above: *community of interest* among the workers, *effective representation*, and *efficient operations*.[4] Depending on local circumstances, applications of the criteria can produce a variety of results concerning whether both professionals and nonprofessionals should be in the unit. A small district may have so few paraprofessionals, for example, that a separate unit would be both ineffective and inefficient, while in large cities quite the opposite could be true. And so it seems inadvisable to go beyond these general criteria to specify detailed rules for professionals and nonprofessionals in the same bargaining unit.

The matter of managerial and nonmanagerial employees is even more complex. Most statutes include some dividing line between these classes of workers, with managers either being prohibited from entering into a bargaining relationship or being allowed to do so only in a separate unit. Contracts follow this same basic pattern, but where to draw the dividing line is a persistent issue. Stephen Hayford and Anthony Sinicropi have divided the way supervisors are treated in statutes into four categories: exclusion of all super-visors, exclusion of bona fide supervisors, supervisors with full bargaining rights, and supervisors with the right to meet and confer.[5] In reviewing the law in ten states with comprehensive bargaining statutes for public employees, they found that six had definitions of management or supervisory jobs consistent with those in the private sector (Labor Management Relations Act).[6] This definition is based on managerial or supervisory functions rather than on job titles. Only the statute in Iowa excludes all supervisors by job title.

Among the six states that have a functional definition of super-vision, three (Connecticut, Oregon, Wisconsin) exclude supervisors and management from coverage of the law. One state (Pennsylvania) allows only meet-and-confer rights. The remaining two (Minnesota and Hawaii), along with three states without statutory definitions of supervisors, allow full bargaining rights. Only in Iowa is the presence of supervisors in the bargaining unit clearly removed from the bargaining table. In the other states the definition of who is a bona fide supervisor remains a matter for negotiation and adjudica-tion, as is also true, of course, in states that allow bargaining for school employees but have not legislated clear definitions or ex-clusions of supervisory workers.

Confidential employees, even if they are not supervisors, may be excluded from bargaining units. This category might include secre-taries to key administrators or other professional or clerical workers with access to data that could affect bargaining. The information might be related to finances, board strategy, or related questions.

Defining who may bargain is a ticklish problem in schools because of the great variation in organizational patterns and the blurred lines dividing supervisory functions from the rest of the work of education. Curriculum directors and coordinators, grade-level supervisors, department heads, assistant principals, and other workers often share teaching and supervisory functions. In smaller schools principals may also be part-time teachers. Where federal or special state-funded projects are involved, teachers may move into the role of project director on a part-time or temporary basis. Where direction and evaluation of employees is concerned, teachers with full-time classroom duties have supervisory functions. They direct teacher aides and clerical staff, evaluate their performance, and, in many instances, assist in evaluating their teaching colleagues.

As programs and internal structures of the school change over time, these supervisory functions will shift as well. A clear delineation, if once achieved, would still require revision, which suggests that the negotiation of supervisory-nonsupervisory distinctions should be a matter for local review and control.

The problem of contractually dividing supervisors from teachers is related to and, in fact, exacerbated by the pattern of tension and conflict between supervisors and teachers. Supervisors are expected to both help *and* evaluate teachers and other workers. Arthur Blumberg states the conflict succinctly in terms of a central question: "How can a supervisor be expected to develop an open, supportive, and trusting interpersonal climate when he is also expected to evaluate the teacher?"[7] The negotiation of the contractual division between supervisory and other workers in terms of membership in the bargaining unit affects this conflict. Those excluded from the unit are thereby cast into an adversarial relationship with members, and an "open, supportive, and trusting" relationship is more difficult to maintain. While such a division is necessary to the contract and to the orderly management of the school, the language of the contract should be carefully constructed in an effort to avoid unnecessary conflict on these grounds.

This can be done by making the language as precise as possible. While a statute should be in somewhat general, functional terms, the contract should be specific, naming positions whenever possible. Where positions cannot be named, functions that identify supervisors should be fully described. Of course, both sides of the table have an interest in making their team as inclusive as possible. But the problem of conflict of interest is central, particularly for management. In the committee report accompanying the Labor Management Relations Act, the U.S. Congress points out the reasons for avoiding the conflict of interest: "Management, like labor, must have faithful agents . . . no one, whether employer or employee, need have as his agent one who is obligated to those on the other side, or one whom, for *any* reason, he does not trust."[8] By making the division clear, confusion of loyalty and responsibility can be reduced.

The way some contracts have handled the problem of department heads in secondary schools is an example. Typically, department heads spend most of their time teaching, but they also have important supervisory duties that can include hiring, evaluating teaching, assigning teaching and paraprofessional staff, and assisting in budget preparation. They are clearly on the border line. One solution has been to remove the strictly supervisory duties (evaluation, assignment, and so forth) to a member of the administrative staff such as an assistant principal. Department heads can then be members of the bargaining unit and function effectively as support to teachers without serious role conflict.

Scope of the Agreement

Once the parties to the bargaining process are determined, the central issue of the structure of the relationship remains: What is in the contract? "Scope" is the term that refers to what is negotiable and what is covered by the contract. A topic that one party simply refuses to negotiate will clearly not be in the contract. One that is accepted as a legitimate subject of bargaining may not get into the contract in any particular year. But the fact that an item can be bargained does affect the contract, both because it can be a trade-off with other issues and because it can be included in a later contract. Items that are negotiated but not settled in one series of negotiations have a way of appearing again in the next. And so in discussing scope of the agreement we include by extension those subjects that can be bargained, whether or not they become part of the contract.

The important distinctions in the legal definition are among items that are *mandatory, permissive,* and *excluded* (or illegal). Mandatory items are those that both parties have a positive duty to negotiate. Refusal to do so can lead to a charge of unfair labor practice that will be sustained in court action. The duty to bargain an item does not, however, require any particular concession — only that the parties bargain in good faith.[9] Permissive items are those that are allowed in the contract but are bargained by mutual consent of the parties. Refusal to bargain is not considered an unfair labor practice. Excluded or illegal items are explicitly prohibited from bargaining by law. For example, under most state codes, a school board cannot negotiate the power to hire or dismiss employees.

Where there is no statute or court decision imposing a positive duty on employers to bargain, there are no mandatory items. Employers can refuse to bargain any and all items, provided they are prepared to take the consequences. Where a statute does impose a duty to bargain, however, the central issue becomes what the employer *must* negotiate. That may be settled in the statute, where the mandatory and excluded items are spelled out in detail, leaving little in the permissive category. In such cases, the scope of the bargaining is determined away from the bargaining table. In most other states with any appreciable level of bargaining, the law sets only boundaries within which there is much bargaining leeway. In these instances, the scope of the agreement is settled at the table.

At the bargaining table, scope is determined in two ways. The most obvious and most important is simply an item-by-item struggle over whether a proposal is to be discussed at all or accepted into the agreement. Once a bargaining relationship is established, a few topics—usually wages, benefits, length of the work day and year, and duration of the agreement—are readily accepted as negotiable by both parties. Beyond these, the scope may depend on the legal framework, the history of the relationship, and the immediate objectives of the parties. In general, of course, the union prefers to expand the scope of the agreement. The more that is negotiated, the larger the union's role. Management's goal is usually to keep as much out of the contract as possible in an effort to preserve its area of discretionary action. Apart from mutually acceptable core areas or items already included in the contract, scope is an inherent consideration when discussing each proposal and making decisions.

In sophisticated bargaining, these are not a series of ad hoc decisions; rather, they are a set of carefully planned and coordinated strategic moves. Each party has a number of significant proposals that it wants to include in, or omit from, the agreement. Teachers' unions may, for example, wish to negotiate some procedures for teacher evaluation; the board may feel that this is strictly a management prerogative that is nonnegotiable. This would be a permissive subject in most states, with no legal compunction either to include or exclude it from consideration. The eventual outcome would be determined by the bargaining behavior and power of the parties. The teachers might force the board to accept such an item by threatening a strike, especially if the board were unwilling to accept the costs of a strike. The board could keep evaluation off the table altogether by refusing to discuss it. If the union were unwilling to "go to the mat" over that issue, it would be dropped. Or the board might be willing to accept an evaluation clause in the contract in return for a sufficiently large concession by the union in some other area, such as salary level. By contrast, the teachers might be willing to drop the demand for evaluation in the contract in return for a sufficiently large concession by the board elsewhere. In this manner, the boundaries of the contract and of management's rights are established incrementally.

The agreement may also include a so-called management's rights clause. This section of the contract spells out, in detailed or general terms, the definition of the boundaries of the negotiations. While there is some disagreement among negotiators about the purpose and value of such a clause, the dominant view is that it is unnecessary to establish management's "rights" in a contract. These "rights," better referred to as "discretion," are established in the constitution, school code, and bargaining laws of the states. From the union's point of view, it is desirable to negotiate such a clause since it is unlikely to expand the extensive areas of discretion that already exist, and it may actually move more of the substance of school operation into the negotiations mode. Conversely, there seems to be little incentive for management to seek such a clause. In short, the best clause, from management's point of view, is none at all.

Scope of Bargaining and the Public Interest

The central policy issues embedded in the question of management's rights are, of course, *where* should the boundary be drawn and *how*. This problem lies at the center of the power relationship between the parties, according to Lewis Kaden[10] (see Chapter 5). Management's desire to keep scope narrow and labor's pressure to broaden it are clearly understandable in terms of power. Because the union has greater power in the bargaining mode of governance, pressure to increase scope increases the power of the union at the expense of management.

If it were simply a matter of relative private power, the private sector's concept of balance would be appropriate. But the public school as an employer is responsible to the public. An erosion of management rights through an expansion of scope is thus seen as damaging to the public interest, primarily because it diminishes the sovereignty of the local government. As Joan Weitzman puts it, "sovereignty, as it applies to labor relations, refers to the government's power to fix, through law, the terms of its employees' employment. This power is unique, unalterable, and unilateral."[11] This power is vested in government so that it may act on behalf of all citizens. The union, in contrast, acts to further the private interests of its members. To the extent that it allows decisions to be made contrary to the interests of all citizens, a broad scope of bargaining is seen as evidence of excessive union power. From this perspective, public policy should tightly limit scope through law, which would prevent public school (and other public-sector unions) from exerting undue influence on the working of local government.[12]

This argument rests on the questionable assumption that employment in the public sector is fundamentally different from that in the private one, particularly because it is monopolistic and provides essential services. Determination of the scope of bargaining cannot, therefore, be left to the dynamics of the bargaining process, but must be controlled by a higher level of government, supposedly removed from the undue influence of unions. But this clear distinction between public and private sectors has been seriously challenged by a number of writers.[13] The view they express is, in essence, that the differences between the private and public sectors, while they are real, are neither consistent nor large enough to warrant policies that treat them as fundamentally distinct. In their opinion, labor-management peace is best ensured by policies that rely primarily on balance of power and mutual accommodation at the bargaining table. Scope of bargaining determined through reasonably balanced local agreement may fit local needs better than a narrower, more uniform one set at the state level. If management has insufficient power to protect the public interest in bargaining, that problem should be addressed directly. State policies and organizations to increase the managerial or political strength of school boards would be such direct means.

Maintenance of Standards

Closely tied to scope are the so-called maintenance of standards clauses, which bind the board to negotiate with the union on *any* change in existing policies related to teacher welfare, working conditions, and related items (for example, class size). The language may be subtle or obvious. It may apply only to one section of the contract, or it may apply to all terms. In any case, it is clearly in the union's interest to insert maintenance-of-standards-type clauses whenever possible. They work to bring large areas of board policy-making discretion into the bargaining arena. From management's point of view, all language must be carefully scrutinized to determine whether it has implications for the maintenance of standards.

Wages, Benefits, and Work Load

The core of bargaining is, of course, over salary and work to be done. The details of pay and work load can be as simple as using a single salary schedule and calendar, or so complicated that they require dozens of contract pages covering leaves, insurance, special duty pay, class size, and many other items. These items may be the most difficult ones to bargain over, in terms of both conflict between parties and the many details to be resolved. Yet, paradoxically, they are the least problematic elements of the contract because, by their nature, the specification of salaries, hours, the school calendar, and benefits is usually quite unambiguous. If the salary schedule says beginning teachers with a B.A. get $9,500, then that is what should be paid. Much time and effort may be expended in reaching the figure, but, once reached, it is easy to interpret and administer; deviations from the contract are usually obvious and can be readily remedied. Not all wage and work load elements are quite so precise, but the generalization still holds.

Writing, understanding, and interpreting the wage and work load section of the contract is, therefore, less troublesome than other areas, which is why it receives less attention here. Instead we briefly cover the range of issues and concentrate on those that pose more serious problems of interpretation.

Salary

The objectives of employees' organizations, when they are negotiating salaries, are to obtain as much as possible and to remove the manipulation of salary from administrative control. Aside from the amount to be paid, the negotiations include the imposition of uniform rates and mechanisms for allocation. Thus, base pay is determined by uniform schedules, where placement of individuals on the schedule is controlled by clear rules and criteria. The same rules and criteria apply to advancement in pay by moving to different parts of the schedule. Unions typically oppose merit pay systems, where salary increases are contingent either in part or completely on administrators' evaluations of teachers' work. The same principle applies to pay for extra duties, longevity, or substitutes. Thus, the salary portions of contracts typically contain both the numerical wage rates and the rules for determining which employees receive each rate. This can extend in large, complex contracts to hourly rates for attendance at workshops, separate schedules for different work years, and rules for evaluating educational credits where those credits affect wage rates.

It is useful to note here that negotiations may produce salary terms that never appear in the contract, and the contract itself will not indicate the overall cost of the salary settlement to the school system or the increase for employees. Translating the contract language into the actual costs and benefits involved is complex. Without knowing how many teachers receive wages at each step of the salary schedule, the total cost cannot be calculated. Negotiations may take place in terms of percentages of increase, or total dollars, which are later reflected in a salary schedule and pay rate clause. Calculating the costs of alternative proposals becomes an integral part of the negotiations process, but one that is not evident in examining the contract itself.

Insurance

Several forms of insurance—for example, life, health, income maintenance, dental coverage—are typically part of a fringe benefit package, whether or not there is a negotiated contract. And so any particular compensation package represents trade-offs among salary, insurance, and other fringe benefits. For one thing, estimates of insurance premiums are often inaccurate, which means that school districts may have to increase payments during the term of a policy. Also, employees may be unable to predict their own use of various items, which makes the distribution of benefits among the bargaining unit unclear. And, since insurance premiums paid by the employer are not taxed as income, the amount of benefit to the individual employee varies with the persons' family income tax bracket. Besides, the details of insurance coverage are seldom spelled out in the contract, but, rather, covered in other documents.

Pension Funds

Most states require pension funds for public school teachers, and private school systems also usually have retirement funds. Whether to offer such a benefit is seldom an issue, but the percentage to be paid by the employer is. Increasing the employer's contribution increases take-home pay, but not tax liability, which makes it attractive to employees. And where the retirement system is locally controlled, it may be politically attractive for the employer to increase retirement benefits rather than salaries. The costs to the taxpayer are less visible and have less impact in the short run. The larger pension fund liabilities that result only become political and financial problems in the future, when those making the decision will probably no longer be in office.[14]

Leave

It is difficult, when negotiating leave policy, to produce a system of long- and short-term leaves in which costs can be estimated and controlled. And, when writing the contract, it is also difficult to find contract language that is clear and can be administered effectively. Short-term leaves—sick leave, personal business, and other limited absences from teaching duty—are more difficult in this respect. They involve larger costs, because they affect many employees and allow more opportunities for abuses and arbitrary administration. Long-term leaves—sabbatical leaves, military service—affect fewer employees, involve lower costs, and have more clearly defined terms and purposes.

The costs of a short-term leave policy are determined by the total number of days allowed, the tightness of restrictions governing their use, and the pattern of use in the system. Not all teachers use all allowed sick leave or personal business days, and tight regulation further reduces use. The historical pattern of past behavior or records from comparable school systems, can serve as a guide for writing the contract or estimating costs.

Factors that affect cost are how many unused days employees can accumulate ("banking"), the conditions under which these days can be either used or compensated for, and whether the unused days are transferable from one employee to another. A typical sick leave clause would allow, say, for fifteen days of paid sick leave per year. Any days not used in one year would be available in the next, accumulating either without limit or to some fixed amount (such as 180, equivalent to a school year). Teachers may sometimes receive some proportion of their unused sick days upon retirement as additional severance pay. Welfare or sick leave banks are also found in some agreements. In these clauses, the members of the bargaining unit transfer some sick days to a "bank" that is then available to other teachers who exceed their allowance.

All of these provisions have the obvious effect of increasing the overall cost of a leave provision. But predicting the cost, especially if the arrangement is new to the system, is quite difficult. As a result, neither side has a clear idea of what they are giving up in order to include banking provisions in the contract.

Perquisites

Depending upon the bargaining power and creativity of the unions, a number of minor benefits or professional perquisites may be included in the contract. These can run from such common-place matters as providing each teacher with a desk, to lounges, special work areas, parking, and so forth. These items are typically low-cost ones for the district and, as such, provide useful small-scale bargaining items for the union. Management may counter minor demands for perquisites with minor additional demands for teachers' duties. Although such items are of little consequence in themselves, they indicate the character of the labor-management relationship. The presence of a large number of minor perquisites in an agreement also provides that many more opportunities for grievances.

Work Load

The contract specifies both benefits to workers and work expected in return. In teaching, this can be expressed in terms of the number of students per class, the number of classes taught, or the amount of time spent teaching. For noninstructional personnel covered by contract, the work load is expressed in conventional terms of hours per day or per some other measure of work to be performed. Since the units of production in education are not easily or precisely measured, the employer purchases, in effect, a certain amount of teaching from the staff rather than a certain amount of educational product. It is in the union's interest to limit and control the amount of effort required of the members for a given wage level. Management, on the other hand, is interested in obtaining the most effort for the wage paid, as well as in retaining flexibility in arranging the work process (that is, the curriculum and organization of the school program). Bargaining over the work load revolves around these central issues.

School Year. State school codes usually specify a minimum length of the school year (typically, 180 days). Additional workdays beyond the minimum school year, either for additional teaching or for other duties, can be part of the contract. Besides specifying the number of days to be worked under the contract, there may be a clause detailing the methods to be used to calculate pro rata pay for portions of the school year worked. This latter provision is particularly important in situations where severe financial shortages might result in a shortened school year.

School Day and Class Size. As with the length of the year, school codes typically specify a minimum length of the school day. Contracts usually deal with the hours of work for teachers and other staff members, rather than the number of hours students attend school. The length of time required for teachers before and after the beginning of class time is usually a negotiable item, but not usually one of major consequence. The total amount of time spent teaching within the day and the size of the classes taught are, however, much more important. These provisions directly affect the cost of the program and the number of jobs.

The workday issue is usually expressed in terms of number of periods for which lessons must be prepared as opposed to nonteaching time during the school day. For secondary teachers, it may be a matter of how many classes are taught; for elementary teachers, a matter of total teaching and nonteaching time. These questions determine both work load and the number of teaching jobs for a given student population. There are, of course, no clear professional standards for these questions, although bargaining is often carried out as though it were clear what is best for the students. Where these decisions are made in the bureaucratic-professional mode rather than bargained, the basis is usually professional judgment or available standards within fiscal constraints. Usually patterns of accepted practice with regard to what is considered a "normal" or acceptable school day are used.

The same applies to determining what the size of classes should be. Although it is widely believed that smaller classes are better, there is no definitive way to determine optimum class size. Where class size is not negotiated, it is set on the basis of professional judgment, past practice, and budget considerations. Where it is negotiated, the class size or teacher-pupil ratios expressed in the contract largely determine the cost of the contract and the number of teaching jobs. Since there are different ways to deal with the teacher-pupil ratio question in the contract, those details are worth closer examination.

Ordinarily, teacher and board objectives regarding class size conflict. Teachers, who want smaller classes and more jobs, suggest that "maximums" are preferable. Whenever a class exceeds the maximum, they insist that it be split so that another teacher is needed and the size of the average class drops. Administrators, who want to control costs and retain power, suggest, first, that it is desirable to keep class size away from the bargaining table. If it is to be negotiated at all, management's position would normally be to employ rough guidelines and averages for teacher-pupil ratios, rather than to set absolute maximums. This allows greater flexibility, and the average class size can be larger. When an individual teacher's load exceeds the guideline, for example, that teacher would become eligible for a variety of remedies, such as extra clerical help, to lighten the load.

An additional complication can arise when boards of education have strong policies or feelings about reducing the size of classes in an effort to improve the quality of the educational program. If both sides at the bargaining table seek lower class sizes, there may be an opportunity for integrative bargaining. If there is a tight limit on the budget, smaller classes can only come from either lower salaries or reducing some other expenditure. Choosing among the various alternatives can become a problem-solving process rather than adversarial bargaining. If there is little in the way of a budget limit, other than the political sensitivity of the board, salary and other expenditures can be maintained and more teachers can be employed. In that case, the selection of a class size or teacher-pupil ratio may be even less of a distributive bargaining situation. Either way, the specification of class sizes or ratios in a contract has a direct and substantial effect on both the cost and operation of the instructional program.

Teachers' Aides. Providing help for the teacher in the classroom is an obvious way of reducing the work load. It may also be somewhat lower in cost than reducing class size since aides' salaries are considerably below those of teachers. As with any budget-linked contract item, however, providing teaching aides or increasing their number involves trade-offs. It also calls for negotiated procedures and standards for allocating these people, as well as the specific division of responsibility and duties between teachers and aides. When the aides themselves are organized and covered by a contract, through either the teachers' bargaining unit or their own, there may be conflicts over supervision and duties. To illustrate, teachers' aides were employed in one program to teach reading through a computer-assisted instructional system. The aides, without a teacher present, were to supervise pupils working at computer terminals. But the aides filed a grievance, claiming that, in order to help the pupils do the lessons, such an arrangement forced them to make instructional decisions, a violation of the contract. An arbitrator ruled that there must be a teacher in the room to assist in making instructional decisions.[15] In this and similar cases, the language of the contract should provide clear rules for the use of aides that do not interfere with the general operation of programs.

The use of aides also places teachers in a quasi-managerial position. Where this is a matter of contract, the agreement should include clear statements of the responsibilities of the teachers with respect to the supervision, direction, and evaluation of aides.

Extra Duties. While extra duties may involve a relatively small part of the total program or budget, they may be a ticklish element of the contract because they are either onerous chores teachers would rather avoid or prizes actively sought for extra pay or status. In either case, the allocation of such duties has the potential for considerable conflict. Most contracts recognize that some routine duties—supervising study periods or hallways or sponsoring some extracurricular activities—are considered part of the regular teaching job to be performed without extra pay. The contract may, however, provide a mutually agreed upon and equitable means of distributing the chores.

For the desirable activities for which teachers are paid, the contract can provide for a systematic and uniform method of allocation and compensation. Some flexibility and discretion in these matters is the usual concern of management. Teachers, in contrast, often push for fairly rigid mechanisms to control the allocation of extra duties in an effort to prevent management from using the allocation as a means of rewarding or punishing staff unfairly. And, if the contract covers a fairly large system, there are many extra duties and student activities. As a result, this section of the contract can be more detailed and require more attention during negotiations than would seem necessary in relation to the amount of money or instructional time involved.

Personnel Policies

In a broad sense, "personnel policies" could apply to all that is covered in a negotiated contract. In this section, therefore, we confine the meaning to rules for the hiring, intrasystem mobility, evaluation, and dismissal of staff. In the absence of a collectively bargained contract, all of these decisions are under the control of the school administration, and they are considered part of the bureaucratic-professional mode of decision making. To the extent that these elements of administration become part of the contract, they move into the negotiations mode, with a concomitant loss of administrative discretion and increased power for the teachers' organization. In examining these parts of the contract, it is useful to outline the basic issues and interests of management and labor.

Hiring

The power to employ professional and nonprofessional personnel resides with the board of education. Some contract clauses may, however, apply to hiring policies. In general, it is in the union's interest to keep people outside of the bargaining unit from having access to jobs in the system. In contrast, it is generally in management's interest to keep the selection of personnel to fill positions as flexible as possible. The contract may contain proposals by either side concerning hiring and certification.

These basic concerns must at the same time be balanced with other objectives of the parties. Many of the large-city school systems operate their own certification systems, separate from that of the state. When there is a shortage of teachers, local systems often create temporary and substitute arrangements to fill vacancies for which no regularly certified teacher is available. These "temporary" teachers often remain on the staff for many years as members of the bargaining unit. Contract provisions suggested by unions provide ways for these teachers to obtain permanent positions or certification through modified procedures, such as allowing successful experience to be substituted for other certification requirements.

The unions are interested in making the substitute system smooth and reliable, and it is also in the union's interest to transform a haphazard substitute arrangement into a stable job that allows entry into the bargaining unit. These aims are largely consistent with those of management, which can provide an opportunity for integrative bargaining.

Promotion

The interests of the parties diverge somewhat more in the matter of control of promotion policies. Ensuring teachers mobility in the internal labor market of the school system is a normal objective of the union. This means reducing management's discretion to make promotion decisions and ensuring that members of the bargaining unit have access to advancement opportunities. Management's concern, in contrast, is to use promotions as incentives for high performance and for achieving specific objectives. Since promotion decisions themselves are not bargained, unions seek contract provisions that open access to all members, including the requirements that all vacancies be announced well in advance of hiring and that details of the position be available to all teachers.

Transfer Policies

The internal labor market of the school system is even more active in transferring among jobs at the same level because of the varied desirability of teaching positions within systems. Classes and school buildings have different or better facilities; students differ as to manageability and achievement; the qualifications of staff members differ; and neighborhoods reflect specific problems, particularly in terms of the crime rate. These variations encourage teachers to change teaching positions, even though the pay is no different. In negotiations on these matters, the union's main interest is generally to have the transfer procedure, whether voluntary or involuntary, controlled by contract.

Management, instead, desires flexibility in the control of transfers to achieve its own objectives. Transfers are necessary to meet enrollment shifts, to fit program changes, to comply with external legal requirements (such as faculty desegregation orders) and other conditions set by the government for the receipt of federal funds. Administrators may also wish to initiate the involuntary transfer of staff members they consider to be unsatisfactory. In most of these cases there is the potential for direct conflict between the wishes of individual teachers and the objectives of administrative action, but some degree of administrative flexibility in making transfers is clearly necessary.

Contract provisions concerning transfers usually deal with the maintenance of transfer lists for voluntary transfers and some procedural rights for teachers in the case of involuntary transfers. Transfer lists contain the names of teachers whose request for transfer has been approved but who have not yet been reassigned. The list represents a pool of possible transferees. Contract clauses usually spell out procedures by which teachers can apply for transfers and the criteria for approval, including maintaining the confidentiality of transfer requests. Criteria can include administrative concerns such as staff needs, balance, and programming, as well as teacher preferences and qualifications (including seniority). The following sections of a contract for Buffalo, New York, illustrate:

A. A teacher may request transfer to another school by submitting a written request directly to the Associate Superintendent for Instructional Services. In evaluating such request, it will be necessary to consider:
1. That a balanced staff be maintained at each school;
2. That the probationary teachers be expected to complete the probationary period in the school originally assigned, except where conditions seem to indicate that a transfer is desirable.
3. That the wishes of the individual teacher be honored whenever possible.

*   *   *

E. If the teacher's request for transfer is approved, his name shall be placed on a transfer list, which shall be kept confidential, and the teacher shall be advised by direct mail. In such cases, every reasonable effort shall be made to transfer the teacher as soon as possible in accordance with his wishes. In selecting teachers to be transferred, the following shall be considered in implementing the provisions of Paragraph A above:
1. Length of teaching experience in the school system. This factor shall be controlling where all other factors are substantially equal.
2. Date of request for transfer.[16]

Other contract provisions cover selection among teachers who have applied for transfer to the same position. This is another instance of direct conflict between negotiated and professional modes of making decisions. Unions usually prefer to let seniority govern the choice. Management would usually prefer to base the decision on their judgment of what is best for the program. The degree to which judgmental criteria are specified in the contract and the importance of seniority indicate the degree to which management was willing to concede on this issue. The basic alternatives are that the decision be made strictly by the administration, that criteria and procedures spelled out in the contract include seniority, that seniority be used as the deciding factor when professional qualifications are essentially equal, that seniority be an important or primary factor, and that seniority be the controlling factor. Some examples of each of these alternatives can be found, although strict seniority clauses are rare.

Contract language about involuntary transfers usually deals with the timing of transfer notices and teachers' rights to know why they are being transferred and to discuss administrative actions. Contracts may also limit the reasons why involuntary transfers can be made, such as for shifts in enrollment, changing program needs, desegregation, and so forth. Aside from procedural specifications, however, the administrative prerogative to make involuntary transfers remains a power of the board of education.

Racial segregation and imbalances in pupil costs are special problems involved with staff transfer policies. While these problems are much larger in scope than the labor-management relationship, they deserve some mention here. Federal and some state laws prohibit school systems from promoting or maintaining racially segregated faculties. Voluntary transfer policies may directly or indirectly produce racially segregated faculties, particularly in large-city school systems with concentrations of black and other minority students in some neighborhoods or areas of the city. Concentrations of white teachers in schools with a predominantly white student body and black teachers in schools with a predominantly black student body may be the result of permissive transfer policies rather than an attempt to segregate. But these concentrations may be found illegal by federal or state courts and result in court orders to transfer large numbers of teachers involuntarily in an effort to eliminate segregated faculties. For example, in 1977, Chicago's Board of Education was forced to transfer over

1,400 teachers to balance the racial composition of the faculty and avoid the loss of federal funds.[17] These transfers often require teachers to accept jobs far from their homes, and they can disrupt the programs in many schools. Some of this disruption may be avoided or reduced by wording the contract in such a way that it would encourage transfers that enhance racial balance among faculties or would disallow transfer that contribute to the imbalance.

Permissive transfer policies can allow more experienced teachers (those with more seniority) to move to the most desirable teaching positions. These teachers are generally paid better as well because of the credit for experience on salary schedules. Concentrating more experienced teachers in a building raises staffing costs per pupil, and this could mean a possibly inequitable allocation of funds among buildings. In turn, this could interfere with local or state objectives to reduce inequities in the allocation of resources to schools. As with racial segregation, contract language may be adapted to include the reduction of imbalanced staffing costs as one criterion to be used in approving voluntary transfers.[18]

Evaluation

The conflict between bureaucratic-professional and negotiated modes of decision making is never more obvious than in the issues growing out of evaluation. These include the routine evaluation of teachers and other professional staff members, evaluation for promotion and tenure decisions, and evaluation of programs. In all three cases it is necessary for someone in a superordinate capacity to make decisions about jobs or programs on the basis of evaluative information gathered in part from the teaching process. Salary, advancement opportunity, and professional reputation are at stake for the people being evaluated. And the ability to operate programs most effectively is what is at stake for the evaluators. In short, the conflict is over some of the most important rewards and sanctions within schools. Some control, through the negotiation and grievance arbitration processes, is thus important to the employees' organization. Similarly, maintaining discretion over these same decisions is central to management's objectives. Where evaluation procedures enter the contract, the language reflects the degree to which the union has gained some leverage.

Routine evaluation of teaching is closest to the main job of the teacher. Thus, where evaluation is negotiated, this element is likely to be most extensively covered. The main issues are determining who is to perform evaluations, deciding the timing and methods to be used, allowing access and rights to remediation, providing access to records of evaluations, and developing fair procedures for dismissal for cause. Aside from procedural elements, the criteria or outcomes are not normally considered negotiable.

The matter of who and how in evaluation basically involves protecting the teacher's turf, that is, the classroom (or other teaching space). Contract items in this area include requiring administrators to announce visits in advance, prohibiting the use of intercoms or other devices to listen to classroom activities, and requiring that all judgments or conclusions reached by administrators in the course of visits be shared with the teacher. The contracts may also include provisions for a committee of teachers to work with administrators and others to develop or review evaluation methods.

Some elements of due process for teachers in the evaluation and dismissal process are objectives in other parts of the contract. Access to information in files and the opportunity to remedy problems during a specified time period may be required. The contract may also include a review procedure, with formal hearings and representation for teachers when remediation fails and dismissal for cause is initiated. For tenured teachers, these procedures may parallel or exceed those in the state tenure statute. The procedures may cover dismissal for causes other than poor performance, such as insubordination. When a contract includes such a so-called "fair dismissal procedure," the board of education may be bound to use that process, even if it goes beyond the state tenure statutes. Dismissals under that clause may also be subject to the grievance procedure and ultimately place the dismissal decision in the hands of an arbitrator. This delegation of board power is permitted in some states.

When nontenured teachers are involved in a dismissal procedure, the possibility of conflict with state statutes expands. Many state statutes provide that boards may dismiss nontenured teachers without specifying cause or granting hearings. A contractual "fair dismissal" procedure for nontenured teachers may conflict with such a law and consequently not be enforceable.[19]

Such procedural constraints can have a marked impact on the entire evaluation process. In school systems where evaluation procedures are informal and nonuniform, the development of contractual procedures can impose substantial adjustments in administrative behavior. Principals or other supervisors may be prevented from just "dropping in" on teachers during the course of the day. Where careful evaluative record systems do not exist, they must be developed. Systematic procedures are needed for both gathering evaluative information and providing opportunities for teachers' development and remediation of deficiencies. In short, more extensive evaluative structures are needed. This may clash with informal administrative styles or personal relationships within the building or system. The contract can be seen as making the system more "rigid" or "bureaucratic." It can also be viewed, however, as improving the overall management of the evaluation and staff development process.

Program evaluation provides a somewhat different problem. In response to requirements in federally funded programs and increasing demands for accountability at the state and local level, there has been a considerable increase in the amount of program evaluation undertaken in the school system.[20] Many of the data collected for these evaluations involve the classroom teacher and other members of the bargaining unit. Some of the procedures may conflict with the contract. For example, Michigan's Title I regulations call for collection of what they call "process" data in the Title I programs. Collecting these data places added responsibility on the classroom teacher, as well as revealing much about the classroom behavior of that teacher. The state regulations thus affect working conditions in a way that may be covered by the contract, which may make the contract a set of procedural constraints on program evaluation.[21] This is an aspect of evaluation clauses that should be taken into account when drafting the document. In addition, some other clause may be necessary to exempt certain programs from some or all of the constraints so that they can qualify for state or federal funds.

Reduction in Force

School systems experiencing either declining enrollment or financial pressure often find it necessary to dismiss members of the teaching staff. In some districts normal attrition allows for staff reductions without dismissals. If the declines are sufficiently serious, however, more drastic action might be required. In terms of the labor-management relationship, the problem is fundamentally different from dismissal for cause, where union efforts are primarily intended to protect jobs and limit the possibilities of arbitrary administrative action. In staff reduction situations, however, the jobs are already lost. Negotiated procedures will not save them, but such procedures may help determine the order in which staff members are dismissed or laid off and may limit management's discretion. Imposing contractual constraints on the dismissal process also gives teachers some control and predictability in an otherwise threatening and disturbing situation, especially when long-term, tenured teachers are involved.

Management's objectives in reducing the work force coincide to some degree with those of the union. Both sides desire a procedure that will preserve morale and minimize the disruptive effects of dismissing staff. Management prefers to maintain control of the decision, however, in order to ensure that programmatic and administrative objectives are met. A teacher with less seniority, for instance, may be seen as more effective in a particular department than a teacher with more seniority. If seniority alone controls the decision, the younger teacher will be dismissed. Allowing a decision on the administrator's judgment of merit gives relatively more power to administrators than a decision controlled through the contract, and so unions have traditionally held that seniority is a better overall criterion of quality than merit decisions made by administrators. Although both sides may want a fair reduction procedure that maintains morale, they will certainly differ on the details.

Where reduction procedures become part of the contract, they typically take the form of rules to determine the order in which staff members are to be dismissed. The example below shows one approach:

In the event it becomes necessary to reduce the number of teachers within the school system, then no tenure teacher shall be laid off if there is a non-tenure teacher serving in a position that the tenure teacher is qualified to fill.

In determining the order in which the teachers shall be laid off, within the separate groups of tenured and non-tenured teachers, the Committee shall consider the following factors in laying off teachers within a discipline: professional training, evaluations, the needs of the school system, and length of service in the . . . Schools. In the event that two or more teachers are, in the judgment of the Committee, equal on the basis of professional training, evaluations and the needs of the school system, then the least senior of such teachers shall be laid off first. Continuous employment in the . . . Schools, including periods of leave of absence for which salary credit is granted, shall be used to compute the length of service for such purposes.[22]

The contract goes on to list the areas considered disciplines for the administration of this clause, which resolves most of the central issues in the decision. Tenured and nontenured teachers are treated separately, but the same criteria apply to both groups. Decisions are made within a discipline, that is, the program structure controls the selection process. Professional qualifications come first, with seniority used to break any ties. Seniority is calculated on a system-wide basis, including certain kinds of leaves. But since the discipline or department controls this, the clause amounts to departmental seniority. Elementary teaching is viewed as a single department. But primary and intermediate grades (or some other division) could be used as well. Finally, the decision is clearly one to lay off, rather than to dismiss; that is, if needed, the teacher may be recalled to duty.

Criteria for recall, where needed, are usually part of the reduction clause. Teachers with recall rights are usually given preference, for a specified time period, in filling positions similar to the ones they left—in the above contract, the time period was fifteen months. Laid-off teachers may also be given preference for dissimilar positions if they are as well qualified as new applicants. The contract may also specify whether laid-off teachers retain seniority or other contractual benefits during the period when they are eligible for recall.

When seniority becomes the basis for employment decisions under the contract, detailed provisions may be necessary to determine the precise order of teachers according to seniority. The contract may specify whether seniority is calculated from the first day of work or from the day the individual employment contract was signed. The former system gives many teachers equal seniority since most teachers new to a system start on the same day. In either case, for teachers with equal seniority, a tie-breaking procedure, such as a lottery, is often specified. Including this much detail in the contract may prolong the negotiations process, but it reduces the possibility that grievances or other disputes will arise when difficult decisions concerning layoffs must be made.

Grievance Procedures

An agreement can be no more effective than the means to enforce it. If either party can modify or ignore the provisions of a contract at will, it becomes a useless document. Some mechanism to ensure that the contract is followed is, therefore, often part of the negotiations process, and it has become commonplace for agreements to include such a set of enforcement procedures. These procedures apply primarily to the employer since the initiative in implementing and interpreting the contract lies there. Management can also threaten to discipline or discharge individual employees in an effort to enforce the contract and other work rules. The enforcement of the contract against the union as an organization is discussed later.

The purpose of a grievance procedure is to provide a peaceful and systematic means for resolving disputes arising out of the administration of an agreement, and the procedure can extend to most disputes arising in the workplace. In a sense, it extends the bargaining process to the settlement of the many individual conflicts that can arise during the term of the contract. Mutual agreement and accommodation, in that way, remain the basis for the labor-management relationship. There is also a need, however, for peaceful settlement of disputes that cannot be settled through discussion and accommodation. Left unresolved or allowed to escalate, these disputes undermine the stability of a relationship and can render a contract meaningless. Thus, it is generally in the interest of both parties to have a mutually satisfactory grievance procedure as part of an agreement.

Constructing such a procedure does require resolving a number of points of conflict, for a typical grievance procedure consists of a definition of what constitutes a grievance; some specification of who may initiate grievances; a description of the steps, usually four or five, whereby the grievance is discussed and eventually settled; and additional provisions such as statements of general principles, copies of forms to be used, assurances of confidentiality, and protection against recrimination for those initiating the grievance. Where a procedure culminates in arbitration, the language usually provides rules for selecting the arbitrator or arbitrators, clarifies any restrictions on arbitrability, and provides for sharing costs. Each of these topics contains a number of bargaining issues.

Definition of a Grievance

The foundation of any procedure is the definition of the types of disputes that may be treated as grievances. Consider the following two definitions:

Any claim by the Association, a teacher, or group of teachers, that there has been an alleged violation, misinterpretation, or misapplication of the terms of the Agreement, an alleged violation of their rights, or alleged violation of any School Board policy or practice shall be a grievance, and shall be resolved through the procedure set forth herein.[23]

A grievance is an allegation of violation, misapplication or misinterpretation of this contract. Every teacher or group of teachers or the union shall have the right to present grievances in accordance with these procedures.[24]

The fundamental difference is the *scope* of disputes that come under the procedure. In the first definition the procedure is extended to all policies and practices of the school board, as well as to the vague area of teachers' "rights." The second definition is much narrower and confined to alleged violations of the contract. Under the first definition, virtually any action of the board or the administration could result in a grievance. This gives the individual teacher and the association substantial influence in the full range of policy making and administration. The potential for many more grievances, with the associated costs, is built into the contract, including a greater opportunity for the union to attempt to gain concessions through the grievance procedure that it was unable to gain at the bargaining table.[25] It also brings the bureaucratic-professional and political modes of decision making within or closer to the negotiations mode. The second definition limits the grievance procedure; noncontractual items are excluded. Such a tight definition could be expanded to the same breadth as the first one if a clause elsewhere specifically includes all of the existing policies of the board in the contract.

Parties to the Grievance

The basic principle governing the initiation of grievances is somewhat different in the public and private sectors. Under the Taft-

Hartley Act, individuals are the source of grievances, with the union as representative. Unions have the responsibility to represent all workers covered by the contract, and workers have the right, independent of the organization, to file grievances. This basic principle is not fully accepted in the framework of public-sector laws. Many states and contracts allow groups of employees, including the union itself, to initiate grievances (as in the clauses cited above). And the union similarly bears the responsibility for representing nonmembers covered by the contract.

The power to initiate grievances provides the union with some additional advantages. The grievance procedure can be used to build a bargaining position on issues not gained during the negotiations. If this happens, the procedure becomes more a part of strategy than a means for resolving the specific disputes of individual workers.

Procedural Steps

The key elements of the grievance procedure are its beginning and end. The first step of the procedure is at or near where the problem arose. If the first step is handled properly, many problems and disputes can be settled quickly and smoothly at relatively low cost. Thus, grievance procedures usually provide a first step where an immediate supervisor can meet with the employee and attempt to resolve the difficulty. This may even occur before a grievance is formally filed. It is also at the first step that union representation becomes involved through a grievance committee, chapter chairman, or steward at the workplace (for example, in the school building). To initiate a grievance, the employee confers with a local union official and informs the immediate supervisor, usually in writing.

Once filed, the grievance can be settled at any step. Either the employee (grievant) drops the matter, or the supervisor grants the relief acceptable to the grievant at the first step—usually the department or building level in a school system. If the relief offered is unacceptable at that step, the grievant may appeal to the next higher level in the process, and so forth. At each step a time limit must usually be met by both parties: the administrator must respond within a certain period, and the grievant has a limited time either to accept the answer or to appeal further. At the final step, the award made, usually by the board of education or an arbitrator, is binding on both parties.

Each of the details of the procedure involves conflicts of interests between the parties. The union benefits if a grievance procedure has few steps, short time limits for administrative response, and binding arbitration by a neutral third party as the final step. Such a procedure tightly constrains administrative decision making and keeps management from prolonging a grievance process to discourage its use. Conversely, a procedure with many steps, long delays, and final decisions left to management preserves management's discretion.

The final step of the procedure has the greatest potential for conflict. Binding arbitration by a neutral third party as the last step, which unions prefer, is often viewed as a serious loss of authority by management. Whether to include binding arbitration can, therefore, become a high-conflict bargaining issue. A compromise sometimes employed is so-called "advisory arbitration." A neutral party renders an award, but the board of education may choose to accept or reject the arbitrator's decision. In either case, the details of contract provisions for the final step have much to do with the effectiveness of the entire grievance procedure.

Arbitration

The place of the arbitrator in the resolution of grievances has grown along with the process of collective bargaining. The earliest forms of arbitration date from the late 1800's, and the first state labor arbitration law appeared in Maryland in 1878. Since then a fairly consistent general view of the arbitration process has developed for grievances in both the private and public sectors. The arbitrator is seen as a creature of the contract, employed by the parties to interpret and apply its terms to settle specific disputes in an impartial manner. The arbitrator may not normally ignore, modify, or go beyond any portion of the contract in making an award. Decisions as to what is properly arbitrable, how the process should be handled, and what is admissible as evidence, if these are not specified in the contract, are left to the arbitrator's judgment. There is no standard way for selecting an arbitrator, setting a time limit for decision making, or determining how fees are to be paid; these are specified within the grievance procedure.[26]

The key steps in the process are the selection of the arbitrator, setting limits of arbitrability, and setting the framework for rendering the decision. Selection is usually made from a list of qualified persons furnished by a state labor relations agency, the American Arbitration Association, or the Federal Mediation and Conciliation Service. The parties may agree on one person, strike names until one is left, or select a single arbitrator in some other fashion. If the parties then wish to limit that person's authority to certain areas of the contract, that must be specified in the grievance procedure. Also, whatever rules of procedure concerning timing, witnesses, transcripts of proceedings, and payment of fees and expenses by the parties may be detailed. Then, within the framework of the contract, the arbitrator renders final decisions on grievances, and, if so directed, provides a written opinion explaining the award.[27]

The process of arbitration is not without problems. It can, first of all, be quite costly, especially if long hearings, verbatim transcripts, and written opinions are involved. If the costs are split by the parties, the burden on a small union can be substantial. This is an incentive for the union to be judicious in use of arbitration, but it can also prompt management to force many grievances to arbitration in an effort to drain the union financially. The financial problem is but one indication of a more general danger: excessive use of third-party intervention can undermine the working relationship between the parties themselves.

The matter of fees and the selection of an arbitrator both affect a decision made outside the framework of the grievance procedure, but are important to it (whether to let the matter go to the arbitrator at all). Both parties must weigh the costs of arbitration, the probabilities of winning, and the stakes involved. Both parties have a stake in preserving the credibility of the process, as well as limiting costs and avoiding undesirable precedents. The union's responsibility to fairly represent all workers must be balanced against its share of arbitration costs. Management's interest in preserving its discretion must be balanced against the value of having a neutral party take on a tough decision. Management may even allow a grievance to go to arbitration knowing the grievant will win. If managers only arbitrated cases they were sure to win, the process would lose credibility for all parties. In short, the decision to use arbitration is a complex, joint decision of the parties that is affected by the framework of the grievance procedure and other circumstances of the case.

The grievance procedure should be viewed as a working tool of the parties in an effort to maintain a stable, peaceful relationship, with arbitration remaining as a last, seldom used resort. Such a view allows the overall grievance machinery to retain its place as a central part of a functional labor-management relationship.

Teaching Issues

In terms of general union strategy to move as much of management as possible into the negotiated mode of decision making, a number of elements of teaching practice are commonly represented in the contract, including the participation of teachers in educational policy making (especially concerning curriculum), the discipline of pupils, and the responsibilities of teachers. These matters are by no means universally negotiated, and they fall outside the range of bargaining subjects generally specified as mandatory in state codes. With sufficient bargaining power, however, unions have been able to get these subjects onto the bargaining table in many areas. A survey done by the National Education Association in 1971 showed approximately 53 percent of the contracts examined had some form of teacher protection-pupil discipline clause, about 25 percent had curriculum review language, and about 23 percent involved textbook selection processes.[28] It is not known exactly what the clauses contain, but it is clear that the subjects are involved in the bargaining process.

Pupil Discipline and Teacher Protection

Maintaining discipline and controlling pupils in the schools is a responsibility that teachers and administrators share (assisted by other staff members, such as security personnel). The division of roles and tasks in meeting this responsibility must be worked out in some manner. It is usually in the teachers' interest to have this take place in negotiations, where their ability to influence the outcomes is substantially higher than it is in most organizational decisions. Some negotiations over disciplinary issues may be in management's interest as well, if this produces a cooperative working relationship between teachers and administrators on the day-to-day handling of disciplinary problems. Management may, however, lose substantial discretion by including precise wording concerning discipline, especially since disciplinary problems are likely to vary widely through the system. Administrators may require leeway to cope effectively with local situations.

In a sense, discipline is related to work load. In the absence of contract language on discipline, the administration is free to place the major responsibility for control of pupils on the teacher. Teachers' proposals for contract language on discipline tend to shift responsibilities toward administration and increase support and resources for teachers.

The language may be as general as: "The parties agree that the employee has the primary responsibility for the maintenance of discipline within the classroom. The Board, however, recognizes its responsibility to support and assist the employee in maintenance of control and discipline in the classroom."[29] Or it may be as detailed as the discipline clause in the Chicago Public School agreement. That clause runs over six hundred words and includes procedural details for exclusion of pupils from class, a list of serious offenses, and relief for teachers who suffer from assault.[30] Vague language does not impose any particular constraint on administrative action or costs, but it is open to wide variations in interpretation and could cause many grievances. More specific language does impose costs: administrative time, additional personnel for handling disruptive students, and the time needed to discuss possible difficulties with parents. Legal requirements for due process for students set by the United States Supreme Court in Goss v. Lopez may also conflict with contract language and produce grievances, legal problems, or both.[31]

In places where criminal activities are involved or there are threats to the physical safety of teachers, provisions for security personnel and other measures (such as protected parking) may enter the negotiations. These are more direct economic issues, rather than questions of negotiated versus bureaucratic-professional decision making.

Protection measures may be granted as part of the contract if management can afford them or if the teachers are willing to make a concession elsewhere. The same argument applies to the use of teachers to supervise students in noninstructional settings (hallways, cafeteria, and so forth). If teachers are able to exert sufficient bargaining power or make concessions, they may win contractual restrictions on this use of teacher time, and management will have to employ others for such duties.

Curriculum and Textbook Decisions

The heart of bureaucratic-professional decision making in schools lies in the substance and methods of teaching. Teaching, as it is generally understood, inherently requires the teacher to make some of these decisions—from the minute-by-minute choices of teaching behavior in the classroom to the school-wide review of curriculum. When it comes to bargaining, it is seldom a question of whether or not teachers will participate in those decisions. It is, rather, what the mode of participation will be. A survey of contracts shows that three out of four have no language on curriculum or textbook review. Those decisions are reserved to the bureaucratic-professional mode. In the others, contract language may involve the actual substance of the curriculum, which is rare, or the mechanism by which teachers are to be involved in those decisions. This latter, more common type of language could include the contractual provision of standing task forces or committees of teachers to deliberate on or review curriculum matters. Or the membership of teachers on other committees formed for those purposes may be specified. The contract may also require that administration discuss with teachers all proposed changes in the school program, either at the building or district level. All provisions of this type give teachers contractual rights to participate in such decisions and may give teachers more control over these decisions.

The operational details of decision making on curricular matters are an important part of the policy-making structures of the system. The *final* decision lies, of course, with the board of education. But the process by which issues reach the board may strongly influence the outcome. For example, a negotiated curriculum committee, which is the only place decisions are discussed, is structurally more influential than one that operates along with a parent committee and requires administrative review. It is also important whether the committee is strictly advisory or has the power to change or block proposals. These and other structural details of curricular decision making are critical elements in the process, and, if negotiated, they become the basis for discussing and constructing specific contract language.

Union Security

Contract language includes clauses that directly assist the existing union in maintaining its position as the exclusive representative of the employees in the bargaining unit. The major items in this group are the deduction of union dues or checkoff and agency shop or maintenance of membership provisions. Other minor benefits to the union such as space for meetings and room on bulletin boards, leave for members to hold office, access to school publications, and so forth may also be considered union security items.

The advantage of winning these concessions at the table is obvious. But it may also be in management's interest to promote some level of security for the existing bargaining agent for the teachers (or other employees). Management does not want too weak a bargaining agent, for a weak union, in terms of members' support of the organization and officers, is vulnerable to being replaced by a more militant one, whose officers are unknown. A weak set of officers cannot be said to represent adequately the interests of their members or to speak accurately about what those members would accept. Some concessions on union security items may be reasonable strategy for management, especially if they represent low cost to management but are important to the union. Substantial union concessions can be expected in return.

Agency Shop

Union objectives traditionally include reducing or eliminating the so-called "free rider": the person who gains the benefits of union membership without paying dues. In the private sector the union shop provision is allowed, whereby the employee is required to join the union within a certain period after employment. This is not normally permitted in the public sector, although the state of Pennsylvania does allow a union shop. Some other states allow the bargaining parties to negotiate a provision whereby all employees covered by the contract must either be members of the union or pay a fee to cover the cost of being represented. This is known as an agency shop clause. Paying a fee or dues thus becomes a condition of continued employment, and the free rider is eliminated.

Some employers strongly oppose this type of clause on the grounds that the employee should have the right to work without paying dues or fees to support a union. They feel that this restricts employees' freedom of choice and makes the government, through the employer, the agent of financing the union. Apart from this ideological opposition, bargaining over agency shop language does provide some opportunity for integrative interaction.

Related to and sometimes part of an agency shop provision is a maintenance of membership clause that requires employees who are members of the union to maintain that membership during the life of the contract as a condition of employment. This may be especially important to unions operating under a multiyear agreement.

Dues Collection

Union security may also be enhanced by regular collection of dues through payroll deductions. This assures steady income and saves the union the expense of collection. Since most payroll systems are computer based, the process is relatively easy and inexpensive for management to implement. The only issues are whether management will agree to do it in the first place and whether the system is established to encourage employees to pay or not to pay dues. For instance, the deduction may require the employee to sign an authorization card and renew that authorization each year. This may reduce the number of authorizations since it requires a positive action on the part of the employee. Alternately, the deduction may be automatic, requiring that the employee take action to prevent it.

THE CONTRACT AS LANGUAGE

For each of the main points of bargaining outlined above that actually enter the negotiations, there will be some translation into specific contract language. It is common for both parties to prepare a number of written proposals or demands that are placed on the table at the onset of bargaining. These items then become the subjects of bargaining, and they are either rejected, modified, or eventually accepted as part of the final agreement. Once the contract is accepted, its actual administration depends on the interpretation of that language in the thousands of day-to-day events that have some connection with the labor-management relationship. They can be as routine as a teacher punching a time clock to start the day, or as controversial as a reorganization of the school program. In any of these events, the true meaning of the contract lies in the way the language is worked out in decisions and actions within the school system.

Both the construction and interpretation of contract language are intimately tied to the operation of the system. The parties to the bargain draft, modify, or accept language according to how they believe it will affect their own objectives. An understanding of the drafting and interpretation of any contract should, therefore, rest on a consideration of both the language itself and how it is likely to affect practice.

A contract is, however, also an arrangement enforceable through the courts or through arbitration. Every clause has potential for arbitration or litigation. This is a central fact of the labor-management relationship and can color every action involving the negotiation and administration of the contract. Because outside agents— courts or arbitrators—may be called on to interpret or enforce parts of the agreement, the standards of judgment commonly used by these agencies are relevant.

Elements of Language

To discuss the contract itself, it is useful to identify salient characteristics of the language, five of which are discussed here: precision, semantics or meaning, consistency, specificity, and significance. Each characteristic plays an important part in the analysis of the clauses as well as in their administration.

Perhaps the most common problem in contract clauses is lack of precision. Contract language should supply exact details concerning what actions are to be taken (or avoided), by whom, under what conditions, with what criteria for judgment when judgment is necessary, and by whom the judgment is to be exercised. Precise language avoids the use of words that are inherently undefined or undefinable, such as "good cause," "reasonable," "usually," "appropriate," "whenever possible," and so forth. For example, the drafters of the clause below seem to have gone out of their way to include as many vague words and phrases as possible.:

Specific assignments of TEACHERS shall be considered final after written notification, to be made as soon as possible before the ending of the school year. In emergency situations, assignments may be changed after a reasonable effort has been made to contact the TEACHER, explain the reasons for such change, and hear the opinions of the TEACHER.[32]

The terms "as soon as possible," "emergency," and "reasonable" call for interpretation, and no provision is made for who is to contact teachers or by what means. The vagueness in this case results in a high degree of administrative flexibility. In each case, the judgment about what is "as soon as possible," "reasonable," or an "emergency" rests with the administrators. Compare the clause above to the one below, which retains administrative flexibility but defines much more carefully how the matter of involuntary transfers is to be handled:

Notice of transfers shall be given to teachers as soon as practicable and under normal circumstances, not later than June 1 of each school year. A transfer will be made only after a meeting between the teacher involved and the Superintendent or his designee, at which time the teacher will be notified of the reasons therefor. In the event the teacher objects to the transfer, he may immediately notify the Association. The Superintendent will then meet with the teacher and the Association representative to discuss the matter.[33]

Here judgment is also involved, but some dates (June 1) and standards for judgment (normal circumstances) are specified. Some elements of due process for the transferred teacher are included as well.

Where language is left ambiguous, as in these two clauses, it will be interpreted to place the discretion for transfer decisions with the administration of the system. The clause does not say the teacher must agree with the transfer; the conference or notification is all that is required. In this case, as in any like it, the *language* of the contract, not implications, determines how the clause will be enforced by arbitrators or courts.

Precision, or lack of it, in a contract clause may be part of a conscious strategy on the part of the bargainers or simply the result of careless drafting. Where language is left ambiguous, as in the clauses above, the decision on transfers remains clearly with the administration of the school system. This obviously suits the objectives of the administration. In interpreting such a clause, an arbitrator or court would assume that the parties to the bargain were aware of the ambiguity and that it was their intent to leave the discretion with the administration. If the language cannot be clearly interpreted, however, the doubt must be resolved by some other means. In these cases, the arbitrator or court will resolve the doubt *against* the side that drafted the language. This rule assumes that the drafter was aware of, and desired, the ambiguous language. This serves as an incentive to keep contract language clear.

Where definitions of terms are necessary to interpret clauses, the most common meanings of words will be used. Specialized terms used in labor-management agreement will also be given their most common meaning; for example, "hours" would mean the length of the workday. If certain words have come to have a special meaning through established usage in a particular system, that meaning is assumed to reflect mutual consent of the parties and will be used to interpret the contract.

Consistency of meaning throughout the contract is another element of interpretation. To understand a particular clause or term, the contract must be read as a whole. Consider, for example, the following clause:

If for any reason the Board anticipates a reduction of staff, it shall, prior to taking any formal action, consult with the LSEA to receive recommendations regarding priorities and procedures to be followed.[34]

The key word in that clause is "consult." Without further elaboration, that term could cover everything from a simple phone call from the superintendent to the association president, to a series of meetings between the board and the teachers. If another part of the contract defined "consultation" as a face-to-face meeting between the superintendent and the association's officers, that same definition would apply to this clause. Any lesser form of consultation by the board could be considered a breach of contract.

Specificity of language is another important concern. Where there is conflict within the contract, the more specific language will normally control. For example, one part of the contract may say teachers are exempt from clerical duties, but not including taking attendance. Ordinarily, then, the taking of attendance would not fall within the overall meaning of clerical duties. When lists of items are included in the language, the list is taken to be inclusive, that is, items *not* on the list are *not* included in the category. This rule of interpretation does not, however, apply when a list is designated: "including but not limited to" or some equivalent language.

The overall significance of clauses may also be employed to resolve conflicts in interpretation or effect. In general, the more significant clause will be considered controlling, provided significance can be established. For example, teachers' qualifications may be defined in either a seniority or reduction-in-force clause for the purpose of determining order of layoffs or transfers. The definition of qualifications might conflict with qualifications described for extracurricular assignments. If a court or arbitrator had to choose between competing definitions of teachers' qualifications, the one in the seniority clause would control since that is clearly more significant to the labor-management relationship.

Language and Practice

The principles for interpreting contract language described above refer primarily to an outside review—through arbitration or litigation. While this is an important concern, it is not the main one. All of the clauses of the contract will have some effect on the operation of the program, but not all will be subject to litigation or arbitration. How a contract is administered is another element in the interpretation of the language by an external review. No contract is seen as encompassing all of the possible elements of the labor-management relationship, nor all of the issues that may arise. The law and principles of arbitration recognize that the parties often need to modify or expand the terms of the agreement during the course of its administration. Thus, the record of actual labor-management practices can be construed as an extension of the contract.

Consider the teacher transfer clauses, discussed above, which require consultation between administration and teachers concerning involuntary transfers. The administration may choose to consult with teachers in a face-to-face meeting of the director of personnel with the union president before the transfer is finalized. If this becomes standard practice and goes unchallenged by the union, the procedure can be considered part of the contract. Thus, if the administration were suddenly to drop the conference and simply phone the teachers' association, that action could be interpreted as a breach of the contract.

Beyond the question of past practice, analysis of contract language in terms of impact is central to understanding the meaning of the agreement. John Dunlop's concept of the "web of rules" can be applied to each contract clause.[35] The rule can be seen as a constraint on behavior, either a direct control or an indirect one (through the allocation of resources). A clause requiring teachers to work until 4:00 p.m. is a direct constraint; a clause awarding each teacher a filing cabinet constrains the administration from using those resources for some other purpose. It is the objective of the administration to minimize the degree of constraint in the contract, leaving as much as possible to administrative discretion and, conversely, placing as many responsibilities as possible on the teaching staff.

From this point of view, it is possible to analyze contract language in terms of shifting responsibilities, costs, and constraints from one party to the other. Obtaining permission for teachers' leaves is a case in point. Some contracts have a page or more of detailed rules for how teachers are to obtain permission for personal leaves, including written permissions, approved reasons, and so forth. Other contracts simply grant the leave at the teacher's discretion, with no allowed or disallowed reasons and no requirement to obtain permissions. Obviously, the latter clause restricts administrative control over the use and distribution of such leaves and gives the teachers great flexibility. The former imposes costs on the teachers; the latter, on the administration. By asking the basic questions of where costs, responsibilities, and constraints lie, each element of the contract can be translated into potential impacts on the operation of the school system.

Completing the analysis requires that potential impacts be related to the operational details of the school system. This is where intimate knowledge of the system is necessary. Writing a teacher transfer clause, for instance, should be governed by a detailed knowledge of the patterns of teacher mobility in the system and the particular needs of schools and areas where there are shifts in enrollment. Writing a leave clause requires understanding of past patterns of use, the general availability of substitutes, administrative record-keeping systems, and patterns of administrative behavior with respect to granting permission. For virtually every clause, the same depth of knowledge is needed as a base for constructing effective contract language.

THE CONTRACT AS ARTIFACT

One idea underlying much of this discussion deserves restatement and closer attention at this point: the contract is not a definition of the labor-management relationship but only a product of it. The language does not, nor is it intended to, describe all the elements of the work, the way it is managed, or the overall climate of union-management relations. Nor is the contract a static device; it should be thought of as "a living document." That is to say, the operational meaning of the language, because it is the result of a dynamic process, can change as a consequence of the actions of the parties or the decisions of courts and arbitrators. And any contract is just one of a number of past and future agreements. The content is at once a product of the contract's history and an indication of expectations for the future. Each characteristic is important to an overall understanding of the meaning of the agreement to the parties.

Language and Behavior

The contract sets up a framework of rules for the behavior of both union and management, but those rules are not adequate descriptors of the patterns of behavior that occur within that framework, anymore than the rules of a baseball game adequately describe the details of play. In a study of bargaining in municipal government, for example, James Begin found that two city departments with essentially equal contracts and grievance procedures had widely different grievance rates.[36] The high grievance rate occurred in a department where many employees had been fired after the new mayor took office. The other department was insulated from political appointments. Once a contract establishes a procedure or committee structure, its use may also extend beyond the letter of the clause. Elementary principals have been found to consult with building-level union officers on many matters not covered by the contract.[37] Even the example of a broad grievance procedure cited above can be misleading. The scope of the clause would suggest a high incidence of grievances. But in three years of operation of that particular procedure, no grievance had moved beyond the first step. Disputes are handled informally, usually by phone, and settled without recourse to the official machinery.

The creation of contractual committees and task forces is a particularly ambiguous area of the contract. Such a mechanism may be created for a number of reasons: to clear a difficult subject off the bargaining table without loss of face by either side, to serve the demands of a special constituency on either side, or to provide the opportunity for some problem solving away from the bargaining environment. Contracts seldom spell out details of how a committee or task force is to operate or how the results will be treated. Such groups may become a major policy-making mechanism in the system, or they may simply generate reports to take up shelf space. The contract tells little of these situations. In fact, the bargainers themselves may have little firm idea how these mechanisms are to operate when they are created. Only a clear record of intent or a pattern of past performance in this regard is a reliable indicator.

The Contract and Bargaining History

The importance of intent and past performance is an example of the more general place of the bargaining history in the relationship. Any particular contract is an accumulation of many decisions and agreements made over the life of the bargaining relationship, but it is far from a complete history. It does not contain the record of previous items changed or dropped; nor does it give any indication of the items proposed and then dropped by the parties during bargaining. To appreciate the place of the contract in the bargaining relationship, it is helpful to consider both of these elements in the bargaining record.

Change in the scope of the agreement is one important element in the historical picture. If a first contract were quite broad in scope, perhaps as a result of inexperienced management negotiators, management would probably try each year to remove items or reduce the scope. This seems to be a common situation, judging from the frequent admonitions of experienced negotiators not to "give away the store" in early bargaining and statements concerning the difficulty of "getting something back" once it is bargained away. Each item removed from the contract may require substantial concessions by management in some other area. This is quite a different situation from one where a first contract might have been narrow in scope. In that case, management might simply refuse to expand the coverage or have exacted large concessions in return for simply agreeing to discuss a particular issue. No one contract in the series of agreements would show the changes in scope and the history of concessions.

Even an examination of the series of agreements for the same system cannot, of course, reveal what was left out as a result of bargaining. Unless transcripts or detailed records of the negotiations are kept, the information on trade-offs is kept only in the memories of the bargainers. Part of the preparation and strategy involved in bargaining often includes, however, a review both of the contract and of the opponent's package of demands over several years. These patterns of demands can be a clue to the opponent's priorities or changes in objectives. The same is true of a record showing when certain items are dropped from the table. An item dropped early in the bargaining can usually be considered less important than one held for later.

These records and patterns, along with the contract itself, make up the documentary evidence of the bargaining history. They are valuable elements in constructing an understanding of the labor-management relationship, but only if they are viewed as artifacts and not the history itself.

NOTES

1. Robert A. Gorman, *Labor Law: Unionization and Collective Bargaining* (St. Paul, Minn.: West Publishing Co., 1976), 540.

2. The schedule simply lists the salary according to the number of years of experience in the district and degrees held. Some salary increment may be given for nondegree academic credit, such as the M.A. degree plus thirty semester hours.

3. *Agreement between the Board of Education of the City of Chicago and the Chicago Teachers' Union, A.F.T., AFL-CIO*, September 1, 1976 - August 31, 1977, 1-2.

4. Section 9 (a) (5) of the National Labor Relations Act states that the representation unit should be one that is "appropriate" for bargaining purposes. Decisions as to appropriateness are to be handled by the NLRB, with mutuality of interest as the primary criterion (99 NLRB 777). State boards and courts have employed similar standards. See, for example, the California Educational Employee Relations Board decision in *Sierra Sands Unified School District and California School Employees' Association*, EERB Decision #2, Case #LA-R-710, October 14, 1976, GERR 680:B12, October 25, 1976; the Indiana statute contains representative criteria, Title 2, Art. 7.5, Sec. 10 (a) (2), GERR-RF 51:2314 (June 25, 1973).

5. Stephen L. Hayford and Anthony V. Sinicropi, "Bargaining Rights Status of Public Sector Supervisors," *Industrial Relations,* 15:1 (February 1976), 44-61.

6. The NLRA reads: "The term 'supervisor' means any individual having authority, in the interest of the employer, to hire, transfer, suspend, lay off, recall, promote, discharge, assign, reward, or discipline other employees, or responsibly to direct them, or to adjust their grievances, or effectively to recommend such action, if in connection with the foregoing the exercise of such authority is not of merely a routine or clerical nature but requires the use of independent judgment." U.S. Code Title 29, II, § 152 (11).

7. Arthur Blumberg, *Supervisors and Teachers: A Private Cold War* (Berkeley, Calif.: McCutchan, 1974; 2d ed., 1980), 139.

8. U.S. Congress, House, Report on H.R. 3020, 80th Cong. 1st sess., 1947, H. Rept. 245, quoted in Bernard D. Meltzer, *Labor Law* (Boston: Little, Brown and Co., 1970), 589.

9. A more complete discussion of the good faith concept in bargaining is found in Chapter 5.

10. Lewis Kaden, as quoted in Joan Weitzman, *The Scope of Bargaining in Public Employment* (New York: Praeger, 1975), 4.

11. Weitzman, *Scope of Bargaining in Public Employment*, p. 8.

12. For a detailed exposition of the point of view, see Harry H. Wellington and Ralph K. Winter, *The Unions and the Cities* (Washington, D.C.: Brookings Institution, 1971). See also John H. Metzler, "The Need for Limitation upon the Scope of Negotiations in Public Education," in *Education and Collective Bargaining*, ed. Anthony M. Cresswell and Michael J. Murphy (Berkeley, Calif.: McCutchan, 1976).

13. See John F. Burton and Charles Krider, "The Role and Consequences of Strikes by Public Employees," *Yale Law Journal*, 79:3 (January 1970), 418-443; and Anthony M. Cresswell, "The Public Interest in Public Sector Bargaining: Management Rights v. Management Power," in *Critical Issues in Education*, ed. Lou Rubin (Boston: Allyn and Bacon, 1979).

14. For a more detailed discussion of pension fund finance, see B. Jump, "Teacher Retirement Systems Benefit Structure, Costs, and Financing," *Journal of Educational Finance*, 3 (Fall 1977), 143-157.

15. *Jackson Public Schools and Jackson Education Association* 60 LA 38 (1973).

16. *Master Contract between the Board of Education of the City of Buffalo* (New York) *and the Buffalo Teachers Federation*, July 1, 1973-June 30, 1976, Art. XIV, Secs. A, E.

17. See *Chicago Tribune*, September 3, 1977; and *Agreement between the Board of Education of the City of Chicago and the Chicago Teachers' Union, Local No. 1 A.F.T.*, September 1, 1976 - August 31, 1977, Art. 42.

18. The interactions of federal program regulations with contract provisions are discussed in Anthony M. Cresswell and Michael J. Murphy, "Compensatory Education Policy and Collective Bargaining," Report to the Institute for Educational Leadership, Washington, D.C., 1977.

19. The relationship between tenure statutes and contract dismissal procedures is discussed in Chapter 5.

20. See Mike M. Milstein, *Impact and Response: Federal Aid and State Education Agencies* (New York: Teachers College Press, 1976), 40-44; and Jerome T. Murphy, "Title I of ESEA," *Harvard Educational Review*, 41:1 (February 1971), 35-63.

21. Evaluation procedures for Title I in Michigan are discussed in Cresswell and Murphy, "Compensatory Education Policy and Collective Bargaining."

22. *Contract between the Brookline School Committee and the Brookline Educators Association*, 1975-1977, Art. 7.

23. From *Professional Negotiations Agreement between Moline (Illinois) Board of Education, District #40 and Moline Education Association*, 1976-1978, Art. V.

24. *Agreement between the Dearborn (Michigan) Board of Education and the Dearborn Federation of Teachers, A.F.T.,* 1975-1978, Art. X.

25. The existence of a broad definition of a grievance does not guarantee that there will be a large number of grievances. In fact, the use of the grievance procedure is rare in the Moline (Illinois) public schools where clause a. is in effect.

26. Maurice Trotta, *Arbitration* (New York: American Management Association, 1974), 14.

27. There are, however, standard rules of procedure published by the American Arbitration Association which are often cited in contracts as the applicable standards. See American Arbitration Association, *Voluntary Labor Arbitration Rules* (New York: American Arbitration Association, 1970).

28. "Trends in Negotiation Items for Teachers," *National Education Association Negotiations Research Digest,* 6:3 (November 1972), 13-14.

29. *Basic Model Contract,* Illinois Education Association, 1975, Art. 3(5).

30. *Agreement between the Board of Education of the City of Chicago and the Chicago Teachers' Union, A.F.T.,* 1977-1978, Art. 30.

31. *Goss* v. *Lopez,* 419 U.S. 565 (1975). For a detailed discussion of this aspect of pupil policies, see William R. Hazard, *Education and the Law,* 2d ed. (New York: Free Press, 1978), esp. ch. 4.

32. *Agreement between the Board of Education of Elmhurst Community Unit District and the Elmhurst Teachers' Council, Local 571, A.F.T.,* 1975-1977, Art. IV, Sec. 11.

33. *Agreement between the Denver Classroom Teachers' Association and the School District in the City and County of Denver (Colorado),* September 1, 1970 - April 6, 1975, Art. 14.

34. *Master Agreement between the Lansing (Michigan) Schools Education Association and the Lansing School District Board of Education,* 1973-1976, Art. XII.

35. John Dunlop, *Industrial Relations Systems* (New York: Holt, Rinehart and Winston, 1958).

36. James P. Begin, "The Private Grievance Model in the Public Sector," *Industrial Relations,* 10:1 (February 1971), 21-35.

37. Arthur I. Goldberg and Lisa Harbatkin, "The Teachers' Union Chapter in the Elementary School," *Teachers College Record,* 71:4 (May 1970), 647-654.

9

Impasses and the Resolving of Impasses

If true collective bargaining takes place in education, teachers' unions and school district management cannot possibly reach voluntary agreement concerning hours, wages, and other conditions of employment at all times. Failure to agree in collective bargaining is generally termed an "impasse" and represents a situation when at least one of the parties feels that it is futile to proceed with negotiations. There are ways of dealing with an impasse. The parties may insist on a strike or a lockout. They may appeal for outside help. Usually this help comes from a third, neutral party that either attempts to assist in reaching an agreement or, in some cases, sets the terms of agreement at which the parties themselves were unable to arrive. The courts or government may intervene.

Impasses in collective bargaining appear to be fairly common occurrences. The Federal Mediation and Conciliation Service (FMCS) reports that, in 1976, they processed nearly 20,000 cases. Of those cases, about 45 percent required formal intervention by mediators appointed by FMCS for successful resolution. Of cases handled by the FMCS, the agency reports that their case activity in the private sector remained relatively constant between 1967 and 1976, but showed a 2.2 percent decline between 1975 and 1976.

During the same period, public-sector dispute cases referred to FMCS have increased from zero in 1967 to 757 cases in 1976. The period from 1975 to 1976 shows a 99.7 percent increase in public-sector cases processed by that agency.[1] Our data indicate that about one out of every three bargaining interactions results in an impasse being declared by one of the parties at some time during negotiation.[2]

Although there is an impasse over one or more issues being negotiated, this does not necessarily mean that the teachers will engage in a strike or the district will lock out. In fact, the incidence of strikes growing out of impasse disputes is quite small. The FMCS reports that, of the cases closed in 1976, only about 13.2 percent involved a strike or work stoppage.[3] Over the last ten years, the ratio of strikes to impasse situations has ranged between 12 percent and 15 percent, indicating that many disputes are resolved without resorting to the so-called ultimate weapon in collective bargaining.

In the private sector, the number of strikes has been declining. Strikes by public-sector employees, on the other hand, have been increasing rapidly over the last twenty years. In 1956 there were 5 teachers' strikes recorded in the United States. Twenty years later (1976) the number of strikes was 138, down from a high of 218 in the previous year (see Table 9-1).

This chapter examines the nature of these events in an effort to provide a picture of changes in impasse and impasse resolution over time to the present. It provides a description of the role that the strike plays in labor relations systems and attempts to synthesize the reasons why strikes occur. This includes an examination of the machinery set up by both the private and the public sectors for use in resolving impasses and weighs its importance within the labor relations systems.

And, finally, we discuss issues that seem paramount in any consideration of policy and procedures related to impasse and impasse resolution in the public sector and, more particularly, in educational bargaining. In the matter of impasses, labor relations as practiced in the public sector departs substantially from that practiced in the private sector. David Lewin, in his analysis of unionism in the public sector, takes note of some general similarities as well as differences between practices in the two sectors:

Table 9-1
Work stoppages by teachers: 1959 to 1976

Year	Number of stoppages	Teachers involved	Man-days idle during year	Average number of teachers involved	Average days lost per teacher
1959	2	210	670	105	3.2
1960	3	5,490	5,490	1,830	1.0
1961	1	20	20	20	1.0
1962	1	20,000	20,000	20,000	1.0
1963	2	2,200	2,590	1,290	1.2
1964	9	14,400	30,600	1,600	2.1
1965	5	1,720	7,880	344	4.6
1966	30	37,300	58,500	1,243	1.6
1967	76	92,400	969,300	1,215	10.5
1968	88	145,000	2,180,000	1,647	15.0
1969	183	105,000	412,000	573	3.9
1970	152	94,800	935,600	623	9.9
1971	135	64,600	713,000	478	11.0
1972	87	33,900	207,300	389	6.1
1973	117	51,400	620,700	439	12.1
1974	133	60,100	538,100	451	9.0
1975	218	182,300	1,419,800	836	7.8
1976	138	65,100	713,500	471	11.0

Source: From data supplied in U.S. Department of Health, Education, and Welfare, National Center for Education Statistics, *The Condition of Education* (Washington, D.C.: U.S. Government Printing Office, 1978), 183.

The new governmental labor relations statutes and policies apparently incorporated many characteristics of private sector collective bargaining. These include the principles of exclusive jurisdiction and representation, criteria for determining bargaining units, procedures for union elections, certification and recognition, grievance arbitration, and the development of administrative agencies to regulate governmental labor relations and enforce public policy.

But he notes emphatically that:

state and local governments did not simply ape the private sector in formulating their labor relations policies but departed in several ways from private practice, notably in their treatment of the right to strike. Thus, public employees are prohibited from striking either expressly by legislation or, if the statute was silent on the issue, by judicial decision.[4]

There are many reasons why governmental units are reluctant

to allow their employees to strike. They range from the sovereignty of government to the essential nature of public services, and they are discussed more fully in the sections dealing with impasse resolution. Suffice it to say here that, for a variety of reasons, the private sector has relied heavily on voluntary solution and the strike, while the public depends on mediated or adjudicated solution.

THE STRIKE

It is doubtful that any single occurrence throughout the history of labor relations has had more impact or attracted more attention than the strike. Though it is almost universally outlawed in the public sector,[5] the strike has been extensively used by unions in that sector. The number of work stoppages by public employees increased between 1942 and 1974, as did the number of workers likely to be involved and the number of days idle. Strikes among governmental employees increased from a total of 384 to a total of 478 in 1975—the year with the highest recorded number of strikes in the public sector. More of the strikes involved school employees (54.7 percent in 1974 and 57.9 percent in 1975).[6]

Although public-sector strikes are increasing, it is probably not fair to label the public sector as strike prone. Of the 6,000 or so strikes that occurred in the United States in 1975, the 478 that occurred in government service represented less than 8 percent of the total number, even though government employees represented between 14 percent and 17 percent of the total work force in the United States.

The Strike and Public Policy

It is generally illegal for teachers and other public employees to strike. Though the right individually to withhold one's labor is generally rooted in common law and supported by the Constitution of the United States, concerted or collective withdrawal of labor has been usually interpreted to be an attack on the sovereignty of the state and an untenable threat to the health and safety of the community. The rationale behind prohibition of strikes in the public sector is based, in part, on the fact that most public employees provide services for which there is no substantial or immediately available substitute. When General Motors is struck by the United Auto Workers and production ceases, potential customers have a number of alternatives. They can buy automobiles from a rival manufacturer; they can invest the money they would have spent on the purchase of a new car into the maintenance and improvement of their existing automobile; or, if they live in urban areas, they can use public transportation. There are obvious alternatives in terms of manufactured goods, for it is assumed that, in the competitive marketplace, there are always companies ready to respond to the demand generated by the strike-curtailed availability of a competitor's product.

In the public sector this becomes somewhat more complicated. There are no alternative police services. Similar monopolies exist for some health care services and for educational services. Though parents can and do set up interim educational facilities during an extended strike, it is generally impossible to duplicate the education supplied by the public school system. This is a particular problem in the public sector because services are provided regionally so there is no intermarket competition. Students attending school in District X cannot shop for educational services in District Y or Z in the event that District X is shut down by a work stoppage.

Lewin elaborates reasons for prohibiting strike rights in the public sector as follows:

Denials of strike rights for public employees are predicated on the view that government is not simply another industry and therefore that public and private sector collective bargaining are not closely analogous, as they seem at first glance. This view, in turn, reflects several underlying assumptions: first, that the government is a sovereign, duly elected by citizens, and that its employees have no right to strike; second, that the services provided by government are essential, and that their suspension because of work stoppages would impose severe hardships on the public that must pay for them; and third—related to the second—that public employee unions are in an especially strong position negotiating with a monopolist, i.e., government, and operating, therefore, independent of market constraints. Permitting them to strike would enhance their bargaining power, and, again, allow them to impose substantial costs on the taxpaying public.[7]

Functions of the Strike in the Labor Relations System

Despite problems of sovereignty, service monopoly, and potential political distortion, the general public-sector ban on strikes is not unanimously endorsed. There are many who believe that strikes by the public sector should be legal or at least that prohibitions should be relaxed. Reasons for this belief, as well as reasons for believing that strikes by public-sector employees must be prohibited, will be taken up in detail later in this chapter.

Though the argument over the appropriateness of strikes in public employment continues, in the private sector there is virtually unanimous agreement that the strike is an essential element in a system of free collective bargaining.[8] It is generally held that, to make collective bargaining work, there must be a way to impose extreme costs on both parties as motivation to resolve disputes.

If workers succeed in slowing or shutting down production, the employer will lose business. In addition to business lost during the period of the strike, it is entirely possible that, as a result of the substantial shift or search for alternative suppliers during the strike, customers will not return to the employer's market once the strike is settled. On the union side, a strike imposes substantial economic hardships on employees. It deprives them of their regular income and means not only that they must delay purchases but also that they may have to change their life-style for some time after settlement to repay loans and catch up on mortgage and other payments that came due during the strike. These constitute substantial incentive for both sides to resolve their differences if just the mere threat of a strike hangs over the negotiations.

Certainly, in a historical context, the strike has served an important role in industrial relations in the United States and has been an important factor in breaking the unilateral rule-making discretion of employers. It serves to notify the employer in negotiations that the workers take their demands seriously and are prepared to endure hardships in order to accomplish their negotiating objectives.

Strikes have had many meanings in different settings. In analyzing strikes related to contract expiration or reopenings and those involved in the settling of disputes during contractual periods, John Dunlop identifies four functions for strikes. First, there are strikes that seek to change the structure of bargaining. Of these strikes, he says:

The central purpose of a number of significant strikes and lock-outs in recent years appears to be the desire by one party to change the structure of bargaining;

to change the organization holding the leadership role on one side or the other, the geographical scope of negotiations, or the level of negotiations, national or local, at which various issues are settled. A traditional arrangement of bargaining is unsatisfactory to some party, and the strike is used to try to achieve a transformation. The objective is not to reach agreement within the existing structure of negotiations but rather to change that structure itself. Sometimes the purpose is achieved; sometimes the old resists change; and in other cases the old system is destroyed, but no stable, new arrangement is found.[9]

These strikes may be directed toward expanding or contracting the bargaining unit, influencing the multiemployer bargaining unit, patterning bargaining arrangements, or some other goal.

A second type that Dunlop identifies are "strikes to change the relations between principal negotiator and constituents in unions or managements." As an example, Dunlop says:

In some cases a strike may be designed to solidify or to unite a union or association, to strengthen the internal leadership both in dealing with the opposite side and in accommodating conflicting interests within the group. In rival union situations or where there are active competitors for internal power, a strike may demonstrate to external rivals strength, militancy, and virility, or it may arise because bargaining compromises with management are incompatible with internal political survival.[10]

It is likely that teachers' strikes in the United States have in many cases been motivated by this functional need. Strikes perpetuated by the American Federation of Teachers or the National Education Association have in many cases been designed to impress their opponents and to attract potential members. It has also been clear that there have been cases wherein teachers' unions have struck simply because union leadership was aware that, though they saw rationality in management's proposals, these proposals would never be accepted by union members. Indeed, it might be said that, in some cases, union members were simply itching for a strike.

A further function of the strike is to "change the budgetary allotment or policy of a government agency."[11] This function is probably more obvious in the public than in the private sector. During the early days of negotiations and teachers' strikes in the 1960's, it was common for a teachers' union to strike for higher wages knowing that the board of education did not have the resources to meet their demands. The hope was that the mayor, governor, or state legislature would produce increased revenue for the school district that would enable the board to meet teachers' demands. Often the employer has at least a minimal interest in whether the strike succeeds in achieving its objectives.

And, finally, the main function of strikes is "to change a bargaining position of the other side." Teachers' unions strike their employing district to try to get concessions on contract terms: a further increase in salary, a reduction in teaching load. Strikes occur in these instances because the terms under negotiation are of sufficient importance to both parties that neither will make further concessions in their position to achieve agreement. The strike, in this case, is a tactical weapon used to induce further concession.

It is Dunlop's contention that the means used to resolve a strike should depend upon the function the strike is designed to serve. Mediation and arbitration, for example, are not particularly effective in a strike aimed at changing government policy. They may not help much in the strike aimed at influencing members' attitudes. Strikes frequently serve multiple functions, and, therefore, their resolution becomes much more difficult as the mechanisms compete with the various functions of the strike.

Strikes as Rational Behavior

One notable commonality among most discussions of strikes in labor relations is an emphasis on rationality and the tactical or strategic importance of the strike to the system. It is assumed that a strike or the threat of one can bring about a change in the bargaining relationship or the utilities of the opponents that will promote ultimate resolution of the dispute. Unions employ the threat of a strike to elicit concessions from employers. Employers threaten to lock out workers and deprive them of their income in order to force concessions by unions. Union leaders may discreetly remind their members of the costs of a strike in an effort to have the members redefine their expectations, or they may let them endure a strike in order to modify their expectations, if that is what is preventing serious bargaining and ultimate agreement.

At least two theorists, Jan Pen and J. R. Hicks, have taken note of the functional consequences of strikes in achieving agreement. Pen, in analyzing the relative power of each of the opponents, considers the cost of agreeing or disagreeing with a particular proposal at any given time during negotiations (see Figure 9-1).

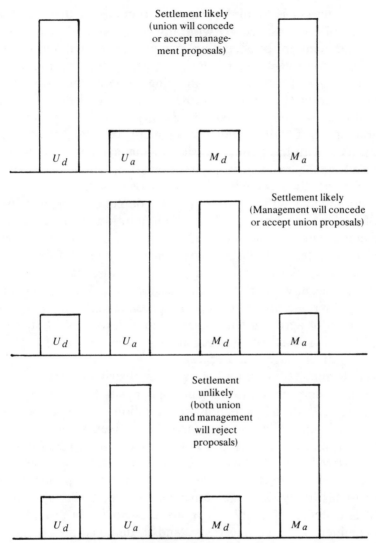

Key:
U_d = Union's cost of disagreement with management's proposals
U_a = Union's cost of agreement with management's proposals
M_d = Management's cost of disagreement with union's proposals
M_a = Management's cost of agreement with union's proposals

Figure 9-1
Simplified Pen model
(adapted from Jan Pen, "A General Theory of Bargaining," *American Economic Review*, 42 [March 1952], 24-42)

Pen's formulation is helpful because it reminds us that there are two types of costs associated with any offer under consideration: costs of agreeing to (or accepting) any given proposal and costs of disagreeing (or rejecting). Costs of agreeing, for the union, can include charges of "selling out," angering union members, prejudicing future terms by settling too low, the likelihood that the union or its officers will be replaced, or loss of jobs and members. Costs of agreeing, to school district management, can be such things as loss of favor with the public, erosion of management authority, or increased management cost, in addition to the money cost of the terms. On the disagreement side, union costs might include loss of members' income as the result of a strike, depletion of a strike fund, loss of jobs, court costs, members' defection. Management costs of disagreeing can include economic or political costs of a strike, lessened morale, and the like. In bargaining, therefore, unions try to increase the cost to management of disagreeing with the union's proposal, while reducing its cost of agreeing. Management will try to increase union costs of disagreeing while reducing costs to the union of agreeing with management's proposals. Settlement will occur when costs of agreeing are less than costs of disagreeing for both parties[12] (see Chapter 12).

Hicks formulated a utilitarian or rational strike explanation. His concession curve model (see Figure 9-2) posits that, under conditions of strike and the expected accumulation of costs to both employer and employees, the resistance to a given settlement point is reduced, and the longer the strike is expected to continue the more it is reduced.[13] This, of course, represents an example of Dunlop's changing of the attitude or utilities of the opponent. Elsewhere in his analysis of collective bargaining, Hicks also argues that it is necessary for unions to strike periodically just to "keep the machinery from getting rusty" and to demonstrate to the employer that the union is capable of entering into and sustaining a strike, that is, to maintain strike-threat utility.[14]

Strikes as Irrational or Uncontrollable Behavior

Much in labor relations literature argues for the functionality or rationality of the strike and its indispensable role in the complete system. There is also, however, considerable evidence that the strike is an accident or a consequence of inadequate or inept

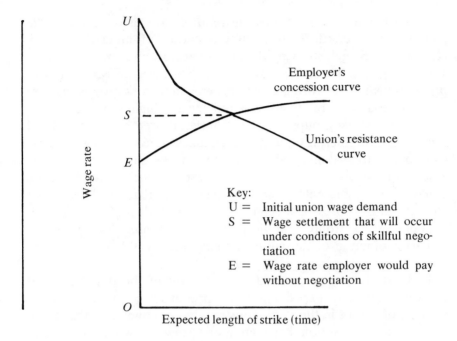

Figure 9-2
Hick's concession curve model
(from J. R. Hicks, *The Theory of Wages* [New York: St. Martin's Press, 1963], pp. 141-146)

negotiations. With the one caveat about the maintenance of the strike machinery, Hicks concluded that a strike results only in a circumstance of imperfect information. That is, if both unions and management were able to estimate their own economic position and the economic utilities of their opponents perfectly, they would in every case reach voluntary agreement without a strike.

Recent work seems to support the "observation that strikes are irrational events emerging from faulty negotiations and, hence, are likely to have a very strong random component. . . ."[15] Others, notably Orley Ashenfelter and George Johnson, have also followed the irrational or unpredictable model for strike explanation.[16] Their work also seems to lend support to relative deprivation models.

Strikes and Work Group Differences

A last major school of thought about strikes uses, as its fundamental construct, differences in the nature of industries. Clark
Kerr and A. Siegel, studying the private sector, and Joseph Krislov,
studying the public sector, have argued that there are certain strike-
prone industries or work groups. It seems that work groups that are
homogeneous and relatively isolated have a higher propensity to
strike than work groups that are more diffuse. Kerr and Siegel
found that lumberjacks and merchant seamen, among others,
were prone to strike,[17] and Krislov found that sanitation workers,
among others in the public sector, were inclined toward strike
behavior.[18] To the extent that one can argue that teachers in the
United States represent a relatively homogeneous, close-knit, self-
contained work group, it would be possible to infer that strikes are
in part a function of the nature or character of this kind of work
group.

Richard Hyman has extended the notion of the importance of
the work group in explaining strike propensity as a result of his
analysis of strikes in the steel industry. He has concluded that there
is a strong interaction between technology of work and social
organization. In the steel industry, which has a high propensity for
strikes, there is a promotional system based on seniority that "not
only ties an employee to the industry and indeed to a single firm,
but also, by establishing a pattern of aspiration and promotion for
his working life, gives him a feeling that he has a real stake in it."[19]

TEACHERS' STRIKES

A strike is a complex affair. It may be directed at the employer
or at the environment. It may result from dissatisfaction with the
bargaining process or with projected outcomes from that process,
or it may be a more general statement of anger. It may be accidental,
stemming from incompetent bargaining, or it may be calculated—
the exercise of "muscle" to achieve a bargaining objective.

It is hard to separate a strike, even for analytic purposes, from
the bargaining system. Strikes stem directly from impasse. In the
fall, when teachers and their employers cannot agree on terms of
employment after negotiating through the spring and summer,
teachers can do one of several things: capitulate and accept the last

offer of the board; refuse to work, that is, strike; agree to extend last year's contract and continue negotiating; or agree (or be forced) to submit the unresolved items to a neutral third party.

In making a decision among these courses of action, leaders for the teachers' union face a number of difficult questions. Obviously they must weigh costs of agreeing with the school board's last offer against costs of disagreeing. They must think about how close the sides are, how close the union is to achieving its bargaining objectives, how important the unresolved issues are, and what the mood of the members is. Further, the leaders must examine consequences of the action they recommend. If the union capitulates, how will it affect membership? Will the district take their demands seriously in future bargaining? If they recommend a strike, will enough teachers withhold their services to make a strike effective? Given the remaining differences, how long will the teachers be able to "stay out"?

If a strike is chosen as the course of action, presumably the school district will take countermeasures. What will they do? If they can get an injunction, there will be court costs and fines if the injunction is defied. Can the board issue contracts unilaterally? Will they fire the teachers?

Deciding to Strike

As with other aspects of the collective bargaining system, the analysis of strikes is made more complex by the fact that the decision to strike (or not to strike) is both a collective (or institutional) decision and an individual decision. In both the institutional and individual cases, two questions, if answered positively, can lead to a strike: Is a strike likely to be worth the effort? Is it necessary to strike, regardless of cost? The first question reflects the strike-as-rational-behavior perspective set forth earlier in this chapter and assumes that strikes are purposeful and undertaken as an investment in present or future gain. They are tactical or manipulative in nature. The second question reflects a strike-as-irrational-behavior perspective and presumes that strikes can be a response to frustration or anger or that they may be accidental—the result of bargaining or tactical error. Strikes in this view are accidental or expressive behaviors.

In bargaining, these two perspectives may exist together. Union leaders may call a strike because they expect to gain a bargaining advantage. Teachers may support a strike because they are frustrated and want to "hit back." Likewise, some teachers may support a strike because they expect a higher salary as an outcome. In fact, a strike in education is likely to serve multiple purposes.

Teachers' union leaders often attempt to manipulate teachers' frustration or anger to serve some tactical purpose. Cresswell and Simpson report an incident in a suburban district in which a board member told the teachers to stop pushing for higher salaries and "try eating dog food." The teachers' union aggressively publicized this statement, and, for teachers, the subsequent strike was motivated by the need to restore their dignity.[20] In a large-city school district we know of, union leaders felt a strike was necessary to increase bargaining power. And yet teachers were apathetic and would not, in all likelihood, support a strike. To develop that support, union leaders set about the task of increasing the teachers' sense of frustration and anger. School board actions to refurbish offices or purchase new cars were publicized. The union succeeded, and one year later the strategically necessary strike occurred.

Causal Models

Although strikes are complex events, often reflecting multiple causes, for analytical purposes we can identify a general model and six variations that have been used to study and explain teachers' strikes. The general model is based on the stimulus-response reaction. Strikes and striking are aggressive behavioral responses to certain situational stimuli. Inter- and intraunit difference in response is assumed to be the result of different individual perceptions and choices among behavioral responses. For instance, teachers' union leaders may be failing to attain settlement levels they believe to be reasonable because district representatives either do not take bargaining seriously or do not take the union seriously. To strike the district is one response to be considered. Whether a strike will be undertaken depends both upon the strength of the stimuli (how great the frustration of demands) and the degree to which the environment would support or frustrate a strike. In the case of an individual teacher's decision to strike, that choice might be in part a consequence of whether that teacher feels personally frustrated by the conditions under which he or she works and the degree to which striking behavior is personally acceptable. The general model is presented in Figure 9-3.

Situational Causes

When one examines the explanations given for teachers' strikes both from the point of view of the union decision to call a strike and teachers' individual decisions to support a strike, six types of situational stimuli emerge: (1) tactical considerations, (2) immaturity in bargaining, (3) individual frustration or relative deprivation, (4) unsatisfied basic needs, (5) sociological forces, and (6) organizational deprivation. The first group, tactical considerations, are those in which striking behavior by a teachers' union assumes some utilitarian purpose. Teachers strike because they expect to gain something or to change or correct some aspect of the labor relations system. Tactical explanations focus on the functional importance of strikes in the negotiating process, and on manipulation of the costs of agreement and disagreement. The assumption that teachers' strikes are largely tactical, a view implicit in much of the literature, has been tested, and one team has concluded that "teachers' strikes are essentially an investment in present and future bargaining power of the teachers' union."[21] These findings are consistent with the ideas of Hicks and Pen that the strike is an important and continuing part of calculating the cost of disagreeing for both parties. It is necessary, therefore, that the strike threat used in negotiations be credible, and, as Hicks pointed out, it may be necessary for teachers' unions to engage in strikes periodically just to maintain credibility.

Immaturity or error in bargaining as a cause of teachers' strikes

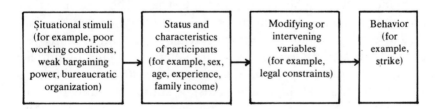

Figure 9-3
Causal model for strikes

borrows another of Hicks's notions that strikes often result from faulty negotiations, inexperience on the part of the negotiators, lack of appropriate and important information, and the like. If one allows these explanations, then it might be expected that, as the negotiations process matures, the number of bargaining mistakes will diminish, and the process will more often yield satisfactory negotiated agreements between the parties. This can happen. For one thing, negotiators will become less emotionally involved and better able to concentrate on the process and content of bargaining. Also, both negotiators and their constituents will become more proficient in estimating both their opponents' and their own utilities. If goals become clearer and the process gains a more objective focus, negotiators will then have a more realistic view about what is possible.[22] As the parties gain a better understanding of each others' limits, they begin to learn how to accommodate those constraints within the framework of bargaining.[23] Also encompassed in this view is the fact that, as collective bargaining becomes more common, the resources devoted to it will be more appropriate to needs. Each side will be better able to estimate the funds available for distribution and the long-term impact of various contract provisions. Union members will develop a better understanding of what is possible and thus have more realistic expectations of what they can expect to receive as a result of contract settlements. Increased sophistication in the use of the bargaining process should, ultimately, reduce the number of impasses and strikes that occur.

The frustration or relative deprivation explanations for teachers' strikes really focus less on collective behavior and more on motivating individual teachers to support the strike. These explanations use situational variables that determine the condition under which teachers work as inputs. For example, teachers and other employees may be frustrated by low salaries, large classes, or lack of supplies and equipment. As explained in Chapter 4, frustration and aggression models hold that the teacher must be sufficiently unhappy with the circumstance or feel sufficient deprivation in terms of working conditions to be willing to undertake an aggressive act, that is, to strike. Stephen Cole, in his study of the United Federation of Teachers, suggests that success in early strikes was a function of the extensive relative deprivation of teachers in New York City regarding wages and working conditions.[24] In another study, school districts in

New Jersey that experienced teachers' strikes between 1965 and 1969 were compared with a similar group of districts in the same state that did not experience strikes during the same period. The districts were found to be significantly different on eleven important economic and organizational variables reflecting wages and working conditions. The variables, in order of importance, are:

Average teacher salary
Average district enrollment
NDEA funds per pupil
Teacher salaries as expenditures per pupil
Expenditures for auxiliary services as percentage of budget
Library and audiovisual expenditures per pupil
Teacher-pupil ratio
Teacher salaries as a percentage of budget
Instructional support services per pupil
Change rate—average salary of teachers
Instructional support services as a percentage of budget

The data from this study suggest that teachers will strike in circumstances where their economic, organizational, and teaching conditions are substandard relative to other districts or in circumstances where these conditions have been deteriorating.[25]

Basic needs models are related to the concept of frustration or relative deprivation, but focus on more fundamental psychological needs. The motivation here comes not from real or perceived lack of job security or poor financial rewards but, rather, from teachers' disappointment in their social status or the need to acquire professional status and respect. A case study of a suburban Chicago school district where teachers ranked "dignity" as the major reason for their strike[26] constitutes a good example of the basic needs model.

Sociological forces or environmental stimuli are often used to explain teachers' strikes. Included here is the view that teachers' strikes are an outgrowth of times in which more people are engaging in overt actions in an effort to correct injustices. In the United States, the 1960's was a period of particularly aggressive use of civil disobedience and other tactics to combat perceived injustices or inequities. The civil rights movement is an example of such a force. It is more acceptable to engage in aggressive behaviors now. Such views extend those elaborated in Chapters 3 and 4 to explain militancy as a response to the sociological environment in which teachers find themselves.

Organizational deprivation explanations hold that strikes are the result of a conflict that occurs between the bureaucratic and professional employees of a school district. There is an inherent conflict between the basic authority structure in a bureaucratic organization and the need of practicing professionals for autonomy and the right to participate in making decisions. The pioneering work in this mode of thought came from Ronald Corwin;[27] his findings have received subsequent support.[28]

Though these six types of causal stimuli are elaborated separately for clarity, it is likely that several may be present in a strike situation. Teachers who have a sense of economic deprivation (relative deprivation) might also believe that they could achieve higher salaries by striking (tactical). By the same token, all teachers who strike may not be responding to the same stimuli. Some may be acting out of relative deprivation; others, from a search for dignity; still others, in response to organizational conflict (organizational deprivation).

The Propensity to Strike

In recent years there has been great interest in attempting to discover how strikers differ from nonstrikers. From the research literature, three categories of teachers' characteristics seem to be useful in describing the propensity of a teacher to strike, and they are the economic condition of the teacher, the professional orientation of the teacher, and general status characteristics.

Economic Condition

Those who are better off economically are not as likely to support a strike by a teachers' organization. In separate studies, teachers who do not hold a second job (are not moonlighting), those who are second wage earners, those whose total family income is higher, and those who have higher salaries generally are less likely to support a strike than those who are less fortunate economically.[29] These findings seem consistent with the relative deprivation explanation of strike behavior. Those who are less fortunate economically are apt to be angrier and, hence, likely to behave more aggressively. By the same token, people who are better off economically may have more to lose and less to gain (that is, lower cost of agreement and higher cost of disagreement) in strike action, which makes them less willing to support it.

Professional Orientation

Teachers' professional orientation is also related to strike behavior. Other things being equal, the teacher who chooses to strike is likely to have a stronger professional orientation than the teacher who chooses not to strike.[30] The nonstriking teacher is more likely to resemble the stereotype of the "organization man."[31] One researcher has noted "teachers who reflect a high professional role orientation will support a strike to a greater degree than their less professional colleagues or their colleagues with high bureaucratic role orientation."[32] Lest there be some confusion, it is necessary to discriminate at this point between professional orientation and dedication to a vocation. The teacher with a "professional orientation" tends to assign importance to professional authority and desires to participate in important decisions within the life of the organization. The teacher who is "dedicated to the vocation" views teaching as a calling that requires self-sacrifice. Those with a high professional orientation are more strike-prone; those with vocational dedication are less strike-prone.

There must be a match between teachers' professional orientation and the nature of the school organization. There is not a universal valuing of organizational characteristics by teachers. Some teachers are more comfortable (hence, happier) in a more bureaucratic teaching environment. Other teachers, because of a stronger professional (hence, autonomy-seeking) orientation, find the bureaucratic environment stifling and alien. It is possible that teachers will be more likely to strike where the match between their bureaucratic-professional disposition and the organizational arrangement of the schools is not good.

General Characteristics

A number of personal attributes or characteristics—religious and political views, sex, age, teaching level, and general satisfaction—appear to be correlated with either the decision to strike or an expressed willingness to strike. Teachers who support a strike are generally less religious and more liberal politically; they are likely to be male rather than female; they are among the younger teachers, though not the youngest; they teach at the secondary level;

and they are generally less satisfied with their work and with teaching as a career.[33]

The profile of the strike-prone teacher that emerges is that of a person who is aggressively unhappy with the organizational, educational, and economic situation in which that person finds himself or herself. Also, the person does not view teaching as a calling or a vocation and is more professionally oriented and less loyal to the organization.

Intervening Factors

A number of intervening factors may affect the decision of individual teachers to strike. Such factors determine whether teachers' frustrations will take the form of a strike or will be vented in some other fashion. Among those variables are the nature of the labor market in education, the professionalism of the teachers, the general antiunion bias of education, and, most particularly, the legal context in which teachers find themselves.

The nature of the labor market and the degree of inflation are both important factors in determining whether there are teachers' strikes.[34] Not only is the employment market for teachers (shortage or surplus) important, but the nature of the general employment market is also important. When the market is tight, teachers recognize that job opportunities outside of education are less readily available. Since teachers do not generally enjoy the same reinstatement rights that workers who engage in strikes in the private sector do, the potential cost of a strike is higher for teachers when the employment market is tight, which makes teachers less willing to engage in a strike. This same reluctance might be expected during periods when there is a surplus of teachers. Teachers are all too aware that boards of education have an alternative supply of labor available if teachers persist in withholding labor from a school district and that eventually the board of education will seek to replace teachers who are on strike with teachers who are unemployed.

In Chapter 3 we discussed the general reluctance of teachers to identify with organized labor and with the mechanisms of organized labor. Although they are reluctant, they do not refuse, in extreme cases, to engage in strikes and similar behaviors. The reluctance does, nonetheless, play a part, particularly in environments where a general antilabor bias in the community reinforces the bias that may exist within the teaching force. It is the reason why most teachers' strikes occur in industrial areas where there is large-scale, private-sector labor organization and where there is more likely to be general public acceptance of striking behavior and of the legitimacy of the strike as a mechanism for achieving one's goals.

Of all the so-called intervening factors, the one that has attracted by far the most attention is the question of statutory or legal framework. Public policy toward collective bargaining and labor relations in the public sector has strongly opposed strikes. This is contrary to the private sector where strikes are not routinely prohibited by law; it is also in sharp contrast to other developed Western democracies, where public-sector employees are relatively free to use the strike as part of their collective bargaining power machinery. Though the intent of public policy is clear, it is not as clear how successful this policy effort has been at constraining or reducing the number of strikes. Burton and Krider, in their analysis of public-sector strikes unrelated to education, found that public policy variables were not successful in explaining strike activity, and they concluded that there was no evidence to suggest that public policy or legislation was effective in reducing the number of strikes.[35] Neither, for that matter, did it produce increased strike activity. Weintraub and Thornton analyzed teachers' strikes that occurred before legislation was passed. They found that from 1946 to 1973 some twenty-seven states had adopted bargaining legislation for teachers that permitted collective bargaining. In sixteen of those states there were no changes in the levels of strike activity over the subsequent twenty-four-month period. In eleven states, where they did find a change in strike activity, there was an increase in seven.[36] They concluded from their analysis that, although it is not clear that legislation will increase the number of strikes that may occur, it is also clear that collective bargaining legislation has not been successful in reducing the occurrence of strikes.

Taken together, these studies would seem to indicate that public policy has had a negligible effect on strike decisions by public-sector and teachers' unions and that it certainly has been generally ineffective in preventing public employee strikes.[37] The key to the explanation of the general lack of relationship between public policy prohibiting strikes and striking behavior may, however, lie in an expanded definition of public policy. A number of states that have experienced a fairly high rate of public-sector and teachers' strikes have had very repressive legislation with heavy penalities for teachers' strikes. If one examines the experience of four Northeastern states (Pennsylvania, Ohio, Michigan, and New York), the relationship of public policy to strikes can be seen in the interaction between the law and the enforcing agencies. In Pennsylvania, strikes are legal; in Michigan and Ohio, they are illegal. In Michigan, however, judges have been reluctant to enjoin strikes, and striking employees are likely either not to be penalized or receive penalties that are minimal. In Ohio, the Ferguson Act prohibits strikes and sets some stiff penalties, but those penalties are rarely applied. In New York, the Taylor Act also provides for penalties for striking employees and their unions, and these penalties, though more modest, are applied consistently. The evidence seems to be that New York experiences a far lower rate of public-sector strikes than the other three.[38] This would seem to indicate that public policy can, in fact, reduce the incidence of strikes but that the courts, the legislature, and the state enforcement agencies must carry out their parts with equal consistency.

STRIKES IN THE PUBLIC SECTOR

Arguments For

The main arguments used to support the call for public-sector strike rights are that strikes occur anyway and, because legislation seems to be ineffective in halting them, this creates an awkward legal system; and that strikes are an intimate and essential part of the collective bargaining process, which means that removal of the right to strike seriously hampers a free collective bargaining process.

Theodore Kheel has emphasized this in his analysis of the role of the strike in public service:

So, from its origin in the battle for recognition, the strike (and lockout) have now assumed indispensable roles in the bargaining process. In my judgment, the prospect of a strike in the vast majority of bargaining situations can never be outmoded, unaccepted, outlawed, or rendered obsolete without doing more damage to collective bargaining than the relief the public would supposedly get. The strike and collective bargaining are Siamese twins.[39]

And, finally, it is argued that, except for a few essential services such as police and fire protection, strikes in the public sector do not pose truly serious threats and, consequently, public-sector unions are in relatively weak positions. When public-sector unions go on strike, they do not usually interrupt the flow of revenue to government. Thus, school districts continue to receive funds from local taxpayers although they are temporarily relieved of their payroll obligations. It is no secret that some school districts have balanced their budgets as a result of strikes and reduced payroll obligations. In the private sector, a strike begins to produce economic hardship for the employer relatively soon. In the public sector the economic hardship would seem to fall most readily and apparently on the employee, not the employer.

Arguments Against

There are two fundamental arguments against the use of strikes in the public sector. The first derives from conceptions of public employment and the representative nature of public bodies acting in the interest of the public and at the same time serving as employers. The so-called "doctrine of sovereignty" holds that a strike against the government must necessarily be illegal, for it represents an attack on the state itself and is, therefore, an intolerable act of aggression against the democratic state. In California, in particular, the courts have held recently that the strike represents a mechanism for forcing the employer to agree to conditions and terms that he would not otherwise agree to and that public decisions made under duress are not consistent with representative democratic decision making.[40]

The second major argument against public employees' right to strike rests on the argument that the strike provides public employees' unions with too much power. The power in public-sector negotiations is derived not from economics but from politics. If unions are allowed to strike, they are given an additional weapon to bring political pressure on their employing governmental agency. In that they generally follow an interest-group model of governmental decision making, this places the union, as an interest group, in an advantageous situation when competing with other interest groups for the allocation of scarce resources, and this is undesirable.[41]

Discussion of Arguments

There are reasons to question these arguments. First, they assume that public employees generally provide monopoly services and that those services are not easily replaced. Second, they assume that, when the public is denied these services, there will be pressure to concede. Implicit in the analysis is the assumption that the public will be so upset by the denial of expected services through the strike that they will support virtually any demands of the unions in their search for a rapid solution. There is reason to doubt that the public can be badgered by unions and that public bodies will therefore grant high wage settlements in an attempt to maintain essential services. In the last three years there have been repeated instances of essential services being cut off by public-sector unions in the United States. In many cases, alternative methods of providing those services have been developed. Where police officers have withdrawn their labor, the National Guard and other military units have been brought in to keep peace. These same units have been used to fight fires while firemen were on strike.

If one looks at the case of Great Britain where unions in the public sector are accorded the same status as those in the private sector, one finds that no favoritism is shown to labor unions in the public sector during negotiations, even though those unions have engaged in strikes quite frequently. In recent years Britain has had a wages-and-incomes policy that has set guidelines for wage changes. Private-sector unions have, on several occasions, been successful in negotiating wage settlements that exceeded the policy guidelines, but they have been unsuccessful in breaking the guidelines. Teachers in Britain are unionized and belong to the trade union council, but they have done poorly in their negotiations with the government.

Recent events in San Francisco have been particularly instructive in showing the resistance of a public angered by wage demands or previous settlements of public employees. On two occasions, public employees sought to increase or maintain their already high wages, and, in both instances, city officials, with a great demonstration of public support, withstood the strike and refused to concede to the demands of the unions. Based on these experiences, assumptions about the relative powerlessness of public bodies to stand up to the political pressure generated by public-sector strikes are questionable.

PROCEDURES FOR RESOLVING IMPASSES

Restriction on the use of the strike in public-sector labor negotiations has led to a quest for effective substitutes. In most cases public policy makers have turned to the use of third-party neutrals to resolve public-sector labor-management impasses. In general, three third-party neutral procedures can be employed in the attempt to resolve impasses: mediation, fact-finding, and arbitration.

Mediation

Mediation is a nonjudicial attempt by one or more outside parties to help unions and management resolve their differences. Maurice Trotta defines "mediator" as

a disinterested third-party, usually a government employee, who helps to settle disputes involving the terms and conditions of a collective bargaining agreement. He is assigned and paid by the state or federal agency by which he is employed. He is not selected by the parties. The mediator renders no final and binding decision. He merely suggests solutions. As a means of avoiding a strike, mediators frequently suggest to the parties that they agree to submit the issue in dispute to an arbitrator.[42]

Trotta's definition of mediator, drawn primarily for the private sector, is based on the fact that the federal government, as a result of the Taft-Hartley Amendment to the National Labor Relations Act, created the Federal Mediation and Conciliation Service. The FMCS not only follows all negotiations in the private sector, but may intervene in contract negotiations if the agency deems it appropriate to prevent an impasse or strike from occurring. Though the mediators of the FMCS have no power to impose settlements on the parties, they do have the legal right to require them to attend mediation hearings and sessions.

Through a recent series of presidential Executive Orders, the FMCS has been authorized to provide bargaining services in the public as well as the private sector. Although the FMCS has no jurisdiction in the public sector, which, except for federal service, is subject to state law, it has been active in public-sector impasse cases. In fiscal year 1976 the FMCS took on a total of 665 mediation cases from the public sector, of which 388 involved school impasses. Other public and private organizations, such as state labor relations agencies and the American Arbitration Association, provide substantial numbers of mediators as well.

Most state laws with a provision for impasse resolution generally require mediation as a first step, and, if mediation proves unsuccessful in resolving the impasse, then the dispute is referred to fact-finding or arbitration. In a recent survey of school districts in the United States, it was found that about 35 percent experienced impasse during collective bargaining. In the districts that experienced impasse, more than 80 percent were submitted to mediation. The evidence in this study of data gathered in 1975-76 indicated that mediators were successful in resolving over half of the cases submitted to them.[43]

The mediator's role is a difficult one, as Paul Staudohar's description of the role shows:

The mediator's stock in trade is persuasion applied through the use of pressure in order to modify attitudes and behavior. Pressure used in mediating a public sector case tends to be more personal, social, and political, but less economic. The dispute in the public sector is not a test of economic strength. Wage criteria such as comparability, cost of living, and ability to pay, are relevant to determining pressure in the public sector, but this pressure is oriented more towards the politics of using the data than toward the economics of the data *per se*.[44]

Another problem for mediators in educational bargaining seems to be the lack of experience that characterizes much of the bargaining in the public sector. Many of a mediator's efforts in the public sector may go toward teaching the parties the basic process of collective bargaining. As experience with collective bargaining in education increases, this function of mediators should diminish.[45]

Fact-Finding

Though fact-finding boards have been used in the private sector (the emergency board procedures in the Railway Labor Act), it is in the public sector that fact-finding has been a major mechanism in resolving disputes. Fact-finding differs from mediation in that a fact finder or fact-finding panel is chosen or appointed and charged with the responsibility of looking into the dispute or gathering the facts. These facts, once gathered, are then made public in the hope that publication will provide the basis for resolving the dispute. The mechanism is intended to work on two levels. First, it is assumed that the fact finders can discover the nature of the dispute in a way that the parties involved will recognize as a basis for solution. Second, a published report represents a political force that will produce pressure on both parties to accept the fact finders' recommendations. Although a number of states use fact-finding as a mechanism for resolving disputes, there is some reason to question its effectiveness. There is some evidence that the public is not generally interested in the reports produced, and, as a consequence, they have little, if any, political impact.[46]

It may be shortsighted to look at the effect of fact-finding solely from the position of its ability to produce political pressure on the parties to settle. Fact-finding and other third-party interventions provide several useful inputs into the negotiation process that can allow for ultimate resolution of the dispute. First, fact-finding can often assist in building or developing consensus among the parties. On this, George Sulzner says, "The method of selecting a fact finder also contributes to consensus building because both parties have had an opportunity to reject fact finders that are unacceptable to them before settling upon a particular neutral."[47]

It is essential to all third-party procedures that the third party not only be viewed as neutral but also prove acceptable to both parties in the dispute. In the private sector the parties generally have some say in the selection, which, in itself, gives them some reason for accepting or moving toward the recommendations made by that party.

Another advantage is "interest pacification." Sulzner points out that mediators and fact finders, by listening to the parties and allowing them to explain their position, often reduce levels of tension and allow the parties to see their dispute in a slightly different light.[48] This would seem to lead to more ready resolution of the conflict. Further, the third party can offer a way out—a face-saving solution that neither party could voluntarily offer or accept if offered directly.

Arbitration

Of all the third-party resolution mechanisms in educational bargaining, the most discussed and most controversial is probably that of arbitration. Arbitration is a quasi-judicial process in which an arbitrator or arbitration panel, after hearing the sides to the dispute, issues an award that may be binding on the parties. The arbitrator or arbitrators act as a tribunal in attempting to resolve the dispute or separate issues in the dispute.

In considering arbitration, it is essential to distinguish the two types widely used in labor negotiations. First, there is "rights" arbitration, in which arbitrators interpret or rule on the meaning of the contract. Most contracts employ a grievance procedure that often results in arbitration if the dispute cannot be successfully resolved by the two parties. If an arbitrator is called in to rule on a grievance, this is called a rights arbitration case (see Chapter 8).

The other major type of arbitration is called "interest" arbitration.[49] In this case, the arbitrator or arbitrators are called upon to make a decision about issues involved in the negotiating of an initial contract or the renegotiating of an existing contract. Trotta points out that about 95 percent of all arbitrations are rights arbitrations and only 5 percent are interest arbitrations.[50]

There are few interest cases because the private sector makes little use of arbitration in settling contract negotiation disputes, though mediation is used actively and widely. If the parties cannot resolve their differences with the aid of a mediator, they generally resort to strike or lockout. Because those avenues are often closed to the public sector, however, much more attention and emphasis are placed upon the process of interest arbitration and, in the event that mediation and perhaps fact-finding has failed to resolve a public-sector dispute, the parties are often required to submit their dispute to arbitration.

There are four types of interest arbitration, three of which are used with some frequency in the public sector. In looking at these types, arbitration can be viewed along two dimensions: one dealing with whether the parties have a choice in submitting their disputes to arbitration; the other, with whether the parties have a choice in accepting the award or judgment of the arbitrator. If the parties must submit their disputes to arbitration under any circumstance, then the arbitration is compulsory. If the parties can choose whether to submit their dispute to arbitration, then the arbitration is voluntary. If the parties agree in advance to accept the award of the arbitrator or if they are forced to accept the award of the arbitrator by governmental decree, the arbitration is said to be binding. If, on the other hand, the parties determine whether or not to abide by the award or judgment of the arbitrator or are free to reject the award, then the arbitration is said to be advisory. These four types are shown in Figure 9-4.

In private-sector bargaining in the United States, almost all interest arbitration is voluntary and binding. The government does not require private-sector bargaining disputes to be submitted to arbitration, but if the parties agree to submit their dispute to arbitration, it is expected that they will abide by the ruling of the arbitrator. In the public sector, on the other hand, because strikes are prohibited it is customary for arbitration to be compulsory. The parties are required to submit their dispute to an arbitrator or arbitration panel. In the past the award of the arbitrator has generally been advisory in nature, and the parties were not obligated to abide by it because there was and is considerable concern about turning over public policy decisions to third parties who can force their decision upon public employers. In recent years, however, there has been considerably more compulsory binding arbitration in the public sector. It began primarily with the essential services (fire and police), but a number of states now require that educational disputes be submitted to compulsory binding arbitration (see Table 9-2).

Are parties obligated to
accept arbitrations award?

		Yes	No
Are parties required to submit impasse issues to arbitration?	Yes	Type I Compulsory binding arbitration	Type II Compulsory advisory arbitration
	No	Type III Voluntary binding arbitration	Type IV Voluntary advisory arbitration

Figure 9-4
Types of arbitration

Table 9-2
Bargaining impasse provisions for each state

State	Bargaining impasse procedures
Alabama	No provision
Alaska	Parties may select mediator, or request resolution by Federal Mediation and Conciliation Service. Advisory arbitration may follow
Arizona	No provision
Arkansas	No provision
California	Mediation, fact-finding, advisory recommendations through EERB
Colorado	No provision
Connecticut	Mediation by secretary of state board of education. Arbitration with nonbinding recommendations by selected panel
Delaware	Mediation, fact-finding, nonbinding recommendations. Binding arbitration by third party is prohibited
Florida	Mediation, "special master" for public hearings, fact-finding. Settlement by appropriate legislative body
Georgia	No provision
Hawaii	May be bargained. May culminate in final and binding arbitration. Mediation, fact-finding, and arbitration available from PERB
Idaho	Mediation, fact-finding, nonbinding recommendations
Illinois	No provision
Indiana	Mediation and fact-finding by EERB
Iowa	May be bargained. Mediation, fact-finding, final and binding arbitration available through PERB

Table 9-2 *(continued)*

State	Bargaining impasse procedures
Kansas	Impasse to be determined by court, using fact-finding. Subsequent procedures include mediation, fact-finding with nonbinding recommendation. Board of education has right to final decision
Kentucky	No provision
Louisiana	No provision
Maine	Mediation and/or fact-finding. MLRB and Maine Board of Conciliation and Arbitration available. Binding arbitration on all matters by mutual consent; if none, binding arbitration on matters other than salaries, pensions, insurance. Court review
Maryland	State superintendent determines impasse exists; mediation, nonbinding recommendations
Massachusetts	Board of Conciliation and Arbitration, mediation, fact-finding, binding recommendations if mutually agreed by parties and authorized by appropriate legislative body
Michigan	Mediation and fact-finding; nonbinding recommendations via PERC
Minnesota	Mediation; binding arbitration by PERB at request of either party
Mississippi	No provision
Missouri	No provision
Montana	Mediation, fact-finding through BPA. Binding arbitration by agreement of both parties
Nebraska	Fact-finding board and nonbinding recommendation. Court of Industrial Relations assumes jurisdiction after procedures of this act have been exhausted

Table 9-2 *(continued)*

State	Bargaining impasse procedures
Nevada	Mediation; labor commissioner may appoint. Fact-finding; American Arbitration Association may assist. Final and binding fact-finding recommendations by agreement of both parties, or on order of governor within 10 days of legislature's adjournment. Deadline dates for agreement prescribe alternate procedures
New Hampshire	Mediation; fact-finding with nonbinding recommendations; renegotiation. Alternate lawful procedures may be bargained. PERLB available
New Jersey	Mediation, fact-finding. Arbitration by mutual agreement
New Mexico	No provision
New York	May be bargained; may provide binding arbitration. PERB available; procedures include mediation, fact-finding with recommendations submitted to appropriate legislative body for necessary action to reach agreement
North Carolina	No provision
North Dakota	Mediation, fact-finding with nonbinding recommendations via Education Fact-Finding Commission. Parties may agree to own procedures
Ohio	No provision
Oklahoma	Must be bargained; final impasse procedure is 3-member fact-finding process
Oregon	May be bargained; may include final and binding arbitration. Mediation, fact-finding through PERB
Pennsylvania	Mediation, with Pennsylvania Bureau of Mediation available; fact-finding per PLRB; voluntary binding arbitration with decisions requiring legislative advisory only

Table 9-2 *(continued)*

State	Bargaining impasse procedures
Rhode Island	Mediation and conciliation services through state education agency or director of labor. Arbitration on request; binding on nonfund items only
South Carolina	No provision
South Dakota	Mediation with Commissioner of Labor and Management Relations available; other procedures optional
Tennessee	Mediation, fact-finding, advisory arbitration. Federal Mediation and Conciliation Service. American Arbitration Association may be used
Texas	No provision
Utah	No provision
Vermont	Mediation, fact-finding, nonbinding recommendations. American Arbitration Association may assist. Employer decision final
Washington	Mediation, fact-finding advisory recommendation through PERC
West Virginia	No provision
Wisconsin	May be bargained. SERC available for mediation-arbitration. If both last best offers in mandatory subjects of bargaining are withdrawn before final arbitration, union may strike. If not, final arbitration is required
Wyoming	No provision
District of Columbia	No provision

Source: Adapted from Doris Ross, *Cuebook: State Education Collective Bargaining Laws* (Denver, Colo.: Education Commission of the United States, 1978), 14-48.

In addition to the legal issues raised by compulsory binding arbitration, there are other questions about its use. One of the main ones has to do with the effect of compulsory use of third parties, particularly binding arbitrators, on the bargaining process itself. Peter Feuille has written about what he terms the "chilling effect" of third-party neutrals on the collective bargaining process.[51] By that he means that bargaining itself is retarded because the parties bargain with the idea that they will or may be submitting their dispute to third-party judgment. They do not wish to compromise that decision by offers made earlier at the bargaining table and entered into arbitration evidence. It is possible that neither party would make a serious attempt to reach agreement or would put forth their best offers in an attempt to influence the arbitrator's decision. On distributive issues, arbitrators will generally split the difference. That means it is in the parties' best interest to stay as far from the position they would be prepared to accept as possible so that the award is more nearly what they would have settled on voluntarily.

Research on arbitration behavior has also shown that arbitrators tend to look at two things in arriving at their decision. First, they seek to construct an award that has the greatest possibility of being accepted and being seen as fair by both parties. In a sense this is the political dimension of arbitration where the arbitrator attempts to please both parties. A second dimension of the arbitrator's decision tends to revolve around questions of equity, fairness, and comparability, that is, the arbitrator will look at other circumstances and other comparable agreements in an attempt to find standards that are generally applied throughout a given industry.[52] In the case of education, that would mean issuing a wage award that was in keeping with general settlements in comparable districts in the locality.

There have been at least two major suggestions for improving this process of arbitration. The one considered most is known as final-offer arbitration. In this system, instead of offering a compromise solution, the arbitrator would have to select one of the two final offers made by the two parties to the dispute; that is, he would have to select either the final offer made by the school board's team or the final offer made by the teachers' team. It is thought that this would motivate the parties to put forth their best offer, and, even if they expected to go to arbitration, there would be motivation to develop a good position so that the arbitrator would be apt to select their offer.

Critics of this system point out that this greatly restricts the arbitrator's ability to construct a fair settlement. It is a particularly difficult situation if neither party has put forth a reasonable offer and the arbitrator, though he may recognize the inadequacies of both parties' final offers, is bound to accept one or the other.[53]

NOTES

1. Federal Mediation and Conciliation Service (FMCS), *Twenty-ninth Annual Report* (Washington, D.C.: U.S. Government Printing Office, n.d.), 27. It must be acknowledged that, whereas all private-sector contract disputes involving twenty-five or more workers must be referred to FMCS, there is no such requirement for state and local public-sector bargaining units. As a consequence, the total number of public-sector cases handled by the FMCS is probably only a small part of the total number of disputes or impasses that occurred in 1976. The tremendous increase in public-sector disputes, as compared with a slight decline in private-sector ones, indicates, nonetheless, that the number of impasses in the public sector may well be on the rise.

2. See Chapter 2.

3. FMCS, *Twenty-ninth Annual Report*, 32.

4. David Lewin, "Public Sector Collective Bargaining and the Right to Strike," in David Lewin *et al., Public Sector Labor Relations: Analysis and Readings* (Glen Ridge, N.J.: Thomas Horton and Daughters, 1977), 238.

5. There are at present only seven states where strikes by teachers may be legal: Alaska, Hawaii, Minnesota, Oregon, Pennsylvania, Vermont, and Wisconsin. In all cases, there are restrictions. In all cases, courts may enjoin the strike if it threatens health, safety, or welfare. In six of the states, strikes may occur only after certain statutory impasse resolution procedures have been exhausted.

6. U.S. Department of Labor, Bureau of Labor Statistics, *Work Stoppages in Government, 1975,* Report 483 (Washington D.C.: U.S. Government Printing Office, 1977).

7. Lewin, "Public Sector Collective Bargaining," 238-239.

8. For discussion of this view, see Reed C. Richardson, *Collective Bargaining by Objectives: A Positive Approach* (Englewood Cliffs, N.J.: Prentice-Hall, 1977), ch. 19, esp. 271-272; and Harold W. Davey, *Contemporary Collective Bargaining,* 3d ed. (Englewood Cliffs, N.J.: Prentice-Hall, 1972), ch. 8, 191-214.

9. John T. Dunlop, "The Function of Strike," in *Frontiers of Collective Bargaining,* ed. John T. Dunlop and Neil W. Chamberlain (New York: Harper and Row, 1967), 106.

10. *Ibid.*, 108.

11. *Ibid.*, 109.

11a. *Ibid.*, 110.

12. For Pen's original formulation, see Jan Pen, "A General Theory of Bargaining," *American Economic Review*, 42:1 (March 1952), 24-42. For a good discussion of bargaining costs of agreeing and disagreeing, see Neil W. Chamberlain and James W. Kuhn, *Collective Bargaining*, 2d ed. (New York: McGraw-Hill, 1965), 170-190.

13. J. R. Hicks, *The Theory of Wages*, 2d ed. (New York: St. Martin's Press, 1963), 140-144.

14. *Ibid.*, 146.

15. G. Scully, "Business Cycles and Industrial Strike Activity," *Journal of Business* 44:4 (October 1971), 374.

16. Orley Ashenfelter and George Johnson, "Bargaining Theory, Trade Unions, and Industrial Strike Activity," *American Economic Review*, 59:1 (March 1969), 35-49.

17. Clark Kerr and A. Siegel, "The Interindustry Propensity to Strike—An International Comparison," in *Industrial Conflict*, ed. Arnold Kornhauser, Robert Dubin, and Arthur M. Ross (New York: McGraw-Hill, 1954), 189-212.

18. Joseph Krislov, "Work Stoppages of Government Employees, 1942-59," *Quarterly Review of Economics and Business,* 1:1 (February, 1961), 87-92.

19. Richard Hyman, *Strikes* (Glasgow: William Collins and Sons, 1977), 64. Hyman provides an excellent summary of research on the strike-proneness of industries and work groups on pages 56 through 65.

20. See Anthony M. Cresswell and Daniel Simpson, "Collective Bargaining and Conflict: Impacts of School Governance," *Educational Administration Quarterly,* 13:3 (Fall 1977), 49-69.

21. Andrew W. Weintraub and Robert J. Thornton, "Why Teachers Strike: The Economic and Legal Determinants," *Journal of Collective Negotiations in the Public Sector*, 5:3 (1976), 193-206.

22. For a good description of how the process of negotiation can be improved, see Richardson, *Collective Bargaining by Objectives*, 106-156.

23. Gilroy and Sinicropi extend this argument by pointing out that one of the main functions performed by third parties in public-sector disputes is the guiding of negotiations that break down, presumably, because the parties lack bargaining experience. See Thomas P. Gilroy and Anthony V. Sinicropi, "Impasse Resolution in Public Employment: A Current Assessment," *Industrial and Labor Relations Review*, 25:4 (July 1972), 498-499.

24. Stephen Cole, *The Unionization of Teachers: A Case Study of the UFT* (New York: Praeger Publishers, 1969), esp. ch. 3.

25. Michael J. Murphy, "Teacher Strikes: A Social-Psychological Analysis," unpub. diss., Claremont Graduate School, 1971, esp. 104.

26. Cresswell and Simpson, *Collective Bargaining and Conflict*, 56.

27. See Ronald G. Corwin, *Militant Professionalism: A Study of Organizational Conflict in High Schools* (New York: Appleton-Century-Crofts, 1970).

28. Corwin's ideas about conflict between the bureaucratic organization and professional employees has been used extensively, as has his concept of "militant professionalism." For supporting research, see Samuel W. Warren, "Striking Teachers: Professionalism and Bureaucracy," unpub. diss., Teachers College, Columbia University, 1974.

29. Economic conditions have been widely studied as potential cause factors in teacher strikes, and there is now considerable evidence that they do play a role. Bruno and Nelken have shown that teachers who carry an extra job (moonlight) and those with lower total family income have a higher propensity to strike. Although Bruno and Nelken were unable to support salary as a related variable, two variables in their list (moonlighting and family income) represent the economic condition of the teacher and would seem to indicate that the economic condition of teachers is indeed important in deciding whether to engage in militant or agressive efforts to change conditions. One would assume that the moonlighting teacher carries a second job, not out of choice but out of economic necessity. The salary earned as a teacher is insufficient to sustain the life-style desired. Similarly, high family income probably indicates that a spouse is also working. The higher total earning, by reducing dependence on the wage rate paid teachers, is less likely to motivate people to acts of aggression. See James E. Bruno and Ira Nelken, "An Empirical Analysis on Propensity for Teachers to Strike," *Educational Administration Quarterly*, 2:2 (Spring 1975), 66-85. Unlike Bruno and Nelken, Warren studied actual behavior during a strike rather than personally stated willingness ("propensity"). Warren's research indicates that salary is an important consideration when teachers decide to support a strike. Warren also found total family income significantly related to strike behavior. See Warren, "Striking Teachers."

30. Cole makes the point that "professional dissatisfactions" are a factor in militancy and the support of the early strikes in New York City. See Cole *Unionization of Teachers*. Warren found that those who participated actively in a teachers' strike were more likely to have a higher professional orientation. See Warren, "Striking Teachers."

31. Alutto and Belasco suggest that organizational commitment is a factor in "attitudinal militancy" that includes attitudes toward strikes. See Joseph A. Alutto and James A. Belasco "Determinants of Attitudinal Militancy among Teachers and Nurses," *Industrial and Labor Relations Review*, 27:2 (January 1974), 216-227. Bruno and Nelken found that teachers whose "colleague orientation toward administration is more positive" are less likely to strike. Also less strike-prone teachers exhibited less belief in peer evaluation. See Bruno and Nelken, "An Empirical Analysis on Propensity for Teachers to Strike," 82. What emerges from these and other studies is the conclusion that organizational loyalty, and perhaps identification with the organizational reward structure, reduce support for strikes. Thus the "organization man" is less likely to be a striker.

32. Warren, "Striking Teachers," 163.

33. This profile of personal characteristics is gathered from many studies. See, e.g., Cole, *Unionization of Teachers;* Warren, "Striking Teachers"; Bruno and Nelken, "An Empirical Analysis on Propensity for Teachers to Strike"; Alutto

and Belasco, "Determinants of Attitudinal Militancy among Teachers and Nurses"; and Alan Rosenthal, *Pedagogues and Power: Teacher Groups in School Politics* (Syracuse, N.Y.: Syracuse University Press, 1969).

34. Weintraub and Thornton, "Why Teachers Strike."

35. John F. Burton, Jr. and Charles E. Krider, "The Incidence of Strikes in Public Employment," in *Labor in the Public and Non-Profit Sector*, ed. Daniel S. Hamermesh (Princeton, N.J.: Princeton University Press, 1975), 135-177.

36. Weintraub and Thornton, "Why Teachers Strike," 204.

37. This point is made also in David Lewin, "Collective Bargaining and the Right to Strike," in *Public Employee Unions: A Study of the Crisis in Public Sector Labor Relations*, ed. A. Lawrence Chickering (San Francisco: Institute for Contemporary Studies: 1976), 145-163.

38. This important point is made in Peter Feuille, "Public Sector Impasses: Symposium Introduction," *Industrial Relations*, 16:3 (October 1977), 265-266; and in David Lewin *et al., Public Sector Labor Relations*, 222-223.

39. Theodore W. Kheel, "Exploring Alternatives to the Strike: Is the Strike Outmoded?" *Monthly Labor Review*, 96:1 (September 1973), 36.

40. *Grasco* v. *Los Angeles City Board of Education*, 31 Cal. App. 3d 297-298 (1973).

41. This point is made most forcefully by Harry H. Wellington and Ralph K. Winter, Jr., in "The Limits of Collective Bargaining," *Yale Law Journal*, 78:7 (June 1969), 1107-1127; reprinted in *Education and Collective Bargaining*, ed. Anthony M. Cresswell and Michael J. Murphy (Berkeley, Calif.: McCutchan Publishing Corporation, 1976), 308-331.

42. Maurice Trotta, *Arbitration of Labor-Management Disputes* (New York: AMACOM, 1974), 24.

43. FMCS, *Twenty-ninth Annual Report*, 21. See also Chapter 2 for data on impasse rates in U.S. school districts.

44. Paul D. Staudohar, "Some Implications of Mediation for Resolution of Bargaining Impasses in Public Employment," *Public Personnel Management*, 2:4 (July-August 1973), 300.

45. See Gilroy and Sinicropi, "Impasse Resolution in Public Employment."

46. This argument that fact-finding fails as a political force developed in William Word, "Fact-findings in Public Employee Negotiations," *Monthly Labor Review*, 95:2 (February 1972), 60-64. It is also made in George T. Sulzner, "The Impact of Impasse Procedures in Public Sector Labor: An Overview," *Journal of Collective Negotiations in the Public Sector*, 4:1, 1975, p. 7.

47. George T. Sulzner, "The Political Functions of Impasse Procedures," *Industrial Relations*, 16:3 (October 1977), 293.

48. While mediation is generally endorsed, fact-finding is a more controversial process. It is fairly clear that fact-finding does not have much impact on public awareness; nor does it seem to generate public pressure for an equitable settlement. Employers reject the recommendations of fact finders at least twice and perhaps four times as often as do unions. On the other hand, there is evidence that fact-

finding "works." Gilroy and Sinicropi estimate that 90 percent of the cases going to fact-finding are resolved at that step. See Gilroy and Sinicropi, "Impasse Resolution in Public Employment," 501. In general, the evidence seems to be that the facts of the dispute gathered by fact finders and their recommendations are more useful to the parties than the public and often serve as the basis for renewed negotiations. For an excellent review of research on fact-finding, see Ralph T. Jones, *Public Sector Labor Relations: An Evaluation of Policy-Related Research* (Belmont, Mass.: Contract Research Corporation, 1975), 162-167.

49. Harold Davey (*Contemporary Collective Bargaining*, 3d ed. [Englewood Cliffs, N.J.: Prentice-Hall, 1972], ch. 8, esp. 191-214) prefers the phrase "future-terms disputes" to describe contract or interest impasses. In many ways it is more accurate and descriptive.

50. Trotta, *Arbitration of Labor-Management Disputes*, 25.

51. See Peter F. Feuille, "Final Offer Arbitration and the Chilling Effect," in Lewin *et al., Public Sector Labor Relations*, 297.

52. For a good review of criteria used by arbitrators in public sector interest disputes see Jones, *Public Sector Labor Relations*, 179-189.

53. For a discussion of the dangers in final-offer arbitration see Hoyt N. Wheeler, "Closed-Offer: Alternative to Final-Offer Selection," *Industrial Relations*, 16:3 (October 1977), 298-305.

10

Unions and Their Impact on School Governance and Politics

Unions have become an important influence on school governance. Unionization has required new, specialized decision-making structures that allow for collective bargaining, attempt to resolve impasses, and provide for the process of grievances. What is perhaps less well recognized is that unionization profoundly affects governance modes other than those generally associated with labor relations. In fact, unionization, as it has developed in the schools, has evolved a structure in which there is a potentially strong influence on the full range of decision mechanisms used in education.

In terms of the school governance model introduced in Chapter 6, it is apparent that there has been a shift toward the public (political) and labor relations (negotiated) modes of decision making. This does not, however, indicate that the more traditional bureaucratic-professional mode has simply been replaced. There is even some indication that unionization has increased the extent to which management uses its bureaucratic control mechanisms. What has been taking place, instead, is a continuous process of deciding which of the coexisting decision mechanisms are to be coupled with what

This chapter was written by Charles T. Kerchner, Claremont Graduate School.

issues and what participants. Where there is conflict, it is often over which mechanisms to use rather than what the substantive outcome of the decision will be. This continuous conflict over the choice of decision modes indicates that labor-management relations are substantially more complex than the formal or legal processes of negotiating a labor contract and administering it. The broader view suggests a world in which negotiation is virtually continuous, labor and management meet in places other than the bargaining table, and labor and management are dependent on each other and on third parties to find acceptable solutions to problems.

One of the results of the continuous tension over choosing which decision mechanism to use has been the creation of relatively porous organizational structures that are subject to either direct intervention or external influence at multiple points. Thus, the question of who participates in decisions becomes both important and problematic. Consider wages, for example. In any jurisdiction in the United States, wages are clearly within the province of collective bargaining. Consequently, there has been a tendency to associate wage determination largely with the labor relations mode of decision making. In reality, the process is not that simple. At least three decision modes are commonly part of wage formation in the public schools. The first is political: funds for school districts are allocated by the state and the federal governments. Labor and management lobbyists frequently coalesce in their efforts to increase this allocation. The second mode is largely bureaucratic-professional: school district administrators acting as managers estimate income, develop their priorities for expenses, and calculate the wage settlements they feel they can afford. (They may also act in a political mode by balancing the claims of competing employee groups, members of the school board, program specialists, and externally voiced or anticipated interests.) Finally, there is the labor relations mode in which collective bargaining may alter the perceptions of the funds available to the district and management's previous priorities, in addition to allocating those funds according to contract.

DECISIONAL COMPLEXITY

Because it is not always clear which decisions are to be made through which decision mode, there is a complex, often tense process in which participants seek to link issues in which they have an interest with decision processes in which they are influential. This process is a complex one for at least three reasons. For one thing, schools are highly sensitive to their environments. A second consideration is that participants change from issue to issue, with many decision situations being characterized as having low salience or little importance to one or more of the participants. Then, labor relations is an unfinished process.

The openness of school systems and the interaction they have with the environment require that we describe and characterize the school organization in the context in which it operates.[1] To look at one without understanding the other invites misunderstanding. Declining enrollments, the apparent loss of public favor, and the tightness of the labor market for teachers are all aspects of the environment indicating that the relative influence of labor unions will be substantially different in the decades ahead than it was in the late 1960's. State statutes and enforcement practices create situations in which similar acts can have highly different consequences. A strike in Pennsylvania can take place with the protection of law; the same act, although it is illegal in Illinois and California, occurs, and usually those who participate are not punished. In New York, strikers have usually been fined; in some other states they have occasionally been fired.

Just as the law varies from state to state, so also do organizations vary from setting to setting. The presence of such extreme variability challenges the assumption that there is a single "industrial model" of labor relations that has been imposed upon education. Not even in industry is there a single, universal model.[2]

The second factor that complicates the analysis of labor impacts in education is the changeability of participants; this idea and much of social governance is consistent with the concept of loosely coupled organizations.[3] Many decisions are nonissues, and many issues are unimportant to one or more of the potential participants who choose to spend their limited time attending to other things. In discussing the impact of labor on governance, therefore, we consider those structures and issues that tend to link labor and management, to bring them together in situations where choices must be made. The labor contract is an obvious one, but there are many others where labor and school district interact. The fundamental fact to remember is that there is no single tight control over who participates in these events or necessarily over who participates in which decisions. Understanding labor relations requires understanding how the choice to participate is made.

Finally, labor relations is made more complex because the process is never finished, which simply means that the defining of employee-employer relations is continuous.[4] Rather than signaling arrival at a destination, the recognition of a union as a bargaining agent is better thought of as a stop along the way. The journey is not the same for all travelers. Nor does a relationship that exists at any particular time necessarily exist in the future. Relationships of trust, harmony, conflict, and cooperation—all change over time and are always in the state of becoming something else. This instability is consistent with the pragmatic desire of American labor to protect the worker from today's perils, rather than conceiving a new tomorrow, which Samuel Gompers called, "a new society constructed from rainbow materials—a system of society on which even the dreamers themselves have never agreed."[5]

These three complicating factors—the sensitivity of schools to their environments, the changeableness of participants, and the unfinished nature of the labor process—lead us to conclude that describing labor impacts in terms of mixed decision-making modes is both useful in understanding labor relations in education and profitable in practice.

Multiple Governance Modes

The simultaneous existence of different decision-making modes produces interesting, complex interactions as issues move from one mode to another. Such issues need not be heroic agreements hammered out by governors, chief state school officers, or the heads of legislative finance committees, as this example from a California school shows:

At Orange Blossom Elementary, the weekend vandals have struck again. This time they not only broke in and did minor damage, but they ransacked the office and stole the master key to all the classrooms, which had been inadvertently left out of its own lockbox.

The teachers feared for the safety of their classrooms and of personal property they had brought to school to help them in their instruction—tape recorders, typewriters, tanks of topical fish. They joined the principal in asking the central office to get the locks changed.

"No," the answer came back, "it's too expensive. We'll just wait to see if the vandals are caught. The police think they know who they are." The disappointed principal took the news back to his school.

Before there was a union, that would have been the end of things. Precious personal belongings would have had to have been locked up or removed to the teachers' homes until the crisis passed. But the situation had changed.

Mrs. W. was an experienced teacher, and also the California Teachers Association's building representative. "Just wait and see!" she said. "You tell the superintendent that if those locks aren't changed and so much as a fin is missing on my tropical fish that the district is going to catch a big grievance."

"You tell him yourself," the principal countered. She went to the teachers' lounge to telephone the central office.

The principal retired to his own office and smiled a cat-like grin for the rest of the day.

Within days workmen arrived to replace the locks.[6]

The teacher moved the issue to a decision mode that would accommodate it. There was nothing that specifically joined the vandalism question to the formal mechanisms of labor relations. The union's representative in the school building threatened to file a grievance, but one was never actually written. Instead, what transpired was the coupling of the issue to political and bureaucratic decision modes. The principal's initial attempt to resolve the security problem administratively (bureaucratic-professional mode) was unsuccessful. He entered into an unspoken (political) coalition with the building representative, and she used the threat of disturbance (labor relations) to change what appeared to be an administrative decision.

The process of choosing which decision mode to use is repeated many times as school and union continue to coexist. And joining existing modes of governance to that of collective bargaining has had impact in several identifiable areas. These, as we shall see later, have had implications for the structure and process of organizational functioning and for the ways in which managers approach their jobs.

RULES AND FIVE AREAS OF IMPACT

The most common representation of the impact of unionization is that there are new rules to follow. The contract and the policies that flow from it are the most visible examples. The most commonly used studies of union impacts on management are those prepared by Sumner Slichter, James Healy, and Robert Livernash (private sector) and by David Stanley and by Harry Wellington and Ralph Winter (public sector).[7]

Private-sector studies found that unions diminished management's decision-making scope, particularly through contractual limitations on work assignment and requirements for consultation and review by the union.[8] They also found that they had a leveling effect among employees, that they reduced management's judgmental decisions, and that they increased pressure for equality of treatment and less dependence on the merit principle. Disciplinary procedures also became less discretionary. Because the body of written policy was enlarged, ad hoc decisions were replaced with ones that took into consideration the possible consequences of management actions on the stability of the labor-management relationship. Management structure was changed to accommodate more staff specialists to handle personnel policy, pensions, insurance, and other concerns that often entered the organization as the result of collective bargaining. Staff specialists, along with their organization and management, became a factor in administration. Finally, despite a diverse and unpredictable set of relationships, these studies perceived a general trend toward mutual adjustment and accommodation on the part of labor and management.

Besides discovering many of the same impacts in the public sector, Stanley found a preference for political over economic means in efforts to resolve conflict.[9] Wellington and Winter suggest that, in the public sector, the quality and nature of services become issues, particularly in cities with multiple unions where the government must choose between competing interests (and unions) in the division of available revenue.[10]

Assuming the context of a set of rules that bind behavior in new ways, we can suggest some generalizations about areas of impact on governance:

1. The breakdown of the unitary command structure and its replacement by a multilateral bargaining system, or, in some cases, by a bilateral system.
2. The introduction of new participants into school decision making, including labor professionals (both advocates and

neutral third parties), organized and unorganized citizens, and elected officials outside of education.

3. The movement of the locus of decision making to central offices within school systems and to locations outside of school systems, including legislatures, courts, and public administrative agencies.

4. The broadening scope of issues that fall into the labor relations arena—both issues raised during formal negotiations and those joined to the collective bargaining process during the administration of contracts.

5. The changing nature of managerial work since there is evidence that school administrators face different types of issues, new constituents, different managerial roles, and new criteria for success in their jobs.

In each of these areas, the generalizations suggest using more than one decision mode or moving decisions from one mode to another. For instance, breaking down the unitary command structure pushes school organizations toward political means to reach agreements simply because the legitimate authority within the established school structure is not sufficiently influential to meet its goals by itself. The school must at least bargain with the union and, quite possibly, create coalitions with others outside of the organization if the school's goals are to be advanced.

Breakdown of the Unitary Command Structure

Just as schools came to embrace Weberian bureaucracy and the legitimate authority of the superintendent, they have come to doubt it. The attack on the technocratic control structure and oversight by "blue-ribbon" trustees forms a major chord in the recent literature on school politics.[11] While the extent to which a single hierarchical control mechanism existed unfettered has probably been overestimated, it is nonetheless apparent that the zone of tolerance for independent action by school superintendents, boards, and teachers is growing smaller.[12]

The simple intrusion of labor unions into the strongly hierarchical setting would be enough to cause a breakdown in the old order since the essence of collective bargaining, as depicted in labor texts, is bilateral decision making. The same lore has been transferred to the public sector. A training manual for state and local government administrators defines collective bargaining, sometimes called "bilateralism," as "a process through which employees elect a representative who deals with management within a systematic framework to seek agreement on the terms and conditions of employment."[13]

In the public sector evidence showing that the relationship between labor and management is not that simple is mounting. Labor unions, moreover, are not alone in their challenge to the authority structure. They have risen to prominence at the same time that citizens' groups, legislative investigators, federal agencies, and others have penetrated deeply into school operations, which has further complicated the relationship between employer and employee.

Bilateralism, in fact, is often an inaccurate description. Kenneth McLennon and Michael Moskow introduced the words "multilateral bargaining" to describe what was occurring in the public sector.[14] Other parties became involved or had interests perceived as legitimate, and they were making demands on the system. As Theodore Caplow points out, the kind of transactions involved in multiparty bargaining are fundamentally different from the kind involved when there are only two parties.[15] This is the case because coalitions must be formed among parties and because the parties may choose to meet in any one of many different arenas. Consider the following vivid example paraphrased from Hervey Juris's work on police unions.[16]

Several years ago there was a difference of opinion between the students at a major university and the local police department. During the altercation, the officers removed their badges—they said it was to avoid being stuck by the pins. The students said that the badges had been removed so the officers could not be identified if they roughed up a student.

The mayor of the city intervened to say that he would have name tags sewn on the officers' uniforms. It was hard to get stuck with a cloth tag. The officers replied that, if they put on the name tags, their families would be harassed, and the mayor responded by ordering cloth tags showing just the officers' badge numbers.

Members of the International Ladies' Garment Workers' Union were contacted to come to the police station to do the sewing, but the policemen formed a picket line and the ILGWU members would not cross it. An arbitrator was asked to decide whether the mayor had a right to order officers to sew their badge numbers on their shirts.

In a bilateral situation the arbitrator would have made a decision, and the story would have ended. But that did not happen. The union went to the state legislature and got enabling legislation that said cities, by local option, could forbid the sewing of badge numbers on police officer's uniforms. The mayor went to the governor and had the bill vetoed. The police officers went to the legislature and had the veto overridden. Then, they went to the city council to exercise the local option banning the sewing on of badge numbers.

Meanwhile, the arbitrator ruled in favor of the mayor. "Badge numbers could be sewn," he said. But his decision was moot because in that city it was against the law to wear a police uniform with the badge number sewn on.

While it is a bit unusual, this example of multilateral bargaining makes the concept clear: there are participants other than labor and management, and the parties can meet in arenas other than the bargaining table. School officials can take action away from the bargaining table that would affect the outcome of formal negotiations, or they might undertake an act during the course of the contract that would change the meaning of the agreement. Multilateral bargaining might also include community interest groups that become involved in negotiations, either through direct participation or through making demands on school or union officials. Elected officials outside of education may attempt to influence settlement or serve as mediators in reaching agreement.

Multiple participants and multilateral bargaining can also be seen at work in this country's school systems. Examples from Chicago, New York, and Los Angeles follow, and there is growing evidence that multilateralism can be found in smaller cities and towns.

Bargaining over School Decentralization in New York

New York City's Ocean Hill-Brownsville controversy stands out in educational history because it brought together so many of the issues that typified the late 1960's—decentralization, unionism, Black power, a penchant for activism, and intervention of external change agents. The issues converged on the question of whether teachers could be removed from their classrooms by a community school board, despite contractual rights in a city-wide contract. Conflict on this question shattered whatever alliance had existed between parents and teachers.[17] The United Federation of Teachers struck three times in the fall of 1968. Frank Cassell and Jean Barron show how, in the fifth week of the long strike, the many participants edged toward settlement.[18] They included:

—The community school board and its president, civil rights attorney, John Doar.
—The state education commissioner, James E. Allen, who attempted to serve a mediation role by proposing a stream of compromise solutions including one to draw the controversy away from the school administration by having a representative of his office oversee the experimental district.
—The governor, Nelson Rockefeller, who by refusing to call a special session of the legislature forced the others to reach a negotiated settlement.
—New York labor leaders, most supporters of Shanker, but some, particularly black and Puerto Rican union officials, showing signs of switching positions.

Together with the teachers' union and the administration, they or their representatives entered Gracie Mansion, Mayor John Lindsay's official residence.

So many groups were involved that they were spaced out in different areas of the mansion. Shanker and his aides were in the main ballroom . . . . In a basement conference room were city and state education officials . . . . Across the hall, Lindsay waited with two deputy mayors.

Theodore Kheel, crack arbitrator, and Kenneth Clark, the Black psychologist who served on the state board of regents, called Lindsay that morning with some new suggestions for settlement, and they were invited to the mansion. Whitney Young of the National Urban League was invited to join the group, and then Rhody McCoy (the superintendent of the decentralized experimental district) and some of the Ocean Hill governing board . . . . The Ocean Hill group met with Young and Clark in a room of the mansion's residence wing . . . .[19]

The settlement did not favor the community school organization; in fact, by the time the settlement was reached, the Ocean Hill people had left. Questions still remain about what the standing of the community organization was or whether it was adequately represented in the negotiations. It would be difficult, however, to argue that what occurred represented bilateral bargaining.

The multilateral relationship has appeared in New York in at least two other ways. The first was a period of codetermination in which the process of year-round consultation allowed the union to become a powerful force in school administration, while other, older forms of representation were abandoned.[20] This introduced a type of multilateralism involving subgroups within both labor and management bargaining over issues that affected only part of the organization, something that James Kuhn recognized in studying industrial unions and called "fractional bargaining."[21]

More recently, New York City experienced financial difficulties. By investing its pension fund in municipal notes, the teachers' union pulled the city back from possible bankruptcy. Collective bargaining was changed, along with other things. The city government became the financial ward of the state and federal governments, whose stewardship is felt as labor agreements are reached. Old agreements have actually been abrogated and promised raises withheld as powerful forces external to the bargaining relationship shaped the continued employee-employer relationship.

This, in turn, is forcing changes in the expectations that the union has for itself and its members. As Albert Shanker said in 1977 in an interview with Nat Hentoff: "Of course, I'd like to have the money back and I haven't given up trying to figure out ways to get some of the cuts restored, but there isn't a trade union, a police force, any organization that, on losing 22 per cent of its budget wouldn't sit down and ask itself if there are different ways of doing things . . . ."[22]

Multilateral Bargaining in Chicago

"Chicago," Alderman Paddy Bauler was said to have pronounced, "ain't ready for reform." The alderman was ungrammatical but correct. The disengagement of the schools from city hall, a standard feature of the school reform movement of the 1920's, was never completed. The ties of the school to municipal government are still strong, even though many of them are informal. Paul Peterson's study of Chicago school politics is particularly illustrative—in part because it openly looked for relationships between labor, management, and city hall and in part because it considered bargaining as one of the means by which all school decisions may be analyzed.[23] Although Peterson does not use the term "multilateral," his pluralist bargaining model is clearly that. Groups concentrate their energies on narrow interests and on the creation of specific demands, and then, reaching for a broad constituency, they may change and modify their positions. Alliances may change with every issue, and relationships may cut across religious and ethnic bounds.

The dramatic rise in teachers' salaries in the late 1960's is of particular interest. Beginning salaries increased 72 percent—from $5,500 to $9,572 a year between 1965 and 1972. Most of those gains were, however, achieved in the years from 1967 to 1969, immediately after the union gained the right to bargain. In the following years, salaries just kept pace with the cost of living.[24] During the period of the rapid increases, the school board was split. Reform members, increasingly concerned that salary increments were interfering with educational improvements, opposed the union's salary demands. They were also concerned that the fiscal destiny of the school system was not being determined at school headquarters, but in the state capitol (frequently, the school district would pledge more to its teachers than it had, and then representatives of school unions and the city would appeal to the legislature to make up the difference).[25]

The board's behavior, according to Peterson, was best explained as "ideological" bargaining, that is, as bargaining that occurs when the questions at issue involve the interests of the regime, in this case, the school. Mayor Richard Daley, on the other hand, was seen as a "pluralist" bargainer. Managing conflict was more important to him than particular reforms. Daley supported the union generally, but not always. He did not provide revenues from the city's income tax or other sources to support teachers' demands in later years. Peterson comments that, "perhaps he knew power relations had changed on the school board; perhaps he realized the teachers did not want higher salaries with the same intensity as they had in earlier years; *perhaps there were too many competing claims for him to consider.*"[26]

Having the mayor act as the primary bargainer contrasts with the way teacher-board relations were handled immediately prior to the first collective bargaining contract in 1968, when relations were governed by a norm that required organizational unity among educators in an effort to protect "the autonomy of educators from outside pressures."[27] That norm broke down during collective bargaining.

Unity was shattered further in November 1979. Mayor Jane Byrne was instrumental in disclosing a concealed $450 million school deficit. Superintendent Joseph Hannon and several board members resigned. The schools became wards of the state, and the financial community demanded cutbacks requiring salary decreases or teacher layoffs. Paydays were missed, and the Chicago Teachers' Union struck, saying it would accept no contract violations. In addition, the school crisis called attention to the city's own financial health.

Changes in Los Angeles

In contrast to Chicago, the relationship between city government and school governance in Los Angeles is almost incidental. Yet, as Conrad Briner and George Blair point out in their study of the Los Angeles Unified School District, there are plentiful mechanisms through which various interest groups present themselves, build agendas around their interests, and create support for those agendas.[28] Labor relations is a part of this web.

Employee-employer relations has been a multiparty affair in Los Angeles from the outset. Under California's Winton Act (1970-1975), bargaining was explicitly multilateral, with employees represented on a bargaining council in proportion to the membership strength of each union. With teachers there were only two primary groups, but with classified employees there were, at times, up to fifty groups represented in bargaining. The state's bargaining statute was changed in 1976 to the more usual form of exclusive representation and binding contract. Still, numerous mechanisms and events have come together to make labor-management relations multilateral. The statute adopted in 1976 requires that initial proposals of both management and labor be made the subject of a public hearing.[29] Although the process has been variously interpreted, frequently abused, and sometimes ignored, there is some evidence that the intervention of public opinion has helped shape the resistance points of both management and labor and that in other cases bargaining issues have been introduced by various public groups. In Los Angeles, specifically, there is an established citizens' advisory committee for collective bargaining.

Aside from the legislated structure of collective bargaining, other issues have made the process multilateral. Taxes and integration have focused public attention on the school in Los Angeles. Under state court order, the district initiated an integration plan in September 1978. The plan involves limited use of school pairing and busing to achieve racial balance. The integration controversy, already more than a decade old, has intensified. It has involved the use of outside experts and court-appointed monitors, white flight and the withdrawal of children from school, proposed state legislation and constitutional amendments forbidding busing, and recall elections that have successfully removed a school board member. The chronicle changes daily, and it would be impossible to recount it fully here.

Along with the battle over integration, there have been tax reductions. Proposition 13 passed by a 65 percent plurality in 1978, amending the state constitution and substantially reducing property tax revenue. Summer school was canceled, but massive layoffs were prevented because the legislature distributed an accumulated state surplus of $5 billion to assist local governments. Other tax initiatives and school finance measures followed, effectively removing many money decisions from contract negotiations.

These external events are clearly linked with labor relations. Salary demands have been muted. Great attention has been paid to the right of employees to transfer, terminations, and severance provisions. The integration issue, in particular, has caused grave internal problems for the combined NEA-AFT United Teachers of Los Angeles. While union leadership has tended to favor integration, the rank and file is far from united on the subject, and the question of involuntary transfer continues to be an issue. The union's integration activities have tended to be low-key. It has supported the plan and encouraged its members to help make it work. It has run a training program for member teachers. It was also active behind the scenes in forming plans that both the court and a majority of the school board could accept. The union's role in financing has also become more public. The financial decision process has clearly moved to the state capital, where the union, often in concert with the school district, runs a strong and active lobby.

Finally, the school board itself, because of its disunity, has become a point of multiple entry into the labor relations process. In 1979 the election of school board members switched from a city-wide basis to a district one. This gives particular interest groups, including the unions, increased ability to find and support candidates. School board membership, moreover, has come to be considered as a stepping-stone to higher political office.

The point of these illustrations from all three cities is that the area of labor relations has become inherently multilateral. Unions do not simply deal with labor contracts; nor are they active only at the bargaining table. And, they are not alone. Courts, legislatures, active citizens, and elected officials outside of school districts play an active part in the same issues. Certainly, governance is moved toward public or political modes and away from professional or bureaucratic ones. But the change is not simply a substitution. All processes continue to exist, and they interact with one another. Thus, the questions of who participates and how assume prime importance.

New Participants

Even if there were no active community interest group and collective bargaining could somehow be restricted to labor and management, the bargaining process would introduce new participants. There are the "professionals," that is, negotiators for both management and labor and consultants (including university professors) who teach the participants what labor relations is about and how to practice it. There are also neutral third parties, such as mediators, fact finders, arbitrators, and staff members from the administrative agency (public employment relations board and others), who often wield both executive and quasi-judicial power simultaneously.

These professionals, particularly the attorneys, tend to make the practice of employer-employee relations more formal and legalistic, which means that great importance is placed on proper procedure and technicalities. Ray Gonzales, a member of the California Public Employment Relations Board, writes that the teachers' collective bargaining law in California has been drolly referred to as the "Lawyers Unemployment Act,"[30] and this has become somewhat of a self-fulfilling prophecy. Each of the three board members has two personal legal counselors. The first board chairman was a law professor. This, added to the general counsel's staff of hearing officers, raised the number of lawyers to twenty out of a total of thirty-one members of the professional staff. Thus, writes Gonzales, "the agency entrusted with the implementation of the new law signaled to the parties appearing before it that its approach would be almost entirely legalistic."[31]

Many of the state's 1,172 school districts responded by engaging private law firms. In most areas of California, the county counsel's offices, which normally serve as legal advisers to school districts, proclaimed that they would be unable to handle questions related to labor relations. One law firm had sixty-three cases before the employment relations board during the first year of the California law; another, fifty-eight cases.[32]

The culture transmitted is one of dependency, consistency, and advocacy. Dependency occurs because of a cycle of unpreparedness. At the advent of unionization, school personnel are seldom ready to deal with the complexities of the law with just their in-house staff. When this has been attempted, the results, which have often proved less than satisfactory, led one labor attorney to assess the situation by saying, "the curse of amateurism is rampant." The parties may also be unprepared to deal with negotiation. There is some evidence that early and frequent resort to fact finders, mediators, and arbitrators can have a narcotic effect. That is, once such people are used, they are more likely to be used again, and labor and management are hampered in learning how to negotiate a contract.[33]

Consistency in the application and interpretation of rules is one of the hallmarks of labor relations. Such consistency partly stems from the nature of labor contracts in which organizational practices become the precedent for interpreting rules. It also reflects union desires to bind management to a consistent interpretation of events. Particularly in situations where the trust level is low, uniformity of behavior allows the parties to avoid continuous conflict. The negative face of consistency, of course, is that it honors the past and directs attention to it rather than anticipating the future.

Advocacy is also important because, although the goal of labor relations is compromise and settlement, limited combat is often required. The shift from the extended family metaphor in explaining educational organizations has doubtless been overdrawn, but it is nonetheless true that, at the outset of collective bargaining, the relationship of the parties becomes more distributive. Cooperative behavior is learned later, if at all.

The Locus of Decision Making

If one accepts the idea that collective bargaining in education is inherently multilateral because of the number of access points to the system, including labor professionals, then the conclusion that the locus of decision making has changed should not be surprising. In general, the trend has been toward centralization, although this is not universally true. There are, for example, instances in which school principals said they assumed more autonomy because they knew that the central office, preoccupied by bargaining, would be less inclined to question day-to-day decisions made at the school level.[34]

The usual trend has been in the other direction. Contract administration usually places great reliance on uniformity. Indeed, one of the stated purposes of labor relations is to avoid capriciousness in the treatment of employees. The objective reality behind this goal is that uniform rules for the treatment, payment, and discipline of employees are a part of every labor agreement. This, in respect to school control mechanisms, means standardization, the use of common rules to control behavior, centralization, and the determination of those rules well up in the school's hierarchy. Generally speaking, substantive and procedural rules follow the signing of a labor contract and make it operational. These rules are violated only on pain of inviting a charge of unfair labor practices, of having to go through a grievance procedure, or, in some instances, of endangering the intended interpretation of a hard-won contract clause. One president of a community college has reported that a failure to administer uniformly a work rule clause resulted in an arbitrator's ruling that the contract clause was not enforceable. That clause had been a major goal of management in previous negotiations, and the administration had agreed to a $1.2 million fringe benefit package in order to achieve a change in the work rule.[35]

The involvement of higher authorities or powerful actors may change the outcomes. In Peterson's study of politics in Chicago, the entry of labor unions reinforced the presence of city hall in educational decision making, something that the school reform movement (ironically favored by teachers' organizations) had only recently limited.[36] John Bowen, in his description of negotiations at City Colleges of Chicago, suggests that the governance role of department chairman has changed, particularly with regard to campus presidents. Early agreements between the board and faculty had the unintended effect of establishing a strong department system, even though it was not clear that either side intended such. The presidents were placed in the untenable position of having to ensure that departmental procedures provided for due process when the presidents had no part in establishing those procedures.[37]

Fiscal decisions also seem to have been centralized. In New Jersey, the courts have held that institutions of higher education can bypass their own boards of control, the chancellor's office, and the state board of higher education to bargain directly with the governor. For public schools in Chicago and in California, the fiscal reality of their contract often depended on labor and management going together to the state capitols to secure increased appropriations. The situation in New York State has become so centralized that Donald Wollett, the state's former labor relations executive, comments that it hardly looks like collective bargaining at all: "what is emerging after 10 years in New York appears to be closer to the direct political action model of collective activity (practiced by employee associations and such unions as the Firefighters and the PBA's prior to the rush to collective bargaining in the sixties) than it is to the conventional trade union model . . . ."[38]

In California, legislative hearings have been held on the feasibility of moving toward a state-wide salary schedule.[39] Unions and school boards vigorously opposed such a move, but, despite general opposition to state-wide bargaining, centralization of salary decisions has already occurred, regardless of the locus of bargaining. The legislature or governor may intervene directly to attempt to control school wage decisions, as they did in California in 1978, or the move toward equalization of school funds may make salary equalization inevitable.[40]

The Expanding Scope of Bargaining

Regardless of what ought to be bargainable, there is always pressure to expand the scope of bargaining. There are two common explanations. One is that labor leaders, as heads of political organizations, are constantly pushed to deliver more. In turn, management is often pressed to find something that it can give away to labor when times are financially tight. Thus, an agreement is reached on a noncost item such as joint consultation or continuous review of safety programs.

The second explanation of the expanding scope of bargaining is that the parties come to know and depend on each other. Labor, as a system for making decisions, falls within the organization. As Ida Klaus points out in her history of the early years of bargaining in the schools of New York City, by the fourth contract the process of year-round consultation was a reality (see Chapter 3). Other, older forms of teachers' representation were abandoned.[41]

The scope of bargaining tends to expand both because of legal interpretation and because the parties themselves act to increase the
number of issues being discussed.[42] Even if statutes attempt to
restrict the scope of bargaining, the relationship of wages and hours
is an important consideration in the nature of the services rendered.
The enactment of an overtime provision in teachers' contracts may,
for instance, affect the extent to which the school district calls
meetings between teachers and parents' organizations. The line
between wages and salaries and policy is a difficult one to draw.

Changes in Managerial Work

As the scope of bargaining expands, new people and new authority structures come into play. When organizations change, the content of managerial work can be expected to change also. The impact
of collective bargaining can partly be determined by looking at
how managers accommodate negotiations and other formal structures of bargaining. But these formalities represent only a part
of what most school superintendents do, and leadership of the bargaining team and the handling of grievances may be delegated to
others. As a result, changes in managerial responsibility include the
full range of contacts between labor and management that occur
during the administration of the labor agreement.

Management is usually pictured as hectic, as indeed it usually
is—composed of ten- to twelve-hour days, interruptions in schedules,
eight-minute phone calls, and ten-minute meetings. There are
variety and fragmentation of duties, often requiring very brief
interpersonal contacts. Managers prefer oral to written communication and current information (including gossip) to formal reports.[43]
The manager gravitates toward the more active elements of his or
her job—the current, the specific, and the well defined. What must
be done first is done first. In this kind of a world, just getting the
attention of the manager can be a formidable task.

New participants in the labor relations sector can push their
way to the front of this enormous queue of activities because they
have the potential for causing a disturbance if they are not dealt
with immediately and because they frequently have the influence
needed to press for solutions to problems. The Orange Blossom
school, in which the union's building representative, rather than
the principal, succeeded in getting the locks changed, stands as an

example of fractional bargaining. In a continuous relationship labor has the ability to insert items into the school's decision-making agenda. While the legal-formal picture of labor relations would suggest that grievances are simply mechanisms for adjudicating differences of opinion about rights granted in the contract, Kuhn found that they also served as mechanisms for organizational control, communication, and even the advancement of management's goals.[44]

As in the Orange Blossom school, first-level supervisors at times actively utilize work-group-level union officers to assist them in resolving their own problems. In Kuhn's factory, "You'll find the stewards doing things that the foremen ought to do. If a problem comes up—a man is sick or a worker has a shortage in his check, or a guy's been drinking too much—they send it to the chief steward."[45]

In education, too, there has been the development of site-level relationships between administrators and employees that have little or nothing to do with the contractual boundaries or formal organizational roles. In New York City, teachers wanted a role in decision making, yet they were somewhat protective of the principal. ("Their emphasis is on the decision-making process rather than on the results.") For instance, the elementary school chairman was outraged that the principal was evidently coming to many decisions without consulting the chapter leadership prior to making decisions. Although the principal's actual decisions were never challenged, the issue became the decision-making process itself. The chapter leadership wanted to feel that they had at least some influence on the principal's decisions.[46]

Just as in the factories, the chapter chairmen for the teachers learned how to bargain fractionally with their principals:

In the high school, the chapter chairman has learned to play on the principal's idiosyncrasies. The principal, it was claimed, considers the filing of a formal grievance a personal affront. Indeed, he bragged that only one grievance, with the exception of the excessive class-size grievance, has been filed while he was principal . . . . consequently, the chairman found that the mere threat of a formal grievance was enough to make the principal more amenable.[47]

Administrators also learn how to alter the relationship during the course of the contract. One study showed that presidents of community colleges consciously changed their communication patterns in order to stem the influence of their faculty unions or to turn that influence toward their own goals.[48]

Harmonious, mutually supportive relations are, however, far from usual. Managers encounter problems of role identification, stress, and ambiguity as schools become unionized. Pressures are such that line managers usually have to identify with the school as an organization and thus form a more cohesive management unit, or they band together and form a separate organization. In New York City this has been done under the banner of collective bargaining for administrators, while in Chicago there is a principals' organization that has a contract masquerading as a "memorandum of agreement." Edwin Bridges and Bruce Cooper estimate the number of supervisory units at about 1,275 nation wide, concentrated in the seventeen states with enabling legislation.[49] Management also copes with collective bargaining by boosting the importance of staff positions. Technical specialists fill boundary positions and act as buffers and links between the school and labor organizations. The number of these positions grows, and the people filling them gain power within the management organization as unions themselves become stronger.[50] Their presence also sets up internal negotiations within management known as intraorganizational bargaining. One of the tasks of the labor professional is to convince the members of his or her own organization that they might have to lower their aspirations. Indeed, labor and management negotiators may collude in order to convince their respective employers that a particular settlement is the best that is mutually achievable.[51]

Implications

In a setting in which issues are often connected to more than one decision mechanism, and often simultaneously connected, the participants' problem is to guide and direct processes toward those mechanisms where the resulting decision is most likely to be favorable. Thus, substantial conflict over which decision mode to use can be expected. Also, because there are so many variables, the results of making one particular choice do not necessarily remain constant. As one might expect under the circumstances, labor relations practice in schools has often become a function either of trial and error or of following an orthodox belief. Unfortunately, the errors of "trial and error" are often costly, and orthodox beliefs are often ill suited to educational settings. If one is to move beyond either of these forms of decision making, it is important to understand particular governance modes such as bureaucracy or politics. It is important to understand how events, participants, and issues are coupled to different governance modes, what prevents them from being coupled, and how one gains influence in those situations.

PARADIGM FOR GOVERNANCE IN A LOOSELY COUPLED SETTING

In a governance situation where there are many participants and potential decision mechanisms, there is need for some way to understand how participants and decision points should be brought together with issues to be decided. This process is called coupling. Suppose at the outset that there is little coupling and much independence, that is:
—Issues exist, but no single decision mechanism is associated with any issue.
—Events take place, but not necessarily to resolve particular issues.
—Individuals and organizations participate, but sometimes irregularly.
This would be called a loosely coupled setting in organizational theory, and it appears to be the best way to characterize the interchange between governance modes in education (see Figure 10-1).

Issues are present. There are continuing questions about finance, desegregation, the adequacy of instructional programs, and so on. These may be active issues in the sense that they are involved in decision processes currently underway. Or they may be passive, the dozing alligators of organizational life, seemingly asleep but waiting for an opportunity to snap.

There is a continuous stream of events. But frequently they are not triggered by issues. They are situations in which the organization is supposed to make choices—some important, some not. In many, if not most, cases these events are not the result of management's desires, its grand strategy for the organization, or even its sense of organizational maintenance. The decision process is triggered simply by calendar or external fiat: the legislature meets in the spring; budget documents are due in the county superintendent's

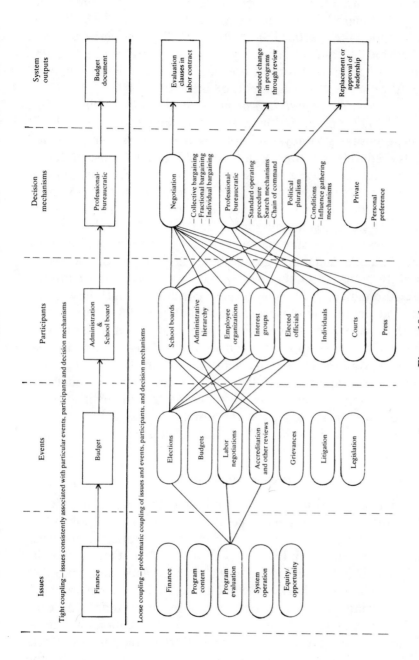

Figure 10-1

Schematic description of tightly and loosely coupled systems in education

office on August 15; applications for federal project refunding are due in Washington at the end of March. For any of these events, labor and the other parties in a multiple mode governance situation may be able to gain influence by becoming part of the decision events in progress. If this does not occur automatically, it may be triggered by unions, management, or others.

Events are coupled with one or more in the field of participants. The field may include union presidents, school superintendents, staff negotiators, attorneys, school board members, other elected officials, federal and state education officers, parents, students, angry crowds, mortgage bankers, or others—not necessarily in that order. Some events carry with them implications for who may or may not participate, so that once an event is triggered, certain participants are automatically drawn together. The expiration of a labor contract, for instance, automatically draws representatives of labor and management together. The participants and the events are rightly coupled. Other events may not draw participants together automatically, but may create conditions that allow interaction. The decision to close a school building is such a case. Union leadership may be tightly coupled to such a decision in terms of a contractual right to approve changes in working conditions that would arise from the closing of a school. Conversely, the union may not be tightly coupled to the decision to close a school because it lacks bargaining or consultation rights in the area of changed working conditions. In such a case, the union may be able to couple itself to the decision through threat of disturbance or other processes.

Decision Mechanisms

Decision mechanisms can be considered as roughly parallel to the four modes of governance presented earlier in the book. Decisions can be made through negotiation, bureaucratic mechanisms, political pluralism or individual preference. Negotiation may involve collective bargaining between management and union or fractional bargaining between work groups and supervisors, such as school principals. Negotiation may also characterize the relationship between individuals when there is a situation of mutual need and a partial divergence of goals. Bureaucracy involves control by rules, that is, standard operating procedures, and by the legitimate authority of office. It may provide orderly search mechanisms when problems or choices confront the organization. Political pluralism suggests multiple participants, each with interests and objectives. Coalition behavior and the development of influence on the entire system through the combining and recombining of interests are to be expected. Private decision making involves the use of individual choice mechanisms based on concepts of investment return, competing alternatives for resources, and the like. It also implies a legitimate private stake or ownership. In the public sector, of course, ownership is not proprietary in the same sense that is in the private sector, but it is clear that private benefit questions become part of governmental and educational decisions. Ownership of the job is tied to both security interests and the ability to formulate policy inherent in the job.

A decision mechanism may be tightly or loosely linked to a particular event. A labor grievance, for instance, triggers a predetermined process that is reasonably standardized. A protest over the drop in school achievement does not produce a standardized result. It may, for instance, precipitate the naming of a blue-ribbon school review panel where both the outcome of the decision and the processes are quite wide ranging. These unstructured choice situations become what James March, Johan Olsen, and Michael Cohen have called "institutional garbage cans" into which one party's problem may be matched with another's solutions while still a third issue is stirred and mixed with the rest of the effluent—unresolved but going through the motions of consideration.[52]

GOVERNANCE BY COUPLING

The essence of governance, then, would appear to be the successful coupling of the various elements in the decision process: linking participants with events, linking participants with one another in coalitions, and linking events with decision mechanisms that are most advantageous. By implication, uncoupling or blocking the linkages between certain issues and certain decision-making mechanisms is also part of the governance process.

Coupling Issues and Participants with Events

Sometimes one can participate in an event just by being there.
Union staff members, taxpayers' organizations, and members of
the League of Women Voters gain influence in school situations
because of their frequent or constant appearance. In decision situations that are protracted, as many are, the constant presence of a
representative from the teachers' union or other employees' organization provides a greater chance that their point of view will persist and perhaps prevail. The structure of decision making in the
modern school is such that any issue must pass a number of decision points before action is initiated. The continued presence made
possible by an organization with staff resources suggests the ability
continually to couple a particular issue with a succession of decision points. As Cohen and March note, most choice situations suffer
from low salience and divided attention in that most people do not
care a lot about most issues, and there are always competing demands on their time and attention.[53] The curriculum program that
is the superintendent's highest priority in September may still be
his first love in January, but it is more likely that, in the interim, his
attention will have been absorbed by the school's integration project
since the judge monitoring the school's performance wants a report
in two weeks. The participant from mangement, the union, or the
public who continues to press for a decision about the curriculum
may prevail.

Sometimes just being present is not enough to allow one to participate in an event. One may be either legally precluded or unable
to participate because of a lack of knowledge about technical
aspects of the decision mechanism. In these cases, the options for
the would-be participant are to wait for another event or to create
an event.

Perhaps the most important mechanism for creating an event is
the threat of a disturbance. A disturbance, or the threat of one,
will gain the attention of almost any prudent manager. First, a disturbance represents a direct threat to the organization and perhaps
to the manager personally. Second, it provides the manager information that something of substance may be amiss in the organization.
Third, disturbances appeal to the manager's already strong preference for live action and immediate, specific problems.[54] Deadlines rule the creation of executive agendas. The manager may,

indeed, have the long-term guidance of his organization in his hands, but it is exercised through a series of short-term specific actions. Managers are often compared to conductors of symphony orchestras, or both the composer and the director combined.[55] But the metaphor of the director implies a greater degree of order and precision than may be present. Leonard Sayles utilizes the same analogy to suggest the importance of the imposed disturbance on managerial life:

The achievement of . . . stability, which is the manager's objective, is a never-to-be-attained ideal. He is like a symphony orchestra conductor, endeavoring to maintain a melodious performance in which the contributions of the various instruments are coordinated and sequenced, patterned and paced, while the orchestra members are having various personal difficulties, stagehands are moving music stands, alternating excessive heat and cold are creating audience and instrument problems, and the sponsor of the concert is insisting on irrational changes in the program.[56]

The point is simply that handling disturbances is both a larger part of managerial work than we may previously have admitted, and starting a disturbance is an easier way to get the manager's attention than we may have suspected.

Obvious aspects of the union's disturbance-making capability include strike or job action threats, slowdowns, refusal to attend parent-teacher conferences or to undertake monitor or lunchroom duties. Use of the grievance mechanism also provides another disturbance route, which, because of the way cases progress, has a highly centralizing and formalizing effect. Oral protest—speaking at a board meeting, staff meetings, or in conversations with important outsiders who visit the schools to monitor and evaluate—is nearly always available as a means of disturbance. So are informational picketing, protest rallies, sit-ins, and the like.

The disturbance itself may not be necessary; the threat of one may be sufficient. In fact, the threat may be more effective than the actual occurrence. A threat, if credible, is, moreover, a renewable resource. Like a tree, if one threat is harvested, another can grow in its place.

The union may not have to resort to a disturbance or even the explicit threat of a disturbance. The position of the organization and its ability to act may already be recognized. Unions know this, and, as a part of their own socialization programs for members, stress the ability to turn out the members in the case of a needed disturbance. Informational picketing is frequently used in collective bargaining situations shortly after a union is first recognized, even where no serious thought has been given to striking. As one union organizer told me, "we just wanted to show the administration what a teacher looked like with a sign in her fist, and we wanted to get the members used to the feel of a stick in their hands and the bricks underfoot."

Management's agenda may also be penetrated by coupling issues with events external to the school, events occurring in the legislative, judicial, or executive branches of government. Unions frequently have the ability to initiate or advance legislation, state department of education regulations, or in some cases the flow of federal funds into a school district.

More profound than disturbance, or the threat of disturbance, is the influence that common need places on strengthening the links between management's agenda and labor's issues. At the most basic level, of course, schools need the continued flow of services from teachers and other organized groups of workers, and employees need the continued existence of organizations called schools in order to practice their craft and to sustain themselves economically. Neither party alone has sufficient authority to command resources for its programs. In a very real sense, the union as an organization is dependent on the school district's ability to raise money and to continue with a high level of public support. Successful collaboration on, say, school finance measures is a prerequisite to meeting the union's objectives, as well as those of management.

The individual school administrator has a common stake in maintaining a cooperative relationship with union officials. In addition to providing early warning about disturbances, such a relationship also provides the manager important information about his own organization, which to him is an important source of power. As Henry Mintzberg puts it:

With access to many sources of information, some of them open to no one else in his organizational unit, the manager develops a data base that enables him to make more effective decisions than his employees. Unfortunately, the manager receives much information verbally, and lacking effective means to disseminate it to others, he has difficulty delegating responsibility for decision-making. Hence, he must take full charge of his organization's strategy-making system.[57]

The preference for live action drives the manager to current and orally transmitted information. Among other things, the manager may do little with the many routine reports that his organization provides him. Because he wants his information quickly, the manager seems willing to accept a high degree of uncertainty. In other words, gossip, speculation, and hearsay form a most important part of the manager's information diet.[58] As a consequence, substantial amounts of time are spent in conversation.

Coupling Participants

Participants require coupling because coalitions are necessary to advance a proposal from idea to implementation. The adoption and implementation of a program proposal is seldom the result of a single decision, and each decision point along the way allows access to different participants, each of whom may have the ability to advance or delay a proposal. The addition of the labor relations governance mode adds to the likelihood that coalitions will be necessary—that no group or individual will possess sufficient legitimate authority to single-handedly implement a major proposal.[59] Labor unions are not unique in creating situations in which coalitions are necessary; other influences that challenge a single authority structure have the same effect. Labor unions are, however, highly visible, have protection under the law, and have some relatively clearly identifiable rights.

Coalitions are a way to transform weakness into strength. As Theodore Caplow puts it: "Unlimited oppression is only possible when rulers and ruled do not belong to the same social system. Whenever they are linked by interaction in an organizational matrix, . . . the will of the master is always subject at some points to that of the servant."[60] The central objective in coalition bargaining is often to see who can first form and hold a relationship together, a situation not unlike establishing a government in a parliamentary democracy.

The triad represents the simplest case of coalition and the simplest possibility in a multilateral bargaining relationship. There may, of course, be more than three parties, but disorganized multilateral conflict is highly unstable. The impulse to form coalitions with others fighting the same enemy is often irresistible. Combination or coalition will usually continue until all the interested parties are divided into two camps. There has been theoretical work on coalitions among numbers larger than three, but these generally are impractical to investigate in the field.[61]

Triads may be continuous because part of a larger social system causes them to interact. The parent-teacher-administrator triad is a good example, as is the school-union-state labor board. Triads may also be episodic. They may be formed for a particular contest, then separated. Legislative battles and political campaigns often reflect this episodic coalition behavior. In collective bargaining, it would be consistent with any kind of activity in which a primary party moved to join forces with others who might not normally be involved.

The formation of particular coalitions depends on the initial distribution of power in the triad. If all parties have the same strength, coalitions between each pair are equally likely. Each will strive to enter a coalition within which it is equal to its ally and stronger because of the coalition than it was in isolation.

If one party is clearly stronger than the other two, there is no incentive to form a coalition. If one party is only slightly stronger than the other two, however, the two less powerful parties will tend to combine. They could also form a winning coalition by combining with the stronger party, but that coalition would leave them dominated by the stronger member of the winning coalition—not an advantageous position. For the very weak, however, there is no choice. In a triad of two equally strong parties and one weak one, the weak party will try to form a coalition with either of the stronger ones. It will always be the weakest internally, but, by combining, it at least emerges as a member of the dominant coalition.[62]

Forming coalitions involves not only understanding the propensities of labor, management, and others to cooperate but also their capacity for independent action, their agenda (what they want), and their resources (what they have that can be used in trading).

Coupling Issues and Decision Mechanisms

Labor usually seeks to have as many questions submitted to the special machinery of the labor relations mode as possible. Management often wants to restrict the scope of issues. Both parties have shown a willingness to use the legislature or the judiciary when those forms appeared to offer the best chance of a satisfactory resolution. The task is one of directing issues toward or away from particular decision-making mechanisms.

Substantial importance is placed on the task of protecting certain decision mechanisms from the intrusion of other parties. Management is usually vigilant about expanding the scope of bargaining or the scope of complaints that can be brought to the negotiated grievance mechanism. The scope of the contract usually expands in part because of judicial interpretation, in part because of the difficulty of separating conditions of work from educational policy, and in part because labor and management depend on one another and genuinely desire a more expansive relationship.[63]

At least three coupling mechanisms are at work. The most obvious of these is *formal specification*, that is, to say in policy, contract, or statute that particular types of issues are to be resolved in particular ways. Carefully crafted grievance mechanisms are an example of this kind of formal specification. They establish the class of issues that are subject to grievances and the process and the timetable to which those issues are subject. In terms of the paradigm introduced earlier, those issues are examples of tight coupling.

The second and more controversial coupling mechanism is *rationalization*, a process by which a case is made for coupling issues to a decision mechanism when there is no complete formal specification. For instance, in a large school district a corporal punishment clause was recently inserted in a contract despite a statutory prohibition against bargaining educational policy matters. The rationale offered was that corporal punishment was an antidote to school violence and, thus, a statutorily allowed safety condition of employment for teachers.

Finally, there is issue-decision mechanism coupling that takes place because of *reinterpretation*. This process frequently involves taking a dispute over the proper decision mechanism through another decision mechanism. The use of strikes is an example. In terms of our paradigm, strikes are resources or sanctions attached to the collective bargaining mechanism of decision making. In an effort to clarify the extent to which strikes can be used and, thus, the advantages of using the collective bargaining mechanism, the parties often seek justification in different places. Depending on the decision of the parties, a dispute over the use of a strike may be taken to the courts either in the form of a civil suit for damages or as a petition for injunctive relief. It might be taken to the state labor agency as an unfair labor practices charge, or it might be taken to the legislature to have the statute amended.

The choice of what decision mechanism to use is often clothed in ambiguity. The outcome of any decision mechanism can seldom be known in advance. The ability to couple issues with decision mechanisms is frequently in doubt. Finally, there is an ambiguity of consequence—even if decision outcomes are known, they may produce secondary, unintended results.

PROBLEMS AND PROMISE OF AMBIGUITY

The presence of ambiguity in decision-making situations— indeed, in the structure of decision making and organizational control—is decidedly two edged. Its presence offers the possibility for integrative solutions and accommodation of special interests and unique situations. It also makes governance unsure and risky.

There is a strong tendency to avoid ambiguity, to undertake what is called the rationalization of the labor relations process in which disputes become minor and the process "not quite routine." But in imposing controls there may be unintended consequences. In a sense, unionization itself can be viewed as an unintended consequence of an older control mechanism. In Ronald Corwin's words, schools found that "order had caused disorder."[64]

Generally speaking, unions historically wanted changes in wages and working conditions for their membership, a system of "industrial jurisprudence" to safeguard members in disputes with management, and, finally, influence in making school policy. The means that the union used were largely political—recruiting among dissatisfied employees, forming organizations and making symbols of issues to create demands and supports.

Management acted to preserve its independent authority. It

has tended to use the mechanisms most readily available, namely, the legitimate authority of office and the division of labor inherent in a bureaucracy. For instance, board rules are passed to interpret the contract to school administrators, and official memorandums instruct principals in how to handle labor situations.

The unintended consequences of unionization include polarization of at least a temporary nature, the development of strong subgroups within the schools, and the introduction of new goals for the school as a whole. Polarization occurs partly as a matter of strategy on the part of unions as they recruit members and form agendas for school bargaining. Sharpening the differences between labor and management builds union solidarity. It also builds management solidarity. Accommodation between unions and management is rediscovered only after both sides have asserted their independence.

Management's response has had the unintended effect of introducing greater degrees of centralization, formalization, and specialization into the school's decision making and into the control of activities. Uniformity of behavior tends to result, but so does rigidity. Work rules provide cues to behavior, but not necessarily the ones intended. "Specifically, by defining unacceptable behavior, they increase knowledge about minimum acceptable behavior. In conjunction with a low level of internalization of organizational goals, specifying a minimum level of permissible behavior increases the disparity between organizational goals and achievement by depressing behavior to the minimum level."[65]

The rules-upon-rules mechanism, which aided the growth of school unionism in the first place, contains the threat of going beyond structural impacts and penetrating the ethos of educational organizations. It threatens to become a spiral of low-trust relations, in which each party reciprocates with more specific, less flexible demands upon the other. As Alan Fox has put it: "When we bind a man with rules which minimize his discretion in a particular sphere of behavior he may, to be sure, accept the constraints willingly as legitimate . . . . But he may perceive the constraints as indicating that we do not trust him, in which case he is likely to reciprocate with distrust towards us."[66]

Fox connects the tendency toward increasingly low-discretion work with increasingly specific prescriptive rules, thus raising the costs of organizational adaptation to a changing environment by requiring increased managerial input of analytical planning and negotiating skill, energy, and time—resources that may or may not be in sufficient supply.[67]

Low trust and problem solving are antithetical, particularly in complex organizations where substantial discretion is needed to respond to problems, not only by the organization but also by the individual worker. Even in high-technology organizations, such as continuous process production industries, there is an increasing need for commitment and autonomy on the part of the workers. To some extent, this is counterintuitive. The conventional wisdom is that workers are tied to the technology of the machines. But the most striking character of high-technology situations is that workers are required to have a large repertoire of responses to specific problems or disruptions because the exact intervention required is not known in advance.[68] If this is the case in high-technology work settings, how much more diffuse must be the requirements for workers to respond to problems when technology is very weak as it is in education.

The circular aspect of low-trust relations complicates problem solving in another way because it distorts communication. The senders of messages will control information, releasing it only when they feel it advantageous to do so, or they may deliberately miscommunicate. Receivers will reinterpret what they hear.

The disutilities of low-trust—low-discretion relationships were seized upon by participative or human relations schools of management, thus placing an increasing emphasis on flexibility and adaptation of organizational structure. The applications were often patently or covertly manipulative, providing the illusion of organizational choice when, in fact, there was none. The exhortation of "trust the company" (or the school) was often given in situations where the employees had no choice, and the appearance of a trusting relationship was, in fact, a manifestation of employees' powerlessness.

That era has ended. Unionized employees have real resources, and, as we have seen, a substantial ability to coalesce with others to increase their stock of power. Building trust under conditions in which many parties are influential is part of the sum and substance of labor relations. The building of trust is a part of the relationship that largely occurs away from the bargaining table. It is part of what Richard Walton and Robert McKersie call attitudinal structuring.[69] As such, personal familiarity and camaraderie form part of the ingredients, but trust relations should not be confused with personal liking. It is quite possible to be attracted to someone in a personal sense and to have no legitimate reason to trust that person. The person may be erratic and undependable or simply beholden to someone other than yourself and unable to respond to your expectations.

The dynamics of building trust can be seen in an overture followed by reciprocation. Reciprocation is often diffuse and not demanded at the outset. Thus, taking the first steps toward breaking the low-trust—low-discretion cycle is risky. There is always a possibility that attitudes have hardened to the point that an overture by one party will be interpreted as a sign of weakness by the other.

Employees will also accept the greater discretion in their work but reject some of the crucial accompanying elements in the higher-discretion pattern being offered by management.[70] Employees may reject the principles of shared goals and values, open communications, diffuse obligations, and mutual confidence. In the terms of Bowen's commentary on the City Colleges of Chicago: "Unionization has always been put in terms of a battle between the security and protection of the labor contract and the freedom from individual control implied in professionalism. Nobody ever stopped to consider that the faculty would take both."[71] It is possible that teachers may take money and privilege and run. Yet, risk is a requirement of management and inherent in the solution of labor relations problems. As Peter Drucker said in a criticism of management science's risk minimization approach: "The attempt to eliminate risks, even the attempt to minimize the risk, can only make them irrational and unbearable. It can only result in that greatest risk of all: rigidity."[72]

In other words, even though there is a substantial possibility that overtures aimed at high-discretion work and high-trust relationships will be rebuffed by one party or another, school districts and unions have relatively little to lose by trying some judicious experiments in altering their relationships. Many of these experiments are, in fact, taking place, labor relations being, like most human experience, essentially adaptive.

One area of active experimentation is dispute settlement. There are enough variations in state statutes to create an adequate natural field experiment around the outcomes of dispute resolution techniques—to answer the questions that will yield settlements that are both amicable and productive, that will serve as barriers to increasing the trust relations between the parties, and that will serve as substitutes for developing trust relations.

Another variant, which has roots in industry, is multilevel bargaining—master contracts for a school system or perhaps even state and local agreements for school sites or occupational specialties. In terms of the coupling model presented earlier, multilevel bargaining is a procedure to link resolutions of issues to the level in the school organization where those decisions are least complex. The smaller scale of school site bargaining may prove an antidote to the formalization, centralization, and dominance of school labor relations by specialists rather than line administrators whose primary interest is in school operations. It would also provide participative access to site level administrators and to the employees directly.

The addition of legitimate third parties, a commonly advocated bargaining reform, would appear feasible at the school-site level. The aggregation of resources and interests to the level of the school district in all but the smallest community makes the solution of particularistic problems difficult and, by definition, assures elite participation regardless of what the participants call themselves. Attempts at direct third-party participation in negotiation have largely been made in crisis and mediation situations. California statutes require that the subjects of information be made public, and Florida requires bargaining in public, but neither state requires involvement of nonelected citizens in the bargaining process. The more common experiment in direct participation occurs at the school-site level in various parent-site councils or school improvement plans. To the extent that these bodies collaborate in union-management relations, they represent an alternative to the "third force" approach to negotiations. In that approach, parties with interests in the outcome of collective bargaining negotiations are usually barred from direct participation, but they form themselves as an independent pressure group working either through collective bargaining or other decision arenas.

Another area where practice varies is that of employees' autonomy in the sense that autonomy means freedom from close supervision or frequent inspection, but they have not been accorded autonomy in the sense that it means a legitimated right to exercise independent judgment and authority. Indeed, external interventions by administrators, state legislators, courts, and parents have most frequently centered on diminishing the area of unrestrained autonomy both in the means of classroom control and in the content of the curriculum—all such interventions being manifestations of increasingly specific, low-trust relationships.

The reaction to threats from the outside is often to adopt more rules, such as additional procedures for the evaluation of teachers. This in effect produces procedural compliance with the outside threat without substantive internal change. When various levels of autonomy do exist at the workplace, they are frequently the result of informal, fractional bargaining at the school-building level between employees and site administrators. There is substantial variation in these practices, but relatively little is known about how they are carried out in labor relations at schools.

The promise that exists in the relatively ambiguous organizational structure and technology in education is that small experiments are possible and that education as an institution in the United States is sufficiently decentralized so that solutions will, indeed, emerge. The problem with ambiguity is that solutions are often difficult to recognize or to generalize across many institutions.

NOTES

1. For a review of open-systems models as applied to the study of organizations, see W. Richard Scott, "Theoretical Perspectives," in Marshall W. Meyer *et al., Environments and Organizations* (San Francisco: Jossey-Bass, 1978), 21-28.

2. Sumner H. Slichter, James J. Healy, and E. Robert Livernash, *The Impact of Collective Bargaining on Management* (Washington, D.C.: Brookings Institution, 1960), 954-955.

3. James G. March and Johan P. Olsen, *Ambiguity and Choice in Organizations* (Bergen, Norway: Universitetsforlaget, 1976); Michael D. Cohen and James G. March, *Leadership and Ambiguity: The American College President* (New York: McGraw-Hill, 1974); Karl E. Weick, "Educational Organizations as Loosely Coupled Systems," *Administrative Science Quarterly*, 21:1 (March 1976), 1-19; R. B. Glassman, "Persistence and Loose Coupling in Living Systems," *Behavioral Science*, 18:2 (March 1973), 83-98.

4. Weick argues that the process of forming organizations is inherently unfinished. Karl Weick, *The Social Psychology of Organizing* (Menlo Park, Calif.: Addison-Wesley, 1969).

5. Samuel Gompers, *Labor and the Common Welfare* (New York: Dutton, 1919), 7-8; reprinted in E. Wight Bakke, Clark Kerr, and Charles W. Anrod, *Unions, Management and the Public*, 3d ed. (New York: Harcourt, Brace and World, 1967), 42.

6. The Orange Blossom School incident was taken from my own research notes. The school name has been disguised. An earlier version of the five classifications of impact appears in Charles T. Kerchner, "The Impact of Collective Bargaining on School Governance," *Education and Urban Society*, 11:2 (February 1979), 181-207.

7. Slichter, Healy, and Livernash, *Impact of Collective Bargaining on Management*; David T. Stanley, *Managing Local Government under Union Pressure* (Washington, D.C.: Brookings Institution, 1972); Harry H. Wellington and Ralph K. Winter, Jr., *The Unions and the Cities* (Washington, D.C.: Brookings Institution, 1971).

8. Slichter, Healy, and Livernash, *Impact of Collective Bargaining on Management*, 948-951.

9. Stanley, *Managing Local Government under Union Pressure*, 19.

10. Wellington and Winter, *Unions and the Cities*.

11. William L. Boyd, "The Public, the Professionals, and Educational Policy Making: Who Governs?" *Teachers College Record*, 77:4 (May 1976), 539-577.

12. Several authors have used the notion of "zone of tolerance" or similar words to describe the latitude or area of maneuverability granted to school administrators, either explicitly or tacitly. Within the zone of tolerance, school officials are supposedly free to run the school according to personal or professional beliefs. When officials violate strongly held community values, however, they face controversy and opposition. (See Boyd, "The Public, the Professionals, and Educational Policy Making," 551-552; W. W. Charters, Jr., "Social Class Analysis and the Control of Public Education," *Harvard Educational Review*, 24: 4 [Autumn 1953], 268; Joseph H. McGiveny and William Moynihan, "School and Community," *Teachers College Record*, 74:2 [December 1972], 317-356.)

13. U.S. Civil Service Commission, *Collective Bargaining for Public Management (State and Local) Instructors Manual* (Washington, D.C.: Government Printing Office, n.d.), Unit 1, page 7.

14. Kenneth McLennon and Michael W. Moskow, "Multilateral Bargaining in the Public Sector," *Industrial Relations Research Association, 21st Annual Proceedings* (Madison, Wisc.: the Association, 1968), 31-40. The authors suggest four tests for the presence of multilateral bargaining: the existence of an external interest group structure; a broad scope of bargaining; broadly perceived effect of a work stoppage; and bargaining tactics designed to employ outsiders as influences of bargaining outcomes. See also Charles M. Rhemus, "Response [to McLennon and Moskow]," *ibid.*, 59-63.

15. Theodore Caplow, *Two Against One: Coalitions in Triads* (Englewood Cliffs, N.J.: Prentice-Hall, 1968).

16. Hervey A. Juris, "The Economics of Collective Action," paper presented at the National Forum on Hospital and Health Affairs, May 1976.

17. Frank H. Cassell and Jean J. Barron, *Ocean Hill-Brownsville: A Modern Greek Tragedy* (Evanston, Ill.: Graduate School of Management, Northwestern University, 1971); also included in Frank H. Cassell and Jean J. Barron, *Collective Bargaining in the Public Sector: Cases in Public Policy* (Columbus, Ohio: Grid Publishing, 1975).

18. Cassell and Barron, *Ocean Hill-Brownsville*, 47-49.

19. *Ibid.*, 50.

20. Ida Klaus, "The Evolution of a Collective Bargaining Relationship in Public Education: New York City's Changing Seven-Year History," *Michigan Law Review*, 67:5 (March 1969), 1036-1065.

21. James W. Kuhn, *Bargaining in Grievance Settlement* (New York: Columbia University Press, 1961).

22. "Remember Big Al Shanker? Where Has All the Power Gone?" *Village Voice*, January 10, 1977.

23. Paul E. Peterson, *School Politics Chicago Style* (Chicago: University of Chicago Press, 1977).

24. *Ibid.*, 186-187.

25. *Ibid.*, 189-193.

26. *Ibid.*, 200 [italics added].

27. *Ibid.*

28. Conrad Briner and George S. Blair, "Political Costs and Educational Benefits," unpub. MS, Claremont Graduate School, 1975.

29. California Government Code, Sec. 3547.

30. Ray Gonzales, "New Decision Makers in Education," *Sacramento Bee*, January 15, 1978.

31. *Ibid.*

32. *Ibid.*

33. Thomas A. Kochan, "Determinants of Power of Boundary Units in an Interorganizational Bargaining Relation," *Administrative Science Quarterly*, 20:3 (September 1975), 434-452.

34. Charles T. Kerchner, "The Process Costs of Collective Bargaining in California," *Journal of Collective Negotiations in the Public Sector*, 8:1 (1979), 39-51.

35. *Id.*, "An Exploration into the Impacts of Faculty Unions on Community Colleges and Their Presidents," unpub. diss., Northwestern University, 1976.

36. Peterson, *School Politics Chicago Style*, 185.

37. John J. Bowen, "A College Union Contract: Before and After," *Phi Delta Kappan*, 58:8 (April 1977), 616-619.

38. Donald H. Wollett, "Public Employees: Villains or Victims," *California Public Employee Relations*, No. 32 (March 1977), 2-13, esp. 11.

39. John F. Dunlap, "California's Chicken-or-Egg Question: Statewide Union or Statewide Bargaining First? *Phi Delta Kappan*, 59:7 (March 1978), 458-461.

40. In California, the passage of relief legislation following Proposition 13 was, in effect, conditioned by a prohibition against salary increases. Employees' unions sued, and the prohibition against raises was overturned by the state supreme court.

41. Klaus, "Evolution of a Collective Bargaining Relationship in Public Education," 1055.

42. Charles T. Kerchner, "From Scopes to Scope: The Genetic Mutation of the School Control Issue," *Education Administration Quarterly*, 14:1 (Winter 1978), 64-79.

43. Henry Mintzberg, *The Nature of Managerial Work* (New York: Harper and Row, 1975).

44. Kuhn, *Bargaining in Grievance Settlement*.

45. *Ibid.*, 30.

46. Neil G. Ellman, "Union-Administration Cooperation in the Public Schools of New York City," unpub. MS, Teachers College, Columbia University, 5.

47. *Ibid.*, 7.

48. Kerchner, "An Exploration into the Impacts of Faculty Unions on Community Colleges and Their Presidents."

49. Edwin M. Bridges and Bruce S. Cooper, "Collective Bargaining for School Administrators," *Theory into Practice*. 15 (October 1976), 306-314.

50. Thomas A. Kochan, "Determinants of the Power of Boundary Units in an Interorganizational Bargaining Relation," *Administrative Science Quarterly*, 20:3 (September 1975), 434-452.

51. Richard E. Walton and Robert B. McKersie, *A Behavioral Theory of Labor Negotiations: An Analysis of a Social Interaction System* (New York: McGraw-Hill, 1965), esp. ch. 7 on intraorganizational bargaining and the resolution of rule conflict that faces negotiators.

52. Cohen and March, *Leadership and Ambiguity*, 81.

53. *Ibid.*, 206.

54. Mintzberg, *Nature of Managerial Work*, 30.

55. Peter F. Drucker, *The Practice of Management* (New York: Harper and Row, 1954), 341-342.

56. Leonard R. Sayles, *Managerial Behavior: Administration in Complex Organizations* (New York: McGraw-Hill, 1964), 162.

57. Mintzberg, *Nature of Managerial Work*, 5.

58. *Ibid.*, 36.

59. Edward C. Banfield, *Political Influence* (Glencoe, Ill.: Free Press, 1961).

60. Caplow, *Two Against One*, 4.

61. *Ibid.*, 9-10.

62. *Ibid.*, 21-25.

63. Joan Weitzman, *The Scope of Bargaining in Public Employment* (New York: Praeger, 1975).

64. Ronald G. Corwin, *Militant Professionalism: A Study of Organizational Conflict in High Schools* (New York: Appleton-Century-Crofts, 1970), 12.

65. Alan Fox, *Beyond Contract: Work, Power and Trust Relations* (London: Faber and Faber, 1974).

66. *Ibid.*, 14.

67. *Ibid.*, 332.

68. L. E. Davis and J. C. Taylor, eds., *Design of Jobs* (Harmondsworth, Eng.: Penguin Books, 1972), pp. 419-420.

69. Walton and McKersie, *Behavioral Theory of Labor Negotiations.*

70. Fox, *Beyond Contract,* 115.

71. Bowen, "College Union Contract," 618.

72. Peter F. Drucker, *Management: Tasks, Responsibilities, Practices* (New York: Harper and Row, 1974), 512.

11

Finance and Labor-Management Relations

COLLECTIVE BARGAINING AND FINANCIAL DECISION MAKING

The connection between collective bargaining and financial decision making in the schools in obvious and direct. Salaries, benefits, and related expenditures, which are major entries in most school budgets, are also, of course, central elements in negotiations.[1] In fact, most elements of a collectively negotiated contract have at least some financial implications, from the large and obvious costs of salaries and benefits to the less direct but important costs of work rules and of bargaining itself. It is just as clear that many of the financial decisions of school systems, such as setting taxes and making budgets, have major consequences for the conduct of bargaining and the administration of the contract.

Educational Resources

Education is a labor-intensive activity; salary and related costs account, on the average, for three-fourths of the total expense budget of school systems. Using figures from 1976-77, this amounts to about $45 billion for public elementary and secondary schools and an additional $3.3 billion for nonpublic schools.[2] Of course, not all school systems bargain to determine the allocation of these expenditures. But, by our estimates, teachers' wages in more than 80 percent of all public school districts are determined by some sort of collective interaction between the employer and an employees' group (see Chapter 2).

Not only is the amount expended for labor substantial, but work assignments (transfers, number of classes, length of school day, and class size) and rules governing the performance of that labor are often part of the negotiations. Thus, the basic organization of schooling ties financial decisions to the deployment of staff in ways that are common to other organizations where a large proportion of the employees is professional.

Decision-making Arrangements

The financing of public education is a state responsibility. With the exception of Hawaii, all states have delegated some portion of that responsibility to local school districts and boards of education, of which most have elected rather than appointed members. In addition, school districts spend about $6 billion in federal funds per year, much of which is administered by the separate state governments. Each state has, in addition, its own financial system. The range of financial structures and allocations in this three-level arrangement can vary considerably, as is illustrated in Table 11-1.

Variation in the proportion of total revenue from each source reflects patterns of past practice and tradition among the states, different distributions of wealth, and, in the case of federal aid, variations in distribution among the states. While the proportions reveal some part of the basic financial structure, they do not directly reflect decision-making patterns. The objects of expenditure for most state and federal grants to local school systems are determined by decisions made locally. For example, compare New Hampshire and New Mexico. State-level decisions determine the *gross amount* each district will receive from state sources: two-thirds of the budget, on the average, in New Mexico; less than one-tenth in New Hampshire. What this means is that the overall size of the school budget is much more affected at the state level in New Mexico than it is in New Hampshire. Within that budget, however, local boards of education have the discretion to set salary levels, determine class sizes, and establish other aspects of policy governing wages

Table 11-1

Sources of revenue and expenditures of public elementary and secondary school districts for selected states, 1976-77

Revenue	State				
	Connecticut	New Hampshire	Mississippi	New Mexico	United States
Sources					
Federal					
Amount (thousands)	$ 58,301	$ 13,007	$115,000	$ 68,646	—
Percent of total	4.8	5.1	21.2	16.9	8.2
State					
Amount (thousands)	$ 367,670	$ 21,940	$300,000	$273,386	—
Percent of total	30.3	8.6	55.2	67.2	43.4
Local					
Amount (thousands)	$ 787,104	$220,294	$128,000	$ 64,536	—
Percent of total	64.9	86.3	23.6	15.9	48.4
Expenditures					
Total (thousands)	$1,189,762	$223,232	$549,000	$448,908	—
Per pupil[a]	$ 1,888	$ 1,261	$ 1,072	$ 1,354	$1,578
Index of variation within state[b]	2.29	1.78	1.80	1.41	—

[a] Expenditure per pupil in average daily attendance.
[b] Ratio of expenditure per pupil of district at 95th percentile of expenditure rank to that of district at 5th percentile, 1975 data.

Sources: National Center for Education Statistics, U.S. Department of Health, Education, and Welfare, *Statistics of Public Elementary and Secondary Day Schools, Fall, 1976* (Washington, D.C.: U.S. Government Printing Office, 1978); id., *The Condition of Education, 1978 ed.* (Washington, D.C.: U.S. Government Printing Office, 1978).

and working conditions. The ability of a local board to increase the budget by increasing local revenue varies considerably from state to state.

There are significant differences among states in levels of spending as well. The range in average expenditure per pupil (Table 11-1) demonstrates this, with a ratio of almost 2:1 between Connecticut and Mississippi. Within the states, wealth- and revenue-generating capacity also varies considerably among school districts. The index of variation, also shown in the table, reflects the range between high- and low-expenditure districts. In Connecticut, for example, the district at the 95th percentile spends over twice as much per pupil as the district at the 5th percentile. These ranges in expenditure affect the range of teachers' salaries among and within the states as well. The average instructional staff member in Connecticut for instance, earned $12,051 in 1974-75, while the corresponding salary in Mississippi was $8,338.

The overall picture is one of a finance structure combining decisions on the local, state, and federal levels of government. Most allocations within the budget are made at the local level, but decisions about the overall size of the budget are shared among the three levels. Among the states there are wide differences as to the funds available and as to the level of government at which decisions about total amounts are made.

Interactions between bargaining and financial decision making in this environment are made even more complex because of the different decision structures. The construction of local budgets proceeds on a timetable different from negotiations, often a timetable set by law. State decisions about the level and distribution of funds for education require that state budgets be prepared in the governor's office and that appropriations be made through the legislature. Participants in labor-management relations may be political actors in these processes (as described below), but state financing is not tied directly to the negotiation of contracts. Decisions about federal aid are even further removed from local negotiations, even though bargaining issues are part of financial decision making at the federal level. Federal aid programs may be the subject of local bargaining in some cases, but the amount of a grant has little effect on the negotiation of contracts.[3] Local decisions about revenue involve setting tax rates and quite often require the approval of voters.

Most school districts are special governments. That is, they set their own tax rates and have their own financial decision-making process—independent of municipal, county, and other units of general government. But the funds for operating the schools come from the same taxpayers as other revenues, which means that schools compete with other governments for the same tax resources. Collective bargaining is a part of this competition since both school boards and employees' unions are part of the political environment in which overall tax rate decisions are made. School districts do, however, have one special characteristic in this local tax environment where competition for resources is particularly keen. The school tax rate or budget is often the *only* local public expenditure decision on which taxpayers can express a direct opinion through referenda, and the number of rejections of proposals that would increase tax rates in the past few years has increased.[4] What is usually interpreted as general public resistance to increased spending can be expressed in very few ways: voting against school finance decisions that might require an increase in the tax rate is one.

Interaction between Bargaining and Financial Decision Making

It is useful, at this point, to think of financial decision making and collective bargaining as parallel decision-making processes. Financial matters are primarily part of the public mode of governance, however, with some additional characteristics of the bureaucratic-professional mode. The main participants are the actors in the political arena that make decisions concerning public policy and expenditures: the school board, the administrative staff of the school, local, state, and federal interest groups, other governments, and employees' organizations. The structures for decision making vary from state to state and from one level of government to another. But there are, nonetheless, basic structures for public decision making that are reflected in the main criterion: the decisions are being made to satisfy competing demands and in accord with relative power in a political arena. In other words, both financial decisions and labor-management relations reflect the process of bargaining and political exchange. In financial decision making, on the one hand, the process is more open and pluralistic, with a variety of interests and actors represented. In collective bargaining, on the other hand, many of the same actors may have an interest, but participation is channeled through the mechanism of two-party negotiations. What constitutes a good decision in the collective bargaining mode is determined more by the balance of power between the two major parties to the bargain, rather than the more general accommodation of interests among direct participants found in financial decision making.

Although these processes can be thought of as occurring parallel to one another, there are clearly a number of interactions whereby actions in one path have some influence over actions or outcomes in the other. The influence can be direct and obvious, as in the case of negotiating a wage package for teachers. Any wage package has a certain, fairly predictable cost that must be considered when calculating the budget. A less direct but still important connection would be a local vote to increase the tax rate for education. Such a vote would provide more resources to pay teachers' salaries. But there is no guarantee that the board would increase salaries, or, if it did increase them, by what amount. In either a direct or an indirect interaction, we can think of the parties in either decision-making process as using the means at their disposal to influence decisions to serve their interests and objectives. The same basic means of influence we discussed in general in Chapter 7 apply specifically here: allocation of benefits or punishments, control of information or expertise, formal or legal authority, and friendship or affiliation.

In attempting to influence either bargaining or financial decision making, the participants use whatever means are available in their situation or environment. The environment at each level of government is somewhat different from that at other levels, and the environments for individual school districts vary considerably. The kinds of interaction that work in any particular decision context reflect both these environmental differences and the choices of the participants in the different environments. That is, we can hope to understand the way the financial environment interacts with collective bargaining by examining the elements in that environment that influence bargaining issues and how the mechanisms of influence might work.[5]

FINANCIAL ENVIRONMENT

The aspects of the financial environment of interest to us are: volume of resources, funds available, structure of financial arrangements at each level of government, and how collective bargaining fits into the financial decision-making process. Each of these aspects has some specific elements that combine financial considerations with collective bargaining; we devote some attention to a few of the major ones.

Federal Financing

As we see in Table 11-1, federal funds count for about 9 percent of the total revenues of public elementary and secondary schools. In many school districts, especially those in large cities, the proportion can be much higher. And the place of federal funds in the financial and collective bargaining environments may be more important than the proportion of the total budget would suggest because federal funds can enter into the governance and collective bargaining arenas in a number of ways. The receipt of federal funds usually provides jobs or supplemental income or benefits to workers in the school system. When a district receives federal funds, the regulations and policy structure that accompany them become part of the governance system as well, which means that collective bargaining decisions can be influenced by the nature of federal regulations and policies associated with the receipt of funds.

This is particularly evident in Title I of the Elementary and Secondary Education Act. This is the largest single federal aid program for elementary and secondary schools, and it channels approximately $3.48 billion per year into programs for educationally disadvantaged students.[6] Title I funds cannot be used to supplant local expenditures; Title I programs must, therefore, add additional jobs or educational services to existing programs. In addition, Title I funds must be concentrated where there are substantial proportions of disadvantaged pupils. In practice, therefore, Title I funds are additional resources (beyond state and local revenues) to be distributed in the budget-making process.

Little in the policy structure of Title I conflicts with local bargaining; employees are paid with Title I funds according to negotiated salary schedules; work under contract-specified rules; and in general, fit into the overall personnel policies of the school district. Federal policy is silent as to whether these employees are entitled to the full range of benefits and seniority provisions under existing local contracts, but seldom are Title I employees treated as a separate category. Since Title I has been a fairly consistent source of funds for most districts for almost ten years, Title I and locally funded employees can be considered quite similar under personnel rules.[7]

Another major source of federal revenues for some school districts are those received to compensate for the impact of students living in a district because of the presence of a federal installation or activity. Congress appropriates funds to these school districts in lieu of taxes since federal installations and activities are not usually subject to local property taxes. These funds, received as general grants by local school districts, become part of the local budget. Unlike Title I or other categorical programs, they are not subject to programmatic rules or regulations. The only salient difference between these and local funds in a bargaining environment is simply that the amount available is determined by congressional appropriation rather than local or state decision making.

Labor Unions and Federal Financial Policy

Because the volume of federal aid and the regulations under which it is distributed can be important influences on the local bargaining environment, representatives of employees' groups are active in the federal policy-making process. Because federal policy making in education is part of the larger policy system, it includes participants other than representatives of school employees' unions and employers. It runs the gamut of interest groups and governmental officials who have some stake in the distribution of federal funds.

Among the interest groups and participants, those representing education employees are quite active and effective.[8] The National Education Association (NEA) is considered one of the largest and most effective lobbying organizations in Washington. It maintains a large office and staff involved in legislative liaison. The American Federation of Teachers (AFT) is active in the political process independent of, and in cooperation with, the AFL-CIO. These activities are not limited to federal policies for distributing funds to local education agencies; they extend to the full range of federal activities and issues.

Along with their independent lobbying activities, the NEA and the AFT participate in coalitions of education groups in trying to affect federal financial policy. In general, the consensus among these groups is facilitated because they share a common objective: increased federal support of education. Maintenance of a coalition is easier because bargaining is a local activity, and the conflicts generated at the local level are less important when it comes to federal funding. This is illustrated by the major coalition involved in federal education financing: the Committee for Full Funding of Education. This has been supported heavily by the NEA, the National School Boards Association, the American Association of School Administrators, and other major educational interest groups active at the national level.[9]

The effectiveness of teachers' associations, particularly the NEA at the national level, depends on their expertise, information on resources, and ability to work with and assist federal policy makers. Stephen Bailey describes the way educators can be effective in working at federal policy making and legislation:

Some legislators and a few staff members convey to academic petitioners a sense that a simple request for help is an act of laissez majeste. But there is an in group of a dozen or so legislative types on the one hand and an equal number of education representatives on the other who are in the game together. They may get miffed at one another on occasion and they do not always see eye to eye; but they are basically dependent on one another. This mutual dependence takes a number of forms, but in essence the trade is one of expertise and service from the education side for sympathetic consideration by the political side. If expertise turns out to be wanting, sympathetic consideration dwindles. On the other hand, if relevant expertise is patent and sustained, the education spokesman finds himself on the fringes of legislative mark-up sessions—making history anonymously along with a thirty-two-year-old staff expert, one or two executive branch specialists, and a couple of preoccupied legislators.[10]

The kind of assistance education groups can provide in return for favorable consideration goes beyond expertise. The NEA and the AFL-CIO can mobilize funds and direct participation in congressional and presidential campaigns. Education associations can provide direct communication to members and a forum for politicians. Through these forms of political bargaining, the education groups can influence federal policy to increase the resources readily available to the financial and bargaining environments.

Nonpublic School Issues

An example of the complexity of financial policy making and labor relations is found in the issue of aid to nonpublic schools. Both the NEA and the AFT have taken strong positions against aid to nonpublic schools. They believe such aid programs would draw funds from public schools and, therefore, from their constituents. As a result of these positions, the NEA and the AFT have been losing support among teachers in Roman Catholic and other nonpublic schools. In fact, two major Catholic school teachers' unions, in Philadelphia and Pittsburgh, have disaffiliated from the AFT largely because of the AFT's position on this issue. Thus, a potential field for the organizational efforts of both the NEA and the AFT is diminished because of their positions on this particular question related to federal policy.[11]

State Finance Policy

Most state funds expended by school districts are distributed in the form of general purpose grants. The amount to which a school district is entitled is determined by a formula constructed by the legislature. Legislative decision making on educational finance at the state level centers, therefore, around two major issues: determining the total amount of funds available for grants, and determining the formula by which the funds are to be distributed. Both issues are important to the conduct of labor-management relations at the local level, which makes them the object of considerable political activity on the part of school employees' and employers' groups.

The politics of financial decision making is easily as complex at the state level as it is at the federal level, and educational funding is usually the major state expenditure. Such decisions affect the entire state budget, and they are subject to the influence of many participants in the political process beyond education groups. Because the education groups, particularly school board associations and teachers' organizations, are most directly involved, however, they have been major forces in affecting educational finance policy at the state level. In the past these groups commonly formed coalitions at the state level to obtain more funds. As tensions generated by local bargaining increased at the state level, these coalitions became less stable. Now, in most states, there is limited cooperation between school board and administrator groups on one hand and state-level teachers' associations on the other. They agree that they want more funds for education, but the distribution of funds and the regulation of funding usually divide the groups. As a consequence, state-wide education coalitions are less important than individual actors in the political process.[12]

Finance Reform

The main financial issue involving education at the state level in the past ten years has been school finance reform, or attempts to reduce the variation in resources available to the pupils or school districts in the state. Most state systems allow local property values and tax rates to determine the overall level of expenditure. Consequently, wealthy school districts can spend a great deal more per pupil than less wealthy ones. Efforts are being made to reduce this disparity and produce a more equitable distribution of resources.[13]

Educational groups have been quite active in the reform movements. In general, teachers' associations have supported reform, while school board and administrators' associations have been less committed to any one position.[14] Reform usually means removing the advantage that certain wealthy school districts have in acquiring revenues, and these districts and their political supporters usually resist such movements. Most financial reforms have, however, been accompanied by a general increase in revenues for education, a position consistent with the political objectives of the state school board associations.

It has been argued that reforms, particularly those accompanied by large increases in total expenditure, will produce windfall benefits for teachers in the form of higher salaries, but this does not appear to have happened in states that have enacted such reforms. The pattern of use is quite varied, and only a part of the funds has been used to provide higher salaries.[15]

Expenditure and Tax Controls

After Proposition 13 was passed in California, a number of states tried to limit government spending and tax rates. Expenditure or tax-ceiling controls are becoming a common feature of school finance systems.[16] These constrain local school boards and other governments from increasing taxes or expenditures beyond certain mandated ceilings and put substantial pressure on salary bargaining at the local level. Since funds are restricted, increased salaries can only come from reducing the number of positions or other expenditures. Although education associations and AFT affiliates at the state level have been active in opposing legislation of this type, as have other education groups, this "tax payers' revolt" has gained sufficient momentum to impose ceilings despite the opposition. The full impact on local bargaining is as yet unknown.

Related State Policies

As part of the general school code or finance system, some states have enacted controls tied directly to bargaining. State-wide minimum salary schedules are found, for example, in Illinois, Maryland, and several other states. The schedules are low relative to the actual salaries paid in most districts. In these states, nonetheless, the law sets a floor for bargaining that is determined not by the parties but by the legislature.

A frequent outcome of school finance reform has been that the state's share of the cost of education increases. As it does, the importance of state fiscal decision making also increases. In states with a high percentage of district revenue from state sources, the allocation decision of the legislature sets the wage-bargaining range. In Utah, where about 70 percent of current operating funds come from the state, it is generally conceded by both teachers' unions and school administrators that value of the Weighted Pupil Unit (WPU) set by the legislature is the most important factor in wage determination. If the value of the WPU is increased by 7 percent, the teachers will get very close to a 7 percent wage increase; if the legislature limits the WPU change to 3 percent, teachers on the average will get about a 3 percent salary increase.

Bargaining may also be affected by regional education agencies established by law among several districts. These agencies may have some regulatory functions, but primarily they provide a variety of services for districts, such as specialized vocational education, data processing, and so forth. In so doing, they remove revenue and jobs from local bargaining and provide a possible avenue for contracting out additional services.

Local Finance System

The contract and related compensation arrangements are integral to local resource allocations. But the process of bargaining is removed to some degree from the rest of the financial decision-making process. Setting tax rates and preparing the budget are fiduciary powers of boards of education. As such they are not directly negotiable. Yet labor contracts determine the largest collection of costs. The way decisions in these two modes interact is thus a central concern to the study of either finance or labor-management relations. Those interactions depend in large part on the structure of the financial decision-making process at the local level.

Levying taxes, proposing budgets, and monitoring educational expenditures are the normal financial functions of school boards. In some cases the board is fiscally dependent, and these powers are shared with some other superordinate government body, such as a county. But in most school districts the only approval necessary is that of the public, and even that may not be necessary in every case. In some states, approval of the budget or tax rate is necessary only if certain ceilings are exceeded. In general, therefore, school boards have substantial discretion in conducting the financial affairs of school systems.

The external limits to this discretion are of direct interest to us since they have some impact on how the financial aspects of bargaining are handled. These external limits can be in the form of ceilings on the amount of funds available for any particular use, of restrictions on the function or object on which funds may be spent, or of rules about the manner or sequence in which these financial and related decisions may be made. Each type may have some interaction with wage setting and other parts of bargaining.

Limits on the Amount of Funds: The Problem of Prediction

Schools must compete for funds with all of the other demands on the local tax base. Other governments levy their own taxes, and households have their own preferences when it comes to private expenditures. There is a limit to the amount of taxes that any household will agree to pay, either in general or for schools in particular. That limit is reached when a sufficient number of households in a school district say no through a referendum or a school board election. Describing such a limit after the fact is one thing, but predicting what it will be in the future is quite another. There is no reliable way for school board members or others involved in school finance to predict when the limit on school taxes will be reached. The limit can only be defined by some absolute ceiling set by law or by seeking public response and adjusting to that response. As Walter Garms and his colleagues have noted, "voters use school budget referenda in part to correct the fiscal policies of local school officials. Districts that increase the tax rate too quickly, or that offer more education than the community prefers, suffer a higher proportion of budget defeats."[17] Experiencing these defeats may be frustrating to school officials. But it seems a proper way for decisions of this type to be made in a local democracy.

In the absence of an absolute legal limit, therefore, it is clear that school officials must rely on their subjective estimates of what the public will bear or of what is a proper level of expenditure. That is, the limits that apply in an actual budget or wage decision-making process are prospective. The officials must predict what will be acceptable and, thus, must depend on their subjective assessment of the community's preferences or on their idea of the desirable limit. The source of information about the limit may be the community, but the actual limit exists in the minds of school officials and others involved in making financial decisions.[18]

It is unlikely that there will be agreement among all involved. As a result, financial decision making involves competition for scarce resources based on imprecise concepts of what the expenditure constraints or limits are. As far as bargaining is concerned, both sides have an interest in accurately gauging the limits in the external political environment. The objectives of employees' organizations are not generally served by achieving a wage settlement that results in sympathetic board members being removed or district taxpayers defeating budget or tax rate referenda. On the other hand, neither side can automatically accept the other's definition of limits since they are likely to be self-serving. Such acceptance can, however, be based on trust or a reputation for accuracy and candor.

A similar argument applies to limits on revenue from state or federal sources, which are normally treated as part of the total resource base available for bargaining. State grants are usually unrestricted, and federal ones are usually flexible enough to fit into local salary and working conditions as negotiated. Predicting what these revenues will be is essential to both budget determination and bargaining. Where a base of trust exists, employees' organizations can accept administrative projections, and both sides then work from the same factual base.

State or local projections are, however, technically complex. Management can take advantage of special expertise or information to misrepresent revenue projections for bargaining purposes. Unless an employees' organization can bring expertise of its own to bear on the questions, it must either accept management's view or reject it without any persuasive alternative. In such a setting, financial predictions are partisan elements of the bargaining dialogue.

Predictions of nonsalary costs may be treated the same way. Management may have limited discretion on expenditures, such as fuel, insurance, debt service, other utilities, and legally mandated retirement contributions. Estimates of these costs affect what is left, or what is seen as being left for negotiation. Overestimating these or other costs can have the same effect as underestimating revenues: funds are effectively removed from negotiations.[19]

Limits on Types of Expenditure: Rules and Sequence

Within the limits of funds available for bargaining and constructing budgets, decisions are affected by expenditure rules and sequences. By "expenditure rules," we mean laws or other binding requirements that determine or prohibit certain expenditures. By "sequence" we mean the limits or conditions imposed on financial decisions because of prior decisions that cannot be readily changed. The two are related, since rules may determine a sequence or control whether prior decisions can be altered. For example, most state codes require that interest and retirement of bonded indebtedness have first claim on local revenues. In other words, school districts must pay principal and interest on bonds first and then allocate to other uses what is left, not vice versa.

Many of the expenditure rules that may, in principle, affect bargaining do not appear to work that way in practice. Some of these are state-wide minimum salary schedules; mandates to provide certain services, such as bilingual or special education; requirements about patterns of spending, such as Title I comparability regulations or limits to variation in spending among buildings or other operating units. Although they are potentially important, state-wide salary minimums appear to be so low that they are not an effective constraint on actual salary decisions. Mandates to provide certain types of services may be state or federal in origin. When the mandate is tied to a grant to be used specifically for that purpose, the rule does not seem to be a bargaining issue. The services are typically provided within the contract, and so the grant simply means more jobs or extra work. Some mandates, such as bilingual or special education, are not directly or fully funded, which may remove resources from other areas, but, because they do not diminish the total number of jobs or the salary available, they are not often of direct bargaining interest.[20] While these rules do not seem to be used to influence bargaining, they are part of the environment and may be exploited at any time.

Requirements about patterns of spending may be more directly tied to negotiations. Most districts receive some Title I funds for educationally disadvantaged pupils, with large districts and cities often receiving substantial amounts. These funds must be concentrated on disadvantaged pupils and used to supplement, not supplant, local funds. (Some state grants—California, Illinois, and Michigan—have similar requirements.) To meet these requirements, districts are to match federal funds with local and state funds and provide as many locally funded staff members for Title I schools and programs as for non-Title I schools and programs. Staffing and funding patterns may be limited or adjusted to meet this so-called "comparability" requirement.[21]

State finance codes or other legal requirements may also limit the variation in expenditure among buildings within a district (for example, in Florida and Washington, D.C.),[22] and staffing decisions and transfers may be controlled by these rules. A building where the staff has a high average salary (owing, say, to more experience) may, for instance, have less funds for nonsalary expense, or the teachers may be involuntarily transferred, and these actions can be bargaining issues as well as finance decisions.

Decision sequence sets up another pattern of interactions. The major sequence issue is whether budget or bargaining decisions come first. If one is locked in, it becomes a constraint on the other, in terms of staffing, program, or other major decisions.[23] Most staff decisions, for example, are made in the spring, before budgets or contracts become final. This commits the district to a certain total salary cost and staff ratio. The district is faced with the choice between two undesirable alternatives: either to decide the total number of teaching staff for the coming year before salaries or revenues are known, or to dismiss more staff than it may be necessary to dismiss and plan to rehire some after budget and salary levels are decided. The first alternative, which restricts the board's ability to adjust the size of the staff or provide salary increases through staff reductions, is especially found in districts with constant or declining enrollment. Dismissal or layoff of staff subject to being rehired can have deleterious effects on morale and risks loss of staff to other positions. Either way, prior staff decisions constrain later budget and bargaining leeway.

Program decisions can have a similar effect. It is not uncommon for districts to have curriculum review and decision procedures that begin early in the school year or even operate continuously. Decisions made by these means can have important budget implications since they involve staff, equipment, or facilities. They can become constraints on the budget or bargaining, depending upon the level of commitment to the decision. Commitment can be developed by integrating the planning of programs and the drafting of the budget, by involving community and staff in the process, by making strong public statements, or by combining these methods. A program decision with a high commitment would then become a constraint by virtue of its having been made before the budget or bargaining processes.

Because the administration is usually able to control arrangements for such program decisions, it is able to influence the degree of commitment and participation. Arrangements for program and curriculum decisions can, therefore, be used to affect bargaining indirectly by removing decisions from the table or setting up constraints. That is why teachers' unions often demand contractual participation in curriculum or budget procedures. It can be seen as an effort by the union to draw both the substance and the process of decision making toward the bargaining table.

Union efforts to participate in or otherwise influence budget decisions point up the importance of the interactions. Drawing up the budget is legally the board's prerogative, and unions cannot directly challenge it. But if the union cannot influence the budget process at all, bargaining becomes an empty sham since all important economic decisions will have been made elsewhere. The main source of union influence is, of course, through direct bargaining power —

forcing the board to allocate resources according to union demands. If the union were strong enough, other attempts to affect the budget would be unnecessary, but this is seldom the case. And so a variety of tactics may be used, from negotiating mandatory participation in the decision process through direct political action aimed at influencing resource flow and budget choices. Examples of all of these can be found in existing bargaining relationships.

Similarly, management has the power in most cases to structure budget and program decisions. This power can be used to diminish union influence or to insulate the process from bargaining. To the extent that management can do this, it retains more unilateral control of resource allocation.

ECONOMIC IMPACTS OF COLLECTIVE BARGAINING

Thus far we have been considering the fiscal policy and allocation context of collective bargaining, and it is clear that the context conditions bargaining behavior and outcomes. In earlier chapters as well as this one, we have suggested that teachers' unions will often try to alter this context so that it becomes more conducive to their fiscal objectives. In general, they try to increase state and federal aid; they oppose tax and spending limits; they try to obtain legislative mandates reducing class size. Sometimes they are successful, and sometimes they are not. In many cases, however, the political successes of unions have no direct or tangible benefit for union members. Increases in the level of state aid do not mean automatic wage increases. It is up to the unions to convert political success to economic benefit (increased wages) through collective bargaining. Thus, a political success at the state level becomes a bargaining advantage at the local level. If the state education association got the legislature to increase the appropriation for education in February, local associations would likely capture a portion of the increase in the wage rate negotiated in August. And it is in August that these events receive the most attention. Unions claim "bargaining victories," and newspapers throughout the spring and summer periodically report bargaining events and settlements in local school districts.

In spite of the interdependence of events, the complexity of bargaining, and the range of issues covered, however, it is the wage package that is the center of attention. To many, that is what bargaining is all about—setting wage rates. Of all the topics in collective bargaining, probably none holds a greater fascination than that of wage or salary negotiation. When teachers bargain with their employers, the things most often reported in the newspapers are the salary demands and counteroffers. When there is a strike of public school teachers, the issue more likely than not is wage rates. Teachers, of course, are no different from any other group of employees in this matter.

There is good reason to expect conflict over wage setting, for it is in economic matters that major differences between employers and employees are revealed. Employees are "income conscious." Employers, on the other hand, are "cost conscious."[24] Employees, including teachers, want to maximize their income; employers, including school districts, want to keep costs to a minimum. Since wages are labor costs, employers are interested in keeping wage rates down to their lowest acceptable level. The lowest acceptable level means, by definition, the lowest level at which employees who have minimally required skills can be attracted. This rate is often called the competitive wage rate.[25] Business employers want to keep wage costs down to increase profit and to make the cost of their products in the marketplace more competitive. Though public employers do not operate within the context of a product market as such, they are interested, nonetheless, in wage economies because an increase in wage rates very likely means an increase in taxation, a move that is likely to be politically undesirable.

Unions and Wage Theory

Explanations of unions' ability to influence wage rates are generally set in two theoretical systems: economic and political. Most economic theory approaches wages and wage setting from the standpoint of the conventional economic pricing system. That is, wages are determined by labor market transactions influenced by both supply and demand. In economic models of wage determination, labor is one cost of production. The price of labor will be determined by labor supply, the degree to which other factors of production can be substituted for labor, and the general elasticity of product demand. In this system, the only way that labor, acting collectively through unions, can influence wage rates is by influencing some segment or factor in the pricing market. Thus, if a union can control the supply of labor, it may be able to influence the price of that labor. It is generally assumed in labor economics, however, that, if labor bids up its price in a competitive product market, the inevitable result will be fewer jobs. The employer will seek to substitute cheaper factors in the production process, or product demand will slacken. Over time the unemployed workers will bid the wage rate down, and the wage will again settle at the competitive level.[26] Though education does not fit all of the assumptions of a competitive product market, there have been recent attempts to apply product market theory to explain wage behavior in the public sector.[27]

The other major explanation for union impact on wages derives more from political theory. As noted, there is not a true product market at work in the usual sense in the public sector. Government usually operates as a monopoly provider of certain goods and services. It also often serves as the producer of last resort.[28] In this system, wage decisions are viewed as being made in a political context. Government, in fact, produces votes *and* goods, both of which are politically important. Rather than maximizing profits, as in the private sector, public officials can be thought of as seeking to maximize votes; more properly, they seek to maximize their political tenure by taking actions that will ensure a sufficient number of votes to win an election.[29] Wage rates in this model must ultimately be judged by their effect on the production of votes, not the price or sales of a product. Politicians have two ways to exercise wage influence: they can "buy" votes by manipulating jobs and wages as patronage or to secure endorsement of public unions; or they can try to manipulate wage rates to affect the cost, quality, and quantity of governmental goods and services that ultimately affect votes. For instance, allowing wages to increase may drive up the cost of city services. This will increase the tax burden and have a negative effect on the production of votes. Or, if wage-employment action reduces the quality of services below some tolerable point, the vote may be negative. Politicians seeking to maximize votes presumably will establish wage rates and engage in employment practices consistent with this maximization scheme.

This position is extended by Wellington and Winter who contend that, although wage decisions in government are political, the important mechanism is the power public unions have through lobbying activity and their ability to disrupt public services. Because of their strategic position, public-sector unions have a disproportionate share of power in the political decision-making process. Policies will be distorted as a result, favoring employees over other participants in the public decision-making process. In this system, the individuals are not viewed as vote producers so much as the collective or union is viewed as an interest group with a power quotient.[30]

But the power of unions may be overestimated. It would appear that recent tax revolts and tax limitation movements act as political constraints, the public-sector equivalent of market constraints. Tax resistance restricts public spending and, thereby, the behavior of wage decision makers and sets up the equivalent of a private-sector employment effect, such that, if wages exceed a certain point, there must be a commensurate reduction in the public-sector work force.

A number of wage goals can direct union behavior. Unions can seek, on the one hand, to maximize the total wage bill. That is, they can seek, through collective bargaining, to gain the largest possible sum of money for wages and salaries. On the other hand, they may seek to maximize average wages. Under conditions of inelastic labor demand, this would be the same as maximizing the total wage bill; under other conditions, however, it would not. Or, the union may attempt to maximize employment and membership, instead. In this case, the union may be seeking to maximize the union's benefit instead of the members' benefit.

The institutionalist view of collective bargaining and the setting of wage rates holds to the belief that unions themselves are political institutions. The system is built on the notion that union officers act like political officials and attempt to maximize their tenure in union office and to build their own personal strength and the strength of the union. Accordingly, they will maximize wage bill or average wages only under circumstances where it benefits the union. Institutionalists posit that there are two prime considerations to the establishment of wage rates: equity and equality.[31] Members of unions, in the institutionalists' view, are not wealth maximizers; rather, they judge their own wages against a benchmark of others in employment. Public-sector concepts of prevailing wage rates and parity pay may originate in this concept of wage equity.

The Nature of the Teachers' Wage Structure

Teachers' wages are almost universally determined using the so-called "single-salary schedule." This schedule, which applies to all teachers in a particular district, consists of a matrix with a row for each year of acquired experience and a column for each level of postbaccalaureate training. A given teacher's salary is the amount in the cell at the intersection of the row for experience and the column for training level. Salary schedules can be seen as an index schedule with the wage rate in the upper left-hand corner of the salary schedule representing the base salary paid to a teacher with a bachelor's degree, no graduate training, and no teaching experience. Wage rates in all other locations in the matrix are an index (or multiple) of the base rate. In general, teachers' salary schedules have an index ratio of about 2:1 between the highest salary and the base salary. An example of a typical schedule and indexes is shown as Table 11-2. The wage bill for teachers in a given district, then, depends on the salary matrix and the number of teachers at that particular salary level.

The single-salary schedule has become so commonly used and standard in form that teachers and managers in education tend to think about salaries in this matrix form. Bargaining activity concentrates on the dollar amount in each cell and differences among cells. Unions try to increase the amount in each cell, and to maintain cell differences at levels seen as equitable by their members. But in that a typical schedule contains sixty or more cells, the cell-by-cell analysis becomes extremely complex.

Individual teachers are interested in the salary they will earn during the contract period and in the pattern of future increases they can expect. Necessarily, therefore, they are interested in the transitional quality of the matrix. They will be affected not only by negotiated increases in cell values, but also by the differences in amount between their present salary cell and the cells they expect to "occupy" in the next few years. Their salary increase will be contingent on increases in the value of cells below and to the right of their present location, as well as the proportional difference that exists between the cells. Thus if a teacher earns a salary of $10,000 in the first year and progresses to a salary of $10,300 by virtue of acquiring one year of creditable experience, that teacher has realized a 3 percent increase. A teacher who had also completed

Table 11-2

Typical teacher salary schedule and index values

Step	Index	B.S. degree	Index	B.S. degree + 30 hours	Index	B.S. degree + 60 hours	Index	M.S. degree	Index	M.S. degree + 45 hours or EDS	Index	Ph.D. degree
1	1.00	$ 8,780	1.04	$ 9,111	1.12	$ 9,822	1.16	$10,203	1.21	$10,604	1.25	$11,005
2	1.04	9,110	1.08	9,461	1.16	10,202	1.21	10,603	1.25	11,004	1.30	11,435
3	1.08	9,460	1.12	9,821	1.21	10,602	1.25	11,003	1.30	11,434	1.40	12,325
4	1.16	10,200	1.21	10,601	1.30	11,432	1.35	11,873	1.40	12,324	1.46	12,795
5	1.21	10,660	1.25	11,001	1.35	11,872	1.40	12,323	1.46	12,794	1.51	13,295
6	1.25	11,000	1.30	11,441	1.41	12,332	1.46	12,793	1.51	13,294	1.57	13,805
7	1.30	11,440	1.35	11,871	1.46	12,792	1.51	13,293	1.57	13,804	1.63	14,335
8	1.35	11,870	1.40	12,331	1.51	13,292	1.57	13,803	1.63	14,334	1.70	14,895
9	1.40	12,330	1.46	12,791	1.57	13,802	1.63	14,333	1.70	14,894	1.76	15,465
10		—	1.51	13,291	1.63	14,332	1.70	14,893	1.76	15,464	1.83	16,065
11		—		—	1.70	14,882	1.76	15,463	1.83	16,064	1.90	16,675
12		—		—	1.76	15,462	1.83	16,063	1.90	16,674	1.97	17,315
13		—		—		—	1.90	16,673	1.97	17,314	2.05	17,985
14		—		—		—		—	2.05	17,984	2.13	18,675

work on a master's degree during that same year would not only move down one row, but would also move over to the master's degree column. This might represent, on the same salary schedule, an increase of $1300 ($300 for one year's experience and $1,000 for the change in the training column). Even if the salary schedule were to remain unchanged for the next year, the teacher would earn $11,300, a 13 percent increase in salary. Now, if the union were to negotiate a 5 percent across-the-board raise, whereby the value of each cell would increase by 5 percent, the teacher would then be earning $11,865 or an 18.65 percent increase as a result of line and step transitions and a negotiated 5 percent increase in all salary cell values. In the ensuing year, the district's wage bill would increase by $1,865 for that teacher. Other things remaining the same, the revenue of the district must increase by that amount, and the teacher enjoys a sizable increase in salary. This same scenario is repeated more or less for all continuing professional employees of the district.

The properties of the single-salary schedule influence bargaining and the way participants think about wages. For one thing, in viewing annual salary changes, individual teachers probably do not distinguish between increases owing to change in row and column locations (usually called "increments") and changes owing to an increase in cell rates (often called "new money" increases). And, except for those teachers with maximum recognized experience and training, wage increases are available to all staff through an experience increment (movement down a column), or training increment (movement across a row), or both. Experience automatically increases salary until the teacher reaches the maximum for that column. Training increments accrue as more education is acquired (usually in blocks of fifteen or thirty semester hours). Salary increases from "increments" are as much a function of individual choice (for example, the desire to stay in the district or a decision to take classes at the university) as it is of district and union bargaining action, and these individual decisions affect the total wage bill, making it subject to large, nonnegotiated increases.

There is considerable disagreement between union and management groups as to whether increments should enter bargaining calculations. Since much wage bargaining in education is carried on with reference to "percentage changes," management groups prefer to make offers "including increments"; unions usually demand a given percentage in "new money" or "plus increments." As a result, in percentage salary settlements it is not always clear whether the amount reflects the average increase in salary schedule cells or the average increase to teachers. Obviously the former will usually be a smaller percentage, and, while it is in the union's interest to limit bargaining to this (and thus make their demands appear more modest), frequently unions will shift after settlement and announce that the average teacher got a certain overall raise.

To the extent that its format is taken as a given, the single-salary schedule makes it difficult to consider variables other than training and experience in salary determination. Difficulty of assignment and quality of performance (merit) are difficult to merge into the schedule and, therefore, more difficult to get on the bargaining agenda.

Determinants of Teachers' Wage Rates

Although most recent studies on wage impact have included collective bargaining in the model, there have been some interesting studies of determinants of teachers' wage rates that did not focus on bargaining effects. Two early studies of this type were those done by H. Thomas James, James Kelly, and Walter Garms, and by Thomas Dye.[32] Both studies, though using slightly different methodology and variables, revealed the importance of environment in the determination of teachers' salaries. Wealth of the community was the most powerful determinant of salary. Dye also found that the average level of education in the community was another important determinant. Both of these determinants are generally correlated, and the influence of community wealth on salaries and other expenditures has been so pervasive that a recent series of court decisions has set in motion programs to try to reduce this influence.

Certain other characteristics of teachers, other than training and experience, have been found to be important determinants of salary levels—specifically, verbal ability and college major.[33] Teachers with high verbal ability and certain majors are paid more. Supply and demand may also play a role in determining wage rates when wealth and certain other variables are controlled. Competition for teachers among school districts indicates that the labor market influences wages. Teachers in geographic areas with multiple districts are paid somewhat more as a result of competition.[34] Levels of per capita income and salaries paid in adjacent industry are other good predictors of teachers' salaries. Teachers in regions where the per capita incomes or industrial wages are higher tend to earn more.[35] Although wealth and per capita income did not prove to be significant salary predictor variables, the school district's revenue was significantly correlated with average teacher salaries in a study done in Utah. Class size was also found to be related. The studies in Utah seem to indicate that districts will first spend surplus income to reduce the size of classes and then transfer the remaining amount into the wage fund.[36]

The Impact of Collective Bargaining

Considerable attention has been paid to the impacts of collective bargaining on teachers' wage rates. Recent studies are not the first, however, to attempt to look at the relationship between collective bargaining behavior and wage levels. In 1930 Paul Douglas wrote:

Unionism, in other words, very probably does give an appreciable increase in earnings during the early period of effective organization, but during the later and more mature years of union development, the relative rate of further progress seems, to say the least, to be no more rapid on the whole for unionists that for non-unionists.[37]

H. G. Lewis also has gathered considerable evidence to support the conclusion that unionism and collective bargaining have not been a source of differential wage advantage in the private sector.[38]

Nearly all of the studies of the impacts of collective bargaining on teachers' wage rates have employed a cross-sectional design that compares wages in organized (bargaining) and unorganized units. In general, one finding appears in nearly every case: collective bargaining does not seem to increase the wage rate by a large amount. Most estimates are in the neighborhood of 5 percent or less, a figure that is generally consistent with estimates in the private sector. A summary of studies of the impact of bargaining on the wage rate is presented in Table 11-3.

All of the regression studies of the impact of collective bargaining on teachers' salaries should be viewed cautiously. There are serious methodological problems in measuring the impact of bargaining on wages. Wage settlements among districts are thought to be highly interactive. For a number of years, many school districts regularly conducted salary surveys to determine wage rates being paid in comparable districts, and the interdistrict interaction of wage rates may be even more systematic. John Sommi has found evidence of the use of pattern bargaining.[39] Districts in the county he studied would wait until wage agreement had been reached in the key or pattern district and then would quickly agree to comparable terms. It was common knowledge in this region that this was being done. The unions collaborated in selecting the district on which they would apply pressure, and the school boards collaborated in determining their common limits.[40] Donald Gerwin has also demonstrated the interaction of districts in wage settlement decisions.[41] In that state teachers' organizations and the National Education Association regularly circulate data on salary settlements during the bargaining season and often supply consultants and advisers, it seems likely that there would be some spillover that would reduce the differences between organized and unorganized school districts. Although it appears that teachers' wages are not significantly influenced by bargaining behavior, it is almost impossible to be sure that is the case.

The cautious conclusion that can be drawn from research on bargaining and wage rates in education is that, although there is some influence, the wages of teachers are probably determined primarily by other mechanisms, such as supply and demand. In a study of the impact of contextual and negotiation variables on wage rates, Herbert Reiter found that, over several years, there tended to be an interesting balance built into the negotiating process. If a district settled higher than most other districts in a given year, they would most likely settle lower than other districts the following year. There seems to be a secular wage line to which the bargains conformed in the long run.[42] Besides the conventional regression analysis method, there are other indications that collective bargaining has not had much impact on teachers' salaries. In Chapter 2 we pointed out that three-quarters of the school districts in the United States are engaged in collective determination of salaries. The data on teachers' wages compared to per capita income and wage changes in the private sector presented in Chapter 4, however, suggest that teachers have not made any substantial gains compared

Table 11-3

Summary of studies of the impact of bargaining on wages

Study	Unit of analysis	Years for which data were analyzed	Sample size	Findings regarding bargaining impact
Kasper (1970)	State + D.C.	1967-68	51	0-4 percent increase in average salary
Thornton (1971)	Cities with population of 100,000 or more	1969-70	83	1-4 percent increase in salary at lower three steps
				23 percent increase at maximum step
Baird and Landon (1972)	School district, 25,000-50,000 enrollment	1966-67	44	4.9 percent increase in minimum salary
Hall and Carroll (1973)	All elementary school districts in Cook County, Illinois	1968-69	118	1.8 percent increase in mean salary owing to bargaining
Lipsky and Drotning (1973)	All school districts in New York State	1967-68	696	15 percent increase in salary change owing to bargaining
				0-3 percent increase in salary level owing to bargaining
				Slightly greater gains at upper steps of pay scale
Frey (1973)	All school districts in New Jersey with more than 750 pupils	1964-70	298	−0.4 to 1.4 percent increase in salary owing to bargaining
Rucker (1974)	School districts in New Jersey	1969-70	556	Less than 0.1 percent increase in base, selected schedule points, average and median salary.

| Chambers (1977) | School districts in six largest SMSA's in California | 1970-71 | 89 | 5.7 percent salary increase in unified districts. 12.2 percent salary increase in elementary districts. 7.5 percent salary increase in unified and 16.8 percent salary increase in elementary districts in regions where 100 percent of the teachers were covered by bargaining. |
| Reiter (1975) | Fiscally independent school districts in New York State with negotiated contracts in 1971-72 | 1969-72 | 703 | Base salary percentage changes not related to changes in negotiating process variables 9 percent of the variance in average salary percentage changes associated with negotiating process variables; larger than average salary increases in one year tended to be offset with lower than average settlements in the following year and vice versa |

Sources: Hirschel Kasper, "The Effects of Collective Bargaining on Public School Teachers' Salaries," *Industrial and Labor Relations Review*, 24 (Ocotber 1970), 57-72; Robert Thornton, "The Effects of Collective Negotiations on Teachers' Salaries," *Quarterly Review of Economics and Business*, 2 (Winter 1971), 37-46; Robert N. Baird and John H. Landon, "The Effects of Collective Bargaining on Public School Teachers' Salaries: Comment," *Industrial and Labor Relations Review*, 25 (April 1972), 410-417; W. Clayton Hall and Norman E. Carroll, "The Effects of Teachers' Organizations on Salaries and Class Size," *ibid.* 26 (January 1973), 834-841; David Lipsky and John Drotning, "The Influence of Collective Bargaining on Teachers' Salaries in New York State," *ibid.,* 27 (October 1973), 18-35; Donald E. Frey, "Wage Determination in Public Schools and the Effects of Unionization," Working Paper 42E, Princeton University, Industrial Relations Section, 1973; Jay G. Chambers, "The Impact of Collective Bargaining for Teachers on Resource Allocation in Public School Districts," *Journal of Urban Economics*, 4:3 (July 1977), 324-339; Herbert David Reiter, "A Study of the Determinants of the Change in Salaries of Teachers," unpub. diss., Teachers College, Columbia University, 1975; Maurice Rucker, "The Influence of Collective Bargaining on Public Secondary School Teacher's Salaries in New Jersey," unpub. diss., Teachers College, Columbia University, 1974.

to these two other measures of income. If bargaining had been very successful in increasing teachers' wages, these tables should have shown teachers getting progressively higher indexes over the years.

Other Fiscal Impacts of Collective Bargaining

Although wage rates have been the economic variable most studied in terms of the impact of collective bargaining, there are others that are subject to the impact, among them, benefits and pensions, work load, and effort. Little empirical work has been done in any of these areas, and the effect of collective bargaining remains relatively uncharted. It is generally known that fringe benefits in the public sector exceed those in the private sector. Teachers generally have excellent medical insurance partly or fully paid by the school district.[43] Many districts provide life insurance plans, and some have dental coverage as well. Teaching has long been noted for its excellent pension system, which is usually provided and managed by the state, and it was in force before collective bargaining became a reality. One thing that makes analysis of benefits difficult to study empirically is the fact that it is difficult to estimate the terms of benefits as a trade-off. Though undoubtedly the district treats them as a wage cost and their total cost is included in wage bill calculations, the impact on given teachers varies. In instances where a district pays medical insurance premiums in full, for example, they may cover single teachers and married teachers with families, with no extra premium being assessed on the married employee. The premiums are obviously different, and the amount accruing to the teacher with a family is higher than that accruing to the single teacher. A discounting of insurance benefits would occur in families where husband and wife were both covered with insurance programs. Other benefits also often have a variable effect for individual teachers.

Productivity and Bargaining

Productivity has become a topic of much concern in the United States. Recently, a presidential report indicated that the productivity of American labor has been declining in recent years,[44] and concern about the productivity of labor in the public sector has grown. Cities have begun to tie wage increases for sanitation workers to an increase in productivity. The same is true for other groups of city and state employees. During its recent financial crisis, New York City indicated that all wage increases for its employees must be self-financing, that is, real wage increases must be matched by productivity increases. Productivity becomes more important as an item for bargaining. As costs of local government increase and the resistance of taxpayers grows, it is inevitable that public negotiators will insist on wage-productivity bargains, long a part of bargaining in the private sector here and in other countries.

Productivity in economic terms is a relatively simple concept. It simply means the efficiency with which inputs are converted to outcomes. Usually, when considering the productivity of labor, this means evaluating the units of goods and services produced in terms of the man-hours required to produce them. In the case of sanitation workers, it means the amount of trash collected per person in an eight-hour shift. This may be reflected in the tons delivered to the city's dumping facilities or in the number of streets covered in an eight-hour shift, or some other comparable measure.

Though it is a convenient and relatively simple term in the abstract, productivity becomes more difficult to deal with in specific instances. There is rarely agreement on either measures of productivity or what governs it. The performance of any job involves many factors. Again, in the case of the sanitation workers, the amount of trash collected is not only a function of the speed with which the haulers work but also of the kind of trash to be hauled, its relative accessibility, and the kind of equipment available. In spite of definition and measurement problems, productivity will grow in bargaining importance. Productivity has economic significance for organizations in that labor has a wage price tag, and the more work that can be extracted from a given input unit of labor, the more efficiently the entire operation will run and, other things being equal, the less it will cost.

In the public schools two questions relative to productivity must be raised: What ways are there of describing or analyzing the productivity of educational institutions and of the labor in those institutions? What are the impacts of collective bargaining on productivity?

Pupil Load and Productivity

Perhaps the most obvious and commonly used index of productivity in education is derived from the size of classes. Productivity is determined by the number of students taught by a given teacher: the greater the number of students, the more productive the teacher.

Education is a labor-intensive industry. It employs very little capital investment per unit of labor purchased. If the number of students taught represents the output, productivity is measured directly by class size or the pupil-teacher ratio maintained by given school systems.

There are at least three distinct reasons why class size enters the bargaining process. First, there are questions of scope. (Can or should class size or staffing ratios be subject to bilateral decision making?) Many states (among them, New York) have held that class size is not an appropriate matter for collective bargaining in education and that this decision should be reserved to the board of education.[45] On the other hand, it is obvious that teachers considered class size to be an important part of their working conditions and are insistent that it should be subject to contract negotiations. In surveys, it is consistently ranked along with salary at the top of teachers' concerns and demands.[46] Thus, although the courts and public employee relations boards often hold that class size is not within the scope of bargaining, it is clear that teachers are anxious to influence class size and will exert considerable effort toward that end. There is much evidence that teachers' unions are being successful in forcing boards of education to negotiate class size, and it is appearing in an ever-increasing number of contracts despite the efforts of the court and state employee relations boards.[47] Further, it is likely, because of its importance, that teachers' unions will attempt to keep class sizes down through lobbying efforts and informal agreement even though this is proscribed from formal bargaining.

A second reason why class size becomes a consideration in bargaining is because it has critical impact on the allocation of educational resources. Obviously, given the labor intensiveness of the education arena, the establishment of class size or a staffing ratio affects the number of teachers employed. A class size constraint in the decision process or in the allocation of resources becomes a staffing limit. Larger budgets are required to provide additional classrooms for smaller pupil-teacher ratios, and vice versa.

A third reason why class size enters into bargaining is that it also affects the wage bill. By creating a relatively inelastic demand for labor through limiting class size, school district employers are not able to trade off wage increases for increased productivity (when that is defined in terms of class size). As a consequence, employment effects are constrained in education. Teachers need not fear that, in attempting to drive their rates up through negotiation, they will decrease the demand for labor. Wage rates and class size or staffing ratios go hand in hand in determining the per unit labor cost in education, By definition, when two teachers are paid exactly the same wage rate and one has a class with twice as many pupils as the other, the teacher with the larger class is functioning at a per unit labor cost that is actually half that of the colleague with the smaller class. Using this definition, then, the teacher with a smaller class is actually considerably less productive because the per unit cost for labor is higher.

In the United States there has been a steady decline in the number of pupils per teacher. According to estimates of the National Center for Education Statistics, this trend may well continue. In 1954, for example, the average public elementary school classroom in the United States had over thirty pupils. By 1976 each elementary classroom averaged less than twenty-two children per teacher. It is likely that, by 1986, the number of elementary children per teacher will be something less than twenty. Similar trends have been occurring in public secondary schools.[48] The decline over the years is depicted in Figure 11-1.

Though this decline in class size can be documented, it cannot be attributed to collective bargaining per se. Though teachers express a strong interest in the reduction of class size, it is also clear that others involved in educational decisions also value small classes. Most surveys of parents consistently reveal their interest in reducing the number of students in the classes their children attend. It is likely that boards of education and administrators value smaller class size, though they are undoubtedly more conscious of the cost implications. If staffing ratios and class size are used as measures of productivity, it is interesting to note that public education in the United States is apparently committed to a steady decrease in productivity. Of course, proponents of smaller classes argue that they are more productive in terms of achievement. There is some evidence that this is true, but it is not conclusive (see below).

Another side to the class size-productivity question that must be considered is the evidence provided by Robert Baird and John

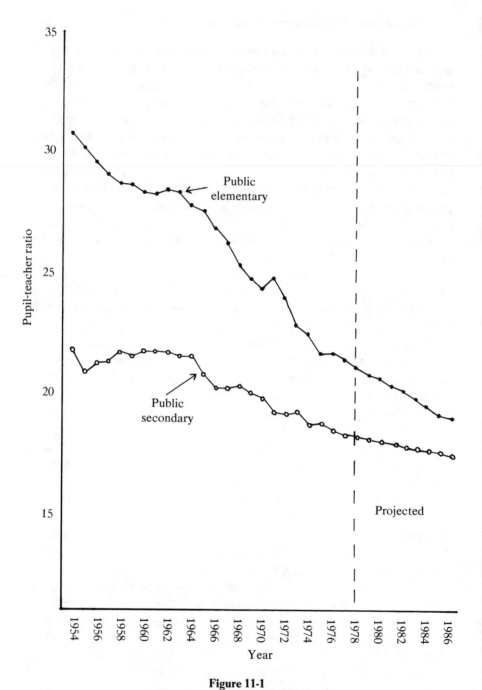

Figure 11-1
Pupil-teacher ratios, 1954-1986
(from U.S. Department of Health, Education, and Welfare, National Center for
Education Statistics, *Projection of Education Statistics to 1986-87*
[Washington, D.C.: U.S. Government Printing Office, 1978])

Landon that teacher wage rates and class size are related.[49] As class sizes become larger, teachers' wage rates also increase. There may be two explanations for this observation. It may be that teachers are willing to exchange or trade off class size for additional earnings and that they will take an additional student or two in return for a higher salary. Or, it may be that, because class size represents an important dimension of working conditions, supply cost considerations dictate that school districts must pay higher wages if they are to attract teachers into districts where the class size is larger.

Educational Attainment and Productivity

Though class size and staffing patterns are ways of thinking about productivity, they may not be either the best or the most revealing. If qualitative dimensions are entered into the equation, we become concerned not about the number of pupils taught but about the amount pupils learn in a given period of time with specified instructional inputs. When this concept is entered, the production function becomes much more complex. We find that we must search for variables that seem to determine the amount of learning that will take place. Although class size has been discounted as an influence in the learning patterns of young people, recent research seems to indicate that there is a relationship between class size and educational attainment. Work by Gene Glass and Mary Lee Smith suggests that there is a definite inverse relationship between the pupil-teacher ratio of a classroom and the achievement that can be expected.[50] This curvilinear relationship (Figure 11-2) suggests that a decrease in class size of a few pupils anywhere above twenty makes a relatively small contribution to learning but that, when there are fewer than twenty pupils, the effect on achievement becomes more pronounced. It may be, therefore, that the increase in per pupil instructional cost incurred as classes are lowered is counteracted by increases in pupil gains, and that it is not adequate simply to consider that productivity diminishes along with class size.

Recent research has suggested that certain characteristics of teachers do in fact relate to learning under various conditions. Experience, for one thing, is related to learning. Low-achieving students generally do better when taught by teachers who are relatively new. High achievers, however, seem to do better with more experienced teachers. All students benefited from teachers

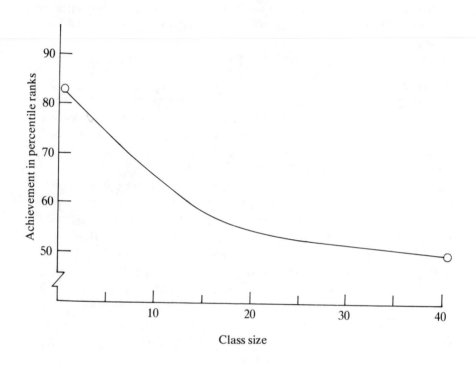

Figure 11-2
Relationship between pupil-teacher ratios and student achievement
(from Gene V. Glass and Mary Lee Smith, "Report on Meta-Analysis of Research on
the Relationship of Class-size and Achievement," University of Colorado, Laboratory
of Educational Research; reprinted by Far West Laboratory for Educational Research
and Development, San Francisco, California, September 1978, page vi)

who graduated from higher-status colleges.[51] Other studies have consistently shown that teachers who had higher verbal scores consistently did better in educational attainment.[52]

If one looks carefully at recent studies and reinterpretations of data on the size of classes, as well as the studies of school inputs into the learning process, the conclusion seems to be that there is a relationship between the quantity and quality of instruction that take place in the classroom. As for quantity of instruction, it is obvious that the amount provided to a given student can vary:

1. It will be influenced by the degree which the student attends class regularly. Students who attend regularly and who are less tardy often do better.
2. It will be a function of the amount of time available in the daily program (time in school) that is not subject to noninstructional requirements (school routine, recesses, clerical and other duties that must be carried out in the classroom).
3. It will be affected by the teacher's skill in managing available instructional time.
4. It will be influenced by the number of unscheduled interruptions that occur in the classroom as a result of housekeeping activities, as well as the frequency with which instruction is interrupted by a pupil who is misbehaving. This latter factor is, of course, influenced not only by the skill of the teacher but by the students assigned to the given classroom.
5. It will be, in part, affected by the number of other students that must share the instructor's attention. This would seem to relate to the size of the class. A large class not only requires that the instructor share attention with a much larger number of students, but it also indicates that, other things being equal, the class will be interrupted more frequently by students who are misbehaving.

It becomes apparent that numerous factors can determine the achievement of students in classrooms and that, if achievement is to be used in the productivity equation, there are numerous ways that collective bargaining can influence productivity. In some ways teachers' unions represent a positive force toward improving productivity. As has been mentioned, they are constantly pressing for reduction in the size of classes. A few years ago the United Federation of Teachers in New York led the way for the creation of units where children with behavior problems could be sent temporarily so that they would not disrupt the classroom. Though it is often criticized, such an arrangement might make a positive contribution to productivity.

It is not as clear how the unions' efforts to influence transfer policy and recruitment efforts will affect productivity. If low-achieving children benefit from association with new teachers and high-achieving youngsters benefit from experienced teachers, it is not obvious that unions will either encourage or permit assignment patterns that would be consistent with these findings. Moreover, the reduction-in-force contracts currently being negotiated in a period of declining enrollment may not permit districts to keep or hire new teachers.

Another dimension of bargaining and productivity that relates to contract provisions is the one that limits the obligations of teachers to certain time periods or provides released time during the school day for preparation. It has become quite common in recent years for teachers' unions to include requests for preparation periods for all members of the teaching staff in their demands, and they have frequently been successful. If one considers that these preparation periods could make for more efficient and skillful teaching, then it might be argued that these provisions will ultimately contribute to productivity. At the same time, providing each teacher with forty-five minutes for preparation during the school day requires the equivalent of one additional teacher for every six teachers already employed. By definition, this increases the teacher-pupil ratio and the unit production cost by that percentage.

The Psychological Contract

Cost factors and even achievement production functions are relatively simple when compared to the last element in productivity that we will examine. That has to do with the psychological contract that determines how much effort the teacher actually expends. Successful teaching requires both skill and commitment of energy and effort. Teachers must work hard, probably not just during the time they are teaching but for a considerable period beyond the teaching day. It is likely, in fact, that schools were designed with the idea that teachers would invest considerable amounts of individual effort and time. The basic structure has not changed substantially during this century, yet, at the beginning of the century, expectations as to the amount of time teachers would commit to teaching were considerably greater than they are today. One necessarily wonders whether effective schooling requires so much commitment and dedication.

It is not clear at all how teachers' unions and collective bargaining have influenced the willingness of teachers to commit their available time to the school. One thing we do know is that contracts frequently specify the amount of time and the conditions under which the school has a claim on the teacher, including the amount of time the teacher must be present before school and after the close of school. It also usually specifies the number and type of occasions that the teacher can be expected to attend outside the normal working day, such as parent conferences, PTA meetings, and so forth.

In addition, the contracts have become much more explicit in defining the conditions under which teachers can take time off. Most districts allow time off for illness, personal business, family matters, and other conditions that may occur. Reports seem to indicate that teachers are taking more sick days and personal time than they have in the recent past.[53] Again, it has not been established that this is a result of unions and collective bargaining. It is possible, however, to imagine that the increasingly specific approach to the time expectations and duties of teachers have encouraged them to exercise their privileges and to take time off when they feel it is owed to them. The nature of the collective bargaining process, with its generation of demands and publishing of attainment, may have increased their awareness of these provisions and their ability to use them. One hears stories about teachers working late in their classroom who are reminded, in a friendly way, by the local union building representative that this is not appropriate. In any case it is possible that the psychological aspect of bargaining has been to bring about a reduction in the degree to which teachers are willing to commit themselves to the function of education and to the school district employer in particular. It is possible to speculate that collective bargaining has contributed to a decrease in productivity. This is not necessarily bad. In fact, it may well be that schools have expected far too much of teachers in times past. Solid answers to these points of speculation must, however, await the development of more effective measures of teacher productivity. In the meantime, the financial aspects of collective bargaining in schools must be understood in terms of the measurable resources and decision processes described above.

NOTES

1. Estimated from National Center for Education Statistics, U.S. Department of Health, Education, and Welfare, *Statistics of Public Elementary and Secondary Day Schools, Fall, 1976* (Washington, D.C.: Government Printing Office, 1978). Salary statistics are published directly. The proportions reported here are derived from the number of employees and average salaries reported and estimated from reported data.

2. *Ibid.*

3. Anthony M. Cresswell and Michael J. Murphy, "Compensatory Education Policy and Collective Bargaining," report to the Institute of Educational Leadership, Washington, D.C., 1977.

4. See the discussion of tax referenda in Walter I. Garms *et al., School Finance* (Englewood Cliffs, N.J.: Prentice-Hall, 1978), ch. 13; see also Arthur J. Alexander and Gail V. Bass, *Schools, Taxes, and Voter Behavior: An Analysis of School District Property Tax Elections* (Santa Monica, Calif.: Rand Corporation, 1974).

5. These ideas are drawn from Hervey A. Juris and Myron Roomkin, "Education Collective Bargaining—Sui generis?" paper presented at the annual meeting of the American Educational Research Association, 1978.

6. This amount is for the President's budget for fiscal year 1980. See Appendix, *Budget of the United States Government* (Washington, D.C.: Government Printing Office, 1979).

7. Cresswell and Murphy, "Compensatory Education Policy and Collective Bargaining."

8. Stephen K. Bailey, *Education Interest Groups in the Nation's Capital* (Washington, D.C.: American Council on Education, 1975), esp. pp. 13-17, 63-70.

9. The Committee for Full Funding is discussed in detail by Bailey, *ibid.* Interest group activities are also described by Norman C. Thomas, *Education in National Politics* (New York: McKay, 1975); and Edith K. Mosher, "Education and American Federalism: Intergovernmental and National Policy Influences," in *The Politics of Education*, ed. J. Scribner, 76th Yearbook of the National Society for the Study of Education (Chicago: University of Chicago Press, 1977).

10. Bailey, *Education Interest Groups in the Nation's Capital*, p. 64.

11. Catholic schoolteachers also differ from the AFT on the issue of abortion. See *Unionism in Catholic Schools* (Washington, D.C.: National Catholic Education Association, 1976).

12. For a more detailed discussion of these and other changes in the state policy and political context, see Laurence Iannaccone, "Three Views of Change in Educational Politics," in *The Politics of Education*, ed. Scribner, 255-286.

13. The overall process of school finance reform is described by Garms *et al.*, *School Finance*, ch. 9; see also Edith K. Mosher and Jennings L. Wagoner, Jr., eds., *The Changing Politics of Education: Prospects for the 1980's* (Berkeley, Calif.: McCutchan, 1978), esp. ch. 6.

14. See Richard Lehne, *The Quest for Justice: The Politics of School Finance Reform* (New York: Longman, 1978); see also Arnold J. Meltsner *et al.*, *Political Feasibility of Reform in School Finance: The Case of California* (New York: Praeger, 1973).

15. Michael W. Kirst, "What Happens at the Local Level after School Finance Reform?" *Policy Analysis*, 3:3 (Summer 1977), 301-324; see also Stephen J. Carroll, "School District Expenditure Behavior," *Journal of Human Resources*, 11:3 (Summer 1976), 317-326; Larry G. Simon, "The School Finance Decisions: Collective Bargaining and Future Finance Systems," *Yale Law Journal*, 82:3 (January 1973), 409-460.

16. A description of the controls for the fifty states is found in Education Finance Center, *School District Expenditure and Tax Controls* (Denver, Colo.: Education Commission of the States, 1978).

17. Garms *et al.*, *School Finance*, p. 337.

18. Anthony M. Cresswell *et al.*, "Budgetmaking and Bargaining in School Districts," paper presented at the annual meeting of the American Educational Research Association, 1979.

19. See John F. Hulpke and Donald A. Watne, "Budgeting Behavior: If, When, and How School Districts Hide Money," *Public Administration Review*, 36:6 (November 1976), 667-674.

20. See Cresswell and Murphy, "Compensatory Education Policy and Collective Bargaining."

21. For a description of Title I funding at the state and local levels, see Anthony M. Cresswell, "Intergovernmental Relations in Education: Professionalism and Policy Administration at the State Level," *Education and Urban Society*, 7:1 (November 1974), 28-51; and Jerome T. Murphy, "Title I of ESEA: The Politics of Implementing Federal Education Reforms," *Harvard Educational Review*, 41:1 (February 1971), 35-63.

22. The details of Florida's finance system are described in Garms *et al.*, *School Finance*, pp. 201-212. The distribution of funds within Washington, D.C., is controlled by a federal court order from *Hobson* v. *Hansen*, 327 F. Supp. (DDC, 1971); see Joan Baratz, *A Quest for Equal Educational Opportunity in Major Urban School District: The Case of Washington, D.C.* (Washington, D.C.: Education Policy Research Institute, Educational Testing Service, 1975).

23. The discussion below of sequence and constraints is based on Anthony M. Cresswell *et al.*, "Budgetmaking and Bargaining in School Districts."

24. Harold W. Davey, *Contemporary Collective Bargaining*, 3d ed. (Englewood Cliffs, N.J.: Prentice-Hall, 1972), 251.

25. There are instances when an employer might pay above the competitive wage rate. This might happen if the employer was trying to keep out a union. It might occur if an employer was trying to create a large pool of applicants from which to select. In education, it might occur if districts had surplus income.

26. The notion of a competitive wage rate derives from equilibrium and competitive theory in economics and is at the core of traditional wage theory. A classic statement of this position will be found in J. R. Hicks, *The Theory of Wages*, 2d ed. (New York: St. Martin's Press, 1963). Traditional wage theory generally holds that it is impossible for labor, organized or unorganized, to raise wages in a perfectly competitive labor market. Thus, by definition unions cannot affect wage rates except where the market is not truly competitive. In recent years traditional wage theory has been subjected to many modifications to make it "fit" empirical evidence. For a discussion of assumptions and weaknesses of traditional wage and labor market theory, see Frank C. Pierson, "An Evaluation of Wage theory," in *Readings in Labor Economics and Labor Relations*, 3d ed., ed. Richard L. Rowan (Homewood, Ill.: Richard P. Irwin, Inc., 1976), 363-376; and Clark Kerr, *Labor Markets and Wage Determination* (Berkeley: University of California Press, 1977).

27. See Robert J. Carlsson and James W. Robinson, "Toward a Public Employment Wage Theory," *Industrial and Labor Relations Review*, 22:2 (January 1969), 243-248; and John D. Owen, "Toward a Public Employment Wage Theory: Some Econometric Evidence on Teacher Quality," *Industrial and Labor Relations Review*, 25:2 (January 1972), 213-223. Fogel and Lewin make the point that private-sector wage rates strongly influence public-sector wages through the prevailing wage principle, and, hence, explanations of wage determination in the private sector must, of necessity, be considered in public wage determination. See Walter Fogel and David Lewin, "Wage Determination in the Public Sector," *Industrial and Labor Relations Review*, 27:3 (April 1970), 410-431. Reder adapts many economic wage theory concepts and approaches in his analysis of public wage determination. For instance, while he assumes public employers are utility maximizers, they are "vote maximizers" rather than "profit maximizers." See Melvin W. Reder, "The Theory of Employment and Wages in The Public Sector," in *Labor in the Public and Nonprofit Sectors*, ed. Daniel S. Hamermesh (Princeton, N.J.: Princeton University Press, 1975), 1-48.

28. By "producer of last resort," we simply mean that the goods and services produced by government are often those that cannot or would not be forthcoming from the private sector. See Reder, "Theory of Employment and Wages in the Public Sector," 24-31, for good discussion.

29. Anthony Downs (*An Economic Theory of Democracy* [New York: Harper and Row, 1957], 35) has observed that winning elections is the prime objective of parties in the governmental arena; hence, actions of public officials "are aimed at maximizing votes." As noted above, Reder has incorporated vote maximization in his public sector utility function. See his "Theory of Employment and Wages in the Public Sector," 7-12.

30. The argument that unions can distort public decisions is perhaps most forcefully made by Harry H. Wellington and Ralph K. Winter, Jr., "The Limits of Collective Bargaining in Public Employment," *Yale Law Journal*, 78:7 (June 1969), 1107-1127; reprinted in Anthony M. Cresswell and Michael J. Murphy, *Education and Collective Bargaining: Readings in Policy and Research* (Berkeley, Calif.: McCutchan Publishing Corporation, 1976), 308-331.

31. For a definition of the institutionalist view by one of the originators, see Arthur M. Ross, *Trade Union Wage Policy* (Berkeley: University of California Press, 1956). For a view of equity and equality as a governmental wage policy issue, see Seymour Martin Lipset, "Equity and Equality in Public Wage Policy" in *Public Employee Unions: A Study of the Crisis in Public Sector Labor Relations*, ed. A. Lawrence Chickering (San Francisco: Institute for Contemporary Studies, 1976), 109-130.

32. H. Thomas James, James A. Kelly, and Walter I. Garms, *Determinants of Educational Expenditures in Large Cities of the United States* (Stanford, Calif.: Stanford School of Education, 1966); Thomas Dye, *Politics, Economics and the Public Interest* (Chicago: Rand McNally, 1966).

33. Henry M. Levin, "A Cost Effectiveness Analysis of Teacher Selection," *Journal of Human Resources*, 5:1 (Winter 1970), 24-33.

34. John H. Landon and Robert N. Baird, "Monopsony is the Market for Public School Teachers," *American Economic Review*, 61:5 (December 1971), 970.

35. John D. Owen, "Toward a Public Employment Wage Theory: Econometric Evidence on Teacher Quality," *Industrial and Labor Relations Review*, 25:2 (January 1972), 213.

36. Michael J. Murphy, "Determinants of Teachers' Wages in Utah," unpub. MS, University of Utah, 1978.

37. Paul H. Douglas, *Real Wages in the United States, 1890 to 1926* (Boston: Houghton Mifflin, 1930), 564

38. H. Gregg Lewis, *Unionism and Relative Wages in The United States: An Empirical Inquiry* (Chicago: University of Chicago Press, 1963).

39. The term "pattern bargaining" is used to describe a structural bargaining arrangement used in the private sector wherein the settlement with one employer becomes the "pattern" for settlements with other employers. When this system of multiemployer bargaining is employed, the union typically selects a target employer with which to negotiate the pattern or "key" bargain. Sometimes this is rotated through the industry; more often the employer selected is the one least able to resist union demands.

40. John B. Sommi, "Management's Response: Bargaining between Board of Education and Teachers' Unions in Rockland County, New York," unpub. diss., Teachers College, Columbia University, 1974.

41. Donald Gerwin, "An Information Processing Model of Salary Determination in a Contour of Suburban School Districts" *American Educational Research Journal*, 10:1 (Winter 1973), 5-20; expanded in *The Employment of Teachers*, ed. Gerwin (Berkeley, Calif.: McCutchan Publishing Corporation, 1974), 152-183.

42. Herbert D. Reiter, "A Study of Determinants of the Change of Salaries of Teachers," unpub. diss., Teachers College, Columbia University, 1975.

43. In Utah, all forty school districts in the state have fully paid health insurance. This is commonplace in other states as well.

44. See *Employment and Training Report of the President* (Washington, D.C.: U.S. Government Printing Office, 1979), 23-25.

45. The New York State Public Employment Relations Board has ruled that school districts may not be required to negotiate class sizes. Recently, the Alaska Supreme Court has ruled that class size and teacher load are nonnegotiable items. See *LMRS News letter* (published by the Labor-Management Service of the United States Conference of Mayors), 9:9 (September 1978), 4.

46. In a survey conducted by the American Association of School Personnel Administrators (*Trends in Collective Bargaining in Public Education* [Seven Hills, Ohio: AASPA], 1978), district and teacher negotiators estimate that class size will be a major issue in future contract negotiations. The Bureau of National Affairs ("Special Report: Teachers and Labor Relations, 1977-78," November 27, 1978) reports that, from September 1977 to September 1978, class size and class assignment were second only to economic issues (wages and benefits).

47. McDonnell and Pascal examined contract provisions in 151 districts. Of those districts, 20 had class size clauses in 1970, and 34 had them in 1975. (Lorraine McDonnell and Anthony Pascal, *Organized Teachers in American Schools* [Santa Monica, Calif.: Rand Corporation, 1979], 12.)

48. U.S. Department of Health, Education, and Welfare, National Center for Education Statistics, *Projection of Educational Statistics to 1986-87* (Washington, D.C.: U.S. Government Printing Office, 1978), 59-60.

49. See W. Clayton Hall and Norman E. Carroll, "The Effect of Teachers' Organizations on Salaries and Class Size," *Industrial and Labor Relations Review*, 26:2 (January 1973), 834-841.

50. Gene V. Glass and Mary Lee Smith, *Meta-Analysis of Research on the Relationship of Class Size and Achievement* (San Francisco: Far West Laboratory for Educational Research and Development, 1978).

51. See Anita A. Summers and Barbara L. Wolfe, "Which School Resources Help Learning? Efficiency and Equity in Philadelphia Public Schools," *Business Review* (Federal Reserve Bank of Philadelphia), 1975.

52. See James W. Guthrie, George B. Kleindorfer, Henry M. Levin, and Robert T. Stout, *Schools and Inequality* (Washington, D.C.: The Urban Coalition, 1969), 113.

53. National Association of Secondary School Principals, "Absent Teachers . . . Another Handicap for Students," *The Practitioner* (May 1979).

12

Collective Bargaining, Management, and Public Policy: Reflections

An open-systems approach has been used to organize this presentation and to provide a way of thinking about and interrelating elements of collective bargaining. By and large, the data and the events have spoken for themselves. What remains are those issues of collective bargaining in public education that transcend chapter boundaries and for which there are no easy answers. In short, most are troubling to serious students of collective bargaining and will be at the center of debate and analysis in the years to come. We cannot assume an objective posture on these issues, but we feel an obligation to raise them and to share our viewpoint.

THE "SECULARIZATION" OF TEACHING

The early chapters examined the history of teachers' union movements and explored reasons why unions attract membership and develop as they do. One of the things that emerged from that analysis was the subtle but rather startling change in the view teachers hold of themselves as working professionals and of their place in the school organization. There has also been a marked change in the way organized teachers conduct themselves, and, perhaps as a result, in the way they are viewed by the public. In times past, teaching has probably been as much a "calling" as an occupation. Teachers have been expected to be dedicated to the students in their charge, unselfishly devoting time and energy to their task. In addition, teachers have been expected to make themselves generally available for community service, including the teaching of Sunday school; to represent the values of the community and, in general, to maintain high moral standards; and to obey the directives of school boards and school management. In many ways, the demands of the profession in the early twentieth century resembled those of a religious vocation.

During the era of collective bargaining, however, teachers' attitudes about their jobs, their obedience to authority, and their dedication have changed. To the extent that it was reasonable to portray teaching as a "calling" or a "vocation," these changes might be termed the "secularization" of teaching. It is not possible to attribute the change solely to collective bargaining. Nor do we think this secularization has been the driving force behind the development of collective bargaining. Rather, it appears that bargaining and secularization have reinforced one another.

It is not likely that individuals who see their occupation as a "calling" are likely to participate in classic union activity. One feature of a "sacred" institution is the shared belief in common goals, objectives, and values. Members of religious orders or others committed to a life of service rarely think of themselves as employees. Rather, they direct their thinking toward the accomplishment of some "good" to which they are committed. Often loyalty to an institution is part of the commitment. It was essential, therefore, that teachers develop a different view of their relationship to their profession, their employer and their clients if they were to become unionized professionals.

The nature of collective bargaining probably reinforced the secularization because it called into question beliefs and objectives among the various parties in the decision arena of public education. It publicized the conflicts that exist between teachers and their employers. It emphasized that teachers are employed professionals, and, in the process, it placed emphasis both on the terms "employed" and "professional." Collective bargaining may have modified the very essence of professional commitment by emphasizing that teachers are paid employees and that they may negotiate their own work energy-pay ratio. Employees, even professional employees, can sell time shares of their skills and commitment to the employing organization and, at the same time, reserve time for interests and commitments that are separate from that organization and, indeed, even from their profession if they wish. The effect of this awareness is that teachers no longer merge their professional commitment into an organizational commitment or interpret one to be the same as the other.

Collective bargaining represents a public expression of the pursuit of self-interest. To the extent that teachers engage in this process, they serve notice to clients, school board members, and others that they are willing to promote their own interests. This has led to more intense questioning of their behavior as professionals because there is confusion as to whether teachers are speaking from a position of professional interest or self-interest and it has left teachers with something of a credibility problem.

Secularization also has great significance for the way decisions within the school system are made, the amount of overt conflict that exists, and the support level that is forthcoming from the environment. During the early period of collective bargaining in public education—that is, during the early 1960's—teachers complained publicly about being underpaid and began to take militant action to try to remedy the situation. The public, reacting in part to the earlier attitudes and views of teachers, responded to the situation as though teachers had finally been pushed to the limit by an unreasonable system that refused to provide a living wage. And so, in early strikes, teachers found support from the public for their position. As the secularization has become more pronounced and as the public has modified its view, public willingness to support teachers has been eroded by worry about the motives of teachers. It is not clear whether they are simply trying to correct an untenable situation or trying to extract as much in the way of wages as is possible. This doubt leads to stiffened public resistance. The messages being sent to boards of education are that they should not yield to the demands of teachers and should be willing to endure a strike if necessary.

The trend toward secularization in education does not pose a public policy problem directly, but there are difficulties. For one thing, the public becomes confused. It is no longer clear whether teachers derive advocacy from positions of professional competence or narrow self-interest. The expert, speaking as such, deserves a certain hearing and response; the lobbyist, another. And yet, teachers' unions seldom specify when they are articulating professional opinion or self-interest propaganda.[1] As a consequence of the public confusion generated by shifting roles, as well as conflict among educational managers and teachers, public support for public schools dwindles along with public confidence.

INVESTMENT IN THE BARGAINING SYSTEM

A major point from Chapter 2 is the fact that public education is making a considerable financial commitment to maintain the collective bargaining system. This is illustrated in Chapter 7 (on the process of bargaining) and in Chapter 9 (on the resolution of impasses). As we have noted, in 1976 the school districts in the United States were spending about $14.00 per pupil, on the average, to manage the bargaining process.[2] This expenditure includes only prorated administrative time and the budgeted expenditures for contracted labor relations services. It does not represent the imputed value of the time spent by teachers or the direct costs of bargaining to teachers' organizations. These estimates do not include the costs to the state of maintaining employee relations boards and impasse systems or the amount paid directly by school districts toward the cost of third-party neutrals. If these additional activities are included, the estimated expenditure per pupil on collective bargaining may approach $20.00 to $25.00 per student, or a total annual expenditure of a billion dollars for collective bargaining in public elementary and secondary schools in the United States.

But the direct costs reflected in a school district's budget represent only one aspect of labor relations in the public sector. There is a growing and extensive legal and political investment in the management of collective bargaining. Over thirty states have passed legislation governing collective bargaining for teachers. Many have established employee relations boards with large staffs to maintain labor relations in the public sector, and legislatures have been deeply involved as well. Passage of a state bargaining law does not usually end legislative involvement, for, even though the majority of states have passed some sort of governing and directing legislation, the history of these laws reveals the need for frequent revision. As a result, legislatures spend considerable time responding to the needs of the collective bargaining system and the needs of the people served by the public sector and the public schools.

The courts are also often involved through the processing of various injunctive relief appeals, as well as the interpreting of both contracts and state law. Besides being a drain on the resources of the judicial system, these activities require lawyers to argue cases, to prepare legal briefs, and to undertake a host of other system-related activities.

Then there is another rapidly growing sector devoted to servicing the collective bargaining process. It includes those organizations and services whose primary mission is providing information for those who bargain or those who manage the process. The Labor Management Relations Service sponsored by the National Conference of Mayors, for example, regularly runs workshops, publishes periodic reports, and issues a regular newsletter. Many state teachers' associations have a staff position for bargaining and also spend considerable time gathering information and providing it to locals. There are, as well, many public-sector labor relations consultants available to work with public agencies or entirely manage their labor relations systems. Something over half of the departments of educational administration in colleges and universities across the country have instituted courses or programs in collective bargaining that are included in the graduate training program for educational administrators. Most of these courses have been started in the last decade.

And, of course, there is the extensive dispute and impasse resolution capacity that has developed. The American Arbitration Association records impasses in the public sector and provides panels of arbitrators for use in school impasses. The Federal Mediation and Conciliation Service has made itself available for school district disputes when requested to do so, even though school matters are not formally within its jurisdiction. With about 35 percent of contract-bargaining relationships ending in impasse in any given year and with 80 percent of the districts referring their impasses to third parties initially, it is obvious that the demand for mediators, fact finders, and arbitrators is extensive and that both public- and private-sector agencies need to respond to that demand.

Then, finally, the financial commitment on the part of agencies and parties to bargaining is extensive. This constitutes, in some cases, a major change in priorities in teachers' organizations. The largest items in the National Education Association's budget relate to field services, many of which develop technical capabilities for and promote collective bargaining in states and school districts across the country. The National Education Association has also developed a section of its research division that does nothing but analyze contracts and provide data for use by its affiliates in bargaining. State teachers' organizations are investing heavily in collective bargaining in the form of workshops and the training of their own personnel. Even in small state associations there is frequently a ranking staff member designated as director of professional negotiations or some comparable title.

Similarly, school districts are expending much organizational time in managing the collective bargaining system. Perhaps 20 percent of the superintendent's time in small- and medium-sized school districts is devoted to this process. Over ten percent of the available administrative time in school buildings, on the average, seems to go to collective bargaining and related matters. All of this represents sizable financial and organizational commitment to collective bargaining and related personnel matters. And, where an organizational function acquires this level of importance, it inevitably attracts the most influential people in the organization and at the same time reinforces the influence of those people who are serving or attending collective bargaining.

The commitment of money and people to the bargaining process has several meanings for the long term. One of these is that bargaining is developing considerable momentum as more money is spent on it and as more individuals derive their organizational importance or their livelihood from it. It is almost inevitable that these individuals will become committed to bargaining and to maintaining a bargaining relationship. As more states develop legal and regulatory mechanisms for dealing with collective bargaining in public education, this investment will increase, and the process will probably become even further entrenched. There is unhappiness with collective bargaining among individual parties and associations, and occasional court decisions would seem to retard its development, but this has not happened. Apparently there is sufficient momentum to sustain bargaining even though it is challenged or found not totally satisfactory to all interested parties. The likelihood of bargaining being replaced becomes less likely with each passing year. And, as the collective bargaining mechanism grows and gains importance, it is also likely that more will be expected of it. It could become a magnet attracting stray issues and problems, and attempts to deal with issues and problems for which it is probably not well suited could strain or distort the process. This concern will be developed more fully in the section of this chapter entitled "Breadth and Scope of Bargaining."

INSTITUTIONALIZATION OF BARGAINING

As the level of bargaining activity increases, as the investment in it grows, and as it becomes more familiar, it seems inevitable that it will be absorbed into the routine administration of the school system. The onset of collective bargaining is often a crisis, and special procedures and behaviors are created to deal with it. There is little reason, however, to believe that the crisis atmosphere is maintained. Instead, the actors develop more or less predictable patterns of activity, and both sides seem to incorporate most activities for the handling of bargaining and conflict resolution into their existing organizational structure.

This is neither a surprising nor a particularly important observation. But the incorporation of labor-management relations into the management routines of school systems can produce both desirable and undesirable consequences. It is probably important that bargaining be reduced from a crisis activity to a more routine occurrence. This would allow both sides to proceed more systematically and less emotionally. As bargaining assumes a regular place in the scheme of things, its ad hoc character dissolves, and parties can look beyond the table to establish a long-term relationship of trust, mutual respect, and awareness of each others' problems. A continued interaction, stripped of some of its crisis character, should result in fewer unnecessary or destructive impasses and other disruptions.[3]

Collective bargaining in public education in the United States has been quite ideological, and adversarial interactions have at times been heavily personal. The orderly conduct of bargaining is confused by the presence of ideological or personal overtones, and they have largely been stripped from the processes in the private sector, where negotiators most often go about bargaining as a job. They do not allow strife to interfere with personal relationships or emotion to overwhelm their judgment. Boards of education, in contrast, might hold out for a quarter of a percent on a salary settlement, not because there is any fiscal justification for the position, but because they are "trying to prove a point." They may become so caught up in the bargaining process that they are willing to risk a settlement for the sake of a strong stand on a principle that has no substantive importance.

As people gain experience with the negotiating process and recognize that it is a way of doing business, it can become less personally threatening. The ideological component begins to diminish. As bargaining in public schools becomes more institutionalized, it will simply be viewed as a way of managing conflict, and less adversarial hostility will carry over to other arenas.

Institutionalizing the process of bargaining and its management could, however, lead to an orthodox approach, and orthodoxy can hinder creative responses to problems and the infusion of new ideas and practices. There is no reason to believe that labor-management relations in schools or in any other part of the public sector are sufficiently well understood to justify such rigidity. This is the basis of our argument against a federal collective bargaining law. The experience of the fifty states, each with its own approach, is a much better basis for developing policy than any single solution imposed at the federal level. The same principle applies at the local level. Diversity in scope should be allowed within states as well. A rich variety of experience seems more likely to lead to the higher levels of professional knowledge about labor-management relations and skill in handling negotiations needed to smooth the process and avoid unnecessary and damaging conflict. The search for better concepts and practices should continue.

Institutionalization and the accompanying routine handling of labor matters can also interfere with the principles of access and representation outlined above. School management bureaucracies, like bureaucracies anywhere, tend to prefer privacy and internal control of their functions. For the process of collective bargaining to be a fair one, in our terms, the parties with stakes, including the public, should have access to, and representation in, the process. That is why the incorporation of collective bargaining and labor-management relations into the regular management routines of the school systems should be accompanied by specific steps to keep the public informed and involved. This helps to ensure public support of the process and the fairness of the results. Differences in the management of school systems prevent us from suggesting specific prescriptions for practice in this regard.

Another, related danger in institutionalization is the possibility that those who conduct the bargaining—chief negotiators, union officers, and others—may become isolated from those they are supposed to represent and conduct the process to suit their own private purposes rather than those of their constituency. Sweetheart contracts favoring the employer are examples of internal corruption in the union.[4] Or management may sell out the interests of the school (or other organizations) through such devices as fiscally irresponsible pension agreements in an effort to reach an agreement with labor. Some institutionalization is, of course, desirable in the interests of stable, predicatable relations. But there should be a healthy tension between unbridled conflict and excessively cozy arrangements. Neither is in the public interest or the more specific interests of school clients or union members.

BREADTH AND SCOPE OF BARGAINING

Breadth

Though many school districts now bargain collectively, breadth of bargaining remains very much at issue. Whether all school districts in a state should bargain is what Robert Doherty and Walter Oberer would call a "threshold" question. Thinking of it in these terms focuses our attention on the effect of bargaining and whether it is needed for all school districts.[5] There are two considerations. One is the differences among school districts, particularly the special problems of small districts. The second is the nature of state legislation and its effects on collective bargaining. Bargaining certainly is more intense in larger school districts; it may even be absent in the smallest districts. Our evidence suggests that most bargaining began in larger districts but that it has successively worked downward in the size spectrum so that only districts with less than six hundred students are not yet likely to be involved. There has been pressure from unions and state law to make every district bargain, even though some districts have no need to do so. They already have effective mechanisms for resolving conflicts and for determining hours and working conditions or other issues that are of direct interest to employees. Where people are on a first name basis, there is more opportunity for communication and expressions of concern than there is in larger, more bureaucratic settings. It may be that bargaining creates an artificial, strained situation in smaller school districts.

Perhaps not all school districts should bargain. Employees in some companies, both large and small, in the private sector have found unions and collective bargaining unnecessary. In most cases the employees conclude that the presence of a union would not improve their situation. The International Business Machines Company (IBM) is one well-known example, but there are others where relationships between employers and employees are relatively harmonious and difficulties are resolved without resorting to bargaining. Bargaining is not mandatory in the private sector; it comes into being when employees are unable to reconcile grievances through any of the available mechanisms and turn to a union for help.

There is, however, a fundamental difference between the organizing patterns of unions in education and those in the private sector. Unions did not arise in schools to force employers to bargain collectively. Rather, as we have noted, both the National Education Association and the American Federation of Teachers became interested in the process of collective bargaining and began to push for it many years after the organizations were founded and their membership base was established. Thus, in most districts, unions or employees' associations exist irrespective of the need for collective bargaining. If bargaining is allowed, state and national organizations are eager for total involvement of districts. Using existing channels, they take steps to ensure that the leadership in *all* teachers' organizations from *all* sizes of districts in the given state opt for and begin to bargain collectively, regardless of need.

This presents a difficult problem in terms of public policy. Some districts have neither the resources nor the skill to bargain successfully. Forcing them to the table simply causes them to fail and results in unnecessary strikes, hostility, and a number of unworkable contracts. On the other hand, if legislation makes bargaining permissive, some boards of education would use this as an opportunity to avoid serious discussion with their employees on matters of mutual concern, and districts where the need is greatest may be those where the employer uses the permissive part of the law to avoid bargaining. A solution may be to require bargaining only where it is demanded. Demand would be determined by an election or certification process similar to those now undertaken by the National Labor Relations Board. Employees should feel they have a real choice as to whether they bargain, as well as a choice of bargaining agents. But even this would have limited effect. At present, most teachers hold membership in large, relatively well-organized teachers' unions. It is not likely that they would reject bargaining. Unlike the private sector, where employees must consciously opt for bargaining and then elect their bargaining agent, teachers already have one. And that agent is being pressed to bargain by state and national leaders. Local leaders would have to go out of their way to reject the process.

As expected, in states where bargaining is mandatory the percentage of districts bargaining is very high.[6] In states where there is no mandatory legislation it is up to teachers' organizations to persuade school districts to bargain. In those states bargaining usually takes place in the larger districts or in those where there is considerable employer-employee conflict. Other districts frequently continue in the consultative mode that has served them for a number of years. This should remain an option if acceptable to both sides.

Scope

Besides breadth, scope of bargaining remains an issue. Management rights and questions of scope are in part a matter of the suitability of the process to deal with all shared interests. As has been discussed elsewhere, there are some matters for which suitable substantive bases for decision exist as, for example, in content of reading programs or building specifications. For those, bargaining is not the best decision-making mechanism. For other issues—budgeting and setting tax rates, hiring administrators, and setting goals—there are clear legal and public policy barriers to bargaining. These are clearly the responsibility of management, and the legal power to exclude them from bargaining is well established. But there are some crucial issues that do not fit fully or clearly into any of these categories; they are on the boundary between educational policy and working conditions. Class size, teacher evaluation, employee transfers, dismissal, and force reduction are among them. Existing public policy varies from state to state as to whether these are allowable subjects of bargaining. This variation reflects the problematic nature of the issues themselves, as well as the different balance of power between employer and employee groups in the separate states.

In such cases it may be that the public interest is best served by allowing the decision on whether these issues should be bargained to be made at the local level. This position is an extension of the argument presented earlier in Chapter 5. It is based on the idea that subsidiarity and flexibility are necessary for local employers and employees to arrange their relationship in a way that best suits themselves.[7] The judgment of outside parties (neutrals, courts, legislatures, or administrative agencies) should be substituted for that of local parties only where it is clearly in the public interest. For fuzzy areas, such as those noted above, the presumption should be that local option controls. The burden of proof should rest on those who wish to make an item mandatory or exclude it from bargaining.

INTERNAL MANAGEMENT AND CONTROL

Conflict and Cooperation

At its core, bargaining can be intense, and the potential for damaging hostility is great. And yet, away from the bargaining table, employees and managers must cooperate in a way that often requires intense personal interaction in order for the school to function. This contrast of conflict and cooperation is an integral part of the labor-management relationship, especially in schools where the need for cooperative relationships among teachers and administrators is pronounced. Coping with these tensions requires a basic understanding of their sources and manifestations.

Bargaining and related activities are best thought of as part of the integrative mechanisms of an organization; conflicts of interest between workers and employers are natural and must be resolved for the organization to avoid disintegration.[8] Integrative mechanisms require balancing the competing values and needs of individuals and groups within an organization with the needs of the organization to exist and attain its goals.

Although unresolved conflict is admittedly destructive and bargaining represents a mechanism for coping with conflict, there are concurrent dangers. Schools require trust and cooperation to attain their goals. Collective bargaining is a system for creating agreement when trust is low. Contracts specify terms for exchanges *where neither party expects to be dealt with fairly by the other.*[9] As a consequence, contracts must be legally explicit, anticipate contingencies, and provide for policing and enforcement. Such a system may well exaggerate the differences and diminish trust between parties.

The need for a contract to be explicit, comprehensive (that is, to anticipate contingencies), and enforceable presents serious problems both for those who negotiate and for those who work with a given contract. To specify all the terms of the exchange between teachers and an employing district within the requirements of a contract would result in an extremely long document. In reality, such a document is an impossibility. The nature of what a teacher gives to the district in return for a specified wage is difficult to articulate. Such things as "commitment," "working as long as necessary to do a good job," and "being available to confer with parents" are not good contract language. What often emerges is a clause requiring that teachers be "at school 30 minutes before the teaching day commences and remain 30 minutes after pupils have been dismissed for the day." Behavioral expectations for professionals do not translate well into legal description. This seems to be another reason for caution before shifting certain decisions to negotiations or relying too heavily on the negotiating mode to specify the nature of professional behavior.

But schools cannot be run just to serve the teachers. It is the educational aims of the society, or the school community, that are to be attained, and they require some conformity within the system and employee performance according to certain external standards. Teachers' and other employees' salary expectations will seldom be consistent, moreover, with the cost concerns of either clientele or managers. Bargaining is only part of this larger system of conflicts and competition that is central to the organizational dynamic.

Maintaining the system's concentration on serving external goals also requires a certain level of bureaucratic structure and controls. These can be in direct conflict with the norms of the teachers and other professional groups—norms that hold that the individual teacher should be autonomous. This is a source of conflict that amplifies the basic tensions of bargaining. Teachers' desire for self-determination in matters of curriculum and work rules is at least as much a result of professional orientation as of the desire to reduce work loads and ease rules. Thus, teachers are doubly motivated to move decision making out of the bureaucratic-professional mode into the negotiated one if bureaucratic decisions are dominated by the administration and characterized by high levels of rigid control and tight supervision.

One way to reduce or manage the conflict arising out of the labor-management relationship more effectively is to remove some of the motivation for teachers to try to move decisions into the negotiated mode. If the bureaucratic-professional mode provides satisfactory mechanisms for teacher participation and there is little arbitrariness, their own professional norms will be better met, and their desire for autonomy can be partly satisfied through that mode. This means that teachers' participation in school governance as individual professionals, rather than collectively as a union, can be an alternative to some parts of bargaining. It is a desirable component of the proper function of the organization. Providing more means for cooperation can reduce the overall level of conflict and avoid loading unnecessary issues onto the bargaining process.

Now we are to the question of what is a necessary bargaining issue. It seems that the adversarial nature of bargaining and the need to compromise and make trade-offs fits best with issues for which rational or substantive criteria are weak or nonexistent or no agreement on criteria is possible. In other words, bargaining is best suited to procedural justice and the resolution of conflict, while many decisions about programming and curriculum are amenable to some substantive standards of judgment. Professional criteria that are empirically based and theoretically sound can be used to determine which mathematics curriculum to use or how to evaluate a certain program or activity. Where such criteria exist, they should be used. Where the best available professional judgment indicates that there is a substantive criterion for deciding, that should be preferable to a procedure such as bargaining. If this general principal is followed, the bargaining process will not become an "organizational garbage can" into which many decisions are "thrown" for convenience or expedience.[10]

Control of information is another source of tension in internal management. Since information can be a power resource in bargaining, husbanding and controlling information is reasonable behavior in the adversarial context. In a professional or collegial context, however, cooperation and rational decision making requires open communication and sharing of information. While not all information is potentially valuable in bargaining, it is certainly not clear what is safe to share and what is not. For example, declining enrollments, common in many areas, require careful planning for staff cuts and changes in facilities. But the involvement of employees in planning gives them access to information about management intentions that could help the union plan opposing strategies. This is more likely where the adversarial elements of labor-management relations are emphasized. Inhibited information flows and ineffective planning are problems that can be avoided, to some degree, by clarifying the boundaries between the content of bargaining and the bureaucratic-professional and political decision modes. Where tension exists over moving issues from one mode to the other, restrictions on the flow of information and on planning increase. If there is mutual acceptance of the limits to the negotiated mode, that is less likely.

Full mutual acceptance of those limits is unlikely in most instances. There is a natural tendency for unions to test the limits of the negotiations mode. Maintenance of boundaries becomes, therefore, a more important management task, both in the interest of maintaining discretion and of stabilizing the potential for conflict and encouraging cooperation within the system. Unions are not likely to cooperate freely in bureaucratic-professional decision processes if they believe the issue could be moved to bargaining. Thus, clarifying the boundaries should be an important management objective.

Collective Bargaining and Rules

Even if decisions are shifted to the negotiated mode, the bureaucratic character of the school organization may be enhanced, and individual professionals may still find themselves working in a rigid environment. James Anderson has identified patterns of control that exist in educational institutions: direct personal supervision and direction, impersonal mechanisms such as job standardization and performance records, bureaucratic rules, and professional standards. These mechanisms may exist together, but it is likely that an organization will favor one method and will invest most directly in it. These functions may be traded off. For example, the standardization of jobs reduces the utility and need for direct supervision.[11]

Several of the mechanisms are difficult to employ in the schools, especially direct personal supervision and direction. The spatial isolation of teachers within most public schools makes it difficult for administrators to observe and supply direction to the classrooms simultaneously throughout the building. Nor has there been much reliance on job standardization in the public schools, largely because of the eccentricities built into the teaching-learning function. It is probably reasonable to say that the schools have depended on professional standards or bureaucratic rules as the principal control mechanisms, which leads one to question what effect collective bargaining will have on the balance between these two control strategies. It would seem that the favoring of one or the other would make a substantial difference in the way the school operates.

Bargaining by definition is a rule-making function. As such, it strongly reinforces the bureaucratic tendency. Teachers, through collective bargaining, seek primarily to gain or share control of the rule-making function. They seldom choose to dismantle it and replace it with the use of professional standards. In fact, one outcome of collective bargaining has been to increase the number of rules and regulations under which teachers operate. The contract is, in fact, a body of rules that is made explicit through publication and debate over its enactment. These contracts explicitly govern teachers' behavior in a variety of settings, specify rights and privileges of administrators and teachers, and set forth minimum performance expectations (for example, the amount of time a teacher must be on campus). In this way collective bargaining may increase the degree to which bureaucratic rules govern behavior.

The resulting goal displacement could lead teachers to view these regulations as minimum performance expectations rather than as boundary conditions. Teachers may then adjust their goals and behavior downward to conform to these minimum expectations. During the process, it is likely that the direct authority of administrators and supervisors will be reduced and that there will be much emphasis on establishing minimum performance standards for teachers. The accountability movement reflects such a direction. Rules themselves may undergo goal displacement, becoming ends rather than means. As a result, school control and management can become less adaptive and responsive to demands. As these rules and regulations proliferate, they inevitably reduce the autonomy of individual teachers and administrators and, hence, can erode the influence of professional standards on their actions. The more expansive the scope of bargaining becomes and the more educational decisions are subjected to collective bargaining, the more likely it is that this pattern will develop.

Collective Bargaining and Pluralization

Bargaining may be an important element in the larger process of pluralizing policy decisions in education. In Chapter 10 we discussed the way labor-management relations can lead to increased coalition behavior when making decisions in a school district. Hierarchical bureaucratic forms of control tend to give way to the participation of groups acting according to their own objectives and interacting with other groups in the process. This transformation is larger than labor-management relations and can be thought of as a more general trend in education. But it is not clear exactly what place union activities and collective bargaining have in the process.

From one point of view, the activities of organized teachers and school employees interfere with the participation of other groups in the school governance process. Some policy or curriculum matters, formerly handled according to the bureaucratic-professional or political mode, become part of the contract; that is seen as excluding the public from those decisions and making the system more rigid overall. Teachers' unions, in particular, are seen as dominant forces in the governance system, discouraging or overwhelming opposition from other interest groups and individual participants.

We do not, however, find this view adequate or persuasive. That collective bargaining has the potential to change school governance is clear. But those changes do not necessarily lead to less pluralism or diminish the participation of other interests in school affairs. In fact, bargaining can have the opposite effect. Along with the development of collective bargaining, the making of decisions concerning school policy is moving away from the monolithic, consensual style controlled by the professional bureaucracy. Bilateral or multilateral negotiations are incompatible with the full maintenance of this form. Instead, the acceptance of union activity legitimizes adversarial activity and militance. As a result, conflict resolution, rather than avoidance, can become an acceptable mode of behavior, and successful militant tactics by teachers can spur other groups to try the same thing. Boards of education and managers, once experienced in open conflict, may be more open to the arena political style. In some cases managers actually encourage and structure the participation of parents and others in school decisions, which has the effect of diluting the power of teachers' or employees' unions.[12]

This type of conflict, inherent in bargaining, does not necessarily lead to other supposedly negative effects. Strong bargaining does not consistently reduce morale or generate continuing hostility in schools. And rigidity in the program is not a direct or necessary consequence of negotiated contracts.[13] In short, expanding pluralism does characterize educational decision making, and collective bargaining is a part of, rather than a counterforce to, this trend.

Decision-Making Processes

We have discussed many types of school governance decisions. There are alternative modes by which those decisions can be made. By way of summary, it is useful to consider how they interact.

Decisions vary, first of all, in the degree to which there are substantive criteria on which to base judgment. For some decisions there are clear, substantive criteria, as well as the data and analytical means to use them. Minimizing the cost of bus transportation through linear programming would be one example. For other issues there are no substantive criteria, or there is little or no consensus concerning them. For the first group, rational decision processes would be most appropriate, with problem solving and optimization as the main activities. For the second group, negotiations and the balancing of competing interests would require either the political arena or formal negotiations process. Selecting school board members or setting priorities would be examples of a political type of decision. When decisions are at the extremes of these dimensions, they may still be difficult, but the methods are not problematic. Away from the extremes, however, the decision-making process itself becomes an issue.

Decisions also vary as to the stakes involved. Decisions made when the stakes are high are more likely to involve the exercise of power by competing interests than when they are low. When the stakes are high enough, even the clearest of rational criteria can become clouded and the need for resolution of competing claims can require a pluralistic or negotiated form of decision making. If the stakes are very high, it may even be necessary to transfer the issue out of the immediate system for external adjudication. The courts are the place to resolve such issues as school desegration. Or a mayor may be called in to "enforce" the settlement of a bargaining impasse in a large-city school. While this may be necessary in extreme cases, it seems better for school managers and workers to resolve as much as possible within the system in order to maintain control over the processes closest to them. In general, however, the higher the stakes, the more likely it is that an impasse will occur, and the more likely it is that outside parties will intervene. Since the stakes in bargaining are often quite high, the occurrence of impasses is frequent and deserves separate attention.

Impasse and Public Policy

We have discussed two types of impasses that may occur in bargaining—those involving interests (which occur during the negotiation of the contract itself) and those involving rights of employees under the contract, that is, grievances. There are three ways that these impasses can be handled. First, the parties can be left to their own devices to force a settlement. This requires that employees' organizations be allowed to strike and that employers be allowed to lock out employees. Of course, other, less drastic devices may be employed to convince the other side to compromise further and help resolve the impasse. A second strategy often used in the public sector is the use of third-party conciliation mechanisms.

These include mediation, fact-finding, and advisory arbitration. The success of these approaches depends in large part on the skill of third parties to manipulate the environment to make a settlement more attractive (see Chapter 9). Third, in the public sector a settlement may be imposed on the parties by some outside agent. Usually this comes in the form of binding arbitration,[14] but it may come through special masters or court proceedings, or it may be imposed by state authorities not directly concerned with the dispute itself.

Of the three processes the one involving nonjudicial third parties represents the least risk both to the parties and to the public interest. Neither party is compelled to accept the award or advice. Neither does the process in and of itself involve a disruption of service. Risks and costs of the two other mechanisms are sometimes higher. Leaving the parties to their own means and providing them with the right to strike or lock out means that inevitably these power tactics will be employed. The result is disruption of service and the possible long-term erosion of public support of public education.

Of the available imposed resolution mechanisms for interest disputes, binding arbitration carries with it the most substantial legal and governance questions. Though it has received considerable attention in the public sector as a means for settling irreconcilable differences, it has had mixed success in securing legal approval. In approximately half of the states that provide for compulsory binding arbitration, the courts have either held that the process is illegal or that the awards may be subject to judicial review.[15]

The legal implications of the use of binding arbitration for interest impasses in the public sector concern the transfer of authority from the board of education to an arbitrator. This can be an illegal delegation of authority. Moreover, the arbitrator is not elected; nor is he or she directly answerable to any public official. The arbitrator can create situations that are financially untenable or that seriously disrupt the governance or instructional process of school districts.[16] We would be reluctant to advocate the use of binding arbitration to resolve interest disputes, even though the process may be acceptable in rights disputes.

The situation and, thus, the power of the arbitrator are substantially different in matters of grievances, that is, disputes about employees' rights under the contract. The contract is the source of the arbitrator's powers. The arbitrator may not legally make an award that goes beyond the contract.[17] If the contract itself is legal and fair, then the action of an arbitrator under its provisions can be seen as fair, thus serving both the parties and the public interest.

This does not mean that the parties will always see an arbitration award in that light. They may have agreed to some contract provisions with one or both sides being unaware of its full implications. Thus, an arbitration award based fairly on the implications of the contract may be quite proper yet strike one or the other of the parties to the contract as quite unfair or beyond the bounds of the agreement. Or they may simply disagree with the arbitrator's interpretation of the contract. These disagreements arise out of interests. The parties' perception of the fairness of an arbitration award is clearly not, therefore, an adequate standard. Thus, if an employer receives a grievance arbitration award that it cannot afford to pay, that must be construed as a fault of the employer in agreeing to the contract in the first place. It is not a problem of the arbitration process itself.

Our examination of mechanisms for dealing with impasses indicates that there is no certain or safe way to deal with them. Maintenance of the adversary system inevitably risks disruption of service. In some government functions, such as police, fire, and health, this can represent a danger to public health and safety. In public education, however, it seems unlikely that disruptions of service represent an immediate threat. Alternatives to the strike or lockout place reliance on third parties. That shifts the decision away from those who are most intimately concerned with the process of education. Neutral parties are not involved in education and most certainly do not have to live with the consequences of an imposed settlement. So it would seem safer in the long run to allow strikes rather than to insist on binding arbitration. Strikes in education are not likely to be of sufficient magnitude or frequency to seriously disrupt the delivery of educational services. The public is capable of enduring work stoppages, and children do not seem to be permanently damaged in the process. There is probably far less danger from allowing teachers to strike under most conditions than from subjecting the process to compulsory binding arbitration.

There are other reasons to believe that strikes may be preferable to alternatives such as binding arbitration now or in the future. We expect that public resistance to union demands will stiffen. Teachers' unions will be unable to extract major concessions from boards of education as easily as they have in the past. Collective bargaining caught the public, school boards, and administrators unprepared to take a tough stance. They become emotionally and somewhat paternalistically caught up in the conflict and were thus unable or unwilling to cope with the adversary process. In some instances, therefore, they made large concessions to teachers' unions without realizing the full implications. In other cases, boards of education were forced to make large concessions because the teachers were able to appeal to the public for support. The public, believing the teachers to be long-suffering, underpaid, and over-worked, allowed or even pressured the boards of education to yield. In yet other cases, the pressure from the teachers' unions gave the boards of education and administrators exactly the leverage they needed to raise the overall level of support for the public schools.

The public no longer seems to take for granted the fact that teachers are dedicated, underpaid, and overworked public servants. This is probably true not only for teachers but also for most other public workers. There also seems to be a genuine tax revolt afoot in the United States. Citizens are demanding, through the political process, that taxes be controlled or reduced. Another source of resistance is that the public and the management of schools have learned that the weapons available to teachers to enforce their demands are not as dangerous as was first imagined. Many school districts have experienced teachers' work stoppages and survived with some discomfort but no catastrophic consequences. It is much more difficult, therefore, for teachers to force concessions from a reluctant school board and public without a good case. Again, recent events in San Francisco are instructive. Not only did the citizens of San Francisco tolerate work stoppages on the part of municipal employees, but they went a step further and restricted the power of elected officials to grant wage increases. Certainly these events will be repeated in other places at other times. So it is not at all clear that the public can be pressured by militant public employees to concede beyond a certain point.

Union and management positions on the resolution of impasses have begun to change as well. Management has generally favored binding arbitration as an alternative to legalized strikes for public education. This position has been favored by legislatures in an effort to minimize disruption of public services. Teachers and other public employees, on the other hand, have sought to legalize the strike. But binding arbitration has begun to lose favor with legislators and school management groups as they have discovered that a strike is not the worst thing that can happen. They have also discovered that arbitrators in some cases are giving awards that seem excessive. Similarly, unions have begun to discover that the right to strike under limited conditions does not necessarily change the balance of power in negotiations. If the threat of a strike is no longer enough to precipitate great concessions from boards of education, unions will probably come to favor alternatives to the strike.

The strike may be an inherently weaker tactic in the public sector, for it lacks the economic leverage that comes from depriving an employer of income and market position. No such threat exists in the public sector. What a public strike does threaten is to deprive the elected school board or elected officials of their political support. This is likely only when the teachers' cause is a good one and they can effectively present it to the public. Otherwise, the public will likely resent the teachers for making unreasonable demands or for causing schools to close and be further convinced that teachers are acting in their self-interest rather than in the public interest. These attitudes make it easier for the public to resist. We believe that the public is wise enough to see the true merit of the demands made by teachers and other school employees. If elected officials are not able to withstand union pressure, the public can be expected to act to restrain the bargaining successes of teachers' unions.

In that regard we are hopeful about collective bargaining. It does not seem likely to us that it will seriously disrupt the educational process. There will, of course, be cases where there will be unnecessary and especially bitter strikes and confrontations. In general, however, each side will discover the nature of rational bargaining processes and will begin to analyze more carefully their interests and the other interests represented. The bargaining process will, we hope, take place under the watchful eye of the public and the citizens who will not be stampeded into making unwise and unnecessarily expensive concessions.

In recent years several states have developed procedures that allow teachers to strike in the event that other mechanisms, such as mediation, fact-finding, and advisory arbitration, fail to resolve an impasse. Pennsylvania has taken such a course of action, and so has Wisconsin. This seems to us to be a sensible route. It increases the chance that the impasse will be resolved by placing the ultimate responsibility for resolution with the parties, not with an impartial judge. The parties to negotiation know what is best for the circumstance and can resolve their own differences.[18]

BARGAINING AND THE PUBLIC INTEREST

We began this book by considering collective bargaining and the public interest. We examined ways of thinking about the public interest and collective bargaining. We argued that, where substantive criteria for decisions are weak or absent, collective bargaining can be used to satisfy procedural criteria (for example, fairness). We have identified both the advantages and the disadvantages of collective bargaining from the standpoint of the public interest and have concluded, in this final chapter especially, with a discussion of the serious problems that the emergence of collective bargaining has posed for public policy.

Though there are problems and potential for distortion, we conclude, nonetheless, that collective bargaining serves the public interest in public education. Our endorsement comes not because we think the problems presented by collective bargaining are trivial; they are not. Nor does it come because we expect that negotiated decisions will prove qualitatively better; most will not. Rather, it stems from the rather simple observation that collective bargaining has failed to bring disaster and from the basic belief that individuals should have a way to influence their work environment. Collective bargaining provides a greater measure of organizational democracy, and, in the absence of evidence linking it to social or economic decay, this fact alone makes it worth cautious support.

NOTES

1. In fact, as Truman points out, teachers and other professionals may use the status of their group to enhance their effectiveness in the political process (David B. Truman, *The Governmental Process*, 2d ed. [New York: Alfred A. Knopf, 1971], 250).

2. See Chapter 2 for the basis of these estimates and the ones below.

3. The problems of new bargaining relationships are described in Charles A. Perry and Wesley A. Wildman, *The Impact of Negotiations in Public Education* (Worthington, Ohio: Charles A. Jones, 1970).

4. For a discussion of union corruption, see Derek C. Bok and John T. Dunlop, *Labor and the American Community* (New York: Simon & Schuster, 1970), esp. ch. 3-5.

5. See Robert E. Doherty and Walter E. Oberer, *Teachers, School Boards and Collective Bargaining: A Changing of the Guard* (Ithaca, N.Y.: New York State School of Industrial and Labor Relations, 1967), 48-56.

6. See Chapter 2 for a description of the extent of bargaining activity.

7. See Anthony M. Cresswell, "The Public Interest in Public Sector Bargaining: Management Rights v. Management Power," in *Critical Issues in Education*, ed. Lou Rubin (Boston: Allyn and Bacon, 1979).

8. Integration as a functional requisite of organizations follows Talcott Parsons. This is applied to schools by R. Jean Hills, "What Educators Really Do," in *Theoretical Dimensions of Educational Administration*, ed. William G. Monahan (New York: Macmillan, 1975).

9. Alan Fox, *Beyond Contract: Work, Power, and Trust Relations* (London: Faber and Faber, 1974).

10. The "garbage can" metaphor is based on Michael D. Cohen and James G. March, *Leadership and Ambiguity: The American College President* (New York: McGraw-Hill, 1974). See also Chapter 10.

11. James G. Anderson, "Bureaucratic Rules: Bearers of Organizational Authority," *Educational Administration Quarterly*, 2:1 (Winter 1966), 7-34.

12. Anthony M. Cresswell *et al.*, "Budgeting and Bargaining Interactions in School Districts," paper presented at the American Educational Research Association Annual Meeting, 1979.

13. Lorraine McDonnell and Anthony Pascal, *Organized Teachers in American Schools* (Santa Monica, Calif.: Rand Corporation, 1979).

14. Where state statutes provide for bargaining, binding arbitration of grievances is typically considered an allowable and enforceable part of the contract. Thus arbitrators' awards are binding on the board provided the arbitrator has not exceeded his or her powers. See, for example, *Acting Superintendent* v. *Liverpool Faculty Association*, 42 N.Y.2d 509 (1977). Even in the absence of a statute,

arbitration can be binding. See *Dayton Classroom Teachers Association* v. *Dayton Board of Education*, 323 N.E.2d 714 (1975).

15. Though eighteen states have compulsory binding arbitration for public employee bargaining, only seven cover teacher bargaining. They are Maine, Michigan, Minnesota, Oregon, Pennsylvania, Rhode Island and Wisconsin. The bulk of the laws are aimed at vital services, usually police and fire. Of the eighteen states that have passed binding arbitration laws, the state courts have upheld the constitutionality of seven, and declared four unconstitutional.

16. There are two criticisms commonly leveled at compulsory binding arbitration in the public sector: the process is illegal or unconstitutional, and the award may be poor, thereby burdening the institution or the public with untenable contract terms. Regarding the former, we presume, as do Lewin and his associates, that the courts can and will deal with this issue. If compulsory binding arbitration of contract terms is illegal, presumably the statutes requiring it will be struck down by the courts as they have been recently in Utah and Connecticut. The fact that the courts have upheld a majority of such provisions leads us to conclude that there is no reason to assume that binding arbitration in the public sector is always an illegal delegation of authority as some have charged. As to the latter point—that awards may be poor and cause harm to the parties, the institution or the public— the evidence is inconclusive at this point. Certainly the potential exists. An arbitrator may award a salary that cannot be met within existing revenues. He may be sufficiently uninformed about the process of education that his award will work to the disadvantage of the educational program. Though there is no direct evidence of this occurrence in school decisions, Horton does observe such occurrences in municipal awards. (See Raymond D. Horton, "Arbitration, Arbitrators, and the Public Interest," *Industrial and Labor Relations Review*, 28:4 [July 1975], 497-507). On examining arbitrators' awards, some have found them essentially the same as those negotiated in comparable situations. Others find that arbitrators' awards sometimes tend to be more generous to unions. For an excellent discussion of these and other public policy issues regarding arbitration, see David Lewin, Peter Feuille, and Thomas A. Kochan. *Public Sector Labor Relations: Analysis and Readings* (Glen Ridge, N.J.: Thomas Horton and Daughters, 1977), 228-232.

17. For an excellent discussion of grievance arbitration and contract interpretation, see Reed C. Richardson, *Collective Bargaining By Objectives: A Positive Approach* (Englewood Cliffs, N.J.: Prentice-Hall, 1977), 205-228.

18. The belief that the parties are best able to handle their own contract impasses is at the heart of the private-sector system in the United States. As a consequence, interest arbitration is seldom used. Yet the days lost to strikes in U.S. industry is among the lowest in the world.

Index

214; growth of, 105, 106-111, 116, 129, 132, 137; organization of, 65-70, 99-100; and professionalism, 61, 62, 70, 91, 97; propositions of, 62; reform and administration of, 60-64, 91-92; Research Division of, 68, 69; salary studies by, 70; and sanctions, 93; and strikes, 347; study committees of, 68; and urban problems, 94-96

National Labor Relations Act (NLRA) of 1935, 20, 80, 109, 120, 147-148, 162, 165, 167, 168, 173, 187, 188, 299, 338. *See also* Landrum-Griffin Act; Taft-Hartley Act

National Labor Relations Board (NLRB), 148, 162, 168, 187, 477

National League of Cities v. *Usery*, 237

National Manpower Resources Study, 25*n*, 26*n*, 31*n*, 32*n*, 33*n*, 37*n*, 40*n*, 43*n*, 45*n*, 46*n*, 47*n*, 50, 100

National School Boards Association, 431

National Teachers' Association, 59-60, 62

National Teachers' Federation, 63-64

National War Labor Board, 147

Nebraska: arbitration in, 179; bargaining units in, 164; collective bargaining laws in, 155; impasse in, 371; state association in, 59

Negotiators. *See* Bargainers

Nelken, Ira, 377

Nevada: collective bargaining laws in, 155; impasse in, 372; state association in, 59; union security in, 174

New Hampshire: arbitration in, 179; collective bargaining laws in, 155; finance in, 424; impasse in, 372; state association in, 59; state funding in, 206

New Jersey: arbitration in, 1979; case in, 187; centralized decision making in, 397-398; collective bargaining laws in, 155; finance in, 450; impasse in, 372; state association in, 59; strikes in, 357

New Jersey Public Employee Relations Commission, 161

Newland, Jessie, 79

New Mexico: collective bargaining laws

in, 155; finance in, 424; impasse in, 372; state association in, 59

New York: arbitration in, 179; collective bargaining laws in, 155; and constraints on public-sector bargaining, 6; and duty to bargain, 159; finance in, 426, 450, 451, 454, 466; impasse in, 362, 372; injunction in, 183; state association in, 59; strikes in, 383; training in, 132; union impact on governance in, 398; union membership in, 141; union security in, 174. *See also* Buffalo; New York City

New York City: bargaining rights in, 150; decentralization in, 232, 233, 389-390; multilateral bargaining in, 389-391; productivity in, 453, 459-460; union development in, 53, 72, 76, 77, 79, 82-85, 87, 88-90, 91, 92, 93, 94; union growth in, 105, 121, 123-124, 132, 136, 356; union impact on governance in, 398, 400, 401; union stance in, 21

New York Public Employee Relations Board, 162

New York State Federation of Teachers, 86

New York State Teachers' Association, 86, 89

New York State United Teachers, 86

Nisbet, Robert A., 117-118, 121, 122, 142, 143

Nixon, Richard M., 120, 149

NLRB v. *American National Insurance Co.*, 187

NLRB v. *Cummer-Graham Co.*, 187

NLRB v. *Truitt Mfg. Co.*, 187

Norris-La Guardia Act of 1932, 147

North Carolina: collective bargaining laws in, 155; contracts in, 153; impasse in, 372; state association in, 59

North Dakota: collective bargaining laws in, 155; impasse in, 372; state association in, 59

Norwalk, Connecticut: bargaining agent in, 21; court case on, 187; strike in,